/N FROM
RARY

ITY OF
WINCHESTER

RACISM AND EDUCATION IN THE U.K. AND THE U.S.

KA 0350872 2

MARXISM AND EDUCATION

This series assumes the ongoing relevance of Marx's contributions to critical social analysis and aims to encourage continuation of the development of the legacy of Marxist traditions in and for education. The remit for the substantive focus of scholarship and analysis appearing in the series extends from the global to the local in relation to dynamics of capitalism and encompasses historical and contemporary developments in political economy of education as well as forms of critique and resistances to capitalist social relations. The series announces a new beginning and proceeds in a spirit of openness and dialogue within and between Marxism and education, and between Marxism and its various critics. The essential feature of the work of the series is that Marxism and Marxist frameworks are to be taken seriously, not as formulaic knowledge and unassailable methodology but critically as inspirational resources for renewal of research and understanding, and as support for action in and upon structures and processes of education and their relations to society. The series is dedicated to the realization of positive human potentialities as education and thus, with Marx, to our education as educators.

Anthony Green Senior Lecturer in the Department of Educational Foundations and Policy Studies at the Institute of Education, University of London, UK.

Renewing Dialogues in Marxism and Education: Openings
Edited by Anthony Green, Glenn Rikowski, and Helen Raduntz

Critical Race Theory and Education: A Marxist Response
Mike Cole

Revolutionizing Pedagogy: Education for Social Justice Within and Beyond Global Neo-Liberalism
Edited by Sheila Macrine, Peter McLaren, and Dave Hill

Marxism and Education beyond Identity: Sexuality and Schooling
Faith Agostinone-Wilson

Blair's Educational Legacy: Thirteen Years of New Labour
Edited by Anthony Green

Racism and Education in the U.K. and the U.S.: Towards a Socialist Alternative
Mike Cole

Constructing Twenty-first Century Socialism in Latin America: The Role of Radical Education (Forthcoming)
Sara C. Motta and Mike Cole

Racism and Education in the U.K. and the U.S.

Towards a Socialist Alternative

Mike Cole

palgrave
macmillan

UNIVERSITY OF WINCHESTER
LIBRARY

RACISM AND EDUCATION IN THE U.K. AND THE U.S.
Copyright © Mike Cole, 2011.

All rights reserved.

First published in 2011 by
PALGRAVE MACMILLAN®
in the United States—a division of St. Martin's Press LLC,
175 Fifth Avenue, New York, NY 10010.

Where this book is distributed in the UK, Europe and the rest of the world,
this is by Palgrave Macmillan, a division of Macmillan Publishers Limited,
registered in England, company number 785998, of Houndmills,
Basingstoke, Hampshire RG21 6XS.

Palgrave Macmillan is the global academic imprint of the above companies
and has companies and representatives throughout the world.

Palgrave® and Macmillan® are registered trademarks in the United States,
the United Kingdom, Europe and other countries.

ISBN: 978–0–230–10379–5 Hardcover
ISBN: 978–0–230–10380–1 Paperback

Library of Congress Cataloging-in-Publication Data

Cole, Mike, 1946–
     Racism and education in the U.K. and the U.S. : towards a socialist
alternative / Mike Cole.
          p. cm.—(Marxism and education)
     ISBN 978–0–230–10379–5 (hardback)—
     ISBN 978–0–230–10380–1 (paperback)
          1. Discrimination in education—Great Britain—History.
     2. Discrimination in education—United States—History. 3. Racism—
     Great Britain—History. 4. Racism—United States—History. 5. Socialism
     and education—Venezuela. I. Title. II. Series.

LC212.3.G7C65 2011
379.2'60941—dc22   2010049025

A catalogue record of the book is available from the British Library.

Design by Newgen Imaging Systems (P) Ltd., Chennai, India.

First edition: June 2011

10 9 8 7 6 5 4 3 2 1

Printed in the United States of America.

UNIVERSITY OF WINCHESTER	
03508722	

Contents

Acknowledgments

I would like to thank Thomas Acton, Wayne Au, Steve Behrendt, Sarah Bell, Thandeka K. Chapman, John Clay, Dave Cole, Richard Delgado, William M. Denevan, David Getches, Edward Ellis, Chien-Juh Gu, Dave Hill, Paul Iganski, Henry Kum, Alpesh Maisuria, Curry Malott, Brian Matthews, Peter Mayo, Sara Motta, Simon Newell, Maria Papapolydorou, Scott Poynting, Paul Warmington, Mandy Williams, Dave Windsor, Richard Woolley, and Frank Wu for various helpful inputs to this book. Special thanks to Anthony Green. Inclusion here does not necessarily imply agreement with the content of this book, and as always, any inadequacies remain mine and mine alone. Last but by no means least, I am indebted to Burke Gerstenschlager and Kaylan Connally at Palgrave Macmillan, New York; and Rohini Krishnan at Newgen Publishing and Data Services in Chennai.

Series Editor's Preface

So far as "race," racism and *racialized* education in the U.K. and the U.S. are concerned, this book by Mike Cole provides a very well-informed introduction, with incisive Marxist analysis while offering a broad overview and critical review of emergent circumstances of struggle for social justice and socialist democracy. As a contribution to necessary debates for action, this could not be more timely for supporting the cause of democratic socialism in and through education. Nor could the bold strategy of offering this analysis with comparative exemplification and profiling current developments in the Venezuelan, Bolivarian revolution would be more appropriate—as Latin American continues to inspire critical modelling for left challenges to neo-liberal and conservative forms. Indeed, more widely, it articulates with voices expressing the need and possibility for establishing a long-awaited Fifth International. Not least, the book provides encouragement and support to the development of social movements through extra-parliamentary progressive forces on either side of the Atlantic. This is a provocative intervention in debates designed for action and implementation of strategies in the broadest senses *in and for education*... all in the spirit of *educating the educators... ourselves in struggles*. Counter-hegemony on a broad scale is the active educative thrust, while more specifically, Mike Cole's focus leads to a proposed new analytical elaboration on the theme of *institutional racism*. Importantly, it is also part of the book's pedagogic and educative function to develop the Marxist vocabulary as it unfolds.

The analysis works with a well-established distinction between *education* and *schooling*. Thus, he mobilizes the generative assumption that *education cannot be separated from society*, and does so by countering and providing alternatives to the repressive and reifying mechanisms of *schooling* which separate and differentiate *within* society. At the heart of the analysis is a neo-Marxist concept of *racialization* (elaborating creatively on Robert Miles' work) embedded within a critique of the capitalist mode of production. Its methodology is educative. The procedure involves recognizing the social and political need for detailed, delicate and multifaceted cultural analysis so far as stereotyping and othering of ethnicity is concerned, for instance, along with articulating some of the key points where resistive action is required. All of this provides materials for feeding back for further critical analysis and reflection and devising practical knowledge; and thus generating really useful collective understanding that can emerge to guide the potential for further radical action and organization building on what is collectively learned in both form and content *as and for transformative education*. Thus, the critical thrust is that s*chooling* signifies the institutional drags on educative progress, working through dominant structures in capitalist economic, cultural and organizational terms and generally having the consequences of the ongoing support of the *myth of social progress through merit*. Schooling policy perpetuates (intentionally or otherwise) selective repression through symbolic and more direct forms of, for instance, institutionally racialized marginalization and incorporation. The analysis thus aims at resistance to social relational forces which are limiting conceptions of horizons of progressive imagination to the immediacy of fatalist acquiescence which serve to embed and consolidate divisive class forms. In these analyses Mike Cole also draws creatively on Gramsci and Althusser who inspire activist challenges to settling for what "they," the dominating voices in the social system of economic relations, can provide and looks to resources in Marxist educational democratic common sense, the good senses which undermine current hegemonies. The targets are commodified and commodifying opportunity structures and state apparatuses, to be attacked through building on such critical good senses opposing possessive individualism and market forms.

Mike Cole's analysis runs counter to developments in the U.K. and the U.S. that instantiate neo-liberal ideological narratives and renewal of oppressive policy initiatives. Such dominant class elite's analyses articulate the trans-Atlantic policy borrowing merry-go-round associated with defaulting *diversity and choice* whereby market models continue to do their class work, consolidating corporate economic, cultural and political class powers from above while appearing to produce support for the narrative of liberating initiatives from below, the pristine individual and romanticized community. Such emergent material and ideological structures are, for instance, arguably reversing social and educational desegregation, in the U.S. In the U.K. the (now late) New Labour regime left most, if not all, the politically and socially significant aspects of the previous Thatcher education policy apparatus intact and developed them further in several respects, notably with policy for institutional differentiation through specialist schools, trust schools and their subsequent academies program presented as bringing support to poor areas; through business focused workforce and human capital development policy and higher education funding to tuition fees policy. In combination, these served to effectively undermine still further the not so far implemented principles of systemic comprehensive education. Thus, New Labour's positive programs on child poverty were unlikely to prove to be significant countervailing forces in the larger social picture of both overt and covert selection in education which has continued largely unchallenged. The small but materially and symbolically very significant private sector continues to reinforce deep social divisions. And selective grammar schools have continued to perform their socially divisive capitalizing roles aided and partly articulated by the housing market for attaining proximity for access to "good" state schools and underpinned by the complex apparatuses of social capitalization.

In the U.S., a penal model of *schooling* through high stakes testing associated with NCLB (No Child Left Behind) is currently going largely unchallenged in material reality by the Obama regime and being re-worked in the U.K. by the current coalition Con-Dem government in the name of "standards." The latter has proceeded to institute an even more reactionary model of New Labour's socially flawed "academies" initiatives concentrating now more overtly on well-performing schools. The Con-Dems are moving to capitalize not so much by stealth, in both welfare and education policy, but boldly reinforcing market forms and corporate interests with the hypocritical front of promoting so-called *free* schools in the inclusive *big* society. The key to such policy is its repressive cuts agenda to further undermine the possibilities of democratic state forms, while maintaining firm control of education funding enabling central government approval of project initiatives. As with New Labour, the Teflon effect is through providing spurious empowerment and responsibility to professionals at the local and point-of-delivery levels.

This book is a part of the fight back against what has become decades of corporate, globalizing neoliberal hegemony, culminating in the latest of the cycles of capital's boom/bust configurations in which the poor and the least well placed will be paying through taxation, interest rates increases, inflation and unemployment to prevent the collapse of wider confidence in finance capital, thereby propping up the divisive system of *socialism for the well off* and *capitalism for the rest*. Mike Cole's work here reinforces the themes that while education cannot compensate for society, and alone is not *sufficient* as terrain, topic and resources in progressive and emancipator struggles, nevertheless, education at all levels and dimensions continues to be *necessary* to and in any of the contexts of these progressive struggles.

ANTHONY GREEN

Preface

This book can be read cover to cover—for example, as individual or collective reading—or it can be used on courses that cover all the themes dealt with in the book. Chapters can also be freestanding. Thus those with a primary interest in the origins of socialism, and in Marxism and neo-Marxism, can read chapter 1; while for twenty-first century socialism there is chapter 5. Similarly for those whose focus is racism in the United Kingdom and/or the United States, chapters 2 and 3 are the ones to look at. Chapter 4 relates racism in these countries to schooling and education. Finally those with a main interest in suggestions as to what to do to promote multicultural anti-racist socialist practice in educational institutions can go straight to chapter 6. It is my hope that for those who start with specific chapters, rather than reading the book from start to finish, there will be a desire to read other chapters, since all the chapters are interrelated, and hopefully the book represents a coherent whole. The Introduction sets out some basic concepts used in the book and gives an outline of each of the chapters.

Introduction

In this book I address racism and education in the capitalist economies of the U.K. and the U.S., and assess the socialist alternative, with specific reference to the Bolivarian Republic of Venezuela.[1] In so doing I examine the efficacy of neo-Marxism (the use of the prefix "neo" is to make a distinction between newer interpretations of a theory or set of ideas and earlier ones) as well as classical Marxism (as originally developed by Karl Marx and Friedrich Engels) in understanding the defining features of the relationship between racism and schooling, and between racism and education. I differentiate "schooling" from "education," viewing the former as oppressive and using *institutions* to socialize young people into the norms and values of capitalism, and the latter as liberating and critical and a lifelong societal process, both inside and outside of institutions.[2]

I look primarily at some important aspects of the work of neo-Marxists Antonio Gramsci (1891–1937), and Louis Althusser (1918–1990), but also at the work of other neo-Marxists; in particular, Robert Miles (1950–). Since their key concepts have much to tell us about the current realities of racialized world capitalism (see later in this Introduction for a discussion of racialization), and given the ongoing crisis in that world system, now is a most opportune time to reconsider Marxist and neo-Marxist analyses and their promise of world democratic socialism as an alternative.[3] At the outset I would like to make some brief comments about socialism and Marxism. These concepts are greatly misunderstood, and often parodied as "state control" or dictatorship or lack of freedom. In actual fact, socialism, as understood by Marx and Engels, was profoundly and genuinely democratic, and not at all the sinister and oppressive system that we are led to believe is entailed by the concept of socialism. Under socialism, wealth is shared equally, workers own and control the means of production distribution, and exchange and make decisions *democratically*, unlike capitalist democracy where, as leading Russian revolutionary Vladimir Ilyich Ulyanov (commonly known as Lenin) (1917 [2002], p. 95) argued, the oppressed workers are allowed once every few years to decide which particular representatives of the oppressing class will represent them and repress them in parliament. Critics rightly cite what became of the Soviet Union and Eastern Europe as being bad examples of Marxism. Modern Marxists acknowledge this and have learned a lot from Stalinism,[4] as practiced in these countries and elsewhere. In many ways, experiences there were the antithesis of Marxists' notions of democratic socialism (for a detailed discussion of common objections to Marxism and a Marxist response, including a rejection of Stalinism and the exaltation of twenty-first century democratic socialism, see Cole, 2008a, chapter 10 and Cole, 2009a, chapter 7).

In order to establish the current relevance of democratic socialism, I begin, in chapter 1, by tracing the trajectory from utopian socialism to Marxism or scientific socialism, and to neo-Marxism, before, in subsequent chapters, specifically applying neo-Marxist theories to schooling and education. Since I address the U.K., the U.S., and the Bolivarian Republic of Venezuela, the book seeks to engage audiences in each country, as well as those interested in developments on both sides of the Atlantic, and those following events in Latin American politics.

In this Introduction I begin by looking at the concepts of "race" and ethnicity. I go on to examine the concept of racism and the neo-Marxist concept of racialization as deployed throughout this volume, before moving on to a general outline of its contents.

"Race" and Ethnicity

"Race" is a social construct. That this is the case is explained succinctly by Marxist geneticists Steven Rose and Hilary Rose (2005; see also Darder and Torres, 2004, pp. 1–12, 25–34). As they note, in 1972, the evolutionary geneticist Richard Lewontin pointed out that 85 percent of human genetic diversity occurred *within* rather than *between* populations, and only 6 percent–10 percent of diversity is associated with the broadly defined "races" (Rose and Rose). As Rose and Rose explain, most of this difference is accounted for by the readily visible genetic variation of skin color, hair form, and so on. The everyday business of seeing and acknowledging such difference is not the same as the project of genetics. For genetics and, more importantly, for the prospect of treating genetic diseases, the difference is important, since humans differ in their susceptibility to particular diseases, and genetics can have something to say about this. However, beyond medicine, the use of the invocation of "race" is increasingly suspect. There has been a growing debate among geneticists about the utility of the term, and an entire issue of the influential journal *Nature Reviews Genetics* (Autumn 2004) was devoted to it. The geneticists agreed with most biological anthropologists that for human biology the term "race" was an unhelpful leftover. Rose and Rose conclude that "[w]hatever arbitrary boundaries one places on any population group for the purposes of genetic research, they do not match those of conventionally defined races." For example, the DNA of native Britons contains traces of multiple waves of occupiers and migrants. "Race," as a scientific concept, Rose and Rose conclude, "is well past its sell-by date." For these reasons, I would argue that "race" should be put in quotation marks whenever one needs to refer to it.

Ethnicity, however, I believe should be retained. There are three reasons for this. First, it is needed at the cultural level, for reasons of collective self-identity. "Ethnic groups" do identify with each other culturally, with respect to religion, language, food, music, and so on. One might call this "cultural ethnicity." Hence there needs to be a general awareness of the specific needs of different "ethnic groups," in order not to perpetrate unintentional or indirect racism. Cultural ethnicity should not be imposed from the outside, as is the case in various versions of "multicultural education," where white teachers teach about others' cultures (for a discussion, see chapters 4 and 6 of this volume). For the most part, cultural identification is not a voluntary process. People, in general, do not choose their language, religion, and social customs—these forms of bodily and social habitus are deeply ingrained in the socialization process. Historically "ethnic identification" has been necessary to survive in racist societies (e.g., Kershen (ed.) 2000; Lesage et al., 2002).

Second, cultural ethnicity is also needed, in racist societies, in order that a self-defined objective description of groups of people is possible. This is for policy issues in, for example, the fields of occupation, health, housing, and education. As long as different "ethnic groups" have differential access to jobs and incomes, to health care and housing allocation, as well as to consumption and life chances, it is necessary to maintain "ethnic classifications." This is, of course, in order to work toward redressing such imbalances. To take one example, in order to understand racism in the U.K. and the U.S., it is necessary to delineate the various constituencies of racialized people in those societies (see chapters 2 and 3 of this volume for a discussion).

Third, "ethnicity" is needed to understand "ethnic conflict." One might call this "racialized ethnicity." In order to understand "ethnic conflict," we need to analyze why self-selected "ethnic groups" perceive other groups of people (whether self-selected as an "ethnic group" or not) as "ethnically problematic" and/or as a threat and/or enemy. History confirms that this is needed both at a local and national level, on a continent-wide level, and on a global level.

For these reasons, I would maintain that, even though its explanatory power is limited, "ethnicity" needs to be retained as a self-selected defining category.[5]

Racism

In chapters 3 and 4, I demonstrate the need for a wide-ranging definition of racism in order to account for the multifarious forms and variations of it that accompany changes in the capitalist mode of production, and immigration patterns in the U.K. and the U.S. It is necessary, first of all, to define what I mean by racism.[6]

I would like to identify nine features of modern-day racism, both in its ideological[7] forms and its material practices. First, contemporary racism might best be thought of as a matrix of biological and cultural racism. I would argue that, in that matrix, racism can be based on biology or genetics. This is the case in notions of white people having higher IQs than black people. With respect to the U.S., see Herrnstein and Murray, 1994; [8] even more recently in the U.S., Nobel laureate James Watson in 2007 claimed inferior intelligence for "Africans" and "black employees" (Herrnstein and Murray, 1994). As far as the U.K. is concerned, see Frank Ellis (Gair, 2006).[9] Racism can also be based on culture and/or religion (as in contemporary manifestations of Islamophobia—see chapters 2 and 3 of this volume). Sometimes, however, it is not easily identifiable as either (e.g., "Britain jobs for British workers," discussed in chapter 2 of this volume), or is a combination of both. A good example of the latter is when Margaret Thatcher, at the time of the 1982 Falklands/Malvinas war, referred to the people of that island as "an island race" whose "way of life is British" (Short and Carrington, 1996, p. 66). Here we have a conflation of notions of "an island race" (like the British "race" who, Baroness Thatcher believes, built an empire and ruled a quarter of the world through its sterling qualities (Thatcher, 1982) and, in addition, a "race," which is culturally, like "us": "their way of life is British."

Second, there are also forms of racism that can be quite unintentional, which demonstrates that you do not have to be *a* racist (i.e., have allegiance to far-Right ideologies) to be racist, or to be implicated in generating racism consequences. The use by some people in the U.K., *out of ignorance*, of the term "Pakistani" to refer to everyone whose mode of dress or accent, for example, signifies that they might be of Asian origin might be an example of unintentional racism. The use of the nomenclature "Paki," on the other hand, I would suggest, is generally used in an intentionally racist way because of the generally known negative connotations attached to the word in the U.K. Another example from the U.K. is the now outmoded term "colored" (coloured in U.K. spelling)—as in the usage "colored people," still used to describe black people. This may or may not be used in an intentionally racist way. "People of color" in the U.S., on the other hand, is not racist, and is routinely used by people who are not white as an inclusive nomenclature. "Colored People," however, is still used in the title of the organization by the National Association for the Advancement of Colored People (NAACP) in the U.S. There are, of course, also terms on both sides of the Atlantic to describe black people that are intentionally offensive.

Third, racism can be direct or indirect. Direct racism is where a person is treated less favorably than another on "racial" grounds. Indirect racism occurs when people from a specific "racial" group cannot meet a rule, condition, or practice that should apply equally to everyone. For example, if school rules require a form of dress to which certain groups cannot comply for religious reasons—it could be because they are Muslims or Sikhs—this would be a form of indirect racism.

Fourth, racism, as practices, can be overt, as in racist name-calling in schools, or it can be covert, as in racist mutterings in school corridors, as a racialized person walks by.

Fifth, whereas for neo-Marxist Robert Miles (1989, p. 79), racism relates to social collectivities identified as "races" being "attributed with negatively evaluated characteristics and/or represented as inducing negative consequences for any other," I would want to inflate Miles's definition to include "seemingly positive attributes."[10] Ascribing such attributes to an "ethnic group" will probably ultimately have racist implications. For example, the subtext of describing a particular group as having a strong culture might be that "they are swamping *our* culture." This form of racism is often directed at people of South Asian origin in the U.K. who are assumed to have close-knit families and to be hard working, and therefore in a position to "take over" *our* neighborhoods.[11] Frank Wu makes very similar observations about Asian Americans (see chapter 3 of this volume for a discussion). In addition, attributing something seemingly positive—"*they* are good rappers" or they are good at sports—might have implications that "they are not good" at other things. In education this is something that facilitates the underachievement of working class U.K. African Caribbean boys and U.S. African American boys who are thought to be (by some teachers) less academically able, and "problems." Stereotypes and stratifications of ethnic groups are invariably problematic and, at least potentially, racist.

Sixth, racism can be dominative (in the form of direct and oppressive state policy) as in the apartheid era in South Africa or slavery in the U.S. (see chapter 3 of this volume), or it can be aversive, where people are segregated, excluded, or cold-shouldered on the grounds of racism (Kovel, 1988), or where they are routinely treated less favorably in day-to-day interactions.

Seventh, in certain situations, racism may well become (more) apparent given specific stimuli. For example, the communications ideological state apparatus (defined in chapter 1 of this volume) can generate racism. In the U.S., conservative mass media opposition to Obama's health care proposals prompted neurosurgeon David McKalip to e-mail an image of the president as a "witch doctor" in July 2009 to the conservative Tea Party, a right-wing pressure group.[12]

Similarly, racist sentiments or responses from a number of people who might be collectively present (physically or connected via the communications ideological state apparatus, or hooked up cybernetically) at a given moment or moments can facilitate further racist sentiments or responses. The Southern Poverty Law Center (SPLC) (2010c) pointed out that extremist "patriot" groups "came roaring back to life" in 2009, their numbers rising nearly 250 percent to more than 500, and with increasing ties to conservative mainstream politics.

Already there are signs of…violence emanating from the radical right. Since the installation of Barack Obama, right-wing extremists have murdered six law enforcement officers. Racist skinheads and others have been arrested in alleged plots to assassinate the nation's first black president. One man from Brockton, Massachusetts—who told police he had learned on white supremacist websites that a genocide was under way against whites—is charged with murdering two black people and planning to kill as many Jews as possible on the day after Obama's inauguration. Most recently, a rash of individuals with anti-government, survivalist or racist views have been arrested in a series of bomb cases. (SPLC, 2010a, cited in McGreal, 2010)

In addition, racism can increase with racist advances in the realm of the political ideological state apparatus (Althusser's concept of the ideological state apparatuses is defined in chapter 1 of this volume). In the U.K., racist attacks tend to increase when the fascist.[13] British National Party (BNP) gains seats in local elections (e.g., Booth, 2010) or in European elections. Thus following the election of BNP leader Nick Griffin to the European Parliament in June 2009, a string of racist attacks took place in the northwest of England, the area from which Griffin was elected (Choonara, 2009, p. 1) (The rise and fall of the BNP is discussed in chapter 1 of this volume.)

Eighth, it should be noted that when somebody starts a sentence with the phrase "I'm not racist but…," the undertone means that the next utterance will invariably be racist.

Ninth, racism is often color-coded, but it can be non-color-coded, or it can be hybridist, where it is not clear whether it is color-coded or non-color-coded. It can also be a combination of color-coded and non-color-coded racism (see chapter 2 of this volume for a discussion).

Racism defined

To reiterate my arguments, racism can be based on cultural and/or religious factors as well as biological ones, or it can be based on a combination of both biological and cultural and/or religious factors; racism can also be not easily identifiable as either biological or cultural. Racism can be unintentional as well as intentional; it can be direct or indirect; it can be overt as well as covert. Moreover "seemingly positive" attributes will probably ultimately have racist implications. Racism can be dominative (direct and oppressive) as well as aversive (exclusion and cold-shouldering). Racism can also become (more) apparent given certain stimuli. It should also be borne in mind that sentences that begin, "I'm not racist but…" should be regarded as introducing a racist feeling or thought. Finally, racism is often color-coded, but it can be non-color-coded, or it can be hybridist, where it is not clear whether it is color-coded or non-color-coded. It can also be a combination of color-coded and non-color-coded racism. There can, of course, be permutations among these various forms of racism.

For these reasons, to underline my arguments, I would maintain that, in order to encompass the multifaceted nature of contemporary racism, it is important to adopt a broad concept and definition of racism, rather than a narrow one based on biological inferiority. Such a biological conception of racism was, of course, the norm in the days of the British Empire in India, Africa, and elsewhere; in the British colonies in America with respect to Native Americans; in the pre–civil rights U.S. with respect to African

Americans; and, just before and after the Spanish Conquest, for the civilizations of Central America. In these historical scenarios, no doubt notions of cultural inferiority coexisted with perceptions of biological inferiority.

The Neo-Marxist Concept of Racialization

Racialization refers to the categorization of people (falsely) into distinct "races." The neo-Marxist concept of racialization is distinct from other interpretations of racialization in that it purports that, in order to understand and combat racism, we must relate racism and racialization to historical, economic, and political factors.

Specifically, the neo-Marxist concept of racialization makes the connection between racism and capitalist modes of production as well as making links to patterns of migration that are in themselves determined by economic and political dynamics. Thus the concept is able to relate to these factors; namely, the real material contexts of struggle (see chapters 2 and 3 of this volume for a discussion of racialization in the U.K. and the U.S., respectively).

Miles (1993, pp. 50–52) has defined racialization as an ideological process, where people are categorized falsely into the scientifically defunct notion of distinct "races." Racialization, like racism, is socially constructed. In Miles's (1989, p. 75) words, racialization refers to "those instances where social relations between people have been structured by the signification of human biological characteristics [elsewhere in the same book, Miles (p. 79) has added cultural characteristics] in such a way as to define and *construct* [my emphasis] differentiated social collectivities." "[T]he process of racialization," Miles states, "cannot be adequately understood without a conception of, and explanation for the complex interplay of different modes of production and, in particular, of the social relations necessarily established in the course of material production" (Miles, 1987, p. 7). It is this articulation with modes of production and with the ideological and the cultural that makes Miles's concept of racialization and my concept of xeno-racialization (Cole, 2004a)—see chapter 2 of this volume—inherently Marxist.[14]

Racialization and "common sense"

For Marxists, any discourse is a product of the society in which it is formulated. In other words, "our thoughts are the reflection of political, social and economic conflicts and racist discourses are no exception" (Camara, 2002, p. 88). Dominant discourses (e.g., those of the repressive state apparatuses [RSAs] and ideological state apparatuses [ISAs])—see chapter 1 of this volume) tend to directly reflect the interests of the ruling class, rather than "the general public."

The way in which popular consciousness is interpellated or hailed (see chapter 1 of this volume) by specters of racialized "others" is via "common sense." "Common sense" is generally used to denote a down-to-earth "good sense" and is thought to represent the distilled truths of centuries of practical experience, so that to say an idea or practice is "only common sense" is to claim precedence over the arguments of Left intellectuals and, in effect, to foreclose discussion (Lawrence, 1982, p. 48). As Diana Coben (2002, p. 285) has noted, Gramsci's distinction between good sense and common sense "has been revealed as multifaceted and complex." For common sense:

> is not a single unique conception, identical in time and space. It is the "folk-lore" of philosophy, and, like folklore, it takes countless different forms. Its most fundamental characteristic is that it is…fragmentary, incoherent and inconsequential. (Gramsci, 1978, p. 419)

Good sense, on the other hand, for Gramsci is exemplified by Marxism. As Coben (1999, p. 206) has argued, good sense, for Gramsci, "may be created out of common sense through an educative Marxist politics." Gramsci believed that " 'everyone' is a philosopher, and that it is not a question of introducing from scratch a scientific form of thought into everyone's individual life, but of renovating and making 'critical' an already existing activity" (Gramsci 1978, pp. 330–331). Gramsci also believed that "[a]ll men are intellectuals,… but not all men have in society the function of intellectuals" (ibid., p. 9). Extending these insights to the whole of humankind (not just men!) forms the basis of the values that inform this book.[15]

Institutional Racism

Both the U.K. and the U.S. are institutional racist societies. That the U.K. is such was recognized by the Stephen Lawrence Inquiry Report (Macpherson, 1999).[16] This definition was given a formal seal of approval by its having been read in the House of Commons on February 24, 1999, by the then Home Secretary, Jack Straw. It is interesting to note, however, that in repeating the definition verbatim in his speech to the House, Straw stresses the word, "unwitting" (http://news.bbc.co.uk/1/hi/uk/285553.stm—audio link available). Institutional racism is defined in the report as:

> The collective failure of an organisation to provide an appropriate and professional service to people because of their colour, culture, or ethnic origin. It can be seen or detected in processes, attitudes and behaviour which amount to discrimination through unwitting prejudice, ignorance, thoughtlessness and racist stereotyping which disadvantage minority ethnic people. (Macpherson, 1999, 6.34)

From a neo-Marxist perspective, there is a need to situate the concept historically, economically, and politically. The Marxist concept of racialization thus also needs to be included to move away from the nebulous and ahistorical definition of institutional racism provided by Macpherson. I believe such a definition also needs to include "common sense," which I argued in the last section of this Introduction, connects racialization with popular consciousness. Finally, in line with my definition of racism formulated earlier in this Introduction, I would also want to add *intentional* as well as unintentional or unwitting racism. Institutional racism is thus reformulated as:

> Collective acts and/or procedures in an institution or institutions (locally, nationwide, continent-wide, or globally) that intentionally or unintentionally have the effect of racializing, via "common sense," certain populations or groups of people. This racialization process cannot be understood without reference to economic and political factors related to developments and changes in national, continent-wide, and global capitalism.[17]

Outline of the Book

The primary aim of this book is to promote awareness of *racism; socialism; Marxism;* and *neo-Marxism* in order to contest world capitalism and imperialism, and to encourage the worldwide export of twenty-first-century democratic socialism from its stronghold in Latin America, and, in particular, in Venezuela. In order to do this, it is necessary to provide an in-depth analysis of the above-italicized concepts.

Having defined racism, racialization, and institutional racism, it is next necessary to establish why I believe we need *neo*-Marxism—in particular the work of Althusser and Gramsci, as well as Marxism—in order to get a full picture of racism, schooling, and education in the U.K. and the U.S. For example, I need to argue why the neo-Marxist concepts of interpellation and hegemony are useful to understand how the ruling capitalist class attempts to forestall a consideration of a humane alternative to world capitalism, such as democratic socialism. At the same time, however, it is necessary to establish how the Marxist concept of counter-hegemonic struggle against racism, capitalism and imperialism makes us aware that resistance is possible and that another world is possible.

At the beginning of this Introduction I made some brief comments about socialism and Marxism. In the first part of chapter 1 of this volume, I discuss the historical trajectory of modern socialism from its utopian origins to classical Marxism or scientific socialism, as formulated by Karl Marx and Friedrich Engels, and as described by the latter. One of two key components of scientific socialism—the materialist conception of history—is then discussed (the other, the labor theory of value, is outlined in an appendix to the chapter). I then address socialism and internationalism, focusing on the first, second, third, and fourth internationals, paving the way for a consideration in chapter 5 of the call of President Hugo Rafael Chávez Frías of Venezuela for a fifth international.

Next, in chapter 1, I assess, within socialist thinking, notions of inevitability and imminence, which are present in certain versions of the materialist conception of history. This prepares the ground for a discussion of neo-Marxism, which was a response to these notions in the sense that the *inevitability* and *imminence* of socialism proved to be ill founded. Specifically, I examine the responses of Gramsci and Althusser, respectively. I go on to argue that we need both *structural* Marxism (stressing the power of the structures of capitalism), as represented by the work of Althusser, and *humanist* Marxism (stressing the importance of the will and struggles against capitalism), as detailed in Gramsci's writings, to get a full picture of the way in which capitalism constrains us, but also of how counter-capitalist strategies and ensuing struggles for socialism are possible, and indeed omnipresent, though of massively varying significance historically and geographically. I concentrate on Gramsci's concept of hegemony as well as both Althusser's analysis of the state apparatuses and his theory of interpellation. In order to exemplify the efficacy of these neo-Marxist concepts to interpret concrete reality, I conclude chapter 1 with a discussion of current U.K. and U.S. politics.

In chapters 2 and 3, I apply a neo-Marxist analysis to racism in the U.K. and U.S., respectively, noting that it takes multifarious forms in both countries, and arguing that the Marxist concept of racialization is best equipped to both understand and to challenge these diverse forms of racism. I begin, however, in chapter 1, by attempting to establish why it is necessary to categorize racism in the first place. With respect to the U.K., I look at older forms of racism—colonial racism, antisemitism, and anti-Gypsy and Roma Traveller racism; as well as at some newer forms—xeno-racism, anti-asylum-seeker racism, and Islamophobia, respectively. For conceptual clarity, I deal with color-coded, non-color-coded racism, and what I call "hybridist racism" separately.

As far as the U.S. is concerned, in chapter 3 I begin by addressing the legacy of Christopher Columbus with respect to racism directed at Native Americans, both historically and contemporaneously, before moving on to a consideration of other major groups affected by racism in the U.S.—African Americans; Latina/o[18] Americans; Asian Americans; and Native Hawaiians and Pacific Islander Americans. I then look at Islamophobia in the U.S., before concluding the chapter with a consideration of antisemitism and the proliferation of hate groups.

In both chapters 2 and 3, I use the Gramscian concept of "common sense" to assess how racialization interpellates popular consciousness. Central to these processes of racialization and xeno-racialization are the roles of the repressive state apparatuses (RSAs) and the ideological state apparatuses (ISAs) as developed by Althusser. I also look at various forms of counter-hegemonic resistance (derived from Gramsci) to racism.[19] With respect to the U.K., in chapter 2, I outline the various groups active in antiracist work. As far as the U.S. is concerned, since Critical Race Theory (CRT) provides a convenient lens through which to view different forms of racism there, in chapter 3, I draw on the work of some key Critical Race Theorists.[20] Key considerations are (different) ways in which, in the U.S., the various constituencies of people of color reject interpellation processes, and engage in (different) forms of antiracist struggle.

In the first part of chapter 4, I make a distinction between schooling (a conforming process), on the one hand, and education (a liberating practice) on the other. To do this, I draw on the work of Althusser and Gramsci. Next, I examine racism and schooling in the U.K. and the U.S. and the ways in which Marxist educators have challenged racism in both countries, and the constraints they have been and continue to be up against.

In order to flesh out the actualities of twenty-first-century socialism, in chapter 5, my concern is with what I consider to be the best currently existing model. That model is the Bolivarian Republic of Venezuela. President Chávez's description of the country as "a giant school" is a most apt description of the processes occurring there, processes that are counter-hegemonic to capitalism and to imperialism. After briefly considering the historical context of the Bolivarian Revolution, I address the ascendancy of social democracy and the moves toward socialism. I then examine the significance of President Chávez's call for a fifth Socialist International. I also look at current (self-) education of the people generally in the theory and practice of socialism. In that context, I address the issue of whether there is a need to amend Althusser's RSA/ISA thesis, specifically and uniquely in the context of Venezuela. Attention is also given in this chapter to antiracist initiatives with respect to Afro-Venezuelans and indigenous peoples. I then address the role of the education system in the ongoing revolution in that country. As a case study, I look at the actual and hidden curriculum of a new school that is being started in a barrio[21] in Mérida. The people working there are revolutionaries, trying to implement socialist change.

In the final chapter of the book, I draw on the preceding analysis in an attempt to provide practical implications for multicultural antiracist socialist practice in educational institutions in the U.K. and the U.S. I insist that the capitalist notion that young people are saddled with varying and hierarchical "abilities" is fallacious, and that, in fact, all learners can learn without limits. The curriculum, I argue, in order to perform an educative role rather than school young people for capitalism, and to facilitate the move toward antiracism and liberation, should include multicultural antiracist education, the teaching of imperialisms,[22] media education, and political education. Political education, I stress, should include a serious consideration of twenty-first-century democratic socialism, of what I call "the last taboo."

One of the features of twentieth-century socialism was its relative neglect (understandably, given the historical context in which it occurred) of issues other than social class. While it is social class that holds capitalism and imperialism together, and while my specific focus in this volume has been racism, twenty-first-century socialists are committed to the promotion of equality for all.[23] To that end, an edited book, *Education, Equality and Human Rights: Issues of Gender, "Race," Sexual Orientation, Disability and Social Class* (Cole [ed] 2011), is due to be published at approximately the same time as this volume. It deals with the equality issues of its subtitle, both per se and with respect to schooling and education.

Appendix

Miles (1989) argues that the concept of racism should not include actions and processes as well as discourses. Indeed, he argues that "racism" should be used to refer exclusively to an *ideological* phenomenon, and not to exclusionary *practices*. He gives three reasons for this. First, exclusionary practice can result from both intentional and unintentional actions (Miles, ibid., p. 78). I have argued, however, that the fact that racist discourse is unintentional does not detract from its capacity to embody racism. For its recipients, effect is more important than intention (see my definition of racism in this Introduction). Second, Miles argues, such practices do not presuppose the nature of the determination; for example, the disadvantaged position of black people is not necessarily the result of racism (ibid.). However, the fact that the "disadvantaged position of black people is not necessarily the result of racism" is addressed by Miles's own theoretical approach, a class-based analysis that also recognizes other bases of unequal treatment. Therefore, I would argue, this recognition does not need the singling out that Miles affords it. Miles's third reason for making racism exclusively ideological is that there is a dialectical relationship[24] between exclusion and inclusion: to exclude is simultaneously to include, and vice versa. For example, the over-representation of African Caribbean children in "special schools" for the "educationally subnormal" (ESN) in the 1960s involves both exclusion from "normal schools" and inclusion in ESN schools (ibid.). I do not see the purpose of this attempt to privilege inclusion. The simultaneous inclusion of black people entailed by exclusion is, by and large, a negative inclusion, as in the case of Miles's own example of ESN schools, which carried a social stigma at the time, and goes against the contemporary consensus in the U.K. for inclusive education. There are, of course, situations where exclusion on account of the application of positive labels leads to positive consequences for those thus labeled. The way monarchies and aristocracies are perceived is an obvious example. They are excluded from everyday life but included in very elite settings with multiple positive benefits. I fail to see how Miles's observation about the dialectical relationship between exclusion and inclusion informs an analysis of racism.

Miles's position on not inflating the concept of racism retains a fervent following among sociologists at the University of Glasgow, where Miles first expounded his views on racism and racialization. I attended a workshop there in 2006, titled *What Can Marxism Teach Critical Race Theory about Racism* (Centre for Research on Racism, Ethnicity and Nationalism [CRREN] Department of Sociology, Anthropology & Applied Social Sciences, University of Glasgow). Some Marxist sociologists who attended were quite insistent on defending Miles's position, and stressed the need to use *Marxist* terminology rather than the concept of racism (though no such terminology was generally forthcoming).[25] One contributor went as far as to express the view that "there is not a lot of racism out there." Another, also following Miles, stated that racism should be narrowed down, and confined to the level of *ideas*, and that *actions* should not be described as racist. The same delegate found the concept of racialization problematic, adding that people "magically becoming racialized" is meaningless (see chapters 2 and 3 of this volume for a discussion of racialization in the U.K. and the U.S.). Another delegate argued that, whereas once people were sure what racism was, now both in the U.K. and globally, it is difficult to understand what racism is (see chapters 2 and 3 of this volume for attempts at explanation with respect to the U.K. and the U.S., respectively).

While I understand Miles's and his supporters' desire to retain a Marxist analysis, and not to reify racism (since describing actions and processes as "racist" may forestall an analysis of various practices in different historical periods of capitalist development), it is my view, as I attempt to demonstrate in this book, that it is *precisely* the neo-Marxist concepts of racialization (and xeno-racialization[26]) that enable, and indeed *require*, a persistent and constant analysis of the multiple manifestations of racism in different phases of the capitalist mode of production in different historical periods. Indeed, I try to show in this Introduction that, contrary to Miles, not only should racism be inflated to incorporate actions, processes, and practices, but that it should, in fact, be inflated considerably to include a *wide range* of actions, processes, and practices. Miles and the Marxist defenders of his position are right to be wary of any tendency to call everything "racist" and thereby to foreclose discussion. However, in my view, there are grounds for believing that if an action or process is perceived to be racist, then it probably is. Indeed this is enshrined in the excellent U.K. Race Relations (Amendment) Act (2000), now under threat from the concept of "community cohesion" (see chapter 4 of this volume for a discussion).

What I think should distinguish a neo-Marxist analysis of racism is the attempt to relate various instances of racism and (xeno-) racialization to different stages in capitalist development (as developed in the rest of this book), but also to relate them to political and other ideological factors. This is not to say that all individual or institutional instances of racism and racialization are reducible to the economy (Miles acknowledges this as a functionalist position), but that racism and racialization in capitalist countries need to be understood in terms of stages and processes in capitalist development.

I take the position that there are striking similarities in actions and processes of racism and (xeno-) racialization directed against different people in differing economic, political, and ideological circumstances (see chapter 2 of this volume for a discussion). Thus, as I have argued, from *my* particular Marxist perspective,[27] the concept of racism should be wide-ranging and fluid.

Chapter 1

Socialism, Marxism, and Neo-Marxism

In order to understand Marxism (which Engels described as scientific socialism) and neo-Marxism, it is first necessary to briefly address earlier visions of socialism. Accordingly I focus on the work of three key utopian socialist thinkers: Henri de Saint-Simon, Charles Fourier, and Robert Owen. I then discuss Engels's assessment of the contributions of the utopian socialists to scientific socialism in the light of his overall critique of utopian socialism as a general theory. I conclude with a consideration of the neo-Marxist response to a key aspect of scientific socialism, the materialist conception of history when interpreted as promising inevitable and imminent socialism. Specifically I outline some of the major theoretical concepts of Gramsci and Althusser. To illustrate the efficacy of these concepts, I outline some recent events in party politics in the U.K. and the U.S.

Utopian Socialism

The common ownership, cooperation, and collective activity that socialism entails are not new to humankind. In fact, in very early history, most, if not all, societies held common property in the soil and were grouped according to kindred. Modern socialism, however, was born in the nineteenth century in Britain and France. The word was first used publicly in English in 1827 in connection with the movement associated with Robert Owen; and in French, in 1835, with respect to the supporters of Henri de Saint-Simon (Berki, 1975, p. 12). I will summarize some key aspects of each of these utopian socialists' work here as well as the other main utopian socialist, Charles Fourier, also French, as they pertain to the development of the materialist conception of history, as analyzed by Engels, and subsequently by Gramsci and Althusser.[1]

Saint-Simon

For Henri de Saint-Simon (1760–1825), the liberation of humanity was to come about when the bourgeoisie (manufacturers, merchants, and bankers) transformed themselves into "public officials" who, holding a commanding and economically privileged position vis-à-vis the working class, would pave the way forward for this liberation. The bankers especially were to be central in this. Given the enormity of the greed of bankers worldwide, particularly transparent in the current crisis in capitalism, one cannot fail to see the irony of Saint-Simon's faith in the bankers.

Saint-Simon's favored society was not intended to be democratic or egalitarian. Wages would be allotted to each, according to their respective contributions to the common good (Crick, 1987, p. 33). His vision was a state of harmony between capital and labor: an elitist vision of a centralized and planned industrial society administered for the common good and looking to the future. As Bernard Crick (ibid.) points out, it is "a picture of a capitalist society without a free-market [and] with a collective capacity to organise and steer the economy for the common good." Like Marxism, as we shall see below, the theory underlying Saint-Simon's utopia is of stages of human development.

What is of greatest significance in Saint-Simon's thoughts for the subsequent development of Marxism is his recognition of class struggle, but in his case, the bourgeois struggle against the aristocracy. Thus Saint-Simon writes of the "struggle between the King and the great vassals, between the chiefs of industrial enterprises and the nobles...the direct action of the industrials against the nobles" (Saint-Simon, 1817 [1975], p. 246). He also refers to "the two classes [that] existed in the nation...before the...industrials...those who commanded and those who obeyed" (ibid., p. 247). As Engels (1892 [1977], pp. 399–400) notes, to recognize the French Revolution as a class war was "a most pregnant discovery."

Fourier

François-Marie-Charles Fourier (1772–1837) believed that "[u]nder a true organization of Commerce property would be abolished, the Mercantile classes become agents for trade of industrial goods and Commerce would then be the servant of Society" (Fourier, 1820, p. 1). Fourier was a strong advocate of communities (phalanxes) where labor would be more attractive, a source of constant joy, rather than sweat and toil. In Fourier's phalanxes, rich and poor would all enjoy that which he described as "trifling work" (cited in Kreis, 2006, p. 7), as well as the work of the artisans.

Like Saint-Simon, Fourier did not believe in economic equality, nor had he any objection to unearned income derived from the possession of capital. Indeed he constantly appealed to capitalists to come forward to finance his envisaged communities. Equality, he believed, was inconsistent with human nature, which dictates that we have a natural desire to be rewarded according to our work (Cole, 1971, p. 67). God, Fourier believed, created human nature, and organized society should respect that and not try to fight it (Kreis, 2006, p. 4).

For Engels (1892 [1977], p. 401), Fourier's greatest contribution to socialism is his dialectical conception of history.[2] Thus Fourier sees societies as having moved through four stages: savagery, barbarism, the patriarchate, and civilization. The last stage is the modern bourgeois society in which he lived. However, whereas Marxists employ dialectical thinking in a progressive way (see later in this chapter for a discussion), Fourier's dialectic view of history ends in the ultimate destruction of the human race. The moral bankruptcy and hypocrisy inherent in the bourgeoisie in the aftermath of the French Revolution exemplifies a stage in this process of destruction (ibid., p. 401).

Owen

Robert Owen (1771–1858) came to prominence when he acquired the New Lanark cotton mills in 1800. Owen's philanthropic capitalism is witnessed by the fact that he worked his employees only ten and a half hours, compared to his competitors' thirteen or fourteen; paid full wages when a crisis in cotton stopped work for four months; and founded infant schools in New Lanark (ibid., p. 402). Believing that everyone is capable of goodness and excellence, he was driven by the need for two great changes: the abandonment of unregulated brutal competition between capitalist employers, and the eradication of false beliefs about the formation of character (Cole, 1971, p. 88).

Owen was concerned about these evils brought on by the Industrial Revolution and deeply revolted by the accompanying poverty, and gradually became convinced that human character was the product of the environments and social systems in which people grow up, rather than character being the fault of the individual (a position that was to become a central tenet of Marxism; see Cole, 2008a, pp. 129–130).

In *Report to the County of Lanark* (1820), Owen put forward his views on the labor theory of value (LTV), soon to become the economic foundation stone of the writings of Marx, suggesting that labor should supersede money as the standard for measuring the relative values of different commodities (Cole, 1971, pp. 94–95) (for a discussion of Marx's LTV, see Appendix 1 to this chapter).

Owen favored a form of "communism"[3] based on businesses funding communist colonies. Thus in 1823, he proposed the relief of distress in Ireland by the foundation of such colonies. In the following year he bought the community village of New Harmony in Indiana (ibid., p. 96) for a similar project of a self-governing community. However, the experiment was racked by sectarianism (ibid., p. 100) and, in 1829, Owen returned to England.

Owen's ideas had a firm hold in the trade (labor) unions, which were springing up all over the country. Owen himself established the Grand National Consolidated Trades Union, which, at its height, had over half a million members (MacKenzie, 1967, pp. 34–35). His ideas also inspired a number of cooperative enterprises and, in 1844, the Rochdale Equitable Pioneers set up the modern cooperative movement (ibid., p. 3) that is still flourishing in Britain today.

For Engels, Owen's great significance in the development of socialism (as noted earlier, the word itself, according to MacKenzie (ibid., p. 35), was first used in an Owenite paper) was his advocacy of "communism," albeit business-based, his commitment to the working class, and his advocacy of cooperatives. As Engels (1892 [1977], p. 404) puts it, "every social movement, every real advance in England on behalf of the workers links itself on to the name of Robert Owen."

Scientific Socialism (i.e., Marxism)

For Engels (ibid.), as we have seen, Saint-Simon's major contribution to Marxism was his recognition of class struggle; Fourier's was dialectical thinking; and Owen's bequest was communism and his dedication to workers' welfare. What these utopian socialists all had in common was that, unlike Marxists who advocate the revolutionary emancipation of the working class in order to change society, the utopian socialists were concerned with liberating all humanity without such revolutionary changes. As Marx and Engels (1847) [1977], p. 60) point out, Saint-Simon, Fourier, and Owen all recognized the class antagonisms in existing societies, but viewed the working class as "a class without any historical initiative." This is primarily because of the "undeveloped state" of the proletariat[4] at the time (ibid.). For the utopian socialists, change was to come about by "peaceful means," by "small experiments," and by "force of example" (ibid.). Marx and Engels, on the other hand, "openly declare that their ends can be attained only by the forcible overthrow of all existing social conditions" (ibid., p. 63).[5]

Although Marx denounced utopian socialism, he never actually referred to his own ideas as "scientific socialism." It was, in fact, Engels (1892 [1977], p. 404) who, believing utopian socialism to be "a mish-mash" of "absolute truth, reason, and justice" based on "subjective understandings" associated with various schools of utopian socialist thought, argued that "to make a science of socialism, it had first to be placed upon a real basis" (ibid., p. 405) (his and Marx's conception of "utopia" accords with its original meaning, "a place that does not exist").

Engels (ibid., p. 428) explains the role of scientific socialists in capitalist society, when referring to the proletarian revolution, which:

> frees the means of production from the character of capital they have thus far borne, and gives their socialised character complete freedom to work itself out...To thoroughly comprehend the historical conditions and thus the very nature of this act, to impart to the now oppressed proletarian class a full knowledge of the conditions and of the meaning of the momentous act it is called upon to accomplish...is the task of the theoretical expression of the proletarian movement, scientific socialism.

The "real basis" of Marxism is the *materialist conception of history* and the *labor theory of value* (LTV) (the basis of *surplus value*). As Engels (1877 [1962], p. 43) argues:

[t]hese two great discoveries, the materialist conception of history and the revelation of the secret of capitalistic production through surplus value, we owe to Marx. With these discoveries socialism became a science.

Since the materialist conception of history is more relevant to my purposes in introducing the relative theoretical contributions of Gramsci and Althusser, I will deal with it in the main text (for a discussion of the LTV, see Appendix 1 to this chapter).

The materialist conception of history

As Engels explains, the materialist conception of history "starts from the proposition that the production of the means to support human life and, next to production, the exchange of things produced, is the basis of all social structure" (Engels, 1892 [1977], p. 411). The materialist conception of history is most clearly explained by Marx (1859) in the "Preface" to *A Contribution to the Critique of Political Economy*. Marx argues that the way we think is fundamentally related to forces of production. As he puts it:

> My inquiry led me to the conclusion that neither legal relations nor political forms could be comprehended whether by themselves or on the basis of a so-called general development of the human mind, but that on the contrary they originate in the material conditions of life...In the social production of their existence, men inevitably enter into definite relations, which are independent of their will, namely relations of production appropriate to a given stage in the development of their material forces of production. The totality of these relations of production constitutes the economic structure of society, the real foundation, on which arises a legal and political superstructure and to which correspond definite forms of social consciousness. The mode of production of material life conditions the general process of social, political and intellectual life. It is not the consciousness of men that determines their existence, but their social existence that determines their consciousness.

Marx argued that societies progress through various stages. Moreover, all past history, with the exception of its most early stage (primitive communism— the original hunter-gatherer society of humanity) is, according to Marx and Engels, the history of class struggles. These warring classes are always the products of the respective modes of production, of the *economic* conditions of their time. Thus slaves were in class struggle with their masters in the historical epoch of ancient slavery; feudal serfs with their lords in times of feudalism; and in the era of capitalism, workers are engaged in a class struggle with capitalists. Like ancient slavery and feudalism, capitalism is viewed merely as a *stage* in human development. Marxists see such stages as containing a number of *contradictions*, which resolve themselves dialectically. Thus when these contradictions become too great, a given stage gives way to another. For example, just as the privileges that feudal lords held and the hereditary basis of subordinating serf to lord in the feudal societies contradicted the need for "free" labor power in emerging capitalism ("free" in the sense that workers were not needed to be indentured to the capitalists; they were, of course, forced to sell their labor power in order to survive), present-day capitalism contains contradictions that Marxists believe, *given the right circumstances*, can eventually lead to its demise, and be replaced by socialism.

It is worth reiterating here what was pointed out in the Introduction to this volume; namely that socialism, as understood by Marx and Engels, is profoundly and genuinely democratic. Under socialism, wealth is shared equally, workers own and control the means of production distribution and exchange, and make decisions *democratically*. Democracy entails decisions being taken by workers, not just in the polity but in the schools, factories, shops, offices. and everywhere else they work, workplaces that would be collectively owned by these workers. Socialism, thus understood, is far removed from many dictatorial regimes that have described themselves as "socialist," even though some, such as the Soviet Union, began with democratically socialist ideals (see Appendix 2 to this chapter for a fuller discussion of socialism; see chapter 5 for a discussion of participatory democracy and twenty-first-century socialism in Venezuela).

Socialism and Internationalism

The First International

As well as being authentically democratic, socialism is also essentially international. The First Socialist International was formed in 1864 in London. As Saul Padover notes (cited in MIA, undated a):

> [t]he meeting was jammed with a large number of assorted radicals...united not by a commonly shared ideology or even by genuine internationalism, but by an accumulated burden of variated grievances crying for an outlet...There was no necessary or integral interconnection among them—except what Marx later tried to provide in the [organization] that followed the meeting.

The meeting unanimously voted to appoint a provisional committee, of which Marx was a member, to work out a program and membership rules for the proposed international organization. Subsequently, the committee formed a small subcommittee to do the actual work. Marx became a member of this crucial subcommittee (Padover, cited in MIA, undated b). As Padover explains, "[h]enceforth Marx was to remain its predominant spirit and the indomitable personality that held the disparate International Association together for eight difficult and often stormy years, until it was shattered by bitter internal dissensions" (cited in ibid.) (for details of the political and social work of the First International, see Eichhoff, 1869). Padover concludes (cited in ibid.):

> In the International, Marx saw a great historic opportunity, and seized it. Indeed, it is questionable whether the organization would have survived, or

would have had any meaning, without him. His steely will and impassioned commitment to the idea of the revolutionary role of the world proletariat prevented the International from passing into the same oblivion as had other dreams of squabbly radicals, confused in their philosophy and at cross-purposes in their aims.

The Second International

Twelve years after the demise of the First International in 1876, the Second International was founded in 1889, with the help of Engels, and was based largely on the organizational success of its largest section, the German Social Democratic Party (Walters, 2001). The Second Socialist International itself was an *instrument* of socialist revolution, which cut across international boundaries that divided the working class (ibid.). As David Walters (2001) explains, the Second International "existed as a loose federation of the world's socialist parties, most of whom described themselves as 'Marxist,'" and "included openly reformist type organizations that saw a gradual implementation of reforms of capitalism to achieve socialism; socialist parties based on unions, or 'Labor' parties; and revolutionary workers parties that saw the need to openly smash the capitalist state structure." Lenin called for the reformists to be expelled from the Second International on the grounds that having two different currents in the organization could only paralyze it (Swain, 2010). After Engels's death in 1895, and into the early twentieth century, class struggle intensified both in the U.S. and in Europe, opening fissures in the Socialist International (ibid.). As Walters (2001) explains, several conferences in 1907 and 1911 strengthened the Second Socialist International's internationalist perspective, by opposing war and colonialism, but also revealing these fissures. For example, the German Social Democratic Party voted against the resolutions against colonialism, even though they were divided on this issue (ibid.). Lenin opposed all colonialism. According to Russian Marxist Lev Davidovich Bronstein (Leon Trotsky), August 1914, the start of the First World War, marked "the effective death of the International" (cited in ibid.). Trotksy made this statement in light of the failure of the International to oppose the imperialist war (ibid.). As Walters (2001) concludes, "[i]nstead of opposing the war, calling for the overthrow of their own capitalists and organizing strikes against it, the various International sections in France, Germany and Britain, voted for war credits and effectively sided with their own capitalist class to wage war." However, in stressing its educative role, Trotsky argued in 1914 that the Second International did not live in vain, but:

> carried out enormous cultural work, the likes of which the world has never seen: the education and rallying of an oppressed class. The proletariat does not have to begin all over again . . . The period now concluded bequeathed it a rich arsenal of ideas. (cited in Swain, 2010, p. 6)

It is because of calls by the Second International that socialists and feminists continue to celebrate International Workers Day on May 1 and International

Women's Day on March 8 (ibid., p. 6). Those who did break with the Second International and oppose the war went on to form a genuine international revolutionary backbone (ibid.).

The Third International

The third "Socialist International," known as "The Comintern" ("Communist International"), was founded by Lenin (see below in this chapter) in the aftermath of the Russian Revolution founded in Moscow in 1919. Its remit was to fight "by all available means, including armed force, for the overthrow of the international bourgeoisie and for the creation of an international Soviet republic as a transition stage to the complete abolition of the State."

Lenin believed that to be successful, the socialist revolution must be worldwide, since the economic and social demands of socialism system could be maintained and able to progress only if on a world scale (MIA, undated a). Lenin felt it essential for workers around the world to be liberated from capitalist exploitation to prevent future wars from sending them to their deaths, and to stop the ongoing growth of capitalism taking away their humanity and freedom (ibid.).

After twenty-three years of annual congresses, the Comintern was dissolved in 1943 by Stalin, who dictated that it was impossible to coordinate communists internationally (ibid.). However, as MIE (undated b) explains:

> [t]he activities and movements of Communists around the world was still closely watched and at times coordinated, but in an explicitly non proletarian-democratic form: behind the walls of the Kremlin. According to the definition of Communist set out by Marx and Engels, supported fully by Lenin (the founder of the Communist International), Stalin's dissolution of the International was one of the most clear and explicit violations of what a Communist is.

As recognized by President Hugo Chávez of Venezuela in 2009, when calling for a Fifth International (cited in Fuentess, 2009), the Comintern "degenerated" under Stalinism and "betrayed" struggles for socialism around the world (see chapter 5 of this volume for a discussion of Chávez's call for a Fifth International).

The Fourth International

Finally, the Fourth International was created by Trotksy in France in 1938, before the demise of the Comintern. Having been expelled from the Soviet Union, Trotsky and many of his supporters considered the Comintern to have been lost to Stalinism and no longer capable of leading the international working class to power (Wikipedia, 2009). During most of its existence, the Fourth International was hounded by the Soviet Secret Police, and repressed by capitalist countries like France and the U.S. (ibid.). Moroever Trotsky died in 1940 and his followers never succeeded in building mass support in the lifetime of the Fourth International (Fuentess, 2009), which suffered a split at the time of Trotsky's death, and a more significant one in 1953 (Wikipedia, 2009). Today Trotsky has a worldwide following, and a number of organizations claim political continuity with the Fourth International. However, these groups are small and marginalized. Hence the call by Chávez for a Fifth International.

Socialism: Inevitability and Imminence

The first proposition of the Comintern was the "inevitability of the replacement of the capitalist system by the Communist social system" (MIA, undated a).This accords with an undercurrent of the inevitability and imminence of socialism in early scientific socialist writing. "Inevitability" could be implied in the citation by Engels above when he talks of the momentous act the proletariat *"is called upon* to accomplish" [my emphasis] (Engels, 1892 [1977], p. 428). A sense of "inevitability" and "imminence" was certainly apparent for Engels in 1886, when he predicted a "permanent and chronic depression" in England and stated that "we can almost calculate the moment when the unemployed losing patience will take their own fate into their own hands" (Engels, 1886 [1965], p. 6).

Some years later, Lenin, principal leader of the Russian Revolution of 1917, writes of the international role of the Russian working class: "the proletariat *will* fight its way to a free alliance with the socialist workers *of all lands*, [my emphases] having crushed that loathsome monster, the tsarist monarchy" (Lenin, 1912 [2002], p. 58). Referring to the end of capitalism, Lenin notes that the workers are "irresistibly advancing to this goal" (Lenin, 1924 [2002], p. 69), and specifically with respect to the materialist conception of history, Lenin writes:

> it is evident that Marx deduces the inevitability of the transformation of capitalist society into socialist society wholly and exclusively from the economic law of the development of contemporary society (Lenin, 1915 [2002], p. 76).

Capitalism is a dynamic system whose aim is to maximize profits. This means that smaller firms are not able to compete and go to the wall, leading to more and more concentration of capital and the growth monopolies. With this development comes the ascendancy of banks to finance monopolies, and the expansion of finance capital. For Lenin, "the growth of large-scale production, capitalist cartels, syndicates and trusts" and "the gigantic increase in the dimensions and power of finance capital, provides the principal material foundation for the *inevitable advent of socialism*" [my emphasis] (ibid.). He notes that "[a]ll nations will arrive at socialism—this is inevitable" (Lenin, 1924 [2002], p. 85) and claims "the final victory of the socialist proletariat the world over" (ibid.). This is because of "[t]he objective process of development," which means that it is *"impossible* to advance from *monopolies*…without advancing towards socialism" [original emphasis] (Lenin, 1917 [2002], p. 88).

Moreover, in 1916 and 1917, Lenin argued that time could be sped up because of the advent of a new stage of history, the imperialist capitalist stage of historical development (Levy, 2009). For Lenin, imperialism was the highest stage of capitalism (Lenin, 1917 [1997]). As such, socialism was imminent. As he put it, "[i]mperialist war is the eve of socialist revolution" (Lenin, 1917 [2002], p. 89). This was not only because war makes the workers revolt, but "because state-monopoly capitalism is a complete *material* preparation for socialism, the *threshold* of socialism, a rung of the ladder of history between which and the rung called socialism *there are no intermediate rungs*"[original emphasis] (ibid.). According to Lenin, the capitalist state, in order to protect profits, needs to shield monopoly capitalism in times of war, and thus the state directs the whole undertaking, making it easier for the workers to seize the state monopoly capitalist apparatus as an entity and direct it in the interests of the workers (ibid., pp. 87–90). Thus:

> [t]he dialectics of history is such that the war, by extraordinarily expediting the transformation of monopoly capitalism into state-monopoly capitalism, has *thereby* extraordinarily advanced mankind towards socialism (ibid., p. 89)[6]

Neo-Marxism

The development of neo-Marxism needs to be seen in the light of the fact that *inevitability* and *imminence* of a general transition to socialism proved to be overoptimistic, and severely compromised. This fact meant that some aspects of Marxism had to be rethought.[7] Specifically, what needed to be understood was the role of capitalist institutions in maintaining their power base. As Leszek Kolakowski (1978) has argued, the common element in theories designated as "neo-" Marxist is a concern with the role of capitalist states' welfare institutions in retarding rather than advancing socialism. The defining features of neo-Marxism are a concern with culture (as in Gramsci's notion of the forging of a hegemonic culture) and with ideology (as in Althusser's ideological state apparatuses). As noted in the Introduction to this volume, neo-Marxist analysis should be seen as a supplement to rather than a replacement of Marxism.

Humanist Marxism and structuralist Marxism

The fundamental difference between the humanist Marxism of Gramsci and the structuralist Marxism of Althusser is, as noted briefly in the Introduction to this volume, that the former emphasizes the power of the human will in breaking through these structures, while the latter reminds us of how powerful the constraining structures in capitalist society are. We should neither overemphasize structuralism (as this leads to determinism and defeatism) nor overemphasize humanism (as this leads to idealism).

Moreover, the structuralist Louis Althusser and the humanist Antonio Gramsci should not necessarily be seen as polar opposites. While it is easy to see how the former's writings have been used to stress domination by structures (e.g., interpellating subjects—see below) and the latter's to stress struggle (e.g., hegemony and counter-hegemony—see below), there are passages in both writers' works that imply the opposite. Both forms of Marxism are in fact predated by Marx's famous dictum that stressed both the power of the structures of capitalist society and the power of workers to change history. I am referring to Marx's famous (1852) observation in the *Eighteenth Brumaire* that we make our own history (humanism), but not in circumstances of our own choosing (structuralism). What is distinctive about my approach in this volume is that rather than relying on Althusserian structuralist Marxism *or* Gramscian humanist Marxism, I argue that, in order to get a full understanding of the relationship between racism and schooling in the U.K. and the U.S., it is informative to utilize some key concepts from both Althusser and Gramsci, as well as those of other (neo-)Marxists, and, of course, those of Marx and Engels themselves.

Gramsci, Hegemony, and Counter-hegemony

As Carl Levy (2009) has argued, the theoretical foundations of Gramsci's work stand in sharp contrast to Lenin's "straightjacket of the most rule-bound 'scientific socialism,'" which, I have noted, for Lenin meant that socialism was inevitable and imminent. With Lenin's interpretation of this aspect of the materialist conception of history in serious doubt by the early 1920s given that outside Russia, the revolution had failed or never taken place, there was a need to develop a *political* theory of Marxism to explain why (Hobsbawm, 1977, p. 208). As Eric Hobsbawm argues, Gramsci was probably the first Marxist to develop the elements of a full political theory within Marxism (ibid). Citing Gramsci's reference to politics as "an autonomous activity" (Gramsci, 1978, p. 134), Hobsbawm goes on, Gramsci is a political theorist inasmuch as he regards politics as such (Hobsbawm, 1977, p. 208). Political passion as in an immediate impulse to action, for Gramsci, "is born on the 'permanent and organic' terrain of economic life but...transcends it" (Gramsci, 1978, p. 140).

The key to understanding political forces in society is, for Gramsci, the concept of hegemony. Hegemony (from the Greek *hēgemonía* "leadership") was used by Lenin to refer to the political leadership of the working class. This was in turn derived from Marxist theorist Pavel Borisovich Akselrod's phrase, "the hegemony of the proletariat in the democratic revolution" (Harding, 1977, p. 47).[8] Hegemony, as theorized by Gramsci, is the fusion of economic, political, intellectual, and moral leadership that is brought about by one fundamental group, and groups allied to it through ideology. Thus a "consensus" culture develops in which the working-class identifies its own good with the good of the bourgeoisie, and helps to maintain the *status quo* rather than opposing it. However, crucially for Gramsci, hegemony is a process of contestation, and counter-hegemonic struggle is always possible. Hegemony has to be constantly worked for by both the bourgeoisie and the workers. As Eric Hobsbawm has argued, what is new in Gramsci is his observation that even bourgeois hegemony "is not automatic but achieved through conscious political action and organisation" (Hobsbawm, 1977, pl. 209).

Thus even in times when the bourgeoisie is decidedly hegemonic as in the U.K. and the U.S. in the first decade of the twenty-first century, the struggle to maintain it continues, as does the struggle to oppose it, even if in considerably weakened forms. Indeed Gramsci famously called for continued determination, even in the direst of circumstances, in the belief that resilience will result in meaningful change even in the face of adversity (Gramsci, 1921).

Gramsci's optimism should not be interpreted as an idealist expression of hope. Indeed, it is important to stress that for Gramsci, hegemony is directly related to the capitalist economy. As he puts it, in describing the concept:

> spontaneous consent [is] given by the great masses of the population to the general direction imposed on social life by the dominant fundamental group; this consent is "historically" caused "by the prestige (and consequent confidence) which the dominant group enjoys because of its position and function in the world of production." (Gramsci, 1978, p. 12)

In countries such as Venezuela, counter-hegemony is much more developed (see chapter 5 of this volume) than in the U.K. or the U.S. With seven million members of the United Socialist Party of Venezuela, the people are more fully involved in politics—a crucial necessity in Gramsci's thinking (Hobsbawm, 1977, p. 212). After the Russian Revolution of 1917, Gramsci emerged as the main theorist of the factory council movement in Turin, Italy, which included the most advanced sections of the working class (Gramsci 1978, pp. xxxiii–xxxiv). Around this time Gramsci began to see the need for the integration of political and economic action with cultural work, which took form as a proletarian cultural association in Turin (Rosengarten, 2007). This represents a further parallel with current events in Venezuela, where great efforts are being made to create economic, political, and cultural spaces that are counter-hegemonic to capitalism and imperialism (see chapter 5 of this volume).

Althusser and the State Apparatuses

In order to theorize Althusser's concept of the state apparatuses, it is first necessary to note that, for Marxists, *the state* is considered to be far more than "government." Moreover, while there has been considerable debate among Marxists as to the nature of the capitalist state (see Jessop, 2002, 2008), they generally agree that the capitalist state is not neutral and acts directly or indirectly in the interests of the capitalist class.

This central regulatory role is both repressive and ideological. Before Althusser, Gramsci had also noted that capitalism maintains control not just through violence and political and economic coercion, but also ideologically (Gramsci's insight is noted by Althusser: 1971, p. 142) through a hegemonic culture in which the values of the bourgeoisie become the dominant elements of "common" sense values of all. Althusser (1971, pp. 142–144) makes a formal distinction between what he calls the repressive state apparatuses (RSAs) (government, administration, army, police, courts, prisons) and the ideological state apparatuses (ISAs) (religion, education, family, law, politics, trade unions, communication, culture).

The RSAs operate primarily by force and control. This can be by making illegal the forces and organizations (and their tactics) that threaten the capitalist *status quo* and the rate of profit. Thus, for example, restrictions are placed on strike action and other trade union activities. More extreme versions of RSA action include heavy intimidatory policing and other forms of state-sanctioned political repression, surveillance, and violence by the police and armed forces (Hill, 2005). The ISAs, on the other hand, operate primarily through ideology—promoting the forms of legitimation, values, and attitudes required by capitalism.

However, it needs to be pointed out that the two state apparatuses—RSAs and ISAs—each function both by violence and by ideology. As Althusser (1971, pp. 144–145) explains, while the repressive state apparatus "functions massively and predominantly by repression (including physical repression)," it functions "secondarily by ideology." He gives the example of the army and the police, which while they form part of the RSAs, they also "function by ideology both to ensure their own cohesion and reproduction, and in the 'values' they propound externally." As far as the ISAs are concerned, Althusser notes that while they "function massively and predominantly by ideology," they "function secondarily by repression, even if ultimately, but only ultimately, this is very attenuated and concealed, even symbolic." He instances schools, churches, the family, and the cultural ISAs that are not *only* ideological but use methods of punishment such as expulsion and censorship.

For Althusser, whereas the religious ISA (system of different churches) used historically to be the major ISA, the ISA "which has been installed in the dominant position in mature capitalist social formations...is the *educational ideological apparatus*...[it is] number one" (Althusser, 1971, pp. 152–153).[9] Althusser argued that schools are particularly important for inculcating the dominant ideology, since they require compulsory attendance of all children for five days a week. This is, Althusser noted, not the case with any other ISA (Althusser, 1971, p. 156). One of the advantages to the ruling class of the educational ISA is that, while given its high profile in party political rhetoric, education, in everyday usage, is no longer perceived as neutral in a party political sense, it is certainly not generally thought of as an agent of cultural and economic reproduction.

The ruling class, and governments in whose interests they act, tend to prefer, in normal circumstances, to operate via ISAs. For example, using parliamentary democratic procedures for introducing trade union legislation to limit the right to strike (secondary picketing for example) or limiting the number of workers allowed on a picket line "for safety reasons" presents fewer problems for the state than physically attacking picket lines that get "out of hand."

The Althusserian concept of interpellation

If the *ISAs* are the source of ruling class hegemony, interpellation is the *process* by which the legitimation, values, and attitudes required by capitalism are instilled in the populace. Interpellation is the concept Althusser (1971, p. 174) used to describe the way in which ruling class ideology is upheld and the class consciousness of the working class—that class's awareness of its structural location in capitalist society—undermined. Interpellation makes us think that ruling class capitalist values are actually congruent with our values as *individuals*. Althusser stressed that it is individuals rather than classes or groups that are interpellated or hailed. This is important in order to bypass counter-hegemonic voices. For Althusser (ibid.), the interpellation of subjects—the hailing of concrete individuals as concrete subjects—"Hey, you there!" (ibid., p. 175) involves a fourfold process:

1. the interpellation of "individuals" as subjects;
2. their subjection to the Subject;[10]
3. the mutual recognition of subjects and subject, the subjects' recognition of each other, and finally the subject's recognition of himself; and
4. the absolute guarantee that everything really is so, and that on condition that the subjects recognize what they are and behave accordingly, everything will be all right: Amen—"*So be it*" (ibid., p. 181).[11] Althusser (ibid.) explains:

[c]aught in this quadruple system of interpellation as subjects, of subjection to the Subject, of universal recognition and of absolute guarantee, the subjects "work," they "work by themselves" in the vast majority of cases, with the exception of the "bad subjects" who on occasion provoke the intervention of one of the detachments of the (repressive) State apparatus. But the vast majority of (good) subjects work all right "all by themselves," that is, by ideology (whose concrete forms are realized in the Ideological State Apparatuses). They are inserted into practices governed by the rituals of the ISAs. They "recognize" the existing state of affairs...that "it really is true that it is so and not otherwise," and that they must be obedient. Subjects recognize that "the hail" was really addressed to them, and not someone else [ibid., p.174] and respond accordingly: "Yes, that's how it is, that's really true!" [ibid., p. 139]. Their subjection is thus freely accepted [ibid., p. 183]. Thus when confronted with the "inevitability" of global capitalism, the response is "That's obvious! That's right! That's true!" [ibid., p. 172]

Althusser (ibid., p. 172) notes that it is a peculiarity of ideology that it imposes, without appearing to do so, "obviousnesses as obviousnesses." There is no point, therefore, for workers to question their social class position under capitalism, let alone consider alternative ways of running the world, such as democratic socialism, or even social democracy[12] (of course, we must not forget that because of their material conditions of existence, participation in struggle, etc., the "bad subjects" might respond differently in a counter-hegemonic way: "That's most dubious! That's wrong! That's a lie").

Interpellation is the process by which ideologies function through concrete social institutions. This means that *individuals* as bearers of structures are transformed ideologically into subjects; that is, they live the relation of their real conditions of existence as if they autonomously determined that relation (Laclau, 1977, p. 100). Interpellation is thus a fundamental process inserted within the ideological apparatus of the state. Subjects "recognize" the existing state of affairs: "it really is true that it is so and not otherwise" (Althusser, 1971, p. 181).

Capitalism has a certain, at times hidden, at times transparent, class-based, racialized, and gendered logic of inevitability and insurmountability, prompted in part by the success of the state apparatuses in interpellating subjects—this is how things are or even should be, and there's nothing we can or even should do. As Stuart Hall (2010) has put it:

> It is when it becomes "just how things are" that it wins consent and enters common sense. And at that point the political regime or philosophy has achieved a more settled, long-term, deeper form of control.

As Anthony Green has pointed out, this is vital, as it does not necessarily speak to positive consensus. It can be more fatalistic, a form of acquiescence for great swathes of participants in the social relations of capitalist production who are simply intent on "making a living," as they see it (his comments on this chapter). In Gramsci's (1978, p. 333) words, such a situation "does not permit of any action, any decision or any choice, and produces a condition of moral and political passivity." What is critical and crucial to the capitalist class and its supporters is that workers do not look to socialist alternatives.

Hegemony and counter-hegemony are important complements to interpellation, something recognized implicitly by Althusser when he noted that the installation of the ISAs must be seen in the context of "a very bitter and continuous class struggle" (Althusser, 1971, p. 185). Hegemony and counter-hegemony are both present in Marx's consciousness, though not theorized in this way, in the sense that Marx was aware of the way in which capitalism had become consolidated (though not perhaps its resilience and capacity for renewal and reconsolidation historically) and how it was perpetuated by ideology on the one hand, and of the potential of class-conscious workers to transcend it on the other. Nevertheless, hegemony fails to explain precisely *how* ideologies work, why they work with certain people and not with others, and crucially why certain ideologies work and others do not. For this we need interpellation. For example, the ruling class's success at keeping Marxism off the agenda, most notably in the U.S., and significantly in the U.K. since Thatcherism and its aftermath, is not logical (indeed, given that Marxism is in the interests of the working class, it is, in fact, *illogical*). However, as Stuart Hall (1978) once remarked, ideologies don't work by logic—they have logics of their own. We act and respond to ideology as if we were the originators of the ideas and values within it. In other words, when ruling class media (in Althusserian terms, the communications ISA) speaks of what "the public" "wants," "needs," "is fed up with," "has had enough of," this strikes a chord with all the other organs of ruling-class ideology— the rest of the media, the various apparatuses of the state. Because the successfully interpellated are largely trapped within one view of the world, it all makes "common" sense to them—"Yes, this is us."

The main effect of interpellation and of the ISAs, then, is to make socialist/Marxist challenges to capitalism redundant; and only specified choices and courses of action viable. Decisions to vote for one pro-capitalist party or another will depend on economic, political, and social conditions at given historical conjunctures. However, as long as the majority of the populace vote for capitalist parties, capitalism itself remains unchallenged. Minority decisions to vote for non-favored parties or not to vote at all may not be particularly important. While interpellation may invoke a variety of responses, the vast majority will be conducive to and supportive of capitalism. To illustrate the contemporary relevance of (neo-)Marxist analysis, I will consider party politics in the U.K. and the U.S., respectively.

Party Politics: The U.K.

As I have argued elsewhere (e.g., Cole, 2005, p. 8), Margaret Thatcher's triumphal discrediting of socialism was directly related to the collapse of the Soviet Union, interpreted by many to mean that Marx's theories and socialism were no longer viable. Thatcher was successful in championing the free market (capitalism with very minimal state regulation) as the only viable way to run economies. She was equally successful in falsely equating the Stalinist Soviet Union with Marxism, with socialism, with the British Labour Party, and militant trade unions, and urging their collective confinement to the dustbin of history. Thatcher thus *appeared* to wipe socialism off the agenda of political change in Britain. This was, of course, essential if Britain were to move in the direction of labor market compliance and labor flexibility. Following the late 1980s revolutions in Eastern Europe and the Soviet Union, Marxism, Thatcher argued, was now extinct. A majority response to Thatcher was: "That's obvious! That's right! That's true!" (Althusser, 1971, p. 172). In this scenario, class struggle, a fundamental tenet of Marxism, becomes outmoded. Therefore the Labour Party was also now extinct. It is precisely the success of this formulation that projected Tony Blair, a believer in the free market, to center stage—a savior of the Labour Party—but only if the Labour Party became reformulated as "New Labour."

"New Labour" was coined as part of an orchestrated campaign to distance the party from its socialist roots, to modernize it—in other words, to establish an unequivocal pro-capitalist base for itself. For Blair, the "founding principle of New Labour" is "the partnership we have tried to build with [business]...and it will not change" (*Guardian*, November 6, 2001, 2). This underlines the crucial importance for Blair of abandoning the anti-capitalist clause IV from the party constitution, which he succeeded in doing.[13] Margaret Thatcher described Blair in Britain's most popular tabloid and one of its most right-wing newspapers, *The Sun*, as "probably the most formidable Labour leader since Hugh Gaitskell" (*The Sun*, July 21, 1995). It is significant that Gaitskell had tried unsuccessfully in 1959 to abolish Clause IV. In 1995, in Hayman Island, Australia, Tony Blair declared to Rupert Murdoch, owner of *The Sun* newspaper, that "the era of the grand ideologies, all encompassing, all pervasive, total in their solutions—and often dangerous—is over" (Blair, 1995).[14]

We are in the midst of a major world crisis in capitalism. In the U.K. we are currently (winter, 2010) witnessing the collapse of New Labour, that ideological formation that continued the Thatcherite revolution with a vengeance. This collapse is not, however, because workers are seizing the opportunity of a counter-hegemonic challenge to capitalism, and not because workers are finally embracing socialism as capitalism's major alternative. On the contrary, successfully interpellated workers have been moving even more to the right. As I have suggested, whether workers or capitalists support one or the other of the mainstream parties will depend on specific historical conjunctures. At the present juncture, the drift has been to the Conservative Party—at least in England—in Scotland and Wales, the Conservatives do not get general support.

Let us continue to exemplify the worth of neo-Marxist analysis, with a brief look at the U.K. in the run-up to and in the aftermath of the general election of 2010. Given that the current crisis in capitalism is clearly *caused* by capitalism—a fact that workers recognized, at least at the time of the onset of "the credit crunch" in August 2007—an interesting question to pose is, "Why are a number of workers not only not questioning capitalism, but are solidly in support of it?" In the crisis, workers are responding to pro-capitalist solutions as required: "Yes, that's how it is; that's really true!" (Althusser, 1971, p. 140). Their subjection is thus freely accepted (ibid., p. 183). Thus in the conventional parliamentary political game, when confronted with the notion that New Labour has failed, and the only solution is to give other pro-capitalist parties a chance, the response is: "That's obvious! That's right! That's true!" (ibid., p. 173).

Such is the power of interpellation that, amazingly, in the wake of the bailing out of the banks which drastically affects workers' living standards and quality of life, a *Guardian*/ICM poll in July 2009 suggested that some workers were opting for greater sacrifices for their own class. The poorest U.K. workers were in favor of cuts in public spending (Glover, 2009).[15]

Voting for capitalism, or not voting at all, means that workers see no point in even considering alternative ways of running the world, such as democratic socialism. Of course, it must again be stressed that because of their potential for class consciousness, participation in struggle, etc., the "bad subjects" have the potential to respond differently: "That's not for me! That's wrong! That's a lie. Things can be different," and vote for socialist parties. Anthony Green has described this as a moment in the struggles in and for "hegemony" invoking *good sense* in Gramsci's terms, thus de-reifying and challenging the interpellative structures, in Althusser's terms (his comments on this chapter).[16]

In actuality, in the general election of 2010, the vote for socialist parties was totally insignificant, and if interpellation was resisted, it was resisted more by a minority who voted for the very right-wing U.K. Independence Party (UKIP) and the fascist British National Party (BNP). The 2010 U.K. election resulted in a hung parliament; that is, no political party with an overall majority. A little over 36 percent of voters voted for the Conservatives, 29 percent for New Labour, just over 23 percent for the Liberal Democrats, and about 12 percent for others (this last figure includes nearly 2 percent for the BNP and over 3 percent for UKIP, the two most popular parties after the three main parties).

The emerging coalition was between the Conservative Party and the Liberal Democrats (in line with the other mainstream parties, its leader and current Deputy Prime Minister Nick Clegg promised "bold and even 'savage' cuts in government spending" prior to the election). Interpellations in the months following the formation of the new government focused on "cuts are the only way" and (in a cabinet where 80 percent are millionaires) "we're all in this together." This was interspersed with "it's all the previous (New Labour) government's fault."

The Socialist Equality Party (2010) describes the ConDem coalition as a "right-wing cabal, dedicated to waging economic and social warfare against the working class." The firmly established hegemony of this ruling bloc, boosted by the highly successful pre- and post-election interpellations of the communications ISAs, militates against the working class seeing the ending of world capitalism and imperialism as a solution to the economic crisis. In the aftermath of the election, prior to the formation of the coalition government, the various organs of the Communications ISAs bombarded the public with the urgent need for the formation of such a government in order to "stabilize the markets"; in other words, in order to "satisfy UK and international capital" that its needs will be accommodated sooner rather than later, and thus attempting to subordinate workers' real needs, and to merge their priorities with those of capitalism.

One hundred days into the new ConDem government, a *Guardian*/ICM poll (August 18, 2010) revealed support for the draconian cuts being implemented and proposed by the government (Elliott and Clark, 2010) (announced in October, 2010, these include £81 billion—$124 billion—cut from public spending over four years). Interpellation was thus once again successful, despite the fact that the cuts that are being made overtly (as well as public spending VAT[17] is being increased to 20 percent) or by stealth (e.g., swingeing cuts in legal aid for those unable to afford to pay for legal assistance).

Interpellation was also successful in spite of the fact that the cuts are *permanent* and the welfare state in danger of destruction. Prime Minister David Cameron is on record as stating that, even after the crisis is over, he will not restore the familiar provisions of public service (Hasan, 2010); a clear attempt to hasten the end of the welfare state. When asked on BBC television whether the welfare state was under threat, Thatcherite Lord Michael Forsyth, who has described Margaret Thatcher as one of the most compassionate people he ever met in his life (Rhodes, 2009), replied with scarcely believable audacity "[n]o, no, this is economics, not ideology" (Hasan, 2010). Judith Orr (2010, p. 12) argues that, following the interventions of Thatcher and Blair, we are witnessing a qualitative shift: "[t]he government is attempting to do something even Thatcher didn't try, a generalised offensive against the whole of the working class and the poor." However Orr (ibid.) notes that this is a "high-stakes" strategy that eventually brought the Thatcher government down after her attempt to introduce the poll tax (a tax on individuals irrespective of means).

Just before the 2010 annual Trades Union Congress of the U.K.'s labor unions, Rupert Murdoch's Sunday tabloid, *The News of the World*, attempted to deal with challenges to this massive assault on the working class, to counter threats to ruling class hegemony by the trade union movement in the form of strikes, with a headline on September 12, 2010 screaming "Halt the Union suicide squad." It interpellated its readers: "Britain demands better, and will not forgive industrial thuggery." In a similar fashion, using Gramscian "common sense," *The Sun's* associate editor, Trevor Kavanagh, declared on page 9 of its October 21 edition, "sensible Sun readers know there is no alternative" to the loss of half a million public sector jobs.

At the time of writing (fall 2010), the U.K. is witnessing a number of counter-hegemonic responses to the government's assault on the working class, particularly from students (incensed at increases in student fees, and at the abolition of the Education Maintenance Allowance (EMA)—introduced by New Labour to encourage young people from poor backgrounds to stay in education and training after the age of 16), but also from labor unions.

At the same time, the rich continue to amass huge profits. It is reported that six "fat cat bankers" are to share £23 million in bonuses. This is a result of U.S. investment bank Citigroup making £4.4 billion in profits in the first half of 2010 (the bank suffered £4.8 billion in losses during the "credit crunch" of 2008 and has received two U.S. government bailouts totaling £27 billion) (Hayward, 2010, p. 2).

Attention to these gross injustices have to be deflected by the ISAs, and one way of doing this, as we shall see in chapter 2 of this volume, is by the creation of a plethora of racialized "enemies," which also serves to redirect workers' attention from the source of its exploitation. The enemy of the working class is not the various racialized minorities discussed in that chapter, but, as I argue throughout this book, the very system that profits (literally and ideologically) from the exploitation of these minorities, as it does, of course, from the working class as a whole. Before turning to a consideration of party politics in the U.S., I will address the parameters of a worrying escalation of racism in the U.K., initiated by a fascist party—the BNP. This will entail a consideration of the general relationship between capitalism and fascism, and a discussion of the concept of "no platform for fascists."

The rise and fall of the BNP

In local elections in 2006, the BNP gained twelve seats in the East London area of Barking and Dagenham, becoming the second party. It also won seats in Epping Forest, Stoke-on-Trent, and Sandwell. In June 2009, two candidates of the BNP were elected to the European Parliament. This minority support of fascism by the electorate can be seen partly as a result of racist interpellation by the communication ISA; particularly, the right-wing tabloids. It should be pointed out that, while this embrace of fascism is not in the general interests of capitalism at this juncture, the traditional pro-capitalist parties do gain by being given the opportunity to claim not to be "racist" when compared to the BNP, whereas of course, in reality, their policies *are* racist.

Nick Lowles, a leading campaigner for "HOPE not hate" (see the concluding section of chapter 2 of this volume), has argued against the widely held and promulgated assumption that the election to the European Parliament amounted to a "protest vote." On the contrary, that fascist vote was based on "political and economic insecurities" that were molded by deep-rooted racism (Lowles, 2009). Lowles cites a YouGov poll that demonstrated that:

> the racism of many BNP voters goes well beyond simple opposition to current immigration and eastern European migrant workers which one might expect if their support for the BNP was prompted simply by economic insecurity. Belief in the intellectual superiority of white people over non-whites, the view of nearly half of BNP voters that black and Asian people can never be British, the almost universal dislike of even moderate Islam and the contempt and suspicion many of their voters have towards a liberal and multicultural society show how hardline much of the BNP support is.

Lowles summarizes the poll that shows that BNP voters are mainly working class, and drawn from former Labour-voting households. Underlining the significance of the interpellation process, Lowles points out that one-third of BNP voters read *The Sun* or the *Daily Star* (like *The Sun* but more porno-graphic, and with less news). YouGov points out that 44 percent (compared to 12 percent of all voters) disagreed with the statement: "non-white British citizens who were born in this country are just as 'British' as white citizens born in this country" (cited in Lowles, 2009), while 31 percent of BNP voters believed there was a difference in intelligence between the average black Briton and the average white Briton (ibid.).

Although only 2 percent of BNP voters deny that six million Jews, Gypsies, and others died in the Holocaust, a further 18 percent accept that the Holocaust occurred, but believe it has been exaggerated. One of the most startling results, Lowles goes on, was the response to the statement that "there is a major international conspiracy led by Jews and Communists to undermine traditional Christian values in Britain and other western coun-tries." One-third of BNP voters "completely" or "partially" agreed. The typical reaction to the BNP of the mainstream political parties is to adopt more and more stringent racist legislation, particularly that aimed at migrant workers and asylum seekers. As Alex Callinicos (2009, p. 4) argues, political leaders probably believe quite sincerely that this is the best means of stopping alienated workers voting for fascism. The mainstream parties also tend to adopt the language of the overt racists, as with Gordon Brown's adoption of "British jobs for British workers" (see chapter 2 of this volume).

These fascist gains were reversed in the 2010 U.K. National Election when the BNP suffered catastrophic losses, which included the failure of party leader Nick Griffin's bid for a seat in Parliament in Barking, and the loss of all 12 of its seats on Barking and Dagenham Council in the council elections of the same year. On this council, it was feared that it might have taken overall control.

Part of the reason for the demise of the BNP might have been the fact that the 2010 Labour manifesto carried a section titled "Crime and Immigration," as if the connection was obvious (Trilling, 2010b). Another contributory factor was the reputation of the victorious Labour MP for Barking, Margaret Hodge. Although she gave a stirring anti-fascist speech at the declaration of results, she had previously proposed that migrants must earn the rights people born in this country take for granted, such as social housing and benefits, in a new points-based system determined by length of residence or national insurance contributions. Moreover, in 2006, shortly before that year's local elections, Hodge told the right-wing broadsheet, *The Daily Telegraph* that eight out of ten of her constituents were considering voting for the BNP, noting, "[t]hey see black and ethnic-minority communities moving in and they are angry. They can't get a home for their children." When the BNP went on to win the twelve seats on the council, the GMB trade union called for Hodge's resignation.

A year later, she said that British families had "a legitimate sense of entitlement" to housing. This prompted the then Education Secretary, Alan Johnson, to suggest that her words were "grist to the mill" for the BNP. Finally, in February 2010, Hodge argued that migrants should be made to wait up to twelve months before they could get access to the benefits system (ibid.). Hodge conceded that "[t]he left don't like what I've been saying, [b]ut I think you can puncture racism by dealing with the feeling of unfairness that people have." "Politicians always shy away," she concluded, "from talking about immigration and the difficult issues that are associated with it. If we don't address those issues, we allow that territory to be captured by the extreme right" (ibid.). Hodge claimed that Barking had experienced, "the most rapid transformation of a community we have ever witnessed" (ibid.).

In reality, as pointed out by social statistician Ludi Simpson, between the 1991 census and the 2001 census, Barking and Dagenham's boundaries were redrawn to include 9,200 people, mainly from nearby Redbridge. So the "rapid" change is partly a statistical anomaly (cited in ibid.). Simpson further points out that the most recent evidence, the 2008 School Census, indicates that Barking and Dagenham still has a lower proportion of minority ethnic pupils than most other London boroughs. "Hodge is wrong,"

Simpson explains, "if she suggests that her constituents' local services, community spirit and jobs will be raised by restricting immigration or by diminishing immigrants' rights as citizens" (ibid).

Perhaps the biggest reason for the demise of the BNP, however, was a concerted and unremitting campaign by anti-fascists; in particular, HOPE Not Hate. Leading member Nick Lowles must take a lot of credit for the coordination of this victory against fascism. In the run-up to the national and council elections, those on his mailing list, including myself, were tirelessly urged, sometimes several times a day, to take action to prevent further victories by the BNP. Lowles commented on the BNP's defeat as follows:

> We mobilised in a way our country had never seen before. In fact, in just the past few weeks, almost a thousand volunteers have joined us in Barking & Dagenham to deliver over 350,000 pieces of literature and nearly 300 volunteers came to Stoke-on-Trent, to distribute leaflets and knock on doors to turn out the anti-BNP vote. Last year's BNP victory was not in our name—but last night's BNP defeat certainly was. We made the world a better place. (cited in Trilling, 2010a)

Capitalism and fascism

While the BNP concentrates on "respectable" party politics, the English Defence League (EDL), like the Scottish Defence League (SDL) and the Welsh Defence League (WDL), is a street-fighting organization. This is typical of fascist complementarity (Mussolini had the "Squadre d'Azione"; Hitler, the "Brownshirts," Smith, 2010, p. 13). The EDL was prominent in 2009 in the wake of the BNP's electoral successes (both at the local council level and in the European Parliament), and are gaining street prominence at the time of writing (fall 2010). While the BNP and the EDL deny links with each other, from the latter's beginnings in March 2009, the BNP has played a major role in building and directing the EDL (ibid., p. 12). For example, the person behind the EDL website, Chris Renton, is a BNP member, as are other key EDL personnel (ibid.). Many EDL activists are also in violent soccer-related gangs—"firms"—forced away from soccer terraces in the light of increased policing and surveillance at stadiums (ibid.). According to Mark Townsend (2010), the EDL has developed strong links with the U.S. Tea Party movement.

Martin Smith (2010, p. 13) cautions, "[f]rom his prison cell in Mussolini's fascist Italy, the revolutionary socialist Antonio Gramsci wrote, 'One of our biggest mistakes was not understanding the sudden rise of the squadre d'azione, and in turn our failure to combat it.'" While the situation in Britain is not, of course, "as serious as Italy in 1920," Smith concludes, "the danger signals are there and we mustn't underestimate the threat from the new fascists" (ibid.).

Anindya Bhattacharyya (2009) succinctly explains the relationship between capitalism and fascism. As he puts it, "fascist organisations offer themselves to the ruling class as a deadly weapon to use against the left. But the use of this weapon comes at a price—stripping away any pretence that capitalism is a fair or progressive system" (ibid). This is because the ruling class has to use the full force of the RSAs rather than just rely on the ISAs. Thus fascism is "a weapon of last resort for our rulers, one that they turn to in periods of acute crisis but keep their distance from at other times" (ibid.). In other words, while the ruling class is quite happy to up the barometer of racism, it tries hard not to admit to doing that. As Bhattacharyya (2009) explains:

> The contradictory political relationship between the ruling class and fascism manifests itself as a contradictory ideological attitude and contradictory action. So the Daily Mail attacks Muslims, but also attacks the BNP for attacking Muslims. The mainstream parties denounce the BNP, but play to its agenda on issues like immigration.

While some on the left argue that we should concentrate on *either* racism *or* fascism, the implications of the above analysis for antiracists, including Marxists, is that there is a need to oppose both, while understanding the distinctions and relationships between them (ibid.). As Bhattacharyya concludes:

> That means understanding that the "right wing anti-fascism" of [sections of the media] isn't simply a matter of hypocrisy. There are material political motives for why the ruling class is ordinarily opposed to fascism...[but we] cannot ever rely on this right wing anti-fascism that can rapidly reverse into support for the Nazis.

The left thus has a responsibility to take on both fascism and the racism that feeds it (Bhattacharyya, 2009).

No platform for fascists

It is my view that antiracists, including Marxists, should make the case for "no platform" for fascists (not allowing fascist groups a joint platform with other political parties and/or interest groups); no access to the media; and against fascists' right to participate in mainstream political debate. These are my reasons:

- giving a platform to fascists makes them appear acceptable and respectable, whereas
- fascists operate by instilling fear and claiming "no right to be here" for specific groups (e.g., Jews; Muslims; Gypsy Roma and Traveller communities; lesbian, gay, bisexual, transgender people; disabled people; and so on);
- "no right to be here" can only be brought about by terror, internment, deportation, and murder (Rosen, 2009);
- the right for fascists to have free speech is less important than the right of those on the receiving end not to be intimidated and abused verbally

UNIVERSITY OF WINCHESTER
LIBRARY

and physically (as pointed out in the Introduction to this volume, physical attack tends to follow fascist victories);

- giving a platform to fascists should not be seen as part of the "democratic process," because if in power, fascists' aim is to smash any form of democracy; and

- whereas Marxists want to destroy an economic and political *system* and replace it with democratic socialism, fascists want to destroy *literally*— if considered necessary and/or expedient—specific constituencies of humankind.[18]

If I am right that it is totally inappropriate for the BNP to be given the "respectability" of mainstream politics, it is even more inappropriate for BNP members to be teachers. However, in March 2010, after fifteen teachers were identified as BNP members in a leaked list, a review commissioned by the British government recommended that teachers should be allowed to be members of the BNP or other racist organizations. Its author, Maurice Smith, a former chief inspector of schools, said barring school staff from joining such organizations would be a "disproportionate response" and a "profound political act." The views of the report were accepted by government ministers.

It is my view that BNP members should be banned from working in the public sector per se, since, as Janice Godrich, cited in Sally Kincaid (2009, p. 9), has argued, the "BNP's message of hate and fear" stands in stark contrast to the values of equality and access for all on which public services are based." As Godrich puts it, when considering schools, "[w]hat would a fascist teacher's response be if there was a racist attack in their school? What if there was a homophobic attack?" (ibid.).

The U.S. and the Election of Barack Obama

Racism

In the U.S., with the election of the country's first black president, interests converged (Bell, 1980)[19] between the wishes of millions of people of color, on the one hand, and those of national (and international) capital on the other, as witnessed, for example, by the massive corporate mobilization for Obama as compared to John McCain in the election run-up (Bhattacharyya, 2008, p. 7).

Moreover, in the terminology of Critical Race Theory, it appears that a major contradiction may have been closed.[20] As I argued in Cole, 2009a, p. 155, "it might now become more difficult to uphold charges of racism in that deeply racist society: how can America now be racist, when a black child can become president?" As I also pointed out (ibid., pp. 155–156), historian Simon Schama told the BBC that the election "wipes away America's original sin" (Weaver, 2008), and shortly after Obama's election, a black reader wrote to the free U.K.-based newspaper (*Metro*, November

10, 2008, p. 18): "[t]here is now absolutely no reason for black people to complain they are mistreated racially."

The election of a black president will not end racism in the U.S. On the contrary, it has created a racist counterreaction among significant sections of the U.S. population. The posting of the image of the president as a "witch doctor," sent to the Tea Party movement, and mentioned in the Introduction to this volume, is but one prominent example. This movement is, in fact, receiving a high profile in the U.S., and epitomizes a racist Republican backlash to Obama. Another example relates to the Tea Party Republican candidate for New York governor, Carl Paladino, whose e-mails included an image of Obama dressed as a pimp and his wife Michelle as a prostitute, and a video clip of African tribespeople in a ritual dance with the heading, "Obama inauguration rehearsal" (Lamb, 2010, p. 28).

Moroever, sponsored by Roger Ailes, the current head of Fox News (Rupert Murdoch's U.S.-based right-wing TV channel), Tea Party activist Glenn Beck uses the language of civil rights to manipulate America's white working class, his argument being that, despite all the evidence to the contrary (see chapter 3 of this volume), it is not people of color who are on the receiving end of racism; rather, it is whites who suffer collectively at the hands of black racists (Williams, 2010). Obama is, of course, the prime and reiterated example. As Beck puts it, "we" will "reclaim the civil rights movement" in the name of individual rights and freedoms. "We will take that movement because we were the ones who did it in the first place" (cited in Williams, 2010). Beck has also insisted: "[w]e are the ones that must stand for civil and equal rights. Equal justice. Not special justice, not social justice, but equal justice" (ibid.). As Patricia Williams (2010) points out, in saying this, he is invoking Plessy's apartheid of "separate but equal." As Williams (2010) argues, "[w]ittingly or not, Beck echoes the very wrong side of battles about affirmative action, school integration, anti-miscegenation, harassment in the workplace, eugenics, segregated graveyards, and so much more."

If the arguments put forward in this book are right, then racism will continue to exist, not permanently as Critical Race Theorists (e.g., Taylor, 2009) claim, but as long as capitalism does. That is not to say that socialism will inevitably bring with it the demise of racism. As E. San Juan Jr. (2009) has argued, capitalism's abolition is a necessary if not a sufficient step in doing away with it.

Capitalism and imperialism

After more than a year and a half of Obama's presidency, the president remains committed to maintaining the hegemony of U.S. capitalism and imperialism. Tom Eley (2010a) describes Obama's speech on the economy in September 2010, where he "outlined a 'jobs plan' based on a series of corporate tax give-aways that have long been championed by the Republican Party." As Eley (2010a) points out, Obama made no proposals for the direct creation of jobs. Instead his "plan" rests almost totally on tax breaks for corporations, based on claims that this will encourage firms to hire more workers. As Obama put it, "I've never believed that government's role is to create jobs or prosperity. I believe it's the private sector that must be the main engine of our recovery" (cited in ibid.). According to economist Mark Zandi, while the program might "a year from now…create tens of thousands of jobs" (cited in ibid.), the *Washington Post* noted that "[t]his would be a drop in the bucket compared with the 7.6 million jobs lost during the recession that began in December 2007" (cited in ibid.). Eley (2010a) goes on:

> One wonders whether Obama and his handlers think the public has forgotten that Obama supported the multi-trillion-dollar bailout of Wall Street under Bush and extended it once he came to power. And that Obama intervened to block legislation that would have imposed modest restrictions on the pay of bank executives, while insisting that government loans to General Motors and Chrysler be made contingent on a 50 percent wage cut for newly hired auto workers.

Eley argues that Obama's speech was two-faced throughout. While appealing to elderly voters by promising to fight "the efforts of some in the other party to privatize Social Security, because as long as I'm president, no one is going to take the retirement savings of a generation of Americans and hand it over to Wall Street," he also pointed out that he was preparing to impose major cuts in basic entitlement programs such as Medicare and Social Security. "[O]nce the bipartisan fiscal commission finishes its work," Obama declared, "I will spend the next year making the tough choices necessary to further reduce our deficit and lower our debt" (cited in ibid.).

Eley (2010a) concludes that "both the Democrats and Republicans are committed to making the population foot the full bill for the economic crisis, the bailout of Wall Street, and the cost of the wars in Afghanistan and Iraq." With respect to the former imperialist adventures, Joe Kishore (2010) explains that the offensive begun in February 2010 against the town of Marjah in Afghanistan "is the largest US military operation in the war since the initial 2001 invasion ordered by George W. Bush." Within a week, there were twenty civilian casualties, including six children (ibid.). With one invading soldier for every five people in the Marjah area, Kishore (2010) speculates there will be many more civilian casualties to come, and explains the military tactics:

> Once US control is consolidated in Marjah and central Helmand province, and as more US reinforcements arrive in the spring, larger and bloodier campaigns are in store, culminating in an onslaught on Kandahar, Afghanistan's second city…With a population of nearly half a million, Kandahar is comparable in size to Fallujah, the Iraqi city that was largely destroyed by US troops in November 2004 and has been cited by military officials as a model for the present campaign.

As Kishore (2010) concludes, Obama and the Democratic Party have done nothing to stop U.S. imperialism or capitalism:

> The Afghan surge has been combined with a sharp increase in US drone missile attacks on Pakistan, which killed 123 civilians in January; the opening up of a new front of the "war on terror" in Yemen; growing threats against Iran; and increasingly provocative actions against China. The expansion of war is determined by the fundamental interests of American capitalism, including establishing control over the geostrategically central regions of the Middle East and Central Asia. War is the outward expression of the predatory interests of the American financial elite. The ballooning military budgets, like the massive bank bailouts, will be paid for through cuts in social programs and the intensification of the exploitation of the working class.

Conclusion

Despite the depressing scenario in both the U.K. and the U.S., given that the inherent instability of capitalism is there for all to see and to experience, there remain grounds for optimism. The inevitability of "boom and slump" in the capitalist system, paradigmatic for Marxists, is firmly on the international agenda, and can provide, in Gramsci's (1921) phraseology, a reason for "optimism of the will" in the face of "pessimism of the intellect," and an impetus for a renewal of energy for all progressive people. Moreover, developments in the Bolivarian Republic of Venezuela (see chapter 5 of this volume) provide space for educators to nail the lie that "there is no alternative" (TINA) to neoliberal capitalism, nor indeed to capitalism per se (for a fuller discussion, see chapter 6 this volume).

In both the U.K. and the U.S., education has played an important hegemonic role in interpellating the populace in the interest of the status quo. It has also played and must continue to play a major counter-hegemonic role. It is this dual role that forms the basis of and the reason for this book. Given the current major crisis in capitalism, a unique opportunity exists for Marxists on both sides of the Atlantic to intervene *analytically* in putting forward the arguments for an antiracist democratic socialism, but also *practically* by making concretes suggestions for practice in educational institutions that might move that project forward. Since teachers can be workers in and against the education ideological state apparatus, crucial here is the importance of the merging of the role of the traditional intellectuals and the organic intellectuals of the working class to forge a counter-hegemonic culture (Gramsci, 1929–35 [1978]).[21]

Ruling class hegemony has been established—in the U.K. by Thatcherism, followed by New Labour and the ConDem government; and in the U.S. by Reagonomics and by Bush, followed by a pro-capitalist black president. Given that hegemony is a process of *struggle*, Marxists will continue to attempt to transcend ruling class interpellation, to engage in counter-hegemonic struggle, and to provide an alternative vision.

In the following chapters I assess the contribution of Althusserian and Gramscian concepts in understanding both racism per se and racism and schooling in the U.K. and the U.S. In the next chapter, I look at some key conceptual issues around racism in the U.K. Specifically I make use of the neo-Marxist concept of racialization and my own neo-Marxist concept of xeno-racialization (e.g., Cole, 2009a, pp. 44–45) to make connections to modes of production. I use the Gramscian concept of "common sense" to understand how racialization interpellates popular consciousness. Central to these processes of racialization and xeno-racialization are the roles of the RSAs and the ISAs. I also look at various forms of counter-hegemonic resistance.

Appendix 1

The Labor Theory of Value

As Tom Hickey (2006) has explained, capitalism has an inbuilt tendency to generate conflict, and is thus *permanently* vulnerable to challenge from the working class. As he puts it:

> The objective interests of the bourgeoisie and the proletariat are incompatible, and therefore generate not a tendency to permanent hostility and open warfare but a permanent tendency toward them. The system is thus prone to economic class conflict, and, given the cyclical instability of its economy, subject to peri- odic political and economic crises. It is at these moments that the possibility exists for social revolution (ibid., p. 192).

An understanding of the source of this incompatibility and permanent tendency toward hostility can be facilitated by Marx's labor theory of value (LTV). The LTV explains most concisely why capitalism is objectively a system of exploitation, whether the exploited realize it or not, or indeed, whether they believe it to be an issue of importance for them or not. The LTV also provides a *solution* to this exploitation. It thus provides *dialectical* praxis—the authentic union of theory and practice.

According to the LTV, the interests of capitalists and workers are dia- metrically opposed, since a benefit to the former (profits) is a cost to the lat- ter (Hickey, 2002, p. 168). Marx argued that workers' labor is embodied in the goods that they produce. The finished products are appropriated (taken away) by the capitalists and eventually sold at a profit. However, the worker is paid only a fraction of the value s/he creates in labor; the wage does not represent the *total* value s/he creates. We *appear* to be paid for every single second we work. However, underneath this appearance, this fetishism, the working day (like under serfdom) is split in two: into socially necessary labor (and the wage represents this); and surplus labor, labor that is not reflected in the wage.

Greatly oversimplifying matters, let us assume that a capitalist employs a worker to make a table. Let us say that the value of the basic materials is £100, and that after these basic materials have had labor embodied in them (i.e., have become a table), that table has a value of £500. Let us further assume that in the time it takes to make the table, £20 of overheads are used up. What happens to the £400 surplus value that the worker has created? The worker is paid, say, £100, and the remaining £300 is appropriated, taken away, by the capitalist. After overheads are paid, the capitalist still has £280 *surplus* that s/he can reinvest to create more surplus. To continue the example, with this £280 surplus, the capitalist can buy £200 worth of basic materials, and employ two workers, and after these basic materials have had labor embodied in them (e.g., have become two tables), those tables have a value of £1,000. Assuming overheads increase to £30, and two workers are each paid £100, the capitalist is now left with £770 surplus that can be thrown back into production to create yet more surplus value, and so on and so on. If the capitalist continues to employ workers, say, seven, the surplus would be over £6,000. It is thus easy to see how surplus value multiplies and how capitalists' surplus (which is converted into profit) is, in truth, nothing more than accumulated surplus value, really the "property" of the worker but appropriated from that worker.[22]

While the value of the raw materials and of the depreciating machinery is simply passed on to the commodity in production, labor power is a peculiar, indeed unique, commodity, in that it creates new value. "The magical quality of labour-power's...value for...capital is therefore critical" (Rikowski, 2001, p. 11). "Labour-power creates more value (profit) in its consumption than it possesses itself, and than it costs" (Marx, 1894 [1966], p. 351). Unlike, for example, the value of a given commodity, which can only be realized in the market as itself, labor creates a new value, a value greater than itself, a value that previously did not exist. It is for this reason that labor power is so important for the capitalist in the quest for capital accumulation.

It is in the interest of the capitalist or capitalists (nowadays, capitalists may, of course, consist of a number of shareholders, for example, rather than outright owners of businesses) to maximize profits, and this entails (in order to create the greatest amount of new value) keeping workers' wages as low as is "acceptable" or tolerated in any given country or historical period, without provoking effective strikes or other forms of resistance. Therefore the capitalist mode of production is, in essence, a system of exploitation of one class (the working class) by another (the capitalist class).

Whereas class conflict is endemic to, and ineradicable and perpetual within, the capitalist system, it does not always, or even typically, take the form of open conflict or expressed hostility (Hickey, 2002, p. 168). This is, in large part, due to the successes of the state apparatuses and of ruling class hegemonic power (as exemplified throughout this volume). Fortunately for the working class, however, capitalism is prone to cyclical instability and subject to periodic political and economic crises. At these moments, the possibility exists for social revolution. Revolution can only come about when the working class, in addition to being a "class-in-itself" (an *objective* fact because of the shared exploitation inherent as a result of the LTV) becomes "a class-for-itself" (Marx, 1885 [1976]). By this, Marx meant a class with a *subjective* awareness of its social class position; that is, a class with "class consciousness"—including its awareness of its exploitation and its transcendence of "false consciousness."

As Hickey (2006) explains:

> Crises provide the opportunity for transition from the oppressive and exploitative, competitive and alienating conditions of the order of capital to a realm of human freedom in which humanity as a whole, through a radically democratic structure, engages collectively in satisfying its needs, ordering its priorities, and constructing new needs and aspirations to strive for, and challenges to overcome.

It should again be stressed that while this scenario is *always* a possibility, it should never be seen as a *certainty*.

Appendix 2[23]

Socialism

Marxists do not have a blueprint for the future (see Rikowski, 2004, pp. 559–560; see also Gibson and Rikowski, 2004 and Cole, 2008a, pp. 80–81). However, there are certain features, which would distinguish world socialism from world capitalism. What follows are just a few examples.

Bowles and Gintis (1976, p. 54) argue that whereas in capitalist societies, the political system is "formally democratic," capitalist economies are "formally totalitarian," involving: the minimal participation in decision-making by the majority (the workers); protecting a single minority (capitalists and managers) against the wills of a majority; and subjecting the majority to the maximal influence of this single unrepresentative minority.

Under socialism, this would be reversed. The workers would own and control the means of production and would encourage maximal participation in decision-making. Public services would be brought under state control and democratically run by the respective workforces. There would be universal free health care for all, incorporating the latest medical advances. There would be no need for private health. There would be universal free comprehensive education for all and no need for private schooling. There would be free comprehensive leisure facilities for all, with no fee for health clubs, concerts, etc. There would be free housing, and employment for all. There would be full rights for women, for the LGBT (lesbian, gay, bisexual, and transgender) communities, for all members of minority ethnic groups, and for disabled people. There would be full freedom of religion.[24] There would be no ageism. There would be no war, no hunger, and no poverty.

Bowles and Gintis (1976, p. 266) capture the essence of socialism as follows:

> Socialism is not an event; it is a process. Socialism is a system of economic and political democracy in which individuals have the right and the obligation to structure their work lives through direct participatory control. [Socialism entails] cooperative, democratic, equal, and participatory human relationships; for cultural, emotional and sensual fulfilment.

Chapter 2

Racism in the U.K.

In this chapter I begin by asking the question, "Why is it necessary to categorize racism?" I then consider older forms of British racism (colonial racism, antisemitism, and anti-Gypsy Roma and Traveller racism), before addressing myself to some newer forms (xeno-racism, anti-asylum-seeker racism, and Islamophobia). I argue that in contemporary Britain, there are a plethora of forms of racism. Given that contemporary British racism is multifaceted, and in order to set the scene for newer forms of racism, I begin by contextualizing them alongside older forms of racism, while also demonstrating that these older forms continue to flourish. For conceptual clarity I deal with color-coded racism, non-color-coded racism, and what I will call hybridist racism separately. I make use of the neo-Marxist concept of racialization, as outlined in the Introduction to this volume, and a newer concept of xeno-racialization, to understand these multifarious forms of racism. I use the Gramscian concept of "common sense," also outlined in the Introduction to assess how racialization interpellates popular consciousness. Central to these processes of racialization and xeno-racialization are the roles of the ISAs and the RSAs. I conclude with a consideration of contemporary counter-hegemonic resistance to racism.

Why categorize racism?

Why then is it necessary to categorize racism?[1] For those at the receiving end, it might well be argued that there may be less concern as to the *origins* of the racism experienced, and more concern about the effects such racism has. Racism is of course racism, irrespective of its origins. I would suggest, however, that there are three reasons for attempting to *categorize* contemporary British racism.

First, in the public perception, racism is assumed to be solely related to skin color. This is a legacy of the British colonial era and its continuing significance. It is useful to the racist state in that it serves to mask other forms of racism. However, I will attempt to demonstrate that, while color-coded racism remains highly significant, in fact, non-color-coded racism also has a long history in Britain, and continues in newer forms, and also that we are witnessing a newer form of hybridist racism.

Robert Miles recognized the salience of non-color-coded racism. Writing in 1993, he identified individuals and communities without skin color markers from Ireland, Italy, Cyprus, Malta, Poland, and Jews from Russia and Germany. The experiences of these communities highlighted, for Miles, that racism does not have to be based on skin color. Miles (1993, p. 149) states that:

> it is not only "black" people that are the object of racism. Such an interpretation constitutes a strange perversion of European history, a history in which the concept of racism was generated to comprehend the use of "race" theory by the Nazis in the course of formulating a "final solution" to the "Jewish question"

Second, and allied to this, is the recent explosion of interest in Critical Race Theory (CRT) in the U.K. (e.g., Preston, 2007: Gillborn, 2008, 2009, 2010),[2] and, in particular, CRT's advocacy of the concept of "white supremacy." Critical Race Theorists argue that "white supremacy" should be used to describe everyday racism in Britain, and not just the racism of fascist and other far right groups. This provides another important reason to stress that both historically and contemporaneously not all racism is color-coded, a fact that de facto limits the usefulness of "white supremacy" as a descriptor.[3]

Third, in order to effectively combat racism, it is important to understand its multiple origins and forms. For the racist state in general, in the struggle to maintain hegemony, while it is important to divide the working class, it is equally important that named racism is restricted to as few scenarios as possible; ideally, merely to describe openly racist political parties and individuals. As noted in chapter 1 of this volume, this can be useful for mainstream political parties to disguise their own racist policies and practices.

Older Color-Coded Racism

The colonial schema[4]

In the Introduction to this volume, I introduced the neo-Marxist concept of racialization. I have developed links with racialization and modes of production at length elsewhere. Noting that racialization is historically and geographically specific, I argued that, in the British colonial era, when Britain ruled vast territories in Africa, India, the Caribbean, and elsewhere, implicit in the rhetoric of imperialism was a racialized concept of "nation." Racism was institutionalized in popular culture in the British Imperial era in many ways: in popular fiction (Miles, 1982, pp. 110 and 119); in missionary work; in music halls; in popular art (Cole, 1992; Cole and Virdee, forthcoming, 2011); and in education. British capitalism had to be regenerated in the context of competition from other countries, and amid fears that sparsely settled British colonies might be overrun by other European "races" (see Cole, 2009a, pp. 42–43).

The empire came home to roost after World War II. The demands of an expanding postwar economy meant that Britain, like most other European countries, was faced with a major shortage of labor. The overwhelming majority of migrants who came to Britain were from the Indian subcontinent, the Caribbean, and the Republic of Ireland (itself subject to British colonization in parts in the sixteenth and seventeenth centuries). Those industries where the demand for labor was greatest actively recruited Asian, black, and other minority ethnic workers in their home countries (Fryer, 1984; Ramdin, 1987). Despite the heterogeneous class structure of the migrating populations (see Heath and Ridge, 1983), migrant workers came to occupy, overwhelmingly, the semiskilled and unskilled positions in the English labor market (Daniel, 1968: Smith, 1977). Furthermore, they found themselves disproportionately concentrated in certain types of manual work characterized by a shortage of labor, shift working, unsocial hours, low pay, and an unpleasant working environment (Smith, 1977). The consequences of this process of racialization were clear. According to Miles (1982, p. 165), these different racialized groups came to occupy a structurally distinct position in the economic, political, and ideological relations of British capitalism, but within the boundary of the working class. They therefore constituted a fraction of the working class, one that can be identified as a racialized fraction.[5]

Today, while some descendants of migrant workers have moved up the social class ladder, racialization continues unabated. A couple of examples will suffice. As far as poverty is concerned, for example, there are stark differences with respect to ethnic group. Lucinda Platt (2007) summarizes this:

> Risks of poverty are highest for Bangladeshis, Pakistanis and Black Africans, but are also above average for Caribbean, Indian and Chinese people. Muslims face much higher poverty risks than other religious groups.

Two years later, Platt (2009, p. 26) noted that white British people had the lowest poverty rates, followed by Indians, black Caribbeans, black Africans, and Pakistanis, with Bangladeshis having the highest risks of poverty.

Another example of the continued racialization of black and Asian people relates to institutional racism in the repressive state apparatus. Ministry of Justice statistics released in April 2009 revealed that black males are now eight times more likely to be stopped and searched by police than their white counterparts (cited in Ryder, 2009). Increasingly, these stops are being performed under section 44 of the Terrorism Act 2000 or under section 60 of the Criminal Justice and Public Order Act 1994 (ibid.). As Matthew Ryder (ibid.) explains, unlike traditional measures, these powers do not require a police officer to have "reasonable grounds for suspicion in making a stop" (ibid.). This means that "curiosity, dubious 'hunches,' even conscious or unconscious racial stereotyping, can go unchecked" (ibid.). The statistics reveal stop and search of African Caribbeans under counterterrorism legislation increased by 325 percent in 2008 (ibid.). In London, half of all section 60 stops were of black males (ibid.). Ryder (ibid.) points out that "only a small percentage of stops glean meaningful information." The Asian communities are also harassed. Ministry of Justice statistics also revealed that the number of Asian people stopped under the same laws rose by 277 percent (Ministry of Justice, 2009, p. 29).[6] While anti-Asian racism (directed at those from the Indian subcontinent), as outlined above with respect to poverty, is a structural feature of U.K. society, police stoppages relate to Islamophobia, which I discuss under the heading of "Newer Hybridist Racism" (see below).

Older Non-color-coded Racism[7]

The schema of antisemitism[8]

While the biological "inferiority" of Britain's imperial subjects was perceived mainly secondhand in the British colonial era,[9] the indigenous racism of the period was anti-Irish and antisemitic (e.g., Kirk, 1985; Miles, 1982). From the 1880s, there was a sizable immigration of destitute Jewish people from Eastern Europe, and this fueled the preoccupation of politicians and commentators about the health of the nation, the fear of the degeneration of "the race," and the subsequent threat to imperial and economic hegemony (Holmes, 1979; Thane, 1982). Jewish people were routinely referred to in the same contemptuous way as the people in Britain's vast colonial empire (Cole, 2004b), described by the communications ISA as "semi-barbarous," unable or unwilling to "use the latrine," depositing "their filth" on "the floor of their rooms" (Holmes, 1979, p. 17) and involved in world conspiracy (thus directly threatening British Imperial hegemony): "whenever there is trouble in Europe," the ILP paper, *Labour Leader*, put it, "...you may be sure a hook-nosed Rothschild is at his games" (Cohen, 1985, p. 75).

With respect to antisemitism today, while such racism is not generally acceptable in the public domain, it comes readily to the surface, in certain contexts. As Soeren Kern (2009) argues, following the Israeli bombardment of the Gaza Strip in 2008–09, antisemitism increased dramatically across Europe. In Britain, the Community Security Trust (CST) reported a sharp increase in antisemitic attacks, including arson attacks on synagogues, physical assaults of Jews in London, and antisemitic graffiti scrawled in towns and cities across the country (Kern, 2009). British police also advised prominent British Jews to redouble their security arrangements after some of their names appeared on a "Jewish hit list."[10]

As Mark Townsend (2009) explains, with antisemitic incidents running at around seven a day as of February 2009, safety fears were so acute that members of Britain's Jewish community were leaving the U.K. He states that around 270 such incidents were reported up until then, whereas attacks recorded during the first Palestinian intifada of the late 1980s averaged sixteen a month (ibid.). Scotland Yard, he goes on, is understood to have put prominent Jewish communities on heightened alert, and the Association of Chief Police Officers' national "community tension team" was issuing weekly patrol directives to chief constables instructing them of threats to Jewish communities in their areas (ibid.). Townsend describes the nature of incidents:

> [They] include violent assaults in the street, hate emails and graffiti threatening "jihad" against British Jews. One disturbing aspect involves the targeting of Jewish children. A Birmingham school is investigating reports that 20 children chased a 12-year-old girl, its only Jewish pupil, chanting "Kill all Jews" and "Death to Jews." (ibid.)[11]

In February 2009, the CST published its annual report on antisemitic incidents for 2008, which revealed that around 550 were recorded in the U.K. that year (cited in ibid.) Mark Frazer, spokesperson for the Board of Deputies of British Jews, said:

> We are seeing an unprecedented level of attacks directed at the Jewish community, both physical and verbal. It is incumbent upon us all to isolate and marginalise those who would derail the legitimate political debate with an extremist and hateful ideology. (cited in ibid.)

One year later, CST (2010) recorded 924 antisemitic incidents in 2009, the highest annual total since it began recording antisemitic incidents in 1984, and 55 percent higher than the previous record of 598 incidents in 2006. There were 124 violent antisemitic assaults in 2009, the highest number ever recorded by CST. Sixty-eight antisemitic incidents involved Jewish schools, schoolchildren, or teachers as targets. Another source, the Stephen Roth Institute for the Study of Contemporary Antisemitism and Racism (2010) (cited in Lemberg, 2010), cited the U.K. as having the largest increase in the number of "violent antisemitic incidents and vandalism" in the world in 2009—374—compared with 112 in 2008.

Contemporary antisemitism in the U.K., like Islamophobia (discussed below), needs to be seen in the context of hegemonic global U.S. capitalism and imperialism, in which Israel is a key player. It is also crucial, of course, to be vigilant against "world conspiracy" "theory," briefly referred to above, and "holocaust denial," which have for so long been part of the rhetoric of fascists and other racists, the former reaching its apotheosis in that exceptional form of the capitalist state (Poulantzas, 1978, p. 123) and associated mode of production in Nazi Germany,[12] the latter mouthed by neo-fascists in various countries whose aim presumably is to reinstall similar exceptional forms of the capitalist state, and related modes of production. It is also vital to make a distinction between antisemitism on the one hand, and anti-Zionism and the State of Israel's close relationship with the U.S. on the other. This is particularly important for Marxists and other Left factions whose brief must be total and unremitting opposition to *all* forms of racism.[13]

Anti-Gypsy Roma and Traveller racism[14]

Gypsy Roma and Traveller communities include English Romani Gypsies, Welsh Gypsies, Irish Travellers, Scottish Gypsy/Travellers, Travelling Showpeople, Circus People, Boat-Dwellers, Fairground Travellers, New Travellers and Romanis from central and eastern Europe who have arrived as refugees or asylum seekers (Clark, 2006b, p. 8, Clark, 2006c, p. 12) (with respect to this last constituency, we have a possible conflation with xeno-racism and anti-asylum seeker racism—see below).

By the late nineteenth century, despite increased statutory controls, such as the 1822 General Turnpike Road Act that charged a 40 shilling fine for camping on the side of a turnpike road (Greenfields, 2006, pp. 60–61) (a law that was still in place until 1980 [Diverse Herts, 2009]), traditional stop-ping places were reasonably freely available (Greenfields, 2006, p. 62), and, as Duffy and Tomlinson (2009, p. 2) argue, always surviving on the margins of society, Gypsy people became a useful source of cheap labor seasonally in the fields, as blacksmiths and as entertainers.

A pattern of traveling on specific circuits continued until the Second World War, when with the need for intensive labor, members of the Gypsy Roma and Traveller communities were recruited into semipermanent work on the land, in the mining industries, in the army, and in factory and muni-tions work (Greenfields, 2006, p. 63).

After the Second World War, with the mechanization of farming, the lifestyle of Gypsies changed drastically (Duffy and Tomlinson, 2009, p. 2.). This mechanization of the traditional rural work started in the 1950s, and previous sources of livelihood in the rural areas were no longer 'sufficient. With industrialization began the migration from rural areas. The changes in society were also reflected in the Romany Gypsy population. No lon-ger wanted for hop or strawberry picking and other traditional trades, they found that they had to adapt. Work was difficult to find for some fami-lies and the motorization of families also changed the travel patterns. Many Gypsies moved from the rural areas to the cities and towns (ibid.), often meeting hostile reactions from the local population and from the authorities (Greenfields, 2006, p. 65). Where caravans were visible to non-Gypsy Roma and Traveller people; for example, next to a roadside, this attracted the atten-tion of the authorities, and thus began a cycle of rapid repeat eviction (ibid., p. 66). Many families reluctantly sought to be rehoused into local authority (council) accommodation (ibid., p. 71). However, in 2006, some 3,500 to 4,000 Gypsy and Traveller families continued to live "illegally" on the road-side (Clark, 2006a, p. 286).

It has been estimated that one-third of the total Gypsy Roma and Traveller population lives in "unauthorised roadside encampments" (Greenfields, 2006, p. 57). As Rachel Morris (2006) has argued, Gypsy Roma and Traveller peoples are in many ways an "invisible" minority. Although "visible" in the literal sense, as Colin Clark explains, while English Romani Gypsies since 1988 and Irish Travellers since 2000 have been regarded in law as "minority ethnic groups," in general terms, this legal status has largely been unrecognized by the majority of the settled population, and those working for local authorities and other agencies that deal with Gypsy Roma and Traveller communities (Clark, 2006a, p. 283). Far from being regarded as a "real" minority ethnic group, they are regarded as an "eyesore" or a "nuisance" (ibid., p. 286). As such, racist acts may not be viewed as such. Clark (2006b, pp. 3–4) gives the example of the torching of an effigy of a caravan with a Gypsy family painted on the side, the registration plate of which was "P1 KEY,"[15] the perpetrators of which were not prosecuted for incitement to racial hatred (Clark, 2006a, pp. 3–4). He also cites the racist murder of a fifteen-year-old Irish Traveller, who was kicked, stamped, and beaten to death. This was also judged not to be motivated by racist hatred, the defendants receiving four and a half years for manslaughter (ibid., pp. 5–6). Given that the barrister in this case argued that the attack was motivated by racist hatred of Irish Travellers (ibid., p. 5), and that the murdered young man had "an identifiable Irish accent," we see here the conflation of anti-Gypsy Roma and Traveller racism and anti-Irish racism.

Duffy and Tomlinson (2009, p. 1) reveal the extent of institutional racism that affects Gypsy and Traveller communities who have the poorest life chances of any ethnic group. There is a greater incidence of ill health among Gypsies and Travellers, and 18 percent of Gypsy and Traveller mothers have experienced the death of a child, as compared to 1 percent of the settled community.[16] With respect to education, in a survey of exam results in the U.K.'s 30,000 secondary schools, children of "Travellers of Irish Heritage" and those of "Gypsy Roma" origin were the worst-performing minority ethnic group at GCSEs (General Certificate of Secondary Education) (Department for Education, Statistical First Release, 2010). At the same time, the proportion of pupils in the "Gypsy/Romany" category reaching the expected level in both English and math has fallen from 28.9 percent in 2008 to 24.8 percent in 2009 (Department for Children, Schools and Families, 2009).

Families with young children, Duffy and Tomlinson point out, are evicted on a daily basis, under Section 62a of the Criminal Justice Act of 1994, which is used to hound homeless families from one district to another (ibid., p. 3), a clear example of the repressive state apparatus in practice. Duffy and Tomlinson (2009, p. 1) list many other issues faced daily by the community, such as the effects of the communications ISA; in particular, in the form of racist media reporting. As Clark (2000b, pp. 1–2) has argued, there has been a collective assumption that tabloid racism against Gypsy Roma and Traveller peoples is seen as "safe ground," since there would be little response to this form of racism. As the then Commission for Racial Equality (now subsumed under the Equality and Human Rights Commission) put it in 2004, discrimination against Gypsies and Travellers is the last "respectable" form of racism (CRE, 2004, cited in Gypsy Roma Traveller Leeds, 2007). *The Sun* both captures and creates working class racism and racialization. In its March 24, 2008 edition, for example, the front page headlines declared, "Gypsy Hell for Tessa." The article was referring to the fact that sixty-four

Travellers had "set up camp just yards from the country home of the then Government Minister Tessa Jowell" (p. 1). Above the headline was the caption, "Easter Holiday Invasion." Other descriptors included "30 caravans swarmed on to the...field'" (p. 1); "Gypsy Nightmare"; "crafty gypsies" (p. 4); "these families" (p. 8). More recently, columnist of the Murdoch Sunday paper, *The News of the World*, Carole Malone referred to "gypsies and travellers" in the following terms: "[n]one of these people have jobs or pay tax and most of them contribute little or nothing to society"; "travellers are constantly moving and don't live ordered lives like the rest of us"; "[a]nd why do these armies of people who descend on peaceful villages all over Britain bringing chaos and distress get special treatment?"; "[I]t's not our fault they choose not to live in a house—although they seem fairly adept at knocking up jerry-built dwellings on land that doesn't belong to them"; "[a]nd how come they're allowed to break the law, particularly planning laws, with impunity, yet the minute one of us does 35mph in a 30 limit we get clobbered?" The interpellation concludes: "[I]t's not fair. It's not right" (*The News of the World*, June 21, 2009). A final example of the ongoing tirade against the Gypsy Roma and Traveller communities occurred at the time of writing. Andy Crick claimed in *The Sun* (August 27, 2010, p. 34) that Irish Travellers wishing to see the Pope had "thrown [his visit] into turmoil amid fears hordes of gipsies will gatecrash a mass." He went to point out that "[w]aves" had already arrived.

Duffy and Tomlinson (2009, p. 1) also note a lack of understanding by service providers. This is either through lack of cultural awareness, racism, or by just failing to understand the needs of the communities. Families cite racist bullying as a major issue for removing children from schools (ibid., 2009, p. 7).

Under the ConDem government, Gypsy Roma and Traveller communities are already faring worse. The Regional Strategies plan that set targets for councils to provide land has been scrapped, and £30 million of funding for Gypsy and Traveller sites has been withdrawn (Robinson, 2010, p. 4). The coalition is drafting new laws that will allow police more powers to evict and arrest people for trespass on public land (*The Observer*, 2010). In addition, planning laws are also being altered to stop applications for retrospective permission to put caravans on private land; regional planning bodies which were to oversee provision of registered sites are being abolished; and grants for councils to provide sites have been slashed. At the same time, an estimated £18m a year is being spent on evictions (ibid.). Founding member of the Gypsy Council, Gratton Puxon, commented, "Gypsies are being squeezed on all sides in this wave of intolerance and racism which is unlike anything I've ever seen before" (cited in ibid.).

Newer Forms of Racism

Liz Fekete (2009) has written at length about newer forms of racism. Her specific focus is on anti-asylum-seeker racism, xeno-racism, and Islamophobia.

Explaining the underlying *economic* dimension of these newer forms, Fekete explains how the combination of anti-immigration movements and an onslaught from the communications ISA in the form of the press became too much for mainstream parties. From the perspective of the political ISA:

> Politicians knew full well that, because of Europe's declining birth rates, an ageing population and shortage of skilled workers, in some areas, and semi- and unskilled workers, in others, Europe was in desperate need of migrant workers. But they also knew that to openly acknowledge this would be to antagonise the electorate. At the same time, governments feared that the globalisation-inspired irregular movements of people, resulting in migratory flows of labour surplus to Europe's economic needs, would derail a political strategy based on micro-managing the migration process quietly and behind the scenes. (Fekete, 2009, p. 6)[17]

Gareth Dale (1999, p. 308) notes how migrant workers are a perfect solution in times of intensified labor market flexibility, but also recognizes the contradiction between capital's need for (cheap) flexible labor and the need for hegemonic control of the workforce by racializing potential foreign workers:

> On the one hand, intensified competition spurs employers' requirements for enhanced labour market flexibility—for which immigrant labour is ideal. On the other, in such periods questions of social control tend to become more pressing. Governments strive to uphold the ideology of "social contract" even as its content is eroded through unemployment and austerity. The logic, commonly, is for less political capital to be derived from the [social contract's] content, while greater emphasis is placed upon its exclusivity, on demarcation from those who enter from or lie outside—immigrants and foreigners.

Exemplifying institutional racism in the political ISA in the U.K., and as a precursor to Gordon Brown's infamous racist interpellation in September 2007: "British jobs for British workers," Fekete notes how, in the run-up to the 2001 General Election, Conservative leader William Hague, in a speech to the Conservative party conference, used the phrase "We will give you back your country" eight times (Fekete, 2009, p. 7). Current institutional racism of this form might be seen as the zenith of England's historic interconnection between racism and nationalism. As Robert Miles (1989) put it, "English nationalism is particularly dependent on and constructed by an idea of 'race,' with the result that English nationalism encapsulates racism" and that "the ideas of 'race' and 'nation,' as in a kaleidoscope merge into one another in varying patterns, each simultaneously highlighting and obscuring the other." "British jobs for British workers" and "getting our country back" can be perceived in Gramscian terminology as "common sense"—"it's only common sense that we should put jobs for British workers first and keep the immigrants out; this will make sure we get our country back and keep our nationality in the face of this immigrant threat."

Newer Non-color-coded Racism

Xeno-racism

On May 1, 2004, ten more countries joined the European Union (EU): Cyprus, the Czech Republic, Estonia, Hungary, Latvia, Lithuania, Malta, Poland, Slovakia, and Slovenia, bringing the total from 15 to 25 member states. On January 1, 2007, two more countries, Bulgaria and Romania, joined the EU. This fact has given rise to a new form of non-color-coded racism, directed primarily at Eastern European workers: xeno-racism.

Sivanandan (2001, p. 2) has defined xeno-racism as:

> a racism that is not just directed at those with darker skins, from the former colonial countries, but at the newer categories of the displaced and dispossessed whites, who are beating at western Europe's doors, the Europe that displaced them in the first place. It is racism in substance but xeno in form—a racism that is meted out to impoverished strangers even if they are white. It is xeno-racism.

Fekete's interpretation of xeno-racism is a wide one that incorporates not just racism directed at European migrant workers, but also Islamophobia (e.g., Fekete, 2009, pp. 43–44, p. 69) and anti-asylum-seeker racism (e.g., ibid., p. 15, p. 19, pp. 41–42). While Sivanandan (2001) does refer to asylum seekers under this definition of xeno-racism, and indeed to those with darker skins from the former colonies as in the quote above, it is my view that conceptually it is better to restrict xeno-racism to that form of racism directed at Eastern European migrant workers. Indeed, in the Foreword to Fekete's book, Sivanandan writes of non-color-coded racism directed at East European workers as follows: "the treatment meted out to (white) East European immigrants [stems] from a compelling economics of discrimination, effectively racism under a different colour, xeno-racism" (Sivanandan, 2009, p. viii).

There are two reasons for my preference for restricting xeno-racism to (white) Eastern European migrant workers (and their families). First, those Eastern European migrant workers who are inhabitants of an EU country have the right, unlike other migrant workers, to work anywhere in the U.K. Second, xeno-racism thus defined is region-specific, or even country-specific (unlike anti-asylum-seeker racism and Islamophobia, which is not region-specific). Moreover, "xeno-racism" is, of course, derived from "xenophopbia," and, if the Online Etymology Dictionary (2001) is correct, the latter was first used just before World War I, in 1912, and itself had early Eastern European connections—between 1914 and 1917, in response to xenophobia aimed at citizens of the Austro-Hungarian Empire arising out of the First World War, 8,579 Eastern Europeans were interned (Berryhill and Sturgeon Ltd, undated).

There is abundant evidence of xeno-racism in this restricted definition of the term. Eastern European workers are also xeno-racialized and pathologized by the communications ISA; and certain tabloids (in particular, *The Sun*) have unleashed anti-Polish and other anti-Eastern European racist rhetoric on a regular basis, alleging a drain on resources, whereas in fact, Eastern European workers make positive contributions to the society on a number of levels (Ruddick, 2009, p. 8). Nevertheless, such workers are on the receiving end of institutional racism on a number of levels—having fewer rights than British workers, being subject to immigration raids, having a higher rate of unemployment and lower wages (ibid.). Jane Hardy (2009, p. 137) notes how legally employed migrant workers, "face huge problems at work." She describes the abuse of such workers over employment contracts and wages, and lists complaints of "excessive working hours with inadequate breaks and no enhanced overtime" (ibid.). She cites evidence (Fitzgerald, 2007; Hardy and Clark, 2007; Anderson, Ruhs, Rogaly and Spencer, 2006) of "recruitment and temporary labour agencies" imposing "high charges for finding employment, lower payment than promised and the withholding of wages" (ibid.). In East Anglia, workers from the new EU countries, she states, are widely used in agriculture, food processing, distribution, and supermarkets, where "there is evidence of terrible working conditions and bullying" (ibid.), and of "gangmasters running some small towns" (ibid., pp. 137–138). Truck drivers from the new EU countries working in supermarket distribution centers, she concludes, are often on zero-hours contracts (contracts that do not guarantee work and pay only for work actually done), and Polish workers she interviewed in a fruit-packing factory were continually told to work faster to meet supermarket demands (ibid., p. 138).

Following Jordan and Düvell, 2002, Hardy also notes complaints from migrant workers concerning overpriced, overcrowded, and shoddy housing (ibid.). There is well-documented evidence of contemporary racist attacks on Polish workers in the U.K. (see BBC News, 2008a, b, c, d, e, f, g, 2009a, b, c, d, e).

Like the migrant workers from the former British colonies in the immediate postwar period, the structurally distinct position in British capitalism of racialized Eastern European workers (Cole, 2009a, pp. 44–45) means that they also constitute, adapting Miles (1982, p. 165), a xeno-racialized fraction of the working class. I will thus restrict the usage of the term xeno-racism, and deal with anti-asylum-seeker racism and Islamophobia separately, under the heading of what I will call hybridist racism.[18]

Newer Hybridist Racism

Under this heading I am including anti-asylum-seeker racism and Islamophobia. My reason for using the term "newer hybridist racism" is because, unlike the forms of racism described above that are on the one hand essentially color-coded, and, on the other, essentially non-color-coded, anti-asylum-seeker racism and Islamophobia can be either color-coded or non-color-coded. These forms of racism can also encompass a combination of color-coded and non-color-coded racism. For example, most asylum seekers come from Iraq, Zimbabwe, Somalia, and Afghanistan (Refugee Action, 2009).[19] This means that, while the racism directed at most Zimbabwean asylum seekers is color-coded, that meted out to Somalis, given that Somalia is in "sub-Saharan Africa" (itself a term with color-coded racist implications), will be color-coded, but may also be Islamophobic, which is not necessarily color-coded (see below), or it may be a combination of color-coded (anti-black) racism and non-color-coded racism (Islamophobia). That form of racism experienced by Afghans and Iraqis is also ambiguous, and may or may not be more Islamophobic than color-coded.

Anti-asylum-seeker racism[20]

We are interpellated that it is "common sense" to keep out asylum seekers, just as we are interpellated that is "common sense" to have "British jobs for British workers" and "get our country back" and keep our nationality. This is dealt with both by the political ISA and the communications ISA; in particular, the right-wing tabloids. From the 1990s, political and legal ISAs laid the groundwork for the rendering of asylum seekers illegal. Fekete describes how "both center-Right and center-Left parties began to implement laws that criminalized asylum seekers" (Fekete, 2009, p. 8). She provides painstaking documentation of the multifaceted horrors of anti-asylum-seeker racism in contemporary Europe. While no one can deny the exploitative nature of the smuggling networks that bring asylum seekers to Europe, she reminds us that it is the blocking of legal routes that "throw them into the arms of smugglers and traffickers" (ibid., p. 23). Institutional racism directed at asylum seekers by government RSAs is apparent throughout the continent. It is now an offense all over Europe, she notes, to assist anyone trying to cross an "illegal" border, whether they are in need of protection or not (ibid.). "Dealing" with asylum seekers also entails the brute force of the RSA—in the form of detention. Institutional racism exists also in the form of a separate prison complex for asylum seekers, where the "use of measures more germane to serious criminal investigation, such as the compulsory finger printing of all asylum seekers...has become routine" (ibid., p. 39). Moreover, asylum seekers can be detained indefinitely under the Immigration Acts, as long as they are being detained "with a view to removal" (ibid., p. 40). The aim of detention is "to break down the will of detainees, so as to make them compliant to their own removal" (ibid., p. 15). Thus, Fekete concludes, those "who challenge their proposed deportation may be asked to choose between lengthy detention in the host country or return to torture in their country of origin" (ibid.). Fekete quite rightly describes this as "psychological torture" (ibid.).

Although the detention of children has now ended, families with all legal rights exhausted are given two weeks to leave the U.K. voluntarily. If they do not, children and parents are forcibly removed from their homes and taken directly to the airport to board a plane. In the event of parents of affected families resisting on the day, the family could be separated, with children possibly taken into care, while police/immigration officials deal with parents.

Fekete (2009, p. 137) explains that the motor that sets "the brutal deportation machine" in motion is "targets," initiated throughout Europe by respective government RSAs. For example, in 2004, Tony Blair established a deportation formula based on the "monthly rate of removals" exceeding "the number of unfounded applications" (ibid., p. 137). As Fekete argues, the imposition of such targets "necessarily undermines the whole humanitarian principle of refugee policy—'need not numbers'—and becomes its obverse, 'numbers not need'" (ibid.), with failed asylum seekers being reduced to "a statistic for removal, even when they have strong claims to remain on humanitarian grounds" (ibid.). Forced removal involves "officially sanctioned state violence" (ibid.) on both routine passenger flights and on chartered special flights and military jets (ibid.). The latter are increasingly favored, since passengers, pilots, and crew on commercial flights object to the violence, which can include:

> crying children frogmarched on to planes…violent control and restraint methods against adult deportees, who may be bound head and foot, gagged (with special adhesive tape) or have their heads forced into the special deportation helmet (a chin strap prevents the deportee from moving [the] lower jaw, an additional strap covers the detainee's mouth). (ibid)

The tabloids are not the only element of the communications ISA brought into play to justify and effect asylum-seeking. Sometimes, for example, the deportations are filmed to discourage attempts at seeking asylum. For example, the U.K. government sent a film crew to film the deportation of about twenty-four Afghans from Gatwick airport, to be broadcast in Afghanistan as a warning to those considering coming to Britain (ibid., p. 138).

With respect to health, free National Health Service (NHS) treatment was removed from failed asylum seekers in 2004, except in the case of emergency, adversely affecting cancer sufferers, newly diagnosed HIV/AIDS patients and pregnant women (Fekete, 2009, p. 37). The Department of Health in the U.K. even tried (unsuccessfully) in 2007 to ban failed asylum seekers from primary care at doctors' surgeries (ibid.).

In 2009, the Borders, Citizenship and Immigration Act came into force, designed to simplify immigration law, strengthen borders and extend the time it takes to gain citizenship.

According to a report published by the Institute of Race Relations (IRR) in October 2010 (IRR, 2010), racist-asylum-seeker and immigration policies in the U.K. have led to the deaths of 77 asylum seekers and migrants over the past four years. Of these, seven are reported as dying after being denied health care for "preventable medical problems"; more than a third are suspected or known suicides after asylum claims have been turned down; seven are said to have died in prison custody; and fifteen to have died during "highly risky" attempts to leave the country (ibid.).

Islamophobia

The first recorded use of the term "Islamophobia" in English was in 1991 (Richardson, 2009, p. 11), which coincided with the first Gulf War (1990–1991) and the upsurge of anti-Muslim racism and hate crime that accompanied it (Poynting and Mason, 2001).[21] Islamophobia is a major form of racism in the modern world. It is important to stress that, while Islamophobia may be sparked by skin color, like the forms of non-color-coded racism described above, Islamophobia is not necessarily triggered by skin color—it can also be set off by one or more (perceived) symbols of the Muslim faith. As Sivanandan (2009, p. ix) puts it, referring to British Muslims—"the terrorist within"—"the victims are marked out not so much by their colour as by their beards and headscarves" (ibid.).

As far as the communications ISA is concerned, Fekete points out how Muslim cultures are presented "through the grossest of stereotypes and sim-plification," (ibid., p. 48) whereas in fact, such cultures are no more of a monolith than Christian ones (ibid., p. 85). Nevertheless they are treated as all the same, both in terms of the racism directed at them and in terms of being a threat—the "repressive force [of] global Islam" (ibid., p. 125). The "repressive force of global Islam" is met by the RSAs of the British state. Fekete (2009, p. 55) discusses the growing trend whereby arrests and pros-ecutions are based not on material evidence but on "crimes of association"; that is, "association with terrorists or with the associates of terrorists." Thus the trustees of mosques fall under suspicion if they have been fund-raising for international causes, such as humanitarian relief for Palestinian refugees in the occupied territories on the spurious ground that "even though the emergency relief was not destined for terrorist organisations, some of it may have ended up in their hands" (ibid., p. 50).

The U.K. Terrorism Act of 2000 further cemented institutional racism aimed at Muslims by creating new offenses based on the circulation of infor-mation useful for terrorism (Fekete, 2009, p. 109). The possession of cer-tain books, for example, is an offense. Even accessing the Internet, perhaps merely out of interest, for information on political or radical Islam can lead to imprisonment (ibid.). Finally, measures introduced throughout Europe make it possible to deprive citizenship of those with dual nationality who display symptoms of "unacceptable behaviour" such as the glorification of terrorism (ibid., p. 119).

Unlike anti-asylum-seeker racism and xeno-racism, Islamophobia has less to do with immigration and more, in its contemporary form, to do with the aftermath of the 9/11 attack on the Twin Towers in New York in 2001, and the suicide bombings of July 7, 2005 (7/7) in Britain, when a coordinated attack was made on London's public transport system during the morning rush hour. Islamophobia is closely related to both old U.K. and new U.S. imperialisms (e.g., in Iraq and Afghanistan) to hegemony and oil. The fact that "Bin Laden" became a playground form of abuse for children perceived to be of Asian origin bears witness to this.

Contemporary Counter-hegemonic Resistance to Racism

If we assess the 1950s and 1960s, it is clear that apart from isolated cases, there is little evidence of collective counter-hegemonic resistance to racism per se (Cole and Virdee, forthcoming, 2011). However, from the mid-1960s, such resistance intensified (for a summary of resistance to racism from then until the onset of the ConDem government, see Cole and Virdee, forthcoming, 2011; for more extensive analyses of resistance, see, for example, Sivanandan, 1982, 1990; Virdee, 1999a, b; Virdee and Grant, 1994).

Key "single issue" organizations are active today such as the Board of Deputies of British Jews, which dates back to 1760; JCOR, the Jewish Council for Racial Equality, founded in 1976; the Palestine Solidarity Campaign, founded in 1972; the Muslim Association of Britain, formed in 1997; and the National Coalition of Anti-Deportation Campaigns (NCADC), open twenty-four hours a day, seven days a week, 365 days a year since it was founded in 1995. While centralizing their particular concerns, all take a general antiracist stance against institutional racism, and the various racist interpellation processes of the ISAs and the brute force of the RSAs. Prominent in generalized antiracist activity in the twenty-first century are Unite Against Fascism; Searchlight, HOPE Not Hate, the Stop the War Coalition, and Love Music Hate Racism. The first three organizations focus on defeating the BNP, although campaign against racism generally, while the Stop the War Coalition coordinates campaigns against modern imperialist wars. Combining antiracist counter-hegemony with cultural resistance is Love Music Hate Racism.

Unite Against Fascism is a campaigning group that has the aim as "a matter of the greatest urgency" of "calling for the broadest unity against the alarming rise in racism and fascism in Britain today...in particular the British National Party (BNP)" (Unite Against Fascism [UAF], 2010. Formed in 2003, UAF aims to unite the broadest possible spectrum of society to counter the threat of the BNP, and more recently the EDL, SDL, and the WDL (see chapter 1 of this volume). Its members include a number of members of Parliament of all political persuasions, as well as the Socialist Workers Party (SWP), trade union leaders, and some music bands.

The remit of Searchlight, a British anti-fascist magazine founded in 1975, is to publish *exposés* of fascism, antisemitism, and racism in the U.K. Searchlight disaffiliated from the UAF in 2005, partly because of tactical issues (Searchlight favors a local rather than a national strategy).

HOPE Not Hate, an offshoot of Searchlight, mobilizes everyone opposed to the BNP's politics of hate. It was formed in 2005 as a positive antidote to the BNP and has the support of the *Daily Mirror*, trade unions, celebrities, and community groups across the country. It is involved in localized campaigning, working within the communities where the BNP is attracting its support.

The Stop the War Coalition was formed in 2001 at a public meeting of over two thousand people in London. Its aims are to create a mass movement to stop the war currently declared by the U.S. and its allies against "terror-ism," and to oppose any racist backlash generated by the war against ter-rorism (Stop the War Coalition, 2009). While Stop the War condemns the attacks on New York and feels the greatest compassion for those who lost their life on September 11, 2001, it argues that "any war will simply add to the numbers of innocent dead, cause untold suffering, political and eco-nomic instability on a global scale, increase racism and result in attacks on civil liberties" (ibid.).

In its own words, "Love Music Hate Racism uses the positive energy of the music scene to fight back against the racism being pushed by Nazi organisations like the BNP" (Love Music Hate Racism, 2009). As the orga-nization puts it:

> Our music is living testimony to the fact that cultures can and do mix. It unites us and gives us strength, and offers a vibrant celebration of our multicultural and multiracial society. Racism seeks only to divide and weaken us.

Love Music Hate Racism was inaugurated in 2002 in response to rising lev-els of racism and electoral successes for the BNP. Its aim is to use the energy of music "to celebrate diversity and involve people in anti-racist and anti-fascist activity—as well as to urge people to vote against fascist candidates in elections...in the tradition of the **Rock Against Racism** (RAR) movement of the late 1970s" in order "to create a national movement against racism and fascism through music" (Love Music Hate Racism, 2009).

Conclusion

In this chapter I have attempted to outline some of the main forms of rac-ism in contemporary Britain. In the 1970s and the 1980s, it was fashionable to draw a distinction between "white" and "black" with all racialized con-stituencies falling under the latter category. If that was inadequate terminol-ogy then, it is most certainly lacking in twenty-first-century Britain. From a Marxist perspective, the real enemy is not, of course, the various racialized minorities discussed in this chapter, but the very system that profits (literally and ideologically) from the exploitation of these minorities. In diverse ways, racism and (xeno-)racialization serve the "divide and rule" tactics of capital-ism and direct workers' attentions away from that real enemy and toward their racialized sisters and brothers. This was recognized by Marx some 140 years ago:

> In all the big industrial centres in England there is profound antagonism between the Irish proletariat and the English proletariat. The average English worker hates the Irish worker as a competitor who lowers wages and the stan-dard of life. He feels national and religious antipathies for him. He regards him somewhat like the poor whites of the Southern states regard their black slaves. This antagonism among the proletarians of England is artificially nourished

and supported by the bourgeoisie. It knows that this scission is the true secret of maintaining its power. (Marx, 1870 [1978]), p. 254)

Racism is a fluid process. It is unlikely that before the demise of Stalinism anyone would have predicted the xeno-racialization of Eastern European workers in the U.K. In the current crisis in capitalism, as many of these workers return home, future trends in (xeno-)racialization are uncertain. What is clear from a Marxist perspective is that past, present, and future trends can be best understood with references to ongoing changes and developments in the economic and ideological manifestations of the capitalist mode of production, related patterns of migration, and the onward march of imperialism. From a neo-Marxist perspective, these changes and developments will be reflected in ongoing changes in state interpellative and hegemonic strategies. For (neo-)Marxist counter-hegemonic resistance to be effective, these changes and developments merit close monitoring.

Chapter 3

Racism in the U.S.

Racism in the U.S. differs in many, though not all, aspects from the U.K. This is, in part, because of the two countries' different economic and political histories, not least, respective differences in colonization (the U.K. were early colonizers; the Americas, and what was to become the U.S., early colonized) and migration patterns. However, what both countries have in common is that in both, there exists a multitude of different forms of racism. In chapter 2 of this volume, I argued that one of the reasons it is important to categorize various forms of racism is to effectively challenge it. I then proceeded to delineate the plethora of manifestations of racism in the U.K. I concluded with a consideration of contemporary counter-hegemonic resistance to racism. I do the same in this chapter with respect to racism in the U.S., considering respective forms of resistance.throughout the chapter. I begin by looking at the legacy of Christopher Columbus, addressing myself to the situation of Native Americans both historically and contemporaneously. Next I move on to a consideration of the history of slavery in the U.S., followed by some issues connected to the lives of African Americans, post-slavery and today. After that I look at racism experienced historically and currently by Latina/o Americans, before moving on to trace the history of and the current realities for Asian Americans. I conclude my analysis of different groups with a consideration of Native Hawaiians and Pacific Islander (NHPI) Americans. I then address Islamophobia, particularly rampant since 9/11. Next I consider some antisemitic groups in the U.S., before concluding with one major difference between the U.K. and the U.S.—the proliferation of hate groups. Since Critical Race Theory (CRT) provides a convenient lens through which to view many of the different forms of racism in the U.S., I draw critically on some of CRT's insights in the course of the chapter, while also stressing its limitations.

Five Hundred Years of Institutional Racism

Edward Taylor (2006, pp. 80–81) has succinctly summarized the essence of institutional racism in the U.S.:

> The United States was honed from a split stone—Whites would have certain unalienable rights to property and capital, and Blacks, American Indians, and

other people of color would provide these rights, in the form of land (American Indians) and labor (enslaved/ oppressed people). The justification for this was based on a broad consensus that Europeans were innately superior.

It is necessary to deal with the historical reality of institutional racism in the U.S. in some depth. There are four reasons for this. First, there is a tendency to restrict racism to the experiences of African Americans, what some critics (e.g., Delgado and Stefancic, 2001, p. 142) have referred to as the "black-white binary," which "considers the black-white relation as central to racial analysis," or "black exceptionalism," (e.g., ibid., p. 69) which holds that black people's history "is so distinctive that placing it at the center of analysis is…warranted." While, as we shall see, anti-black racism was and continues to be a prominent and abhorrent reality for African Americans, horrific institutional racism existed before enslaved Africans were brought to the Americas, and continues to oppress a wide constituent of peoples. This brings me to the second reason. Institutional racism has existed on what is now U.S. soil for half a millennium, starting with the racialization, exploitation, and pillage of America's indigenous peoples.

Third, the repressive and ideological apparatuses of the State (RSAs and ISAs)[1] have been applied excessively, unremittingly, and mercilessly to maintain hegemony, to uphold and reproduce different forms of institutional racism. A variety of forms of intense counter-hegemonic antiracist resistance has been apparent for five hundred years, too.

Fourth, an in-depth discussion of the history of hegemonic institutional racism and counter-hegemonic resistance is required in order to more fully understand key features of contemporary U.S. racism. This is particularly important given that few U.S. teachers or their students know much about the country's racist past, and "[a] common occurrence in discussions about race [in U.S. classrooms] is a tendency not only to render the complex simply, but to disregard the historic conflict in which it was spawned" (Taylor, 2006, p. 75).

The Legacy of Christopher Columbus and Native Americans

The colonial invasion

In an attempt to find a new trade route to India, in 1492 Christopher Columbus "discovered" America, which, at first, he assumed was part of the coast of Asia. Marx and Engels described how (unknown, of course, to Columbus at the time) the "discovery of America paved the way" for the establishment by European modern industry of the world market (1847) [1977], p. 37. As they put it:

> The discovery of America, the rounding of the Cape, opened up fresh ground for the rising bourgeoisie. The East-Indian and Chinese markets, the colonisation of America, trade with the colonies, the increase in the means of exchange and in commodities generally, gave to commerce, to navigation, to industry,

an impulse never before known, and thereby, to the revolutionary element in the tottering feudal society, a rapid development. (ibid., p. 36)

After landing in "the new world," Columbus wrote in his log that the indigenous people were "utterly convinced that I and all my people came from Heaven" (cited in Okihiro, 1994, p. 17) prompting Gary Okihiro (1994, p. 17) to describe Columbus's venture as "Christian imperialism." Columbus reported back to the King of Spain on the Arawaks as follows: "should your Majesty command it, all the inhabitants could be taken away to Castile, or made slaves on the island. With fifty men we could subjugate them all and make them do whatever we want" (cited in Permanent Revolution, 2008). It has been estimated (Denevan, 1992, pp. xxviii-xxix, 2010) that, at the time of Columbus's arrival, there were between 43 million and 65 million indigenous peoples in the Americas as a whole, and about 3.8 million indigenous peoples in North America alone. Of these, about 3.3 million were in what is now the U.S. (Denevan, 2010). Following on from Columbus's assessment of the potential of this new category of people to exploit, there then ensued, in the words of the Marxist organization, Permanent Revolution, 2008, "force; pillage conquest, mass murder, torture and religious bigotry." As they put it, "[t]hat was how the 'civilised' Europeans stamped their authority on the peoples of what came to be called 'the Americas.'" Maria Paez Victor (2009) has described Columbus as "a mass murderer, an unrelenting racist, who carried out one of the most complete and extensive genocides in history upon the original peoples of our America." The indigenous Arawaks and Caribs were almost wiped out, and later, black slaves[2] from Portuguese Africa were brought in to establish and work the highly profitable sugar plantations (Permanent Revolution, 2008). (See later in this chapter for a discussion of slavery.)

In 1565, Don Pedro Menendez de Aviles and six hundred Spanish soldiers and settlers colonized St. Augustine, Florida,[3] and by 1570, the new continent had been named "America" (Permanent Revolution, 2008). The origins of the term "America" are disputed (see Cohen, 2010 for an interesting account).

The manipulation period

From the 1590s through the seventeenth century, the Americas then experienced what has been described as "the manipulation period" in indigenous-white relations (Coffer, 1979, p. 47; Nederveen Pieterse, 1986, p. 36) where the imperialist powers of Spain, Britain, and France struck alliances with indigenous peoples for colonial trade gains and in which indigenous peoples took part (Nederveen Pieterse, 1986, pp. 36–38). Roxanne Dunbar Ortiz (cited in ibid., p. 37) has described alliances such as those between the Miskito and Iroquois nations with the British against, respectively, the Spanish and the French, as "indirect colonisation." However, Nederveen Pieterse (ibid.) cautions that we should not underestimate the role of these nations as active agents.

Surrounded by white men

From the late seventeenth century to the end of the eighteenth century, the main issue was land rather than trade. This was a period in which, with England in control of the Atlantic seaboard; the French entrenched in Canada and along the Mississippi river; and Spain in Florida and the south-west, "the Indians in the east found themselves surrounded by white men" (ibid., p. 38). After successful rebellions led by the indigenous war chief Pontiac, a member of the Ottawa tribe, one of the colonizers, General Amherst, wrote to a fellow general, "[c]ould it not be contrived to send the small pox among the disaffected tribes of Indians" (cited in ibid., p. 39). This could be seen as part of Amherst's efforts to "extirpate this execrable race" (cited in ibid.). In large part, as the result of Pontiac's rebellion, and in order to stop the rebellion and prevent further ones, the British Crown in 1763 set an official line of demarcation prohibiting white settlement west of the Appalachian Mountains and outlawed private purchase of Indian property (ibid.).

The American Revolution and counter-hegemonic struggle

As Jan Nederveen Pieterse (ibid.) argues, this was the end of an era. The next period saw the settlers angry with the British Crown over the proclamation of 1763, which, along with Crown taxes on tea and other goods, precipitated the American Revolution of 1776 (and the founding of the U.S. of America), during which not a single Native American tribe of consequence joined the colonists. This was because the Native Americans knew they could expect nothing from the colonists, and since "Anglo-Saxon hegemony was secure" (ibid.), the "politics of playing off European rivals against one another and against rival tribes no longer worked" (ibid., p. 40). Following the success of the American revolution, Native Americans, after 300 years of dealing with rival European powers, faced a single enemy: the U.S. of America. Prominent in the counter-hegemonic struggle against this new nation was Tecumseh, a Shawnee leader, who preached for the first time that Native land belonged to all tribes in common (ibid.). He argued in 1810 that the only way forward was:

> for all red men to unite in claiming a common and equal right in the land; as it was first, and should be yet; for it never was divided, but belongs to all, for the use of each. That no part has a right to sell, even to each other, much less to strangers (Clink (ed.)). (1961, p. 74, cited in Nederveen Pieterse, 1986, p. 41)

The strategy of the U.S. government was to turn Native Americans from hunters into agriculturalists, so they would not need so much land. Tactics included getting chiefs into debt at state trading houses so that they needed to sell off land, and exterminating the economic base of the hunting tribes: the buffalo (Nederveen Pieterse, 1986, pp. 41–2). In addition to economic warfare through trade and debt, RSAs were used in military campaigns, and in attempts to annihilate the buffalo, while RSAs and ISAs combined to try to terminate the Native American traditional way of life with "germ warfare, psychological warfare using alcohol…ecological warfare using the reservation system [and] cultural warfare prohibiting Indian ceremonies" (ibid., p. 42).

Tecumseh's vision of a return to common and equal ownership of the land was not to be realized, and, during his absence, Tecumseh's base was raided and destroyed. Native Americans' counter-hegemonic response was to wage guerilla warfare, which the Americans alleged was supported by the British from their forts in Canada, one of the factors that prompted the U.S. declaration of war on England in 1812. Tecumseh fought on the English side and died in the war. (ibid.). As Nederveen Pieterse explains, the English were fighting with reluctance, since England and the predominantly "Anglo" Americans had a common interest in outmaneuvering the Spanish in South America (ibid.). Nederveen Pieterse (ibid.) concludes that Tecumseh, "the harbinger of Indian nationalism perished in the last battle involving Indians which was based on a conflict between Europeans."

Opening up the West

The next period identified by Nederveen Pieterse witnessed the Indian Removal Act of 1830, when, under the presidency of Andrew Jackson, the "West" was opened up for the "American way of life" (ibid., p. 43). As Nederveen Pieterse (ibid.) notes, "Jacksonian Democracy" excluded both Native Americans and black Americans. The U.S. military crushed the resistance, planters occupied Native lands, and their occupants were moved to Oklahoma territory, heralding the "wars of the plains," associated with the names of famous war chiefs such as Crazy Horse, Sitting Bull, and Geronimo (ibid.). While the plains Indians were a formidable foe, in the end it was the annihilation of the buffalo along with U.S. modern weaponry that won the day. In 1871, the practice of signing treaties with Native people ended. Nevertheless a Native American land base remained, however narrow (ibid., p. 48).

The General Allotment Act of 1887

According to Perea et al., (2007, p. 221) "[t]he single most destructive achievement of the nineteenth century movement to break the structure and sovereignty of Indian tribes was Congress's passage of the General Allotment Act of 1887." This act, also known as the Dawes Act, allowed the president of the U.S. to break up lands held jointly by tribes and reallocate them in separate parcels to individual tribal members, effectively converting indigenous peoples from hunters to farmers (Perea et al., 2007, p. 221). David Getches et al., (2005, p. 141) have argued that the act had two goals: "to open up more land for white settlement and to end Indian tribalism."

As they explain, the aim of the act was:

> to turn reservations into campuses for training Indians in the "arts of civilization." The Bureau of Indian Affairs took unprecedented control of

everyday Indian life, seeking to squeeze out Indian government, religion, and culture...."Surplus" lands were sold for non-Indian settlement; the result was a loss of about two-thirds of all the Indians' lands. (Getches et al., 2005, p.141)

President Theodore Roosevelt was brutally honest about the intentions of the act, describing it as "a mighty pulverizing engine to break up the tribal mass" (cited in ibid., p. 186). The 1880s to the 1920s was a period of poverty and demoralization, during which time a number of other acts were passed that successively institutionalized the hegemony of U.S. neocolonialism (Nederveen Pieterse, 1986, p. 49). In response to the decimation of tribal lands and culture caused by the General Allotment Act, attempts were made to restore tribal governance and sovereignty. The Meriam Report (1928) described in great detail Indian poverty, ill health, and poor education. As a result, in 1934, the Indian Reorganization Act (IRA) was passed, which sought to negate the General Allotment Act (Perea et al., 2007, pp. 222–223). However, as Perea et al., 2007, p. 223, point out, while the IRA represented an improvement, the improvement was merely partial. As Vine Deloria Jr. and Lytle (1983, cited in ibid., p. 224) argue, "[m]any of the old customs and traditions...had vanished...The experience of self-government according to Indian traditions had eroded and, while the new constitutions were akin to the traditions of some tribes, they were completely foreign to others." In general, they point out, traditional Indians of almost every tribe objected strongly to "the Anglo-American system of organizing people" (cited in ibid.).

The boarding school project

It was perhaps the boarding school project that crystallized how racism was institutionalized for Native Americans. It was organized by Captain Richard Henry Pratt, who declared in 1892, "a great general [General Phil Sheridan] has said that the only good Indian is a dead one...In a sense, I agree with the sentiment, but only in this: that all the Indian there is in the race should be dead. Kill the Indian in him, and save the man" (Churchill, 2004, p. 1, cited in Malott, 2011a, p. 96). Citing Ward Churchill (2004), Curry Malott (2011a, p. 100) lists 129 Indian boarding schools operating within the U.S. between 1880 and 1980. Malott (2011a, p. 101) describes how the process worked, with children as young as four years old who were:

forcibly removed from resistant parents and taken sometimes thousands of miles from home for years on end and prohibited from speaking their native tongue or practicing any of their other cultural traditions. In other words, they were prohibited from being "Indian" and made, sometimes with deadly force, to be something else, that is, a low-level, manual laborer with white values and worldview. (2011a, p. 100)

Churchill (2004, cited in Malott, 2011a, p. 101) estimates that between the late 1800s and the mid-1900s more than half of all Native American children had been removed from their homes in this way. Schooling socialized them into thinking that "white society in general represented everything good and civilized and that 'Indian' ways were shameful and savage" (Malott, 2011a, p. 101). Colonization and genocide was rarely discussed, and if it was, it was "contrasted with the superior future that is now within their grasp thanks to the generous gift of 'Western civilization'" (ibid.). Native children's dress and hairstyles were changed, cultural materials brought from home were destroyed, cultural practices were banned, and Native languages were forbidden, even out of class (ibid.).

Mainstream churches and government were directly responsible for the deaths of at least fifty thousand children as a result of this process of compulsory assimilation. The crimes that these institutions were guilty of included "murder through beating, poisoning, hanging, starvation, strangulation, medical experimentation and forced sterilization" and pedophilia (Smith, 2005, cited in Malott, 2011a, p. 101).

Moreover, as Malott (2011a, p. 102) explains, Native students had to "contribute to the funding of their own cultural destruction through their collective labor power" in sweatshops, laundries, and bakeries. Churchill (2004, p. 51, cited in Malott, 2011a, p. 103) describes their counter-hegemonic responses:

> Native children were not merely the passive victims of all that was being done to them. Virtually without exception, survivor narratives include accounts of subversion, both individual and collective, most commonly involving such activities as "stealing" and/or foraging food, possessing other "contraband," persistence in the speaking of native languages and running away. In many— perhaps most—residential schools, such activities were so common and sustained as to comprise outright "cultures of resistance."

In challenging these attempts at cultural genocide, many Native American communities have taken control of their schools and embarked on a campaign of cultural rejuvenation, emphasizing traditional value systems, customs, and language (for details, see Malott, 2011a, pp. 104–111). Indeed, from the late 1960s, coinciding with mass movements worldwide, a new Native activism arose, of which the takeover of Wounded Knee in 1973 was the most famous.[4] As Donna Langston (2006) has argued, many groups "borrowed strategies, tactics, theory, and vision from the African American movement" (see later in this chapter for a discussion of African Americans). However, Native peoples also drew on their own history. As she puts it, drawing on Winfrey, 1986, pp. 145–146), "their focus was less on integration with dominant society, and more on maintaining cultural integrity":

> While African Americans had been denied integration, American Indians had faced a history of forced assimilation...American Indians also faced problems

that differed from other groups, since they were owners of land and resources. A central focus of their activism was on gaining enforcement of treaty rights, not civil rights…The Indian movement focused more on empowering the tribe, not individuals, the more common reference point for civil rights groups (Langston, 2006).

Civil Rights are discussed later in this chapter.

Native Americans Today

Cankú Lúta (2009), a national nonprofit organization committed to education, service, and preservation of American Indian culture, documents the plight of today's survivors of the neo-colonial project against Native Americans, who are, it argues:

> struggling with massive problems, such as emotional and psychological trauma, substandard and inadequate housing, frequent lack of food and heat, alcoholism and drug addiction, and high rates of poverty-related diseases. Large tracts of reservation land are leased to white ranchers by the Bureau of Indian Affairs and tribal governments created by the U.S. government Indian Reorganization Act of 1934. Grassroots Indian owners are paid only a fraction of the real value of the leases and rarely offered resources to develop self-sustaining enterprises on these lands. Instead they are offered meager welfare payments and commodity foods with little nutritional value.

Referring to U.S. policy toward indigenous peoples within federal Indian law, Critical Race Theorist[5] Rebecca Tsosie (2005–2006, p. 43) explains that Indian tribes had only a "right to occupancy" rather than the territorial rights of a "real" nation. Moreover, because tribes were perceived to be in a rudimentary state of governance, they were deemed to be "wards" of the federal government (ibid.).

Because the privilege and power resides in federal and state governments rather than with tribal governments, she concludes, the ensuing problems such as lack of meaningful tribal jurisdiction over assaults and domestic violence between non-Indians and Indians, for example, are treated as a "social condition" (ibid., p. 44), "amenable perhaps for federal funding to 'study' the problem" (ibid.). "But no one seriously questions the validity of the basic structure" (ibid.).

Also writing from a CRT perspective, specifically, "Tribal Crit," Bryan Brayboy (2005, pp. 429–430) has argued that colonialization remains endemic to U.S. society, and that U.S. policies towards indigenous peoples are rooted in imperialism.[6]

Tsosie's solution is for Native people "to define, assert, protect, and insist upon respect for the right to be what they always have been: distinctive governments and societies, autonomous and free" (Tsosie, 2005–2006, p. 45). This means resisting the colonial enterprise, which uses external power to define the "other" as subordinate to the colonial nation, and taking back power and constructing tribal sovereignty from *within* Native societies (ibid.).

As Cankú Lúta (2009) put it, if non-Indians want to honor Indian peoples and their traditions, there are a number of things they can do. They can show respect by being thoroughly informed of the conditions faced by grassroots Indians in the past and present; they can help ensure that grassroots people are consulted on all matters pertaining to Indian culture. They can expose self-proclaimed pseudo-experts for what they are; they can also stop the exploitation of Indian culture, the stereotyping, the use of Indian logos and mascots, and the appropriation of ceremonies for personal gain. Non-Indians can offer support to grassroots Indian organizations that are currently involved in recovering illegally seized lands. Moreover, they can pressure politicians to pass legislation beneficial to Indians; and provide material support to grassroots people to ease their physical struggle for survival. Finally, non-Indians can try to incorporate the most basic traditional values of Indian cultures into their own daily living: respect, humility, patience, and making relatives (with other humans and other living beings on our Mother Earth).

With respect to education, Sandy Grande (2009, p. 201) spells out the precepts of what she calls "Red Pedagogy." These include a conception of pedagogy as:

- inherently political, cultural, spiritual, and intellectual;
- fundamentally rooted in indigenous knowledge and praxis;
- furthering understanding and analysis of the forces of colonization;
- informed by critical and revolutionary theories of education;
- promoting an education for decolonization;
- making no claim to political neutrality but, rather, engaging a method of analysis and social inquiry that troubles the capitalist-imperialist aims of unfettered competition, accumulation, and exploitation;
- a project that interrogates both democracy and indigenous sovereignty;
- actively cultivating a praxis of collective agency among indigenous peoples;
- grounded in a hope that lives in contingency with the past—one that trusts the beliefs and understandings of indigenous ancestors, the power of traditional knowledge, and the possibilities of new understandings; and
- about engaging the development of "community-based power."

As such, "red pedagogy" has links with the restoration of indigenous rights in the Bolivarian Republic of Venezuela, including collective ownership of land, and the right to an intercultural and bilingual education, in the context of a firm commitment by revolutionaries to the transition to a future socialist society. This is discussed in chapter 5 of this volume.

Slavery, Segregation, and African Americans

The Middle Passage

Although enslaved Africans were first brought to Spanish Florida as early as the 1560s (Bron Davis, 2006, p. 124), the origins of mass slavery in the U.S. were in the first English colonization of North America in Jamestown Island, Virginia in 1607. The first enslaved Africans were brought there in 1619, and thereafter slavery spread like a cancer, as the English colonists realized its vast financial returns (Kolchin, 1995, pp. 3–4). The slave trade was triangular, in that the ships first departed from Europe to Africa, after which enslaved Africans were taken to the Americas (the "Middle Passage"), followed by the return of the ships to Europe. It is estimated that between the sixteenth and nineteenth centuries, about 12.5 million Africans were shipped from Africa to the Americas, of which approximately 10.7 million actually arrived (Eltis, 2007). Of these, some 390,000 arrived directly from Africa in what is now the U.S. (Eltis, 2008, p. 353). Peter Kolchin (1995, p. 18) argues that, while it was in full swing by the late seventeenth century, slavery was big business in the eighteenth. Successful voyages brought large profits. However, as Kolchin (ibid.) points out, sea travel was dangerous, and on most ships, between 5 and 20 percent of the enslaved Africans (and crew) died in transit. Kolchin (ibid., p. 19) cites the case of the captain of the Zong who, in 1781, ordered the throwing overboard of 132 Africans because the ship was running short of water, and his insurance covered death by drowning, but not from starvation.

He describes graphically the transit to the "new world":

> Marched in chains to points of embarkation, sold to strange-looking men who spoke an incomprehensible language, branded, dragged struggling into long canoes that took them to ships waiting offshore, Africans began their voyage to America in despondency and often in panic. Some had never before seen giant ships, the ocean, or white men...many...feared [they were] about to be eaten. (ibid., p. 20)

This was followed by the transatlantic voyage, where enslaved Africans were usually kept in chains in holds, sometimes so cramped they could hardly move (ibid., p. 21). A doctor (cited in Mannix and Cowley, 1788 [1962], p. 117) refers to conditions in bad weather when they were in temperatures "so extremely hot as to be only bearable for a very short time," when the floors were "so covered with the blood and mucus which had proceeded from them...that it resembled a slaughterhouse." As PBS (Public Broadcasting Service) (undated) explains, people were usually forced to lie on their backs with their heads between the legs of others, meaning that "they often had to lie in each other's feces, urine, and, in the case of dysentery, even blood." In such conditions, diseases like smallpox and yellow fever spread rapidly, with the diseased sometimes thrown overboard to prevent wholesale epidemics. Women were often sexually abused.

Those that survived the journey faced further terror, either with prospective buyers rushing on to the ship, or a public auction where they would be poked, prodded, and examined (Kolchin, 1995, p. 21). As Kolchin (ibid.) puts it, "[o]nce again, anger, humiliation, and fear of impending doom gripped them."

The embedding of anti-black institutional racism in the Americas

Such blatantly inhuman treatment required that African peoples be rendered subhuman. This underlines slavery's close relationship with racism and is related to the racialization of Africans in the English homelands, which has its origins, of course, in U.K. imperialism (see, for example, Cole, 2004b, 2004c). Stereotypes in the Americas centered around three perceived "differences" between Africans and "the English." First, they were black as opposed to white, with all the associated negative attributes related to the former—for example, "dirty," as compared to the positive affiliations of the latter, for example, "pure." Second, Africans were considered "uncivilized" and inferior. Third, they were "heathens" or "non-Christian" (Kolchin, 1995, pp. 14–15). This facilitated the embedding of institutional racism, as decrees by the Southern colonies in the 1660s ensured that all imported "negroes" should be slaves, while whites should be indentured servants (contracted legally for a fixed period in return for transportation, food, clothing, lodging, and other necessities) (Finley, 1967, p. 10, cited in Genovese, 1969, p. 246). Following on from this, a series of laws, primarily in the eighteenth century, established that slaves and the children of slave women would be slaves for life. Such legislation also limited the rights of slaves and of free blacks—they were not allowed to vote, to testify in court against whites, or marry whites. In addition, slaves were forbidden from carrying arms or leaving home without written permission. Severe corporal punishment was introduced for those who challenged white authority. Moreover, the laws had a variety of provisions that discouraged slave owners from freeing slaves (Kolchin, 1995, p. 17). As M. I. Finley (1967, p. 10, cited in Genovese, 1969, p. 246) puts it, "[t]he connection between slavery and racism has been a dialectical one, in which each element reinforced the other."

Exploitation and oppression were both psychological and physical, with slaves being told over and over again that they were "inferior," that they should "know their place," and see blackness as a sign of subordination. They were interpellated "to be awed by the power of their master', to merge their interests with his, thus "destroying their own individual needs" (Zinn, 1995, cited in Perea et al., 2007, p. 101).

This was accompanied by the deployment of both RSAs and ISAs. As Howard Zinn (1995, cited in Perea et al., p. 101) states, all this was accomplished by hard labor, the breakup of the slave family, the creation of disunity by separating "field slaves" from the more privileged "house slaves" and by "the lulling effects of religion." The ultimate power was that of the overseer to "invoke whipping, burning, mutilation, and death" (Zinn, 1995, cited in Perea et al., p. 101). Women were often raped, not merely for reasons of sexual gratification and vilification, but to boost slave numbers and thereby increase profits. As the slave Frederick Douglass (1845) put it:

> in all its glaring odiousness, that slaveholders have ordained, and by law estab-
> lished, that the children of slave women shall in all cases follow the condition
> of their mothers; and this is done too obviously to administer to their own
> lusts, and make a gratification of their wicked desires profitable as well as plea-
> surable; for by this cunning arrangement, the slaveholder, in cases not a few,
> sustains to his slaves the double relation of master and father.

The following graphic account reveals the barely comprehensible depths of inhumanity and depravity of the slave owners, and is indicative of how the designation of black people as less than human stimulated subhuman treatment from the slave owners themselves.

Lavinia Bell, a slave working in Galveston, Texas from the age of thirteen or fourteen, describes how the slaves were allowed no clothes, their hair was shorn close to their head, thus exposing them to the hot southern sun from early morning until late at night. Scarcely a day passed, she points out, without their receiving fifty lashes, whether they worked or not. They were forced to go down on their knees, harnessed to ploughs, with boys riding them and whipping them when they flagged in the work. They were also compelled to walk on hackles (steel combs used for dressing flax), which left them with scarred feet. On one of Bell's many unsuccessful escape bids, her master having difficulty proving her identity, vowed to mark her in such a way that he would have no trouble in future, and proceeded to slit both her ears, branded her on the back of her left hand with a hot iron, cut off a finger on her right hand searing the wound with a hot iron, and branded her on the stomach with a letter. After she refused to tell the master she had been inciting other slaves to escape to Canada, and would not tell him how she found out about Canada, further torture and abuse entailed. She was whipped and the wounds rubbed with salt. She also had her skull broken. As a result, she had to have a silver plate inserted in her head. The master's response was to curse her, saying that she had "a dollar in her head to pay her way to purgatory." At times, she was left without food or drink. On one of such occasions, she was so hungry she tried to tear her eyes out to eat them (Blassingame [ed.] 1977, pp. 341–343, cited in Perea et al., 2007, pp. 119–120).

The Second Middle Passage

The period from the American Revolution of 1776 to the Civil War of 1850 has been described by Ira Berlin (2003, pp. 161–162) as the "Second Middle Passage," a "central event" in the life of a slave between the American Revolution and the Civil War, where they were uprooted or lived in fear of being uprooted. The cause of this total disruption to the lives of slaves was the growing demand for cotton, and the resultant move west in search of suitable land. As Kolchin (1995, p. 96) explains, slave owners moved hundreds of thousands of "surplus" slaves west. With the breakup of families and the forcible removal of slaves to distant parts, the Second Middle Passage replicated many of the horrors, if on a reduced scale, of the international slave trade that was coming to an end (Kolchin, 1995, p. 96). Kolchin (ibid.) estimates that about twice as many slaves were moved west between 1790 and 1860 as had crossed the Atlantic from Africa to what is now the U.S. The slave trade generated its own language, with "prime hands, bucks, breeding wenches, and fancy girls" being common parlance (Berlin, 2003, pp. 166–169). Berlin (ibid., pp. 172–173) compares the passage of slaves on foot as resembling a funeral, with those who survived the journey facing totally new working conditions. Berlin (ibid., p. 174) also points out that, with limited immunities acquired in their previous homes, the death rate was so high that some planters preferred to rent rather than to buy slaves.

While the slave trade was, of course, of great benefit to the colonizers, it also fueled capitalism in the homeland. Marx and Engels argued that slavery was as crucial to English capitalism as the growth of machinery:

> Direct slavery is as much the pivot of our industrialism today as machinery, credit, etc. Without slavery no cotton; without cotton no modern industry. Slavery has given value to the colonies; the colonies have created world trade; world trade is the necessary condition of large-scale machine industry. Thus, before the traffic in Negroes began, the colonies supplied the Old World with only very few products that made no visible change in the face of the earth. Slavery is therefore an economic category of the highest importance (Marx and Engels, 1846 [1977], p. 665).

Counter-hegemonic resistance to slavery

Slave rebellions were commonplace throughout the period of slavery in what is now the U.S. Enslavement was constantly resisted in every way possible, including rebellion and escape. As Howard Zinn (1995, cited in Perea et al., 2007, p. 100) puts it, throughout two hundred years of enslavement, under pain of mutilation and death, slaves continued to rebel. Of course, the odds stacked against the slaves in terms of the high ratio of whites to blacks; the relatively small size and dispersed nature of slaveholdings; the number of well-armed masters; and apart from the War of Independence and the Civil War, relative political stability (Kolchin, 1995, p. 155). Despite all this, there were at least two hundred and fifty reported conspiracies and revolts. As Herbert Aptheker (1973, cited in Perea et al., 2007, p. 126) puts it, arguing against certain conservative historians, this "certainly demonstrates that organized efforts at freedom were neither 'seldom' nor 'rare,' but were rather a regular and ever-recurring phenomenon in the life of the old South." Such rebellions were greatest in number in times of economic depression, when greater numbers of slaves were sold or leased, entailing forced separation.

Another factor was increases in consciousness as a result of various political factors, such as debates on slavery in Congress and the spread of radical philosophy and egalitarian religion. Moreover, slave revolts had a contagious effect (Aptheker, 1973, cited in Perea et al., 2007, pp. 126–127).

In addition to rebellions, tens of thousands of slaves succeeded in escaping to the Northern states, and to the swamps, mountains, and forests of the South. Others, leased by their masters to work in towns and cities, were able to work part time and purchase their freedom. Enlisting in the armed forces was another means of escape. Forms of resistance included terrorism, self-mutilation, and destruction, including mass suicides, occasional strikes, and sabotage, such as the destruction of tools (Aptheker, 1973, cited in Perea et al., 2007, p. 129). As Kolchin (1995, p. 157) explains:

> Throughout the South, slaves dragged their feet, pretended to misunderstand orders, feigned illness, "accidentally" broke agricultural implements, and stole coveted items (especially food).

As Kolchin (1995, p. 157) continues, while sabotage allowed slaves to express their frustrations with relatively little risk, it also served to reinforce aspects of racialization among whites, for example, that black people were "by nature lazy, foolish and thieving." With respect to "thieving," according to Frederick Law Olmstead (1861, p. 106, cited in Kolchin, 1995, p. 157) there was a common adherence to the idea of "the agrarian notion... that the result of labour belongs of right to the labourer." This, of course, accords with the Marxist labor theory of value (see Appendix 1 of chapter 1 of this volume for a discussion).

Last but not least, with respect to counter-hegemonic resistance, it should be stressed that a large number of black people were leaders of agitational and political movements against slavery (Aptheker, 1973, cited in Perea et al., 2007, p. 129).

The American Civil War

The American Civil War, which began in 1861, saw the beginnings of the end of slavery. It was a war for and against the independence of the Southern states. The Republican president, Abraham Lincoln, although overtly racist (he once said, "I... am in favor of the race to which I belong, having the superior position" [cited in Perea et al., 2007, p. 136]), consistently reiterated his belief that slavery was wrong. Although opposed to the expansion of slavery, he initially promised, however, that his administration posed no threat to already-existing slavery (Kolchin, 1995, pp. 201–202). As the war dragged on, however, Lincoln faced mounting pressure to aim for the freedom of the slaves (ibid., p. 201).

W.E.B. Du Bois (1935) put forward the argument that a turning point that tipped the balance in favor of the North was what, in effect, was the engagement of the slaves in a massive "general strike." He describes the beginnings of this movement:

> As soon…as it became clear that that the Union armies would not or could not return fugitive slaves, and that the masters with all their fume and fury were uncertain of victory, the slave entered upon a general strike against slavery by the same methods that he had used during the period of the fugitive slave. He ran away to the first place of safety and offered his services to the [Union] Army.

"The trickling streams of fugitives," he goes on "swelled to a flood," and, once begun, involved poor white people as well as black. As he puts it, "the general strike of black and white went madly and relentlessly on like some great saga." "This was not merely the desire to stop work," Du Bois (ibid.) concludes, "[i]t was a strike on the wide basis against the conditions of work." In the end it involved, "perhaps a half million people," who "wanted to stop the economy of the plantation system, and to do that they left the plantations."

From chattel slavery to wage slavery

At the same time Southern blacks were showing their determination to be free, public opinion in the North was also warming to the idea, and by the fall of 1862, Lincoln decided to move against slavery (Kolchin, 1995, pp. 205–207). At that time he warned the Confederates that unless they ceased their rebellion, he would do just that. On January 1, 1863, the first slaves were freed, and, in 1865, the Thirteenth Amendment banned slavery throughout the U.S. (ibid., p. 207). This was followed, a year later, by the Civil Rights Act of 1866, which gave equal rights to all American citizens; that is, all people born in the U.S.; and in 1869 (ratified in 1870) by the Fifteenth Amendment to the Constitution, which gave the right to vote regardless of "race, color, or previous condition of servitude" (ibid., pp. 210–211).

Despite these measures, inequality remained rampant. As Kolchin (ibid., p. 224) explains, the South continued to lag behind the North in terms of industrialization and urbanization, and remained much poorer, with white racism limiting the opportunities of black people, and the latter continuing to work for white planters with a considerable degree of coercion characterizing relationships. As Kolchin (ibid.) puts it:

> Intense class struggle marked the spread of capitalist relations throughout the rural South, as freedpeople strove to secure what they considered their rightful fruits of freedom and planters endeavored to maintain as much control as possible over their "free" laborers.

Thus exploitation, poverty, and hardship continued, sometimes under a system of "sharecropping," whereby agricultural workers were paid an agreed

UNIVERSITY OF WINCHESTER
LIBRARY

share of the crop, often as little as one-sixth or one-eighth in 1865, and typically one-quarter in 1866 and 1867. The workers also got food, shelter, livestock, and agricultural implements (Kolchin, 1995, pp. 224, 219).

To assist in the transition from the ownership of slaves to wage labor, or as Malott (2011a, p. 80) puts it, "from chattel slavery to wage slavery," the federal government created "rudimentary education and social services" for African Americans (Watkins, 2001, p. 46, cited in Malott, 2011a, p. 80). The schooling provided was of an industrial nature, with an emphasis on discipline, taking orders, and role memorization in order that ex-slaves became accustomed to their new role as low-level wage earners (Malott, 2011a, p. 81). During slavery most states had had no provision for education for slaves (Watkins, 2001, p. 12, cited in Malott, 2011a, p. 81) and many passed "compulsory ignorance laws prohibiting the schooling of blacks," which remained in place until 1868 (Menchaca 1997, p. 36, cited in Malott, 2011a, p. 81).

Segregation

Segregation between black and white became the norm throughout the U.S. Between 1876 and 1965, a number of Jim Crow[7] segregation laws were passed that enforced segregation in all public places. The North, of course, lacked a history of slavery, but not of institutional racism. As C. Vann Woodward (1966, p. 1) explains, the North was "a race-conscious segregated society devoted to the doctrine of white supremacy and [black] inferiority."[8] As a result, segregation developed there early and extensively (Perea et al., 2007, p. 148). Leon Litwack (1961, p. 97) describes the effects of Jim Crow laws in the North as follows:

> In virtually every phase of existence…Negroes found themselves systematically separated from whites. They were either excluded from railway cars, omnibuses, stagecoaches, and steamboats or assigned to special "Jim Crow" sections; they sat, when permitted, in secluded and remote corners of theaters and lecture halls; they could not enter most hotels, restaurants, and resorts, except as servants; they prayed in "Negro pews" in white churches, and if partaking of the sacrament of the Lord's Supper, they waited until the whites had been served the bread and wine. Moreover, they were often educated in segregated schools, punished in segregated prisons, nursed in segregated hospitals, and buried in segregated cemeteries.

The period of the late nineteenth to the mid-twentieth century was a time of great poverty, as well as educational and political deprivation for African Americans (Perea et al., 2007, p. 155). Throughout the South, racist violence erupted. This included threats and warnings, burnings, whippings, and lynchings (Kolchin, 1995, p. 235). Mob violence was inflicted freely on black people, and between 1882 and 1968, the Tuskegee Institute [a historically black university] records 4,743 people lynched, of which nearly 73 percent were black (Perea et al., 2007, p. 155). As Perea et al., (ibid.) stress, this cannot be the full total, since the figure includes only those lynchings recorded.

Counter-hegemonic resistance to segregation

Following a number of legal victories by the National Association for the Advancement of Colored People (NAACP),[9] overthrowing segregation and Jim Crow laws (Perea et al., 2007, pp. 163–168), there was, in the 1950s and 1960s, a move toward collective action, organized in the South by black churches. As Aldon D. Morris (1984, cited in Perea et al., 2007, p. 169) puts it, the "black church functioned as the institutional center of the modern civil rights movement." Prominent leaders included Martin Luther King Jr. and Malcolm X. With respect to the former, Morris (1984, cited in Perea et al., 2007, p. 169) argues that he "had the ability to convey in folksy language the commonalities that the contemporary black movement shared with the great liberation movements of biblical times." For the black masses, "protest was right and even divine" (Morris, 1984, cited in ibid.). Perea et al., (2007, pp. 169–170) cite some of the achievements of the black civil rights movement: the Montgomery Alabama bus boycott; the direct challenge to segregation in Birmingham, Alabama; the student sit-in movement; the Freedom Rides throughout the South registering black voters; and the legislative achievements.

The Montgomery Bus Boycott gives a succinct flavor of the times. It was a yearlong protest by 42,000 black residents that galvanized the civil rights movement and led to a 1956 declaration by the Supreme Court making segregated seating on buses unconstitutional throughout the U.S. First organized as a one-day boycott by the Women's Political Council, it was arranged to coincide with the trial of Rosa Parks, who had been arrested in December 1955 for refusing to give up her seat to a white man on a segregated bus. Such buses had a moving barrier separating blacks at the back from whites at the front. As the bus filled, the barrier was pushed back to make more room for whites and less for blacks (Black American History, undated). As Wayne Au has pointed out, in his comments on this chapter, it should be stressed that the popular version that Parks was tired after a long day of work and refused to move out of fatigue is pure fiction. In reality, she was local secretary of NAACP and her action was a planned civil disobedience (see Loewen, 1996).

After Parks lost her case and was convicted of violating the segregation laws, black leaders met to organize a continuation and extension of the bus boycott. To this end, King was elected president of the Montgomery Improvement Association, making a speech stating there "comes a time when people get tired of being trampled over by the iron feet of oppression" (cited in Black American History, undated).

As the boycott developed, protesters and black leaders were confronted with escalating violence, but maintained both nonviolent resistance and, given that they were without public transportation, their exhausting day-to-day schedule. The Montgomery Bus Boycott had implications that reached far beyond the desegregation of public buses, and propeled the civil rights movement into national consciousness and Martin Luther King Jr. into the public eye. As King put it, "[w]e have gained a new sense of dignity and destiny. We have discovered a new and powerful weapon—nonviolent resistance" (cited in Black American History, undated). King is probably best known for his speech in 1963 during the "Great March on Washington" in support of civil and economic rights for African Americans, when he told his audience, "I have a dream" for full equality between black and white, and rejected "the tranquilizing drug of gradualism" in favor of an immediate end to segregation. Segregation and desegregation are further discussed in chapter 4 of this volume.

Martin Luther King and social class

King, a reformer, pacifist, and Baptist minister, is not generally known for a commitment to socialism (Martin, 2008). However, from the perspective of this book, it is significant that in the year preceding his death, King became notably radicalized. Charles Steele, 2008 president of the Southern Christian Leadership Conference (SCLC) (King was the first president), has emphasized that, toward the end of his life, King had moved on from purely "racial" issues, and that his final campaigns were focused on fighting poverty and on labor disputes (cited in Harris, 2008). Martin Luther King's support for organized labor at this time was not new. A few examples will suffice: in a speech in 1961, King declared, "[o]ur needs are identical with labor's needs...[t]hat is why Negroes support labor's demands and fight laws which curb labor"; in 1962, he supported the coalition of "the Negro and the forces of labor, because their fortunes are so closely intertwined" (American Federation of State, County, and Municipal Employees [AFSCME], 2008); in 1965, he stated that "[w]hen...in the thirties the wave of union organization crested over our nation, it carried to secure shores not only itself but the whole society"; in 1967, that "[t]he Negroes pressed into [service occupations] need union protection, and the union movement needs their membership"; also in 1967, he argued that "[i]t is natural for Negroes to turn to the Labor movement"; and finally to the sanitation workers on strike in Memphis in 1968, he insisted: "[y]ou are demanding that this city will respect the dignity of labor...whenever you are engaged in work that serves humanity and is for the building of humanity, it has dignity and it has worth" (Harrity, 2004). Steele believes that King, who came to Memphis in 1968 in support of striking workers (Harris, 2008), was killed there "because he had started to focus on poor folks, regardless of their colour" (cited in ibid.). As Jerald Podair puts it, "[i]f you thought having a talk about race was difficult in America, then having one about class is even harder" (cited in ibid.). Paul Harris (2008) concludes that "40 years ago King tried to start that debate as well. A bullet cut short his ambitions" (Harris, 2008). On December 8, 1999, a Memphis jury awarded Coretta Scott King and her family $100 in damages for the conspiracy to murder her late husband (Sheppard, 2006, p. 7). According to the jury, Dr. Martin Luther King Jr. was assassinated by a conspiracy that included agencies of the U.S. government (ibid., p. 1). As Sheppard concludes, "[f]rom the beginning it has been clear that the FBI was involved to one degree or another" (ibid., p. 7). As Roland Sheppard (2006, p. 7) notes, Martin Luther King had a different perspective at the time of his death on the 1963 "I have a dream" speech: "he had begun to view the struggle for equality as an economic struggle and the capitalist economic system as the problem." As King, who by 1967 believed that the total elimination of poverty was now a practical responsibility (Sheppard, 2006, p. 8), put it in a speech to the SCLC in August 1967:

> We've got to begin to ask questions about the whole society. We are called upon to help the discouraged beggars in life's marketplace. But one day we must come to see that an edifice which produces beggars needs restructuring. It means that questions must be raised. "Who owns this oil?"...Who owns the iron ore?...Why is it that people have to pay water bills in a world that is two-thirds water? (cited in ibid.)

Perhaps Martin Luther King's most unequivocal declaration of a firm change of direction came earlier, in remarks to his staff at the SCLC on November 14, 1966. King proclaimed that the civil rights reforms of the early 1960s "were at best surface changes" that were "limited mainly to the Negro middle class." He went on to add that demands must now be raised to abolish poverty (cited in Martin, 2008):

> You can't talk about solving the economic problem of the Negro without talking about billions of dollars. You can't talk about ending the slums without first saying profit must be taken out of slums. You're really tampering and getting on dangerous ground because you are messing with folk then. You are messing with captains of industry...Now this means that we are treading in difficult water, because it really means that we are saying that something is wrong...with capitalism...There must be a better distribution of wealth and maybe America must move toward a democratic socialism. (cited in The Democratic Socialists of Central Ohio, 2011)

Malcolm X, racism and anti-capitalism

Like Martin Luther King, Malcolm X, in the last years of his life, expressed, in Kevin Ovenden's (2005) words, "uncompromising resistance to U.S. racism, imperialism and capitalism." After having been jailed for burglary in the 1940s, Malcolm had joined the black separatist Nation of Islam (see later in this chapter) in prison, changing his last name to "X" to express his unknown African name taken away from his ancestors by slave owners. Totally refusing to accept the inferiority of black people, the movement grew in the North and became huge in the South (Ovenden, 2005). After a TV interview in 1959, Malcolm became the Nation of Islam's most well-known spokesperson when having been asked about some modest challenges to racism responded, "[w]hen someone sticks a knife into my back nine inches and then pulls it out six inches they haven't done me any favor. They should not have stabbed me in the first place" (cited in ibid.).

Later responding to accusations of black racism, he replied, "[i]f we react to white racism with a violent reaction, that's not black racism. If you come for me and put a rope around my neck and I hang you for it, to me that's not racism. Yours is the racism, but my reaction has nothing to do with racism" (cited in ibid.). However, as Ovenden (2005) points out, the Nation of Islam did not react and engage in the civil rights movement, attacking it for working with white antiracists, something that later Malcolm acknowledged was a major mistake (Ovenden, 2005).

Following disagreements with the Nation of Islam, Malcolm left the movement in 1964, after which he felt free to speak out. After traveling to the Middle East and Africa and addressing a large number of meetings across the U.S., he declared, "I don't speak against the sincere, well meaning, good white people. I have learned that not all white people are racist" (cited in ibid.). Like Martin Luther King, he came to see the root of the problem as capitalism and imperialism, stating, "[w]e are today seeing a global struggle of the oppressed against the oppressor, the exploited against the exploiters" and "[s]how me a capitalist and I'll show you a bloodsucker" and "[y]ou can't have capitalism without racism," adding, if you find someone who "makes you sure they do not have this racism in their outlook, usually they're socialists." Perhaps his most famous declaration was the need to fight the system "by any means necessary" (cited in ibid.).

Sheppard, a contemporary of both King and Malcolm X, makes reference to both of them at the time of their assassinations:

> both Martin Luther King and Malcolm X were embarking on a course in opposition to the capitalist system. It is clear from reading and listening to their final speeches that they had both evolved to similar conclusions as to capitalism's role in the maintenance of racism. That is why they were neutralized.

Sheppard, who was present at Malcolm X's assassination in 1965, argues that there is "irrefutable proof that the government had the motive to assassinate Malcolm X and the ability, through its...spy operations, to orchestrate his assassination. It is now time to open up all the files of the CIA and the FBI, as well as the thousands of pages of files of the New York City Police Department, so that the truth about the assassination of Malcolm X can be exposed" (Sheppard, 2006).

The Black Panthers and socialism

The Black Panther Party was formed in 1966 in Oakland, California by Bobby Seale and Huey Newton. Other prominent members included Stokely Carmichael, H. Rap Brown, Fred Hampton, Fredrika Newton, Eldridge Cleaver, Kathleen Cleaver, David Hilliard, Angela Davis, Bobby Hutton, and Elaine Brown. Initially, an organization to protect local communities from police brutality and racism, the Black Panthers went on to run medical clinics and to provide free food to school children (Spartacus undated).

According to Spartacus (undated) within a few years, the group was feeding over 10,000 children in Oakland every day before they went to school. The Black Panthers had chapters in some major cities and a membership of over 2,000.

Harassed by the police, members were involved in several shoot-outs (Spartacus, undated). For example, in1968 eight members, including Cleaver, Hutton and Hilliard, were ambushed by the Oakland police. When Hutton left the building with his hands in the air he was shot twelve times by the police and was killed instantly (ibid.). Later the same year, Hampton founded the Chicago chapter of the party, immediately established a community service program that included free breakfasts for schoolchildren and a free medical clinic. Hampton also taught political education classes and instigated a community control of police project (ibid.). One of his major achievements was to persuade Chicago's most powerful street gangs to stop fighting against each other, announce in1969 at a press conference a non-aggression pact between the gangs and the formation of a "rainbow coalition" of black, Puerto Rican, and other poor young people. The Panthers were influenced by the ideas expressed by Malcolm X in the final months of his life, espousing Marxism, and arguing for international working class unity and joint action with white revolutionary groups. They were described by director of the FBI, J. Edgar Hoover as "the greatest threat to the internal security of the country" (cited in ibid.).

In 1969, the Panther headquarters in Chicago was raided by the police, with the latter claiming that the Panthers opened fire, after which a shoot-out took place. Hampton and Clark were killed. Ballistic evidence afterwards revealed that only one bullet had been fired by the Panthers whereas nearly a hundred came from police guns (ibid.).

In the 1970s, the Panthers renounced violence and concentrated on socialist community programs.

African Americans Today

Echoing the preceding analysis in this chapter, Frank Chapman (2010) has noted that contemporary institutionalized racism in the U.S. "is rooted in the historical reality of 250 years of slavery followed, after a brief period of Civil War and democratic reconstruction, by over seventy years of Jim Crow terror and state sanctioned racist discrimination." African American communist Claude Lightfoot was right, Chapman goes on, "when he said that present day racist practices and attitudes carry the stench of the slave market." "Ever since the great powers of Europe turned Africa into a commercial warren for hunting and enslaving Black people," he goes on, "racism has been an instrument of capitalist exploitation for super profits."

Chapman (2010) gives the example of the prison-industrial complex, referred to in Note 16 of the Introduction to this volume, which had its origins in the incarceration of African Americans in the era of repression initiated by the FBI and CIA against the black liberation and the civil rights movements. Today Chapman points out, "[w]hites and non-African Americans make up about 87 percent of the general population but are only 26 percent of the prison population."

As Vicky Pelaez (2008), who describes the prison-industrial complex as a new form of slavery, points out, the prison privatization boom began in the 1980s, under the governments of Ronald Reagan and George H. W. Bush Sr. The prison-industrial complex is one of the fastest-growing businesses in the U.S. As Pelaez (2008) explains:

> This multimillion-dollar industry has its own trade exhibitions, conventions, websites, and mail-order/Internet catalogs. It also has direct advertising campaigns, architecture companies, construction companies, investment houses on Wall Street, plumbing supply companies, food supply companies, armed security, and padded cells in a large variety of colors.

Mention should be made of what has been referred to as the "School To Prison Pipeline," which refers to "the trend of criminalizing, rather than educating [mainly African American] children. The pipeline encompasses the growing use of zero-tolerance discipline, school-based arrests, disciplinary alternative schools, and secured detention to marginalize our most at-risk youth and deny them access to education" (see American Civil Liberties Union, 2008).

With respect to the current economic crisis, Arthur Perlo (2010) has argued that, like previous recessions, it has fallen most heavily on people of color and immigrants. As he explains, this applies to all aspects of the crisis, including foreclosures and evictions, state and local government layoffs, and cuts in services. This crisis has hit all workers, including white workers, with employment levels the lowest since the 1930s (Perlo, 2010).

However, even before the crisis, African Americans had difficult and worsening employment opportunities. As Perlo (2010) explains:

> during the best boom years of 1988–90 and 1998–99, the percentage of African Americans employed in each age group just about reached the levels that white workers have fallen to today. Put another way, white workers today are just beginning to face conditions that African Americans faced in the best of times.

Between a quarter and a third of all working-age African Americans and three-quarters of black teenagers are unemployed. As Perlo (2010) goes on to point out, according to the Bureau of Labor Statistics, the "official" overall unemployment figures for December 2009 are 10 percent with 9 percent for whites, 13 per cent for Latina/os, and 16 percent for African Americans. These figures relate to all those actively looking for work. However, figures that include the "invisible unemployed"—"those who want a job but are not actively looking, and who want a full-time job but can only find part-time work" are 17.3 percent for all workers, 22.3 percent for Latina/os, and 28 percent for African Americans (Bureau of Labor Statistics, Employment Situation for December 2009 Table A-12, cited in Perlo, 2010; figures are

rounded). Perlo (2010) estimates for "African American men of prime working age (25–54)" the real jobless rate is 26 percent, and for African American
teenagers (16–19), real unemployment is 74 percent. This means that in
many communities there is almost no chance of finding a job.

Latina/o Americans

In 2009, the U.S. Bureau of the Census (cited in CNN.com/US [2009])
reported that the U.S. is becoming even more diverse, with more than
one-third of its population—an estimated 104.6 million—belonging to "a
minority group." Latina/o peoples are the fastest-growing constituent, with
nearly one in six residents, or 46.9 million people. The latest data from the
2010 U.S. Census shows that the two largest groups among Latinas/os are
those of Mexican origin, constituting 63 percent, and Puerto Ricans, 9.1
percent.[10]

Latina/o peoples are the largest minority group in the U.S. According
to the U.S. Census of 2010, Cuban Americans form 3 percent. Other
Latina/o peoples are from parts of Central America (other than Mexico),
the Dominican Republic, South America, and Spain (cited in Perea et al.,
2007 ibid., pp. 287–288).

I will consider the history of peoples of Mexican and Puerto Rican
origin in turn, but first it is worth pointing out that people of Latina/o
heritage have lived in what is now the U.S. since early colonization in
St. Augustine in 1565 (see earlier in this chapter). However, the population of areas originally conquered by Spain, as Perea et al., 2007, p.
286, point out, became ethnically mixed "through intermarriage between
Spaniards and Indians, as well as rape and the Spanish importation of
enslaved Africans, who also intermarried with Indians." Thus, for example, the first census of Los Angeles in 1781 (then part of Mexico) revealed
that, even where there was considered to be a pure Spanish population,
the majority were identified as mulatta/o, mestiza/o,[11] Indian, and black
(cited in ibid., p. 286).

Mexicans and Mexican Americans

As Perea et al., (2007, p. 288) explain, as a result of a peaceful revolution
in 1821, Mexico became independent from Spain. At the time, Mexico was
about twice the size it is today, and included Texas, California, Arizona,
New Mexico, Nevada, and parts of Utah, Colorado, and Kansas. After
independence, American settlers began arriving in the Texas region, and
in 1836, Texas claimed independence from Mexico, a claim not recognized
by the latter. The ensuing war between the U.S. and Mexico (1846–1848)
was fueled by a white supremacist belief in the superiority of the Anglo-
Saxon "race," which was ideologically fueled from the mid-1830s to the mid-
1840s. Mexicans were racialized as "a mixed, inferior race with considerable
Indian and some black blood" (Horseman, 1981, cited in Perea et al., 2007,

pp. 290–291), "an idle, thriftless people," as Richard Dana described them (cited in Perea et al., 2007, p. 292). T.J. Farnham in 1840 viewed Mexicans as "an imbecile, pusillanimous, race of men [sic], and unfit to control the destinies of that beautiful country." "The old Saxon blood," he insisted, "must stride the continent" (cited in ibid.). To take lands from such "inferior barbarians" was thus no crime; on the contrary, it was God's work (cited in ibid.). Indeed, according to George Kendall, most Mexicans were content if they could satisfy their animal wants, and "will continue to be until the race becomes extinct or amalgamated with Anglo-Saxon stock" (cited in Horseman, 1981, cited in Perea et al., 2007, p. 292). For Rufus Sage, there are "no people on the continent of America, whether civilized or uncivilized, with one or two exceptions, more miserable in condition or despicable in morals than the mongrel race inhabiting New Mexico" (ibid.). One government minister, Waddy Thompson, described the general Mexican population as "lazy, ignorant, and, of course, vicious and dishonest" (ibid., p. 293).

The events that I will now unfold need to be seen in the light of this Anglo-Saxon racialization of Mexican peoples, which in many ways paralleled the Anglo-Saxon racialization of African and Asian peoples during and after the demise of the British Empire (see, for example, Cole and Virdee, forthcoming, 2011; Cole, forthcoming, 2011). In 1845, the U.S. annexed Texas, and as a result of this, and of a dispute over where Texas ended, war ensued between the two countries between 1846 and 1848. The war, in which the U.S. forces were consistently victorious, resulted in the U.S. acquisition of more than 500,000 square miles of Mexican territory, extending westward from the Rio Grande to the Pacific Ocean (Encylopaedia Britannica, 2010). Henceforth, while the Treaty of Guadalupe Hidalgo (1848) that ended the war granted federal citizenship to all Mexicans who remained in the 500,000 square miles, *darker skinned* Mestiza/o Mexicans residing in this area were denied citizenship and meaningful political participation by state and territorial legislatures (Perea et al., 2007, p. 301).

The history of Mexican Americans is one of back-breaking farm labor. Given that the border between the U.S. and Mexico is two thousand miles long, separating the two countries by a fence, or merely an imaginary line in the sand or by the Rio Grande, cheap Mexican labor, both "legal" and "illegal," has fulfilled the requirements of U.S. businesses (Carrasco, 1997, cited in Perea et al., 2007, p. 341). As Gilbert Paul Carrasco puts it, "Mexican laborers have … become the U.S." disposable labor force, brought in when needed, only to fulfill their use and be unceremoniously discarded, a trend that has been recurring for over 150 years" (cited in ibid.), starting with the Gold Rush to California in 1848. From then until the 1930s and the Great Depression, which lasted from the stock market crash in 1929 to about 1941, Mexican workers were generally welcome in the U.S. as cheap labor. (Prior to then, U.S. immigration restrictions applied mainly to Asians and southern and eastern Europeans [Carrasco, 1997, cited in ibid., p. 342]). During the Depression, many Mexican migrant workers returned to Mexico, often driven from the U.S. by racist violence, and also by reduced welfare. By the end of the Great Depression, over 400,000 Latina/os, including thousands of U.S. citizens, had been "repatriated" to Mexico, without any formal deportation procedures (Carrasco, 1997, cited in Perea et al., 2007, pp. 343–344).

After the entry of the U.S. into the Second World War in 1941, and Mexico in 1942, the U.S. and Mexican governments signed the Bracero Program, which laid down basic conditions, and allowed Mexican citizens to work in the U.S. for temporary renewable periods (ibid., p. 344). Both the U.S. government and the employers, however, ignored the stipulated conditions and exploited and oppressed the workers in the most brutal way:

> Braceros across the country were compelled to endure poor food, excessive charges for board, substandard housing, discrimination, physical mistreatment, inappropriate deductions from their wages, and exposure to pesticides and other dangerous chemicals. (ibid.)

The Bracero Program provided cheap labor in two senses: first, it freed employers from the constraints of supply and demand or collective bargaining agreements; second, unlike Americans who tended to have their families with them, braceros were often males traveling alone, making it easier to provide transportation and housing (ibid., p. 345).

The Bracero Program came to an end in 1947, after the end of the Second World War, as U.S. troops returned to work. However, this did not end the use of cheap Mexican labor, and a new Bracero agreement was signed in 1949, and another in 1951, in response to the start of the Korean War.

As a result of labor union complaints about undocumented workers revealed by immigration authorities, a crackdown on "illegal immigration" ensued in 1954. The commissioner of immigration and reputed "long-time Mexican hater" coordinated border patrols and organized roundups and deportations between 1954 and 1959. "Operation Wetback," named because many "illegal immigrants" had entered the U.S. by crossing the Rio Grande, deported over 3.7 million Latinas/os, almost totally without formal proceedings, and accompanied by the violation of human rights (ibid., p. 347). The Bracero Program, however, continued during this period, to be followed by the McCarran-Walter Immigration Act in 1952, which allowed permanent admission to the U.S. By 1977, there were about one million Mexican resident aliens in the U.S., and many crossing the border backwards and forwards to get work (ibid., p. 348). Carrasco (1997, cited in ibid., p. 349) explains the ongoing nature of the exploitation and oppression of Mexican migrants:

> Due to intense exploitation [of] migrant workers, their productive capacities are used up early in their lives and they have to be replaced by...younger workers. For the United States, employment of migrant workers represents a significant savings in producing and reproducing "human capital" because they stay in the United States only temporarily. Even though the United States needs Mexican labor, migrant workers arrive to face more than exploitation and brutal working conditions. They face racism.

Mexicans, like the black slaves, were the victims of lynchings and killings throughout the nineteenth century, and also like the black slaves, Mexican people resisted U.S. hegemony, in this case, employing border warfare, social banditry (where "bandits" enjoyed the support of their local communities), community upheavals, long-term skirmishing, and coordinated rebellions (Rosenbaum, 1981, after Hobsbawm passim, cited in ibid., p. 324).

Language-based subordination and segregation was a major feature of the twentieth century for Mexican Americans. Attempted assimilation into whiteness and English monolingualism was also a dominant feature (Perea, 2004, cited in ibid., pp. 329–333). So was schooling Mexican American children for their future roles in society.[12] Juan F. Perea (ibid., p. 330) cites one Texas school superintendent who shows full awareness of the importance to capitalism of cheap Mexican American labor. As the superintendent put it, in a way that reverberates with the definition of schooling as opposed to education employed throughout this volume:

> Most of our Mexicans are of the lower class. They transplant onions, harvest them, etc. The less they know about everything else the better contented they are ... If a man [sic] has very much sense or education either, he is not going to stick to this kind of work.

As Perea (2004, cited in Perea et al., 2007, pp. 330, 340) notes, Anglo farmers, many of them on school boards, were keen to keep Mexican Americans uneducated, "guaranteeing a plentiful labor supply for their cotton fields." Unsurprisingly, given the racialization during the previous century outlined above, studies from the 1960s and earlier show that Anglo teachers viewed Mexican American students as "lazy, and favored Anglo students in class participation and leadership roles," with many Anglo teachers and parents seeing Mexican American children as "dirty and diseased" (Perea, 2004, cited in ibid, p. 331).

By the 1960s, strikes, boycotts, and "street politics"—marches, walkouts, confrontations, civil disobedience—became a feature of what became known as the "Chicano movement" (Acuña, 1988, cited in ibid., pp. 352–355). Corky Gonzalez was an iconic leader of the movement, which also held demonstrations against police brutality and marched against the Vietnam War (Democracy Now, 2005). In 1968, Gonzalez led a Chicano contingent to the Poor People's March on Washington, D.C., where he issued a "plan of the Barrio," demanding better housing, education, and the restoration of indigenous land (ibid.). This urban movement made alliances with others on the Left, including Mexican American workers' movements involved in rural struggles, such as those led by César Chávez, a Mexican American migrant farm worker.

As Richard Delgado points out (his comments on this chapter), whereas the Chicano movement tended to be nationalistic, the movement led by Chávez was more ecumenical. In 1952, Chávez joined the Latin civil rights group, Community Service Organization. During his time with this organization, Chávez fought against racism and labor exploitation. Ten years later he founded the National Farm Workers Association (also known as United Farm Workers of America), whose motto is "Sí, se puede," was later to be adopted by Barack Obama as "Yes we can." In 1965, Chávez and the National Farm Workers Association led a strike of California grape pickers, which, as Helen Zia (2000, p. 38) points out, was initiated by Filipino American labor activists, a fact that not many are aware of. The strike lasted five years. Despite financial setbacks, Chávez kept the union going, and by 1970 he managed to get union contracts accepted by local grape growers. Relying heavily on nonviolence (in 1968, Chávez staged a 25-day water-only fast to bring attention to the dismal working conditions of the farm workers), and instead empowering the people to stand up for themselves, he was able to direct U.S. popular attention to the exploitation and suffering of the farm workers. As he once put it, "[w]e make a solemn promise: to enjoy our rightful part of the riches of this land, to throw off the yoke of being considered as agricultural implements or slaves. We are free men [*sic*] and we demand justice" (Time magazine, 1969). Because of his and fellow workers' ceaseless counter-hegemonic struggles, farm workers eventually got fairer wages, medical coverage, and pensions (Cochran, 2010).

Mexican Americans have historically also been active in contesting and ultimately overturning segregation, often through legal channels (see, for example, the cases described in Perea et al., 2007, pp. 333–338).

Puerto Ricans and Puerto Rican Americans

In order to understand the situation of Puerto Rican Americans, it is necessary to make a brief detour to European economic history in the nineteenth century. That century saw a scramble for markets by Germany, France, Britain, and Belgium as they all struggled to gain possession of territory, raw materials, and spheres of influence. This led to the establishment of colonies and empires in Africa, Asia, and the Middle East. In the Pacific region, Japan gained a foothold in China. As a new imperialist power, the response of the U.S. to its disadvantageous position with respect to the older powers, was to look toward Cuba, which had been colonized by Spain and where U.S. capitalists had large investments—$50 million worth of Cuban property, including sugar and tobacco plantations and iron mines. In 1895, the Cuban people rebelled against the Spanish colonial regime, the weakest of the European imperialist states (In Defence of Marxism, 2007). The response of the government in Madrid was to send two hundred thousand soldiers to the island. The Cubans responded with guerrilla war, and the Spanish imperialists' reaction was to round up suspected rebels and place them in concentration camps. American property was being destroyed and the reaction of the U.S. communications ISA was to report every Spanish atrocity, real or imaginary, in a campaign that became known as "yellow journalism" (ibid.), a forerunner of the sensationalism of newspapers like U.K.-based *The Sun*. This was accompanied by rhetoric from the political

ISA. As Senator Thurston of Nebraska proclaimed in an unambiguous statement of the diverse advantages that war brings to capitalists:

> War with Spain would increase the business and earnings of every American railroad, it would increase the output of every American factory, it would stimulate every branch of industry and domestic commerce. (cited in ibid.)

On April 19, 1898, Congress declared war on Spain, achieving victory in a very short space of time not before, however, the U.S. had taken advantage of the situation to expel Spain from Puerto Rico, and to annex that island. Puerto Rico was seen as important to U.S. hegemony for both military and economic reasons. Militarily, it was in an important location to control the Gulf of Mexico and the Canal linking the Gulf to the Pacific Ocean; and economically, Puerto Rico provided a welcome market for U.S. surpluses of goods. The Treaty of Paris (1898), which ended the war, required that Spain relinquish all claims of sovereignty over Cuba, and that Puerto Rico be ceded to the U.S. The treaty empowered the U.S. Congress to determine the "civil rights and political status" of Puerto Ricans (Perea et al., 2007, pp. 357–358). Subsequent debates on whether to grant full U.S. citizenship to Puerto Ricans were, as usual, racialized. Thus one member of the House of Representatives, anxious about conferring U.S. citizenship, claimed that "75 or 80 percent of those people are mixed blood in part and are not the equal of the full-blooded Spaniard and not equal, in my judgement, to the unmixed African, and yet they were to be made citizens of the United States." Another member, also exalting biological rather than cultural racism, believed that the problem was not in language but in color, and that the climate and geography of Puerto Rico were not conducive to Anglo-Saxon government since "the Tropics seem to heat the blood while enervating the people who inhabit them." He felt that "many people in this country who want to sever the tie that binds us to tropical and alien people take that position, because they see in it danger for us." Just to underline the biological and genetic nature of his racialized view of people living within the tropics, he concluded that the "many people" to whom he was referring, agreed that those living in lands within 20 degrees of the equator could "neither comprehend nor support representative government on the Anglo-Saxon plan" (cited in Weston, 1972, cited in ibid., pp. 370–371).

In was not until 1917 that Congress gave all citizens of Puerto Rico citizenship of the U.S. While residing in Puerto Rico, Puerto Ricans cannot vote in U.S. presidential elections, but they can vote in primaries, one of the first steps in electing the president. Puerto Ricans who become residents of a U.S. state can vote in presidential elections.

A quarter of a century passed before the first legal efforts were made to address the Puerto Ricans' lack of autonomy. Given that the U.S. was endorsing self-determination principles as a result of the Atlantic Charter (a published statement issued by the U.S. and Britain during the Second

World War as a blueprint for the postwar world), the Puerto Rican legis-lature demanded that the U.S. Congress end "the colonial system of gov-ernment...totally and definitively." President Roosevelt responded with the enactment of laws that amounted to only a modicum of autonomy. Despite the birth in 1952 of the Commonwealth of Puerto Rico, and the first popu-larly elected Puerto Rican governor, Puerto Rico's political status remained unchanged (Roman, 1997, cited in ibid., pp. 376–379).

Latina/o Americans Today[13]

Class exploitation and racist oppression of Latina/o people continues today, as does, of course, counter-hegemonic resistance. According to Delgado and Stefancic (2001, p. 69), counter-hegemonic priorities are challenging inter-pellative processes such as those that hail Latina/o peoples, for example, as "foreigners" with "unpronounceable last names." In addition, the repressive state apparatuses oppress Latina/o Americans by demanding to "to see their papers."

On May 1, 2005, more than one million immigrants took part in a day of action that forced many businesses to close. Named "A Day Without Immigrants," it involved boycotting school and work and refusing to spend money to show their worth to the economy, to protest against proposed immigration "reform" to further criminalize immigrants and increase "bor-der security" (BBC News, 2005). Wayne Au (his comments on this chapter has argued this day of action put immigration and Latina/os "on the map" in terms of extending mainstream dialogue about racism, which was until then often relegated to the black-white binary.

Despite this higher profile being accorded to Latina/o communities, a report four years later by the Southern Poverty Law Center (SPLC) (2009) noted how Latina/o people "are routinely cheated out of their earnings and denied basic health and safety protections." The repressive and ideological apparatuses of the state are fully involved. As SPLC (2009) put it:

> [Latina/o people] are regularly subjected to racial profiling and harassment by law enforcement. They are victimized by criminals who know they are reluctant to report attacks. And they are frequently forced to prove them-selves innocent of immigration violations, regardless of their legal status. This treatment—which many...liken to the oppressive climate of racial sub-ordination that blacks endured during the Jim Crow era—is encouraged by politicians and media figures who scapegoat immigrants and spread false propaganda.

The Southern Poverty Law Center (2009) further notes the role of the com-munications ISA in that "as a result of relentless vilification in the media, Latinos are targeted for harassment by racist extremist groups, some of which are directly descended from the old guardians of white supremacy." "Instead of acting to prohibit and eliminate systematic exploitation and discrimination," they point out, "state and local governments in much of the South have exacerbated the situation." They go on:

> A number of Southern communities, for example, have enacted ordinances designed to limit services to undocumented immigrants and make their lives as difficult as possible, with the ultimate goal of driving them away. In addition, many law enforcement agencies in the South, armed with…agreements with the federal government, are enforcing immigration law in a way that has led to accusation of systematic racial profiling and has made Latino crime victims and witnesses more reluctant to cooperate with police. Such policies have the effect of creating a subclass of people who exist in a shadow economy, beyond the protection of the law.

Latina/o workers provide cheap labor for the South's economy, "building skyscrapers in Charlotte, harvesting onions in Georgia, slaughtering poultry in Alabama and rebuilding New Orleans after Katrina" (SPLC, 2009).

"Many of the difficulties faced by undocumented immigrants," the Southern Poverty Law Center (2009) notes, "are, no doubt, the result of their lack of legal status, which makes them easy prey for unscrupulous employers and puts them at constant risk from law enforcement." This, of course, does not apply only to "illegal" workers. Legal residents and U.S. citizens of Latina/o descent told the center that "racial profiling, bigotry and myriad other forms of discrimination and injustice are staples of their daily lives." "The assumption is that every Latino possibly is undocumented," as one immigrant advocate put it. The Southern Poverty Law Center (2009) concludes that systematic racism in the region by both private and public entities "constitutes a civil rights crisis that must be addressed."

In April 2010 a new anti-immigrant law was passed in Arizona. The law allows the police to stop anyone and demand identification without a warrant if they have "reasonable suspicion" that the individual is an "illegal immigrant." This racist harassment of the Latina/o communities by the repressive apparatus of the local state marks the first successful attempt to make residence without "legal papers" a criminal offense, defined as "misdemeanor trespassing" (Martin, 2010). Other provisions of the law make it illegal for "undocumented immigrants" to work or to seek work, to impede vehicular traffic by picking up a day laborer who is offering work, and to harbor an "undocumented immigrant" (ibid.). Tom Eley (2010b) has noted that the law has caused widespread shock and anger and led to "a wave of protests in Arizona and across the US." It should not be forgotten that Arizona also has an "English language only" policy that includes an audit of teachers "who are not fluent in English, who make grammatical errors while speaking, or who have heavy accents" (African American English, 2010). This can lead to restrictions on government funding for bilingual education and the repeal of laws allowing multilingual ballots and voting materials. This also affects African Americans, since "such legislation reinforces the ideologies around the African American English not being a valid dialect of English" (ibid.).

The State of Arizona also passed House Bill 2281in 2010 in an effort to eliminate Latina/o heritage and solidarity from its schools.

With respect to immigration nationally, in 2010, President Obama signed into law legislation that will further militarize the U.S.–Mexico border, including "the deployment of Predator pilotless drones, like those used in Afghanistan and Pakistan, to conduct surveillance against immigrants crossing the border" (Van Auken, 2010a). A couple of months after this legislation, U.S. Department of Homeland Security (DHS) Secretary Janet Napolitano told a press conference that the Obama administration had once again deported a record number of undocumented immigrants in fiscal year 2010, with the number expelled of 392,000, surpassing the previous year's 389,000, but still falling short of the administration's "goal" of 400,000 (Olmos, 2010).

As far as schooling and education are concerned, twenty-first-century research demonstrates that students from Latina/o communities are tracked toward vocational and technical courses rather than college preparatory courses, are overrepresented in remedial classes, and underrepresented in classes for "gifted students." So-called "high ability" classes are populated almost exclusively by Anglo students, and so-called "low ability" classes are overpopulated with Mexican American students (Perea, 2004, cited in Perea et al., 2007, p. 332) (for a critique of the whole basis and rationale for fixed ability and arguments for the promotion of learning without limits, see chapter 6 of this volume).

Asian Americans[14]

While Asian American peoples are small in number when compared to Latina/o Americans, making up about 5 percent of the population according to 2008 U.S. Census Bureau figures, they are one of the fastest-growing minority ethnic groups in terms of percentage increase in numbers (Asian-Nation, 2010). Asian-Nation (2010) identifies the main Asian American groups as Cambodian Americans; Chinese Americans; Filipina/o Americans; Hmong Americans; Indian Americans; Japanese Americans; Korean Americans; Laotian Americans; Pakistani and Bangladeshi Americans; Taiwanese Americans; and Vietnamese Americans.[15] I will deal briefly with the histories of each group in turn, before dealing with some commonalities with respect to experiences of racism today.

Cambodian Americans

Halfway through the Vietnam War (1955–1975) (see later in this chapter), the neutral Cambodian government began to allow North Vietnamese troops to move supplies through Cambodia. In 1970, after a U.S.-supported military coup in Cambodia, the U.S. extended the Vietnam War by bombing North Vietnamese supply lines inside Cambodia itself. Five years later, the North Vietnamese captured Saigon (now Ho Chi Minh City). By then, the

U.S. had withdrawn its troops from Vietnam, and Cambodia's government, plagued by corruption and incompetence, had lost its American military support. Taking advantage of the opportunity, the Khmer Rouge marched into the capital of Cambodia, Phnom Penh, seized control, and renamed the country Kampuchea (Takaki, 1989, p. 468; The History Place, 1999). Once in power, Khmer Rouge leader Pol Pot declared "Year Zero" and, instigating a thoroughly and dangerously distorted reading of Marx, and claiming inspiration from Mao Zedong, proceeded to purge "class enemies." Pol Pot declared that society was to be "purified" of capitalism, Western culture, city life, religion, and all foreign influences in favor of "peasant communism." Millions of city-based Cambodians, under a mass location of the urban population to the countryside, were forced into slave labor in Pol Pot's "killing fields" (ibid.). It has been estimated that some two million people, a third of the entire population, died of starvation, disease, and murder. In 1978, Vietnam (then and now one country) invaded Cambodia, and early in 1979, Pol Pot was deposed.

Following a U.S. decision to accept Cambodians from refugee camps in Thailand, over one hundred thousand Cambodian refugees settled in the U.S., mostly arriving in the 1980s. Understandably, many suffer from "post-traumatic stress disorder" (Bankston, 2010; Takaki, 1989, p. 469). By the early 1990s, prospects of a political settlement in Cambodia removed much of the perceived urgency of accepting Cambodian refugees, and immigration from Cambodia to the U.S. decreased to very small numbers. The largest concentration of Cambodian Americans is in California (Bankston, 2010). At nearly 38 percent (Reeves and Bennett, 2004, p. 17), next to Hmong Americans, Cambodian Americans have the highest individual poverty rates.

With respect to overt and violent racism directed at Cambodian Americans, in 1989, a white man, who had often expressed his resentment of Asians, donned military fatigues and a semiautomatic rifle, drove to his old school, which was predominantly Asian, and killed five children—four Cambodian and one Vietnamese—thirty others were injured (Zia, 2000, p. 91). Cambodian Americans, like Korean Americans, were affected by the racism of the Los Angeles riots of 1992 (see later in this chapter under the heading "Korean Americans") when hundreds of Cambodian American businesses in Long Beach, just south of Los Angeles, were looted and burned (ibid., p. 191).

Chinese Americans

In January 1848, gold was discovered during the construction of a saw mill along the American River northeast of present-day Sacramento. As the news spread, among the thousands flocking to California in 1849 were 325 "forty-niners" from China. In 1852, over twenty thousand Chinese arrived, and by 1870 there were over sixty thousand Chinese in the U.S. (Takaki, 1989, p. 80).

In the 1860s, Chinese migrants served as a source of cheap and exploited labor in the construction of the Central Pacific Railroad. A report to President Andrew Johnson described Chinese workers as follows:

> As a class they are quiet, peaceable, patient, industrious and economical. Ready and apt to learn all the different kinds of work required in railroad building, they soon become as efficient as white laborers. More prudent and economical, they are contented with less wages. (cited in Kraus, 1969)

In addition, as Central Pacific's legal counsel judge put it to a California congressman:

> A large part of our force are Chinese, and they prove nearly equal to white men, in the amount of labor they perform, and are far more reliable. No danger of strikes among them. (ibid.)

Up to the late nineteenth century, approximately four hundred thousand Chinese people had migrated to the U.S., many fleeing from internal wars, but most because of economic hardship (Perea et al., 2007, p. 399).

With respect to minority ethnic groups of Asian ancestry, Chinese Americans are the largest, and have been in the U.S. the longest (Zhou, 2003). As Min Zhou (2003) points out, few realized their dreams of becoming wealthy as a result of the gold rush, and many found themselves on the receiving end of exclusion and racism, both institutionalized and personal. In 1852 and 1855, California statutes imposed license fees on all foreign miners. California also enacted a "commutation tax" intended to discourage Chinese migration to the state. The Chinese district associations protested against these racist forms of legislations but met legislative hostility and increasing violence in the mining districts (McClain, 1994, *supra* at pp. 12–20, cited in Perea et al., 2007, p. 400). A serious blow was dealt to Chinese civil rights when, in 1854, the California Supreme Court decided that a Chinese testimony could not be used against a white defendant in a criminal trial (Perea et al., 2007 p. 400). By the mid-1870s, racist hatred of the Chinese had spread throughout California and had generated anti-Chinese hate groups (see later in this chapter for a discussion of current U.S. hate groups) and an "Anti-Chinese Union" pledged "to unite, centralize and direct the anti-Chinese strength of our country." Members of anti-Chinese clubs pledged not to employ Chinese people; not to purchase goods from the employers of Chinese people; and not to sustain the Chinese or employers of the Chinese (Sandmeyer, 1991, p. 57, cited in Perea et al., 2007, p. 405).

Responding to a complex set of economic hardships caused by economic distress, labor market uncertainty, and sheer capitalist exploitation, organized labor also took part in this racialization process (Zhou, 2003). As the leader of the California Workingmen's Party put it:

> We have made no secret of our intentions…we declare that the Chinaman must leave our shores. We declare that white men, and women, and boys and

girls, cannot live as the people of the great republic should and compete with the single Chinese coolie in the labor market... To an American, death is preferable to life on a par with the Chinaman. (cited in Sandmeyer, 1991, *supra* at p. 65, cited in Perea et al., 2007, p. 406)

In 1882, the U.S. Congress passed the Chinese Exclusion Act, later extended to all Asian potential immigrants up until World War II (Zhou, 2003). The number of new Chinese immigrants dropped from 123,000 in the 1870s to 14,800 in the 1890s to a historically low number of five thousand in the 1930s (ibid.). Zhou (2003) graphically explains the overall effects of massive institutionalized and personal racism directed at the Chinese migrant workers.

Legal exclusion, augmented by extralegal persecution and anti-Chinese violence, effectively drove the Chinese out of the mines, farms, woolen mills, and factories on the West Coast. As a result, many Chinese laborers already in the United States... returned permanently to China. Others, who could not afford or were too ashamed to return home, gravitated toward San Francisco's Chinatown for self-protection.

Others traveled eastward in the search of alternative means of earning a living, and Chinatowns in the Northeast of the U.S., in particular, New York and the Midwest, grew to accommodate those fleeing from the intense racialization and racism that they had experienced in California (Zhou, 2003). Up until World War II, the Chinese American community was predominantly male. However, after the 1950s, hundreds of refugees and their families arrived in the U.S. from the People's Republic of China (ibid.). In addition, in 1965, the Hart-Cellar Act abolished the national origins quota system that had structured American immigration policy since the 1920s, and replaced it with a preference system that focused on immigrants' skills and family relationships with citizens or residents of the U.S. (U.S. Immigration Legislation Online, 2007), thus further changing Chinese (and other minority ethnic) communities from being primarily male to family communities (Zhou, 2003).

Throughout the 1960s and 1970s, Chinatown in San Francisco had the highest tuberculosis and suicide rates in the Unites States, and as a result of high unemployment and underemployment, thousands of new immigrants were subject to intense exploitation in sweatshops and restaurants (Ling-chi Wang, 2010).

However, health and mental health problems exist not only in Chinatowns. The overwhelming majority of Chinese Americans no longer live there (ibid.). The rapid growth of the Chinese American population in the last three decades has been accompanied by further racism (ibid.). Ling-chi Wang (2010) gives the example of San Francisco and Monterey Park in California, which tried to restrict Chinese American population growth by "restrictive zoning" of residential housing. In addition, Chinese American achievements in education have led to the use of racist attempts to slow down or reverse their enrollment in select schools and colleges. Since the early 1980s, there has been a steady increase in incidents of reported racist violence (Ling-chi Wang, 2010).

Filipina/o Americans

Following the Spanish-American War of 1898, the Philippines became a territory of the U.S. This meant that, while Filipina/os were not granted citizenship, they were classified as "American nationals" with the right of entry to the U.S. (Takaki, 1989, p. 315). Migrant workers arrived as laborers, mainly in agriculture and domestic service (Dela Cruz et al., 2003). In 1910, there were just over four hundred Filipina/os on the U.S. mainland; by 1920, over five thousand; and by 1930, over forty-five thousand (Takaki, 1989, p. 315). From the early days, Filipinos were racialized and sexualized. For example, in December 1929 in Watsonville, California, the local newspaper published a photograph of a Filipino embracing his white fiancée (he had previously been arrested for being with her, and was released when her mother explained that they were engaged and that the relationship had her approval) (ibid., p. 327). A month later, the local chamber of commerce passed a resolution declaring that Filipinos were "a moral and sanitary" threat and "a menace to white labor" (cited in ibid.). In the following month, about two hundred Americans hunted Filipinos on the streets, and a dance hall where Filipinos were dancing with local women was raided. Two days later, a number of Filipinos were beaten and one was killed by a mob of five hundred white Americans who also destroyed the Filipino quarters. Concerns of "racial purity" and "mixed race" offspring prompted changes in the antimiscegenation laws to include Filipinos (The Philippine History Site, undated).[16]

The Philippines was granted independence in 1935, and Filipina/os were reclassified as "aliens" with immigration becoming limited to fifty individuals per year. However, after the U.S. had entered World War II, thousands of Philippine-born Filipinos were recruited to the military, this population comprising the second phase of immigration (Dela Cruz et al., 2003).

After the aforementioned 1965 Hart-Cellar Act, Filipina/os began arriving in the U.S. for education and work, but also to get away from the repressive political regime of President Ferdinand Marcos. In 1980, the Philippines overtook China and Japan as the Asian country having most workers migrate to the U.S., and by the 1990s, there were more Philippina/o migrants in the U.S. than in any other country except Mexico (Dela Cruz et al., 2003). Currently, with over four million, the U.S. is home to the largest Filipina/o population outside the Philippines (Leano, 2010). Latest available figures show that some 38 percent of Filipina/o Americans work in management, professional, and related occupations; 17 percent in service; 28 percent in sales and office work; and 11 percent in production, transportation, and material moving (Reeves and Bennett, 2004, p. 14). There are strong indications of the feminization of the labor force. Among Asian Americans, Filipinas have the highest labor force participation rate (ibid., p. 13).

Like Bangladeshi and Pakistani Americans, Filipina/o Americans have been on the receiving end of Islamophobia (see later in this chapter), with innocent Filipina/os being victims of racial profiling, interrogation, and selective deportation as a result of the 2002 Absconder Apprehension Initiative, whereby the Philippines was declared "al Qaeda active," despite the fact that this relates to only one of its 7,100 islands (Dela Cruz et al., 2003).

Hmong Americans

Hmong peoples' origins go back some three thousand years in China, with most still living in southwestern China, and in Thailand, Burma, Laos, and Vietnam, where they immigrated in the nineteenth century after centuries of persecution in China (Pfeifer, 2003). Between 1975 (the final withdrawal of U.S. troops from Vietnam) and 1991, more than one million Southeast Asians and Amerasians (the offspring of members of the U.S. military and Southeast Asians) migrated to the U.S. Of these, forty thousand were Hmong people. Like the other Southeast Asian refugees, the Hmong were allies of the U.S. in the Vietnam War (Zia, 2000, p. 256) and fled to Thailand where they were put in refugee camps. After 1994, the number was reduced to a trickle, since the Thai camps were empty and the remaining Hmong had been repatriated to Laos (Pfeifer, 2003). By the time they arrived in the U.S., Hmong people had overcome tremendous hardships, having experienced war and starvation. The Hmong were mainly from the mountainous regions of Laos, and many were illiterate, with few skills that could be used in the U.S. economy. As a result, a high percentage has remained on welfare (Zia, 2000, p. 257).

Like all other Asian Americans, the Hmong are subject to racism. For example, in 1998, a radio talk show host broadcast allegations that a thirteen-year-old Hmong girl had killed her baby after giving birth. Digs were made at the girl, and the Hmong way of organizing families by clans, as well as the diet of boiled chicken that Hmong women eat after childbirth (Zia, 2000, p. 258). Helen Zia (2000, p. 258) describes the banter of the talk show host during the broadcast:

> "I think when you stuff a baby in the garbage can, you forfeit some of these rituals," he said. The broadcast including a recurring fake Asian character named "Tak" who made comments in a mock-Asian/pidgin English accent and joked that it would "take a lot of egg rolls" to pay the criminal fines for concealing a corpse. [The talk show host] recommended the Hmong "assimilate or hit the goddamn road."

Understandably Hmong Americans were incensed, their traditional culture and clan-based system having made survival possible through centuries of oppression and, with other Asian Americans, they organized a street protest

(Zia, 2000, pp. 258–259). It was subsequently revealed that the thirteen-year-old girl had indeed been raped (ibid., p. 261).

The 2000 Census showed the Hmong population in the U.S. as 186,310, including part-Hmong peoples (and the 2010 Census, 236, 434). This, however, is probably an undercount (Pfeifer, 2003). Latest figures show the Hmong people as having, among Asian Americans, the largest number of people (nearly 60 percent) having "less than high school graduate" educational attainments. Hmong men also have the lowest labor force participation rate of Asian Americans (over 40 percent not working) and the lowest median earnings of year-round, full-time Asian male workers. The Hmong have the lowest median family income and the highest individual poverty rates (Reeves and Bennett, 2004, pp. 12–13, 15–17).

Indian Americans

Indians came to the U.S. as early as 1820 (Rao, 2003), the majority coming from the Punjab region of northwestern India (Chan, 1991, p. 18). From the early 1900s until 1922, small male Sikh worker communities emerged all along the West Coast (Rao, 2003). However, the distance from India, combined with restrictive immigration quotas, meant that by the end of the nineteenth century, fewer than eight hundred Indians are recorded to have migrated (ibid.). Indians experienced racism from the early days. For example, in 1907, in Washington, a mob of about five hundred attacked boarding houses and mills, compelling about three hundred Indians to flee (ibid.).

More recent examples of racism occurred during the late 1980s. In New Jersey, a group known as the "the Dotbusters"—the name referring to the decorative bindi many Hindu women wear on their foreheads—violently assaulted several South Asian Americans and created a climate of hostility that eventually resulted in the murder of an Indian American in 1987 (Zia, 2000, pp. 90–91, 221). In 1998, an American-born Indian was attacked with baseball bats by three white men and was racially abused. When his uncle ran to his assistance, he, too, was beaten (Zia, 2000, pp. 219–220).

No significant immigration took place until after the Hart-Cellar Act of 1965, prior to which there were little over seven thousand five hundred immigrants from South Asia (Rao, 2003). By the time of the 2000 census, the population of Asian Indians in the U.S. was 1.7 million, a 100 percent increase since 1990 (ibid.), and in the 2010 Census, 2.73 million, a further major increase.

Attainment at school and university for Indian Americans far exceeds that of white populations, and most immigrants have completed bachelor's or master's degrees. Median earnings for male Indian Americans at nearly $52 was the highest of all Asian Americans, though that of female Indian Americans was much lower at just over $35, still higher than the average Asian female earnings (Reeves and Bennett, 2004, p. 15). Only Filipino Americans had lower poverty rates, with Indian Americans more or less on a par with Japanese Americans (Reeves and Bennett, 2004, p. 17). As a result, there are ongoing debates as to whether Indian Americans should be included in affirmative action programs, and whether Indian-American-owned businesses should qualify for minority status (Rao, 2003). However, as K.V. Rao (2003) points out, the 2000 census showed that many Indian American households had relatives living with them. Thus the larger average household size is arguably a major reason for the larger household incomes. In addition, the concentration of Indian Americans predominantly in East and West Coast cities means that the higher cost of living there offsets higher household incomes (Rao, 2003). As Rao (2003) concludes, the bottom line is that it is very likely that when one controls for achievement at school and university, and experience, Indian Americans may still be earning significantly lower wages than the majority of the population with similar characteristics.

Japanese Americans

Japanese people began entering the U.S. in significant numbers in 1885 when the Japanese government legalized emigration. Between 1891 and 1924, approximately two hundred thousand Japanese people emigrated to the U.S. (Perea et al., 2007, pp. 427–428). In 1907, a so-called "Gentlemen's Agreement" with Japan kept out the Japanese working class (this was the result of efforts by the Japanese and Korean League, formed in 1905, which sought to forbid entry to Japanese and Korean laborers) but allowed entry to certain categories of business and professional people (ibid., p. 428). The 1924 Immigration Act, however, forbade entry to all those ineligible for citizenship, effectively ending the immigration of Asians into the U.S. Protests were made by the Japanese government, and a Japanese citizen committed ritual suicide outside the U.S. embassy in Tokyo. On the day the law became effective, Japan declared a day of "national humiliation" (U.S. History, undated).

Racism restricted the employment prospects of second-generation Japanese young people (nisei). A study of 161 nisei graduating from the University of California between 1925 and 1935 reported that only 25 percent were employed in professional occupations for which the university had prepared them (Takaki, 1989, p. 218). As Perea et al., (2007, p. 436) explain, for Japanese immigrants and their citizen children, their sense of being abandoned was deepened by the events of World War II. They describe the attack on the U.S. naval base in Hawaii (annexed to the U.S. in 1898, and an "official territory" since 1900) that brought the U.S. into the war as follows:

> The bombing of Pearl Harbor on December 7, 1941 plunged the United States into a declared war against Japanese combatants, and an undeclared war against citizens and aliens of Japanese ancestry resident in the United States.

Between February 1942 and December 1944, 120,000 Japanese Americans were excluded from designated areas, removed by the Army, and detained in "relocation centers"—barracks mostly in desolate areas of the West. Most spent the war years behind barbed wire guarded by military police (Report of the Commission on Wartime Relocation and Internment of Civilians, 1982, cited in Perea et al., 2007, p. 436). A Congressional Record of the Senate in 1988 reported that:

> the internment of individuals of Japanese ancestry was carried out without any documented acts of espionage or sabotage, or other acts of disloyalty by any citizens or permanent resident aliens of Japanese ancestry on the west coast; there was no military or security reason for the internment; the internment of the individuals of Japanese ancestry was caused by racial prejudice, war hysteria, and a failure of political leadership; the excluded individuals of Japanese ancestry suffered enormous damages and losses, both material and intangible, and there were incalculable losses in education and job training, all of which resulted in significant human suffering; the basic civil liberties and constitutional rights of those individuals of Japanese ancestry interned were fundamentally violated by that evacuation and internment (Congressional Information Service, 2000).

Between the passing of the Hart-Cellar Act of 1965 and 2000, there were 176,000 Japanese immigrants, a number similar to Pakistanis (204,000), Thais (150,000), Cambodians (206,000), Hmong (186,000), and Laotians (198,000) (Toji, 2003). U.S. Census figures for 2010 give the number of Japanese Americans as 1.3 million.

Korean Americans

After a series of laws barring the immigration of Chinese workers (see earlier in this chapter), between 1903 and 1905, some seven thousand Koreans were recruited and brought to Hawaii as plantation laborers. Before the Immigration Act of 1924 (see the previous section of this chapter) closed the door completely, about 1,100 Korean "picture brides" entered the U.S. (Chang, 2003). The term refers to the matchmaking of brides in Korea with Korean migrant workers via photographs and family recommendations. As Sonia Shinn Sunoo (2002) argues, the women were eager to escape the constricted Confucian society that was early twentieth-century Korea, and the tightening Japanese grip over the country. Students and political exiles also migrated to the U.S. during this period (Chang, 2003). Racist incidents began in 1909. One that drew significant attention was when an orchard owner arranged to hire fifteen Korean fruit pickers. On arrival they were met by several hundred unemployed Euro-Americans who surrounded them, threatening them with physical violence, forcing them to leave on the next train (Chan, 1991, p. 52).

The second phase of Korean immigration was triggered by the Korean War (1950–1953), after which, U.S. soldiers stationed in Korea brought home Korean wives, and adopted war orphans, and sponsored students to come to the U.S. Between 1951 and 1964, approximately 6,500 wives, 6,300 adopted children, and 6,000 students came to the U.S. Nearly 779,000 Korean immigrants entered the U.S. between 1941 and 1998. Korean immigration peaked during the 1980s and has steadily declined since 1987

(Chang, 2003). About one-third of Korean American households have self-owned businesses, with Korean Americans ranking third in this sphere of activity, behind Chinese and Indian Americans. The rate of Korean business ownership is 71 percent higher than their share of the population, highest of all the major Asian ethnic groups (ibid.). To compete successfully, Korean American business owners work long hours, mobilize family labor and minority ethnic resources, often operating without vacations, with husband and wife teaming up to operate the family business, and with children helping during the after-school hours (ibid.).

Korean Americans were on the receiving end of the 1992 Los Angeles riots. The riots were precipitated by the acquittal of four white police officers who had badly beaten African American Rodney King. Over fifty people died and over 2,400 were injured. Damage caused to property was in the billions of dollars (Perea, 1995, cited in Perea et al., 2007, p. 1101). Juan F. Perea (1995, cited in ibid., p. 1101) identifies three media images: "the horrifying image of organized police brutality and violence" meted out to Rodney King, resonating with centuries of similar violence (see earlier in this chapter); the horrible violence inflicted on white American Reginald Denny by African Americans; and armed Korean or Korean American merchants protecting their stores, many of which were barely profitable and uninsured (Wu, 2002, p. 72). Zia (2000, p. 182) describes how, as stores were burned and looted, Korean Americans called 911 (the emergency services). But the Los Angeles Police Department did little to stop the violence; Korean Americans suspected that the police were relieved to have the intense anger over police brutality re-directed (ibid.).

As Perea (1995, cited in Perea et al., 2007 pp. 1101–1102) points out, the media portrayed the events as if they were the outcome of some simmering tensions between Korean Americans and African Americans, with one (the Korean Americans) cast as "good," and the other (the African Americans) labeled "bad." Perea (1995, cited in ibid., p. 1102) explains how the communications ISA served to obscure racist realities:

> Koreans were the good ethnics, "model minority members"—hardworking, quiet, law-abiding property owners striving to climb the ladder of the American dream. Blacks were the bad—violent, criminal, and out of control. The good minority versus bad minority oppositional pairing disguises our traditional racial hierarchy and racism by displacing it onto two oppressed minority groups.[17]

Laotian Americans

By the 1960s, the Vietnam War had extended into Laos, and the U.S. actively increased operations there. In 1975, the "Communist" Pathet Lao defeated the U.S.-supported government of Laos, which led to a panic for safety among pro-U.S. groups in Laos (Takaki, 1989, pp. 460–461). As a result, the vast majority of future Laotian Americans arrived in the U.S. as refugees or as the children of refugees (Phapphayboun, 2003). Resettlement in the U.S. increased dramatically in the late 1970s and 1980s, after hundreds of thousands of Laotians fled across the Mekong River to Thailand, seeking safety in refugee camps. Over 105,000 refugees arrived in the U.S. between 1979 and 1981, and nearly 53,000 Laotians came to the U.S. between 1986 and 1989. Laotian Americans are not a single "ethnic group" but consist of the lowland Tai-Kadai groups (the largest grouping), the Austroasiatic groups residing in the foothills, and the Tibeto-Burman highland groups (Bucholtz, 2004, p. 129).[18]

Many Laotian people arrived without a written language, with little experience of either formal schooling or wage labor. As a result, they had to take low-skilled work (Phapphayboun, 2003). The 2000 census revealed that, among Asian Americans, Laotian Americans had the smallest percentage of people in management, professional, and related occupations, and the highest in production, transportation, and material moving (Reeves and Bennett, 2004, p. 14). Next to Hmong Americans, Laotian men had the lowest median earnings of year-round, full-time Asian male workers (Reeves and Bennett, 2004, p. 15).

Mia Tuan (1999; see also Bucholtz, 2004) notes that while a "racial" status of "honorary whiteness" is sometimes afforded—albeit ambivalently and partially—to *middle-class* Asian Americans, East and Southeast Asians of low socioeconomic class often receive the same "racial" profiling and problematization as African Americans.

Mary Bucholtz (2004) studied two working class Laotian American girls, both refugees, in a "multiracial" high school in California. Given the school's demographics, "a robust racial ideology had developed . . . whereby race was organized in binary terms of black and white," positioned as polar opposites. The social archetypes of these two polar categories were "the gangster" and "the nerd" (Bucholtz, 2004, p. 133). Despite similar life experiences and socioeconomic backgrounds, the two Laotian American girls chose different routes through this racially polarized stylistic landscape, navigated these two contrasting racial ideologies imposed on Southeast Asian Americans by using locally available linguistic and other semiotic resources. As she explains, "[taking different pathways through the local racial terrain, the girls both participated in and refused the binary terms of racializing discourse" (ibid., p. 129).

Pakistani and Bangladeshi Americans

People from present-day Pakistan were among the first South Asians to emigrate to the U.S. Many settled on the West Coast, particularly California, where families can trace their roots back to the early 1900s (Singh, 2003). After Pakistan became an independent nation in 1947, a small number of individuals came under the family reunification provisions of U.S. immigration law. More came as students from the 1950s to the early 1960s (Singh, 2003). After laws in the 1960s made it easier for Asians to enter the country, many Pakistanis took jobs in the professional sectors such as academia, medicine, and engineering. It was not until the late 1980s and 1990s that Pakistanis arrived to work in blue-collar jobs as taxi drivers and shopkeepers (MacFarquhar, 2006). Many continue to come on temporary student visas (Singh, 2003).

In 1971, Bangladesh became independent from Pakistan, after Sheikh Mujibur Rahman (Mujib), proclaimed socialism and a secular democracy. Despite winning the 1970 election, Mujib had been prevented from forming a government. A student leader, and a charismatic and forceful orator, Mujib had become popular for leading the struggle against the institutional racism directed against Bengalis by the previous West Pakistan government (Radhikaranjan, 2009).

New York has the highest number of Bangladeshi Americans, most working in the restaurant and transport industries (e.g., taxi drivers) (Singh, 2003). As Muslims, Pakistani and Bangladeshi Americans are on the receiving end of the virulent U.S.-wide Islamophobia addressed later in this chapter.

Taiwanese Americans

In comparison to the 2.7 million Chinese living in the U.S., the Taiwanese American population is very small—just under 145,000, with more than 75,000 living in California (Lai, 2003). After defeat by the "communists" in the late 1940s, the nationalist government, along with a million and a half Chinese, fled to the island of Taiwan and formed a U.S.-backed government. The Taiwanese first began migrating to the U.S. in the mid-1960s, but by the late 1990s, immigration from Taiwan had considerably slowed down due to a rise in the standard of living in Taiwan (ibid., 2003). As a result of the aforementioned Hart-Cellar Act of 1965, which created a system whereby persons with professional skills and family ties in the U.S. were given preferential status, Taiwanese Americans are mainly well-qualified and well-off. In 2008, over 70 percent of Taiwanese-born adults had a bachelor's degree or higher. As far as employment is concerned, management, business and finance was the dominant occupation of Taiwanese immigrant men (23 percent) and immigrant women (28 percent) (Asian-Nation, 2008).

As Chien-Juh Gu (2003, pp. 5–6) argues, on the surface, Taiwanese Americans "appear to be successful, assimilated, and tend to 'blend' into American society easily such that they are relatively 'invisible' to the U.S. academic eye." Because of this, he goes on, little is known about them (ibid., p. 6). However, Gu (ibid., pp. 6–7) found in his study that more than a half of respondents (57.7 percent) reported experiences of "unfair treatment" at work on account of racism. More than two-thirds of men (68.4 percent) and slightly less than half of women (47.6 percent) said they personally experienced racism. Experiences were skewed with respect to generation, with almost three-quarters (73.1 percent) of first-generation respondents encountering unfair treatment. As far as second-generation adults are concerned, 28.6 percent reported unfair treatment at work. All acknowledged the existence of racism directed at Asian Americans (ibid., p. 7).

Vietnamese Americans

In 1964, there were just over six hundred South Vietnamese students, language teachers, and diplomats living in the U.S. (Takaki, 1989, p. 448). The first major phase of Vietnamese immigration to the U.S. began in 1975. Most were military personnel and their families, fleeing from North Vietnamese troops after North Vietnam had defeated South Vietnam, which the U.S. had supported in the Vietnam War (1955–1975) (ibid., p. 449). It is estimated that over one hundred thousand sought a way to escape (Chuong and Minh, 2003).

The second phase occurred in 1978, with those leaving becoming known as Vietnamese "boat people." Several hundred thousand refugee families left in crowded leaky boats, risking death from storms, robbery, and rape of the women by pirates. It has been estimated that two-thirds of the boats were attacked by pirates, each boat on average more than twice (Takaki, 1989, p. 452). The survivors floated to Thailand where they lived in squalid refugee camps. From the camps, they migrated to various countries, but mainly the U.S. By 1985, there some 643, 000 Vietnamese in the U.S. The U.S. had set up the Orderly Departure Program in 1979 to facilitate entry into the U.S., and in 1987, the Amerasian Homecoming Act enabled over thirty thousand children (and their immediate family members) of U.S. military and civilian personnel stationed in Vietnam during the war to enter the U.S. (Chuong and Minh, 2003).

In 1997, Vietnamese Americans owned 97,764 businesses employing 79,035 people with $9.3 billion in sales. About 16 percent of the businesses were retail shops, reaping nearly $3 billion in sales (ibid.).

Like earlier Asian immigrants, Vietnamese Americans were subject to racism by white workers, as well as by the white supremacist Ku Klux Klan (Takaki, 1989, pp. 453–454). For example, the late 1970s and early 1980s coincided with poor shrimp fishing in the Gulf of Mexico. Car bumper stickers began to appear along the coast, stating "Save Your Shrimp Industry–Get Rid of Vietnamese," the Ku Klux Klan staged demonstrations calling for blood, and U.S. fisherman started carrying guns on their boats (East Asian Times, 2010).

In 1983, in Davis, California, a seventeen-year-old Vietnamese student was stabbed to death by a white student in a high school with a history of racial harassment against Southeast Asian students (Zia, 2000, p. 52). Around the same time, in Lansing, Michigan, a Vietnamese American man and his European American wife were harassed and repeatedly shot at by white men shouting racist abuse (ibid., p. 77).

At the time of the U.S. census in 2000, the number of Vietnamese Americans was 1.22 million [and, according to the 2010 Census, 1.73 million]. Even this number, however, according to community leaders, is under-estimated, partly because of underreporting by the Vietnamese themselves, and partly because many Chinese Vietnamese identify as "Chinese" rather than "Vietnamese" (Chuong and Minh, 2003).

Asian American Counter-hegemonic Resistance Historically

Asian American resistance to racism historically has taken a number of forms, including civil rights struggles and boycotts, and strikes. Once again, dictates of space allow for only a few examples.

Civil rights struggles and boycotts

To begin with, it should be pointed out that Chinese Americans organized early civil rights groups in San Francisco and New York in the mid-nineteenth century (Zia, 2000, p. 28). In the following century too, Asian civil rights was prominent, with the movement spreading throughout the 1970s and 1980s.

Asian civil rights became a national issue in the wake of the racist beating to death of Vincent Chin, a 27-year-old Chinese American in 1982, when his murderers were given probation. Blaming Japanese carmakers for Detroit's problems in the auto industry, one of the two white perpetrators was heard saying, "[i]t is because of you little motherf*ckers that we're out of work," while Chin's dying words were, "[i]t isn't fair" (Ho, 2003). Christine Ho (2003) explains how the Asian American community used the media, raised money, and drummed up support nationwide, organizing rallies and protests and getting support from elected officials to educate the public.

After a campaign that won the support of a wide range of groups (Zia, 2000, p. 50), and the formation of American Citizens for Justice in 1983, the Civil Liberties Act was passed in 1988 (ibid., pp. 48–50).

Events in the following decade also produced an angry response. In 1990, a rebellion by Asian Americans against the Broadway musical, *Miss Saigon*, over the issue of real Asian actors having the chance to play Asian characters, and later over the play's offensive content, resulted for a brief period, in the cancellation of the multimillion-dollar show (ibid., p. 112). In addition, during the 1996 U.S. presidential campaign, Asian American political activists launched a fund-raising drive to help win political recognition for the Asian American community by the Clinton administration, and when it was revealed that a few had breached campaign finance law, the whole Asian American community became the target of intense racialized anger (ibid., pp. 296–297). The result was a profusion of new Asian American and Pacific Islander American organizations using vigorous and militant tactics (ibid., p. 303).

Strikes

As far as strikes are concerned, in 1920, three thousand members of the Filipino Federation of Labor and five thousand Japanese workers struck for higher wages in defiance of attempts by plantation owners at racist "divide and rule" tactics. They were later joined by Portuguese and Chinese workers in what Helen Zia (2000, p. 37) describes as "the first united, interethnic labor action in Hawaii," their strike resulting in a 50 percent wage rise, and a strong labor union movement that survives today (Zia, 2000, p. 37). As noted earlier in this chapter, it was Filipino labor activists that initiated the United Farm Workers' grape pickers' strike that eventually became a movement under César Chávez.

In 1968, inspired by the Black Power Movement, Asian American students, along with other students of color, engaged in militant student strikes in California demanding and winning educational programs in the U.S. that taught their history (ibid., pp. 47–48). Zia (ibid., pp. 16–18) describes how, in the spring of 1971, a joint committee of black, Latina/o, and Asian American students decided to make Princeton University address the issues of racism on campus. The decision was made to occupy the university library and call for a massive rally in the university chapel. They would denounce racism at Princeton, and demand an end to the racist war in Vietnam. Zia spoke before a thousand or more people in the chapel.

Thirty years later, in May 1998, New York taxi drivers—the majority of whom were South Asian, but also including recent immigrants from Russian and Eastern Europe, Africa, Latin America, and the Caribbean—staged a one-day strike, organized by the New York Taxi Workers Alliance. Despite the fact that the workers lacked a common language and basic organizing tools, the strike was successful (ibid., p. 199). One of them explained that, after paying for the car and the gas, all that they make is a few dollars an hour if they are lucky. In addition, they suffer from back pain, exposure to exhaust fumes, the constant threat of robbery, and racist treatment from customers (ibid.).

Asian Americans Today

While, as exemplified in this chapter, Asian Americans experience racism in similar ways to Native American, African American, and Latina/o American communities, they also encounter it in different ways. A key dissimilarity is the aforementioned "model minority" myth. This has been defined by Delgado and Stefancic (2001, p. 151) as the "[i]dea that Asian Americans are hard-working, intelligent, and successful and that other groups should emulate them." As I argued in the Introduction to this volume, in the context of my arguments for a broad concept and definition of racism, there are inherent dangers with "seemingly positive attributes" when applied to given "ethnic groups." I argued that ascribing such attributes to an "ethnic group" will probably ultimately have racist implications. Delgado and Stefancic (ibid., pp. 81–82) explain that exalting Asian Americans as "the perfect minority group—quiet, industrious, with intact families and high educational aspiration and achievement" is not only untrue, but is "injurious" to the many Asian American subgroups who are poor and need assistance (as was demonstrated in this chapter). Frank Wu (cited in BAMN, 2001) argues that "model minority" is a false stereotype, and one should be suspicious of any stereotype no matter how positive because of what it can conceal. For example, the myth causes a backlash for Asian Americans. Describing Asian Americans as hard working very quickly becomes "unfair competition." Also, Wu notes that when Asian Americans are praised for having strong families and strong family values—nuclear families that stay together—they are then criticized for being "too clannish, too ethnic, too insular, not mixing enough, self-segregating" (cited in ibid.).

Robert Chang (2000, p. 359) notes another negative response that results from the "model minority" myth: "when we try to make our problems known, our complaints of discrimination or calls for remedial action are seen as unwarranted and inappropriate." As Chang (ibid., p. 360) concludes, "the danger of the model minority myth [is that it] renders the oppression of Asian Americans invisible."

Benji Chang and Wayne Au (2007–2008, pp. 15–16) summarize the racism inherent in the "model minority" myth, giving a number of examples that have been demonstrated throughout the Asian American section of this chapter. The myth masks: the diversity and ethnic inequity within the Asian American communities; the class divide, sometimes rooted in specific immigration histories; economic circumstance, such as larger household size and residence in high-cost parts of the U.S.; racism and class exploitation; and attributing success and failure of other minority ethnic groups to cultural or "racial" weaknesses. With respect to this last point, other minority ethnic groups are interpellated on the lines of "Asian Americans made it, why can't you?" (BAMN, 2001).

Native Hawaiians and Pacific Islander Americans

As McGregor and Moy (2003) explain, classification of peoples under this category is constantly changing. Until the 1980 census, "Hawaiian" was the only Pacific Islander group listed in census questionnaires. That year, "Guamanian" and "Samoan" were added, and a total of 260,000 Native Hawaiian and Pacific Islanders (NHPI) were recorded. In 1990, the category "Other Asian or Pacific Islander" was added, together with a "write-in" area for all unspecified groups of Polynesian, Micronesian, or Melanesian cultural backgrounds. The census of that year counted 365,000 NHPIs (McGregor and Moy, 2003). In response to calls by NHPI activists, starting with the 2000 census, peoples under this category are now entered as a separate grouping. Thus the 2010 census identifies the following groups: "White," "Black or African American" (it continues to give the choice here of "negro"), "American Indian or Alaska Native," "Asian" and "Native Hawaiian or Other Pacific Islanders." People of Latina/o origin are not considered "races" (U.S. Census 2010 "Official Form").[19]

Native Hawaiians

The native population has been estimated at between four hundred thousand and eight hundred thousand in 1778 when Captain James Cook landed, but as a result of diseases brought in by colonization, it declined rapidly, reducing to 29,800 and a further 7,800 of mixed ancestry by 1900 (McGregor and Moy, 2003). As noted earlier in this chapter, in 1990, Hawaii became an "official territory" of the U.S., having had its monarchy overthrown seven years earlier by U.S. naval forces. In 1959, Hawaii became the fiftieth state of the U.S.

According to the 2000 census, Native Hawaiians and part-Native Hawaiians number 239,655 and are about 20 percent of Hawaii's population. Another 161,500 people with Hawaiian ancestry live in the continental U.S. Native Hawaiians in Hawaii have lower incomes, hold lower-status jobs, and have the highest unemployment rate of all ethnic groups in the islands. Due to their low incomes that hinder access to health care, Native Hawaiians also suffer more from disease, cancer, have higher mortality rates, and eight years' less life expectancy than other groups (ibid.).

Samoans and Guamanians

The Samoan Islands comprise American Samoa and Samoa. The former has a population of around 67,000, and sends a delegate to the U.S. Congress; the latter is an independent country with a population of over 179,000. The economy of American Samoa is undeveloped, with nearly one-third of workers employed in the fishing or canning industry (ibid.). There are more than 130,000 Samoans living in the U.S.

After Samoans, the next largest NHPI group are natives of the island of Guam (also known as Chamorro). The population of Guam is about 157,000, of which about half are Chamorro people. The U.S. military maintains a large, but declining, presence there, with 23,000 military personnel and their families resident on the island. Although Guamanian people have U.S. citizenship, they cannot vote in U.S. presidential elections. Economically, the growing tourist industry catering for Japanese visitors has helped to offset the military downsizing. In the U.S. mainland, there are nearly 93,000 people of pure or part-Chamorro descent (ibid.).

A disproportionate percentage of NHPIs are impoverished, have lower attainment at school, and require public assistance. The "model minority myth" that encircles Asian Americans and is discussed under the heading "Asian Americans Today" in this chapter also does not apply in general to NHPIs. In 1999, their per capita income was $15,054, 37 percent lower than for whites, and 31 percent lower than Asian Americans (ibid.).

Islamophobia

As Omid Memarian (2009) points out, when President Barack Obama addressed the Turkish Parliament in April 2009, he praised Muslim Americans for "enriching the United States." According to Munir Jiwa, however, director of the Center for Islamic Studies at the Graduate Theological Union of the University of California, Berkeley, "virulent Islamophobia" persists across the U.S. (cited in Memarian, 2009). As I argued in chapter 2 of this volume, Islamophobia has less to do with immigration and more, in its contemporary form, to do with the aftermath of the 9/11 attack on the Twin Towers in New York in 2001.

Islamophobia Watch (2010), in its own words, "was initiated in January 2005 as a non-profitmaking project to document material in the public domain which advocates a fear and hatred of the Muslim peoples of the world and Islam as a religion." It was "founded with a determination not to allow the racist ideology of Western Imperialism to gain common currency in its demonisation of Islam." On its website it has 1,543 entries for the U.S.

With respect to schools, Michele Fine (2006) uses the concepts of the specter of *terrorist* (for boys) and *oppressed/uneducated* (for girls) to show the impact of gendered Islamophobia. As she puts it:

> Living in the new "world," they were now outsiders within their own communities and schools. We heard stories of airport delays, dates broken because "my parents wouldn't understand," tongues bitten in history class for fear of being sent to the principal for a dissenting opinion. Abid, a sophomore at a public high school, told us, "My history teacher got mad when I challenged him about the war...I think his son is fighting there." Ahab, at age 11 the youngest and smallest in our discussion group, joined our conversation with a whisper: "I don't like it either when people think me, or my father, is going to throw a bomb."[20]

Here there are clear links here between U.S. capitalism and imperialism, and successful interpellation of the populace in the hegemonic struggle between capitalism and radical Islam. In the Introduction to this volume, I noted how the president himself is indicated in Islamophobia, when I pointed out that some Tea Party supporters view Obama as a Muslim communist. Arguing in a similar vein, Jiwa refers to those anti-Muslims who did not vote for Obama, and who "think we have voted in someone who is, as they say, a 'closet Muslim,' and they think that sometime, he will come out of the closet" (cited in Memarian, 2009).

A survey in April 2009 by the Pew Research Center for the People & the Press found that 12 percent of the U.S. public believe Obama is a Muslim. This misconception is shared equally by Republican and Democratic respondents (ibid.).

Antisemitism

While the increase in antisemitic incidents in the U.S., rising from 98 to 116 from 2008 to 2009 (Lemberg, 2010), is small compared to the U.K. (see chapter 2 of this volume), these figures mask the existence of what the Southern Poverty Law Center (SPLC) (2010a) describes as serious antisemites in America. The largest group is perhaps "radical traditionalist catholics" (not to be confused with "traditionalists" who prefer the old Latin mass), who "routinely pillory Jews as 'the perpetual enemy of Christ.'" Antisemitism is a predominant feature of a number of U.S. hate groups, a consideration of which forms the last section of this chapter.

The Proliferation of Hate Groups

One major difference between the U.K. and the U.S. is the proliferation of hate groups. The Southern Poverty Law Center (2010b) has provided what it describes as a "Hate Map," featuring 932 active hate groups throughout the U.S. in 2009. As the center explains, "[a]ll hate groups have beliefs or practices that attack or malign an entire class of people, typically for their immutable characteristics" (Southern Poverty Law Center, 2010b). At 66, the state of Texas has the highest number of such groups, ranging from the most visible neo-Nazi group in the U.S., the National Alliance, through U.K.-based racist skinhead group, "Blood and Honour"; the Christian identity group, "Aryan Nations Revival"; the antisemitic, black supremacist "Nation of Islam"; to various Ku Klux Klan groups. Full details of all of the hate groups are given on the Law Center website (Southern Poverty Law Center, 2010b). A formidable and a constant often physical threat, these organizations represent a different dimension to the everyday mundane institutional racism that saturates U.S. society, as discussed throughout this chapter.

Conclusion

This chapter has entailed a wide-ranging analysis of the histories of and current realities pertaining to racialized groups in the U.S. The distinctive differences in the experiences of these racialized groups do not, of course, detract from the commonalities of racism experienced by racialized communities there and, indeed, worldwide. Overall, similarities and differences between Native Americans, African Americans, Latina/o Americans, Asian Americans, NHPI Americans, Muslim Americans, and Jewish Americans underline Adrienne Dixson's (2006a) analogy with jazz—in unison and out of unison at the same time. As is argued throughout this volume, in order for these differences and similarities to be fully understood, they need to be linked to racialization processes and articulated with ongoing changes in the capitalist mode of production and developments in imperialism. Racialization processes are themselves intimately connected to migration patterns, which are in turn related to the needs and demands of the capitalist economy, imperialism, and interrelated sociopolitical factors.

Having noted in chapters 2 and 3 that racism takes multifarious forms in both the U.K. and the U.S., in the next chapters I turn my attention to the issues of schooling and education, respectively: the former the processes by which young people are attuned to the requirements of capitalism; the latter a more liberatory process of education from birth to death. In doing so, I draw on Althusser for his analysis of the role of ISAs and of interpellation; and on Gramsci for the potential of counter-hegemony. I then examine the process of racism as it relates to schooling and antiracist education (or education against racism) in the U.K. and the U.S., respectively.

Chapter 4

Racism, Schooling, and Education Against Racism in the U.K. and the U.S.

In the first part of this chapter I make a distinction between schooling (a conforming process) on the one hand, and education (a liberating practice) on the other. To do this, I draw on the work of the two main neo-Marxists considered in this volume, Louis Althusser and Antonio Gramsci. Next, having examined key components of racism in the U.K. and the U.S. in chapters 2 and 3, I go on to examine in this chapter racism as it relates to schooling in these countries and the ways in which Marxist educators have challenged racism. I also address the constraints they have met historically and contemporaneously.

Schooling and Education

It is important, I would argue, to maintain a distinction between schooling, on the one hand, and education, on the other. In this volume I conceptualize *schooling* as the processes by which young people are attuned to the requirements of capitalism both in the form and the content of schooling.[1] *Education*, on the other hand (*educare* in Latin means to "bring out") is generally used here to describe a more liberatory process of education from birth to death, a process of human emancipation and socialism (see chapter 5 of this volume for the example of the Bolivarian Republic of Venezuela).

Schooling played an important part in Althusser's analysis of society. He argued that schools are particularly important for inculcating the dominant ideology, since they require compulsory attendance of all children eight hours a day for five days a week (Althusser, 1971, p. 156). He further suggested that what children learn at school is "know-how"—wrapped in the ideology of the ruling class. Althusser explains succinctly how the school prepares us for our prospective niches in capitalist societies:

> It takes children from every class at infant-school age, and then for years, the years in which the child is most "vulnerable"...it drums into them, whether

it uses new or old methods, a certain amount of "know-how" wrapped in the ruling ideology...Somewhere around the age of sixteen, a huge mass of children are ejected "into production": these are the workers or small peasants. Another portion of scholastically adapted youth carries on: and, for better or worse, it goes somewhat further, until it falls by the wayside and fills the posts of small and middle technicians, white-collar workers, small and middle executives, petty bourgeois of all kinds. A last portion reaches the summit, either to fall into intellectual semi-employment, or to provide, as well as the "intellectuals of the collective labourer," the agents of exploitation (capitalists, managers), the agents of repression (soldiers, policemen, politicians, administrators, etc.) and the professional ideologists (priests of all sorts, most of whom are convinced "laymen"). (Althusser, 1971, p. 155)

Althusser (ibid.) concludes that "[e]ach mass ejected en route is practically provided with the ideology which suits the role it has to fulfil in class society" (ibid.).

While this is a very structuralist determinist position, typical of structuralist Marxism (which emphasizes the power of the structures of capitalism—see chapter 2 of this volume for a discussion), Althusser (ibid., p. 157) does note the existence of counter-hegemonic practices when he asks "the pardon of those teachers who, in dreadful conditions, attempt to turn the few weapons they can find in the history and learning they 'teach' against the ideology, the system and the practices in which they are trapped." He describes them as "a kind of hero."

Like Althusser, Gramsci argued that schooling was one way in which individuals were socialized into maintaining the status quo. As he put it, "each social group has its own type of school, intended to perpetuate a specific traditional function, ruling or subordinate" (Gramsci, 1978, p. 40). There is not much on schooling in Gramsci's main work, *Prison Notebooks* (written while imprisoned under Mussolini's fascist regime from 1929–1935). What he did write was in essence against increased specialization in Italy and for a more "comprehensive" model (Burke, 2005). He argued that changes in Italy were not merely perpetuating social differences but crystallizing them (Gramsci, 1978, p. 40).[2]

It is in the realm of *education* that Gramsci can be singled out as a major figure. As Paula Allman (1988, p. 99) has put it, Gramsci's most important contribution to socialism in general is his reformulation of revolutionary strategy, a strategy that is in essence "education for socialism." While previous socialist strategy was based primarily on seizing the apparatuses of the state, it was Gramsci who made the case that "in western capitalist societies a great deal of pre-figurative work must be done first" (ibid.). Complementing Allman's analysis, Burke (2005) argues that it is for informal educators that Gramsci stands out as a major thinker:

The importance he placed on critical self awareness, on critical social awareness, on the importance of the intellectual being part of everyday life, on the part played by so-called "common sense" in maintaining the status quo and the transformational possibilities of education. All of these are now common-place in the formation of informal educators.

The importance of "informal education" for socialism is readily apparent in Hugo Chávez's concept of Venezuela as "a giant school," discussed in the next chapter of this volume.

Gramsci recognized that education for socialism was a task of gargantuan proportions. In his own words, "if our aim is to produce a new stratum of intellectuals...from a social group which has not traditionally developed the appropriate attitudes, then we have unprecedented difficulties to over-come" (Gramsci, 1978, p. 43). As we have seen (Note 23 of chapter 1 of this volume) Gramsci made an important distinction between traditional and organic intellectuals, and wrote of the need for the working class to produce its own organic intellectuals, but also of the importance of a significant num-ber of "traditional intellectuals" coming over to the revolutionary cause.

As a practical example of changing the system to produce a new stra-tum of organic intellectuals, in chapter 5 of this volume I discuss critical and popular education in Venezuela in the context of a participatory model of endogenous socialist development, which has at its forefront struggling to translate policy into practice in authentically democratic ways, ways that promote critical reflection and participation above formalistic and uncritical learning (Griffiths and Williams, 2009). Later in this chapter, I look at how Marxist educators have theorized and promoted education against racism in the U.K. and the U.S. For such educators the counter-hegemonic struggles against racism and for socialism are part of the same pedagogical process.[3] In the final chapter of the book, I turn to a consideration of the implications for practice in educational institutions for multicultural antiracist socialist education.

Racism and Schooling in the U.K.

The imperial curriculum

In chapter 2 of this volume I noted that racism was institutionalized in pop-ular culture in the British Imperial era in many ways, including education. The curriculum of the early twentieth century was overtly racist, geography and history texts being the prime conveyers of racialization. To give a few examples, in Nelson's *The World and its Peoples* (c. 1907), the anonymous author described the African as "an overgrown child, vain, self-indulgent, and fond of idleness," while the "wretched bushmen [were] the lowest and most debased human beings on the face of the globe" (ibid.). Asia was simi-larly demeaned by Nelson as a continent of dying nations rapidly falling back in civilization (ibid.) and Australian Aboriginals were "among the most miserable of men [*sic*]" whose "great poverty led them to practise vices like cannibalism and the murder of the sick and helpless" (A.J. Herbertson, *Man and his Work* [1902], cited in MacKenzie, 1984, p. 185). The "English," by way of contrast, were portrayed as morally irreproachable. As one history text put it, "[t]hey all show the bold, frank, sturdy character which so strongly marks out the Anglo-Saxon race" (T.J. Livesey, *Granville History Reader* (1902) (cited in Chancellor, 1970, p. 118). In another (Cassell's *History of England*, c. 1900, cited in ibid., p. 122), references were made to "the barbaric peoples of Asia" and the most frequent impression conveyed about Indians and Afghans was that they were cruel and totally unfit to rule themselves (see Cole and Blair 2006, pp. 74–75 for a more detailed analysis of racism and schooling during this period).[4] Imperialist texts could still be found in school libraries well into the 1980s.[5]

The empire comes home to roost

In the light of an expanding postwar economy in the 1950s, the empire came home to roost as the U.K. recruited labor from Britain's colonies and ex-colonies, with the children of these migrant workers eventually entering U.K. schools. Schooling was then, and is now predominantly monocultural; that is, serving to promote so-called "British culture" and "British Values." Given that the culture and values are those of capitalism, monocultural education fits easily in with the definition of "schooling" that I proposed at the beginning of this chapter. However, given the fact the term monocultural *education* has a long history, I will resist the temptation of using monocultural *schooling*, even though in the context of the terminology used in this volume, describing it thus would be more accurate.

Processes of racialization and racism led to the underachievement of minority ethnic children in the 1960s and 1970s (Cole and Blair, 2006, pp. 75–79). Specific concerns about African Caribbean children prompted the government to commission in 1979 an inquiry into "the education of West Indian children." The Rampton Report (1981) confirmed what African Caribbean parents and carers had been saying all along—that racism was a major factor in their experience of school (Cole and Blair, 2006, p. 79). It required courage to say this at the time, and the communications ISA, in the form of the media, attempted to discredit the report before it was published, and Rampton was subsequently sacked by the minister of education.

Multicultural Education

The government then commissioned another report, whose brief was extended to cover other minority ethnic groups. The ensuing Swann Report, *Education for All* (1985) confirmed some of the findings of the Rampton Report but also made some wide-ranging suggestions for education in an ethnically diverse society. Among these was that children in all schools should be educated for their life in a multicultural society. One of the underlying principles was that if children were taught about each other and each other's cultures, this would help to reduce "prejudice," especially among white children (Cole and Blair, 2006, p. 79).

The Swann Report's predominant focus on culture set the trajectory of multicultural education along a superficial line in which children were taught about the food, the clothes, and the music of different countries usually by white teachers, without also understanding the structural and institutional inequalities that had been at the core of community campaigns (Sarup, 1986; Troyna, 1993). Again, this approach is more to do with *schooling* rather than education, but given the long history of the term "multicultural *education*," I will retain it here. The exoticization of minority ethnic group cultures and customs served to reinforce the notion that these cultures were indeed "other" and drew the boundary more firmly between "Them," the "immigrants" or "foreigners" and "us," the "real" British people (Cole and Blair, 2006, p. 80).

Nearly thirty years after Rampton, the colonial legacy remains. For example, while a higher percentage of Indian and mixed white and Asian students reach the expected level in English and mathematics than their peers (probably related to socioeconomic factors), a lower percentage of Black African, Black Caribbean, and Pakistani students reach this level (Department for Children, Schools and Families (DCSF) "Statistical First Release," 2009b)

Antiracist Education in the U.K.[6]

Antiracist education has a long history in the U.K., and has traditionally been associated with Marxism and other radical left thinking. Antiracist educators are critical of both monocultural and multicultural education. The antiracist critique of monocultural education is that in denying the existence of, or marginalizing the cultures of minority ethnic communities, it was and is profoundly racist. The antiracist critique of multicultural education is that it was and is patronizing and superficial. It was often characterized as the three "S's": "saris, samosas, and steel drums" (for a discussion, see Troyna and Carrington, 1990).

Antiracist education starts from the premise that U.K. society is institutionally racist, and that, in the area of "race" and culture, the purpose of education is to challenge and undermine that racism. Over ten years ago (Cole, 1998, p. 45), by way of example, I suggested the way in which an antiracist version of the Australian bicentennial of 1988 might have been taught in primary (elementary) schools in Britain. Here, in order to illustrate the fundamental differences between monocultural, multicultural, and antiracist education, I will update this analysis, and extend it to incorporate how traditional monocultural and traditional multicultural approaches might manifest themselves today (my description of these three approaches applies to Britain, but could easily be extrapolated to other contexts).

In the monocultural classroom, children would be taught that Australia was discovered about two hundred and forty years ago by Captain Cook, a British man, and that, although Australia is on the other side of the world from Britain, the people there are like us, eat the same food, and have the same customs and way of life. The climate is much hotter and people can swim on Christmas day, and at many beaches Santa Claus arrives on a surfboard, or even on a surf lifesaving boat. There are still some Aborigines[7] in Australia and the government has enacted laws that safeguard their communities against drunkenness and other forms of antisocial behavior.

With the multicultural approach, children would learn that Australia is a multicultural society, just like ours, with lots of different cultures and religions making the country an exciting place in which to live. As well as "the British," other people have emigrated to Australia from most of the rest of Europe, and indeed the world. The multicultural nature of Australian society means lots of different foods, music, dance, and national costumes. The Aboriginal people—the original inhabitants—have a thriving culture, and produce very original music and art.

The antiracist approach would focus on the fact that the indigenous peoples of Australia and their supporters view what happened two centuries ago as an imperialist colonial invasion. Given access to a comprehensive range of resources pertaining to life in Australia, children would discover that in reality, multicultural Australia is a racialized capitalist society stratified on lines of ethnicity, class, and gender, with Australian-born and English-speaking white male immigrants a the top of the hierarchy and Aboriginal women at the bottom. They would learn about "land rights" and other counterhegemonic struggles, and the economic and ecological arguments pertaining to these rights. They would discover that Aboriginal communities have faced ongoing exploitation and oppression since the invasion, and how this has intensified in recent years. They would relate Australian indigenous struggles against injustice to other struggles for social justice in Australia, and to struggles worldwide.[8] The children would be encouraged to resist racist interpellations from the ISAs that attempt to distort and mask realities.

This example of antiracist education is provided to schematically emphasize the basic differences between the three approaches. It is not intended in any way of course to deny the importance and salience of indigenous cultures. Given advances in technology, most notably the World Wide Web, to facilitate authentic voices, I believe that a form of radical and critical multicultural antiracist education is now possible (see chapter 6 of this volume for a discussion). With respect to this example of indigenous Australians, there is now a wealth of cultural information about the various communities (see, for example, Cultural Survival: Australia, 2009).

The (neo-)Marxist underpinnings of the above example of the antiracist approach should by now be clear. I am not suggesting that the language of (neo-)Marxism is necessarily appropriate to children at primary (elementary) level. However, it is my belief that, given appropriate use of language and resources, and in the context of sensitivity to age, almost anything can be taught to anyone.

The anti-antiracist backlash

Up until the late 1990s, with their prognosis that Britain is an institutionally racist society, antiracists were branded by many as "loony Lefties" and ostracized by national and local government.[9] In her memoirs, for example, Margaret Thatcher (Thatcher, 1993, p. 598) expressed extreme concern that I was teaching antiracist education in the late 1980s at what was then Brighton Polytechnic. At the time (1987), she also opined, with particular respect to primary mathematics:

> In the inner cities where youngsters must have a decent education if they are to have a better future, that opportunity is all too often snatched from them by hard-left education authorities and extremist teachers. Children who need to be able to count and multiply are learning anti-racist mathematics—whatever that is. (cited in Lavalette et al., 2001)

Similarly, her successor, John Major, declared at the 1992 Conservative Party annual conference speech:

> I also want a reform of teacher training. Let us return to basic subject teaching, not courses in the theory of education. Primary teachers should teach children to read, not waste their time on the politics of gender, race and class. (cited in ibid.)[10]

The Stephen Lawrence Inquiry Report

It took the Stephen Lawrence Inquiry Report (Macpherson, 1999) to change all this. As noted in the Introduction to this volume, the report followed a lengthy public campaign initiated by the parents of Stephen Lawrence after the murder in 1993 by racist thugs of black teenager Stephen Lawrence. The report looked at racism in the Metropolitan Police and other British institutions. While it could have gone further in its castigation of the inherent racism in British society, for antiracists, (Macpherson, 1999) it is nevertheless a milestone in being the first acknowledgment by the British State of the existence of widespread institutional racism in the police, in the education system, and in other institutions in the society. Leading U.K. antiracist campaigner and writer, Sivanandan rightly describes the inquiry as "not just a result but a learning process for the country at large" (2000, p. 1). He argues that through the course of the inquiry, "the gravitational centre of race relations discourse was shifted from individual prejudice and ethnic need to systemic, institutional racial inequality and injustice" (ibid., p. 1). Gillborn (2008, p. 132) is also right to describe the Stephen Lawrence case as "one of the single most important episodes in the history of British race relations."

The report led directly to the very progressive Race Relations (Amendment) Act (2000), which places a general duty on specified public authorities to promote "race" equality. The report, however, is less to do with any caring intentions on the part of the capitalist state and much more to do with public campaigning. As David Gillborn (2008, p. 135) has insisted, the Lawrence inquiry was "not granted by a benign state" that wanted to put right an injustice, but as a result of "high profile protests and public demonstrations."

Threats to antiracist education from New Labour

Initial official state endorsement of the Stephen Lawrence Inquiry Report's acknowledgment of the existence of institutional racism, however, was short-lived. While there was a massive public outcry following the report, with its findings dominating the media, this was followed within weeks by skeptical comments from teachers unions' leaders (ibid., p. 126). There were also signs that the Education Department was not keen on pushing forward the recommendations of the inquiry. While it formally claimed to accept the report, it asserted that things were already in place to sort problems out, with the then Education Secretary, David Blunkett, claiming that the subject of citizenship was already there to "help children learn how to grow up in a society that cares and to have real equality of opportunity for all" (cited in ibid., p. 127).

Later, when he was Home Secretary, Blunkett suggested that "institutional racism" was a slogan that let individual managers "off the hook" in tackling racism (cited in Travis, 2003). He said that it was important that the government's "diversity agenda" tackled the fight against prejudice but also took on the long-standing need to change attitudes:

> That is why I was so worried about people talking about institutional racism because it isn't institutions. It is patterns of work and processes that have grown up. It's people that make the difference. (cited in ibid.)

Questioned about his comments afterward, Blunkett added: "I think the slogan created a year or two ago about institutional racism missed the point. It's not the structures created in the past but the processes to change structures in the future and it is individuals at all levels who do that" (cited in ibid.).

As Gillborn (2008, pp. 130–131) explains, two significant events with respect to the abandonment by the state of the concept of "institutional racism" happened late in 2006 and early in 2007. First, in December 2006, the contents of an internal Education Department review were published in the *Independent on Sunday* newspaper that specified "institutional racism" as the cause of black overrepresentation in exclusions from schools (ibid., p. 130). The review also warned that "[i]f we choose to use the term 'institutional racism,' we need to be sensitive to the likely reception by schools [but] if we choose not to use the term, we need to make sure that the tone of our message remains sufficiently challenging" (cited in ibid.). The relevant minister, Lord Adonis, was quoted in the same newspaper as arguing that "since the report does not baldly conclude that Britain's entire school system is 'institutionally racist,' the term—and the issue—could be quietly shelved" (cited in ibid., p. 144).

The second event happened early in 2007. The BBC, when referring to the David Bennett Inquiry on institutional racism in the National Health Service, reported that "the Department of Health now regards the term [institutional racism] as 'unhelpful' and believes that 'the solutions lie in the hands of individuals not institutions'" (cited in ibid., p. 131).

Gillborn (2008, p. 131) notes that "by 2007 'institutional racism' had been erased from the policy lexicon." A final blow to state endorsement of the concept came when the Commission on Equality and Human Rights (a body that oversees all equality issues) replaced the Commission for Racial Equality and the principle of "proportionality" was introduced. This allows public authorities not to take any action "which might be disproportionate to the benefits the action would deliver" (cited in ibid., pp. 131–132). As Gillborn (2008, p. 132) points out, this means that schools can now decide to focus on other issues (e.g., underachieving boys). A school could acknowledge persistent "race" inequalities, but decide that the effort required to reduce them was out of proportion to any benefits, or it could take no action on "race" because it had too few minority ethnic students (ibid.). Gillborn (ibid.) concludes that the "proposals signal a clear end to the period where equalities policy was drawn up with any meaningful reference to the Lawrence Inquiry."

"The mere fact," Gillborn (2008, p. 133) concludes, "of the Stephen Lawrence and David Bennett Inquiries—and the attendant press coverage—is assumed by some observers to denote change." However, the fact that institutional racism has been named explicitly as a factor in Britain's police, education, and health services is not a solution, it is merely a diagnosis. (ibid.).

Gillborn (2008, p. 120) describes the Stephen Lawrence case as "a case that, after years of the most painful campaigning and mistreatment, was supposed to have changed Britain for ever but...now seems to have left little imprint on the system in general, and education in particular." However, he finishes on a positive note, arguing that the lesson from such cases "is not that change is impossible but that change is always contested and every step forward be must be valued and protected. A victory won is not a victory secured" (ibid., p. 134). The whole case, he concludes, emphasizes "the importance of constant vigilance to maintain and build upon each victory" (ibid.).[11]

No Marxist would disagree with this conclusion. Marxists argue that all progressive gains for the working class have been the result of workers' struggle, and make the point that benefits that accrue to workers in capitalist societies, have, in general throughout history, been won by such struggle, rather than capitalist latent morality, or basic kindness. Indeed as Marx (1862, p. 1) put it, referring to the working class as the main source of extra parliamentary pressure in England:

> No important innovation, no decisive measure has ever been carried through in this country without pressure from without...By pressure from without the Englishman understands great, extra-parliamentary popular demonstrations, which naturally cannot be staged without the lively participation of the working class.

There are further threats to the spirit of the Stephen Lawrence Inquiry Report, and indeed the promotion even of multiculturalism as a result of the

UNIVE.... .. ...UrlESTER
LIBRARY

Education and Inspections Act (2006), which came into effect in September 2007. This act introduced a duty on the governing bodies of maintained schools to promote "community cohesion," placing a new emphasis on schools to play a key role in building a society with a "common vision," a "sense of belonging" and making available similar "life opportunities" for all. Following Wetherell, Lafleche and Berkeley 2007, Andrew Pilkington (2008) distinguishes between "soft" and "hard" versions of community cohesion. The former sees community cohesion as complementing rather than replacing multiculturalism. In addition, the "soft" version recognizes that the promotion of community cohesion requires that inequality and racism is addressed. The "hard" version, on the other hand, views community cohesion and multiculturalism as ineluctably at loggerheads and insists that we abandon the divisiveness that is evident in multiculturalism and instead adhere to "British values." The hard version of "community cohesion" is thus monocultural, and to do with schooling rather than education.

The then New Labour secretary of state for communities, Ruth Kelly, favored the hard version. As Pilkington (2008) points out, in announcing the launch of the Commission on Integration and Cohesion in August 2006, Kelly stressed that it was important "not to be censored by PC," wondered whether multiculturalism was "encouraging separateness," and emphasized how Britain needed to tackle ethnic tensions (Kelly, 2006, cited in Pilkington, 2008).[12] Pilkington (ibid.) notes that her speech glossed over any structural roots of any tensions and stressed to migrants "their responsibility to integrate and contribute to the local community" (ibid.). He argues that the tenor of the report can be gleaned from two of its proposals that both warrant separate appendixes: the juxtaposition of English and translation services, with a marked preference for the former; and a recommendation that priority should be given in the allocation of funding to groups making links between communities rather than single groups (Commission on Integration and Cohesion, 2007, cited in Pilkington, 2008). Pilkington (2008) concludes that both proposals implicitly view multiculturalism and community cohesion as in opposition to each other, signal a shift away from accommodating minority concerns, and point toward a cohesion agenda where people are cajoled into learning English and developing cross-community networks.

The U.K. ConDem government

So far, it is not totally clear what the U.K. ConDem government's schools policies will entail, except that we know there will be changes in the curriculum.[13] For example, Conservative Education Secretary Michael Gove will draw on the services of the aforementioned popular historian, also a TV presenter, and Labour Party supporter, Simon Schama to make U.K. history more central to the curriculum. Gove talks of "shame" as well as "pride" in relation to the history of the U.K., and of "our common story," "full of contention, not self-congratulation" (cited in Vasagar, 2010). However, the fact that right-wing pro-imperialist popular historian Niall Ferguson (a TV presenter, too) was earlier tipped for the post provides a taste of what schooling might begin to look like *ideologically* under the ConDem government.

Ferguson (cited in Higgins, 2010) states that children should be taught that the "big story" of the last five hundred years "is the rise of western domination of the world." He argues that the syllabus is "bound to be Eurocentric" because the world is Eurocentric (Higgins, 2010). For Ferguson, the British Empire was relatively benevolent, and in 2004, he argued that the American Empire, which "has the potential to do great good," needs to learn from the lessons of the British Empire. First, it needs to export capital and to invest in its colonies; second, people from the U.S. need to settle permanently in its colonies; third, there must be a *commitment* to imperialism; fourth, there must be collaboration with local elites. Success can only come, he concluded, if the Americans are prepared to *stay* (Ferguson, 2004). Ferguson (2005) also offered the then President Bush the idea of thinking of the U.S. Empire (Ferguson's words, not mine) "as a kind of sequel to the British Empire."

With respect to the teaching of Empire in the U.K. curriculum, Gove has praised Ferguson for his "exciting and engaging" ideas for a "campaign for real history," and has stated that he is "a great fan of Ferguson" (Higgins, 2010).

Despite current realities, Marxist educators will continue to make the case for multicultural antiracist socialist education. In the last chapter of this volume, I will make some suggestions for practice in educational institutions to achieve this. This will include arguments for the teaching of old U.K. and new U.S. imperialism, but from a Marxist rather than pro-imperialist perspective.

Racism and Schooling in the U.S.

In chapter 3 of this volume, I gave some examples of racism as it relates to schooling in the U.S. through history. I noted that, in light of the Meriam Report (1928), which gave an account of poor Native American education, the Indian Reorganization Act (1934) was passed. However, I explained that many of the old customs and traditions had vanished by then, and traditional Indians of almost every tribe objected strongly to the Anglo-American system of organizing people. I also described the "boarding school project," which attempted cultural genocide by schooling Native American children to reject their cultures.

I pointed out that most states prohibited schooling for slaves. I explained how, between the late nineteenth and mid-twentieth century, a number of Jim Crow segregation laws were passed that enforced segregation in all public places, and that this period was a time of great poverty and educational and political deprivation for African Americans. I noted how schooling post-slavery was put in place to ease the transition from slavery to low-level wage labor.

I drew attention to the fact that language-based subordination and segregation was a major feature of the twentieth century for Mexican Americans, as was attempted assimilation into whiteness and English monolingualism.

I showed how the rapid growth of the Chinese American population in the last three decades has been accompanied by further racism, how Chinese American achievements in education have led to the use of racist attempts to slow down or reverse their enrollment in select schools and colleges. I cited figures that show the Hmong people having, among Asian Americans, the largest number of people with "less than high school graduate" attainments.

I also referred to the fact that a disproportionate percentage of Native Hawaiians and Pacific Islander Americans are impoverished, have lower school attainment, and require public assistance.

With respect to Islamophobia, I cited the work of Michele Fine (2006) who, using the concepts of the specter of *terrorist* (for boys) and *oppressed/ uneducated* (for girls), has shown how gendered Islamophobia impacts U.S. schools.

In this section of the chapter, I consider some major current issues of racism and schooling, focusing on segregation, bilingual education, underachievement, and the No Child Left Behind project. I begin by examining the historical context of segregation.

Plessy v. Ferguson *1896*

Segregation on grounds of "race" was discussed extensively in chapter 3 of this volume. A landmark decision on this was made in 1896. In 1892, Homer Plessy, who was classified as one-eighth black and seven-eighths white, but under Louisiana law was considered black, was jailed for sitting in the "white car" of the East Louisiana Railroad. He went to court, arguing that the Separate Car Act violated the Thirteenth and Fourteenth Amendments to the Constitution of the U.S. As we have seen, the Thirteenth Amendment barred slavery throughout the U.S. The Fourteenth Amendment requires each state to provide equal protection under the law to all people within its jurisdiction. Plessy's arguments were rejected and Judge Ferguson found Plessy guilty of refusing to leave the "white car." After an appeal to the Supreme Court of Louisiana, he was found him guilty once again (Cozzens, 1995). As Lisa Cozzens (1995) explains, the Plessy decision set the precedent that "separate" facilities for black people and white people were constitutional as long as they were "equal." This "separate but equal" doctrine was rapidly extended to many other areas of public life, including restaurants, theaters, restrooms, and public schools.

The Lemon Grove incident *1930–1931*

In the 1920s, in public schools throughout Southern California, the children of Mexican migrant workers were segregated in separate classrooms. The first successful legal challenge to such segregation took place in 1931 in Lemon Grove, a rural hamlet near San Diego, where the main employment was citrusgrowing (Griswold del Castillo et al., 2000). In July 1930, the Lemon Grove School Board decided to build a separate school for seventy-five students, the children of migrants who were attending the local school, and most of whom were born in the U.S. No notice was given to their parents. In January, the following year, the principal, standing at the door of the school, directed the incoming Mexican American/Mexican students to go to the new school building, a wooden structure that became known as "La Caballeriza" (the barn) (ibid.). Instead, the students returned home and, with the support of the Mexican Consul in San Diego, their parents decided to oppose segregation by refusing to send their children to La Caballeriza. They subsequently filed a writ to prevent the school board from sending their children there. The San Diego DA argued that the new school was appropriate because it was in a Mexican area, was big enough, and most of the students were below grade level in their knowledge of English. Moreover, it was claimed that it would be to the advantage of the "American" students if they were separated. In 1931, the Judge ruled against the Lemon Grove School Board and ordered them to reinstate the children in the original school (ibid.). In that decision, the judge ruled that children of Mexican origin could not be segregated under the laws of the state of California, because they were "of the Caucasian race," and laws allowing the segregation of "Oriental," "Negro," and "Indian" [Native American] children did not apply (Wikipedia, 2010). While it was a victory for Mexicans and Mexican Americans, it did not set a precedent for districts outside Lemon Grove where segregation remained. Moreover, the "logic" underlying the judgment did not challenge segregation per se, and indeed reinforced it for these considered not to be "white."

In the early 1950s, segregation across the U.S. was the norm. Because of the Plessy v. Ferguson judgment, however, all schools in a given district were supposed to be equal. In reality, most "white schools" were far superior (Cozzens, 1998). Barbara J. Love (2004, p. 239) chronicles in a CRT counter-story[14] how Plessy v. Ferguson was used to "rationalize racial segregation and America's version of apartheid," whereby in U.S. schools, "white people had the best of the books, buildings, materials, and supplies, while African American children got them when they were of no further use to white children." This even included "the milk that was too old and sour for white children to drink" (Love, 2004, p. 239). Jesse Jackson (2010, p. 62) has movingly described his own childhood experiences:

> I remember when I first saw the school closest to our family home. It appeared to have everything—grass, flowers, a merry-go-round and a slide in the playground. But when I started my schooling, I actually had to go somewhere else, in the opposite direction. My school had no grass in the yard, no merry-go-round and no toys. It was farther for me to travel, across dangerous highways and a railway. But I had no choice because I was black.

Brown v. Board of Education *1954 and the desegregation of public schools*

Cozzens (1998) explains the background to the groundbreaking *Brown v. Board of Education* court decision. In Topeka, Kansas, a black student, Linda

Brown, had to walk for a mile through a railway switchyard to reach her "black elementary school," even though a "white elementary school" was closer. When Linda's father, Oliver Brown, attempted to enroll her in the "white school," this was refused by the principal. Brown then approached the Topeka branch of the National Association for the Advancement of Colored People (NAACP) (Cozzens, 1998). Brown was joined by other African Americans parents, and, in 1951, the NAACP requested an injunction to forbid segregation in Topeka's public (nonprivate) schools. The Board of Education's defense was, in part, that segregated schools merely prepared black children for segregation in later life and the court ruled in favor of the Board of Education. Brown and the NAACP appealed to the Supreme Court and their case was combined with other cases that were challenging segregation. Three years later, in 1954, the court ruled in favor of desegregation of public schools on the ground that segregation "deprived [the plaintiffs] of the equal protection of the laws guaranteed by the Fourteenth Amendment" (cited in Cozzens, 1998). The court thus required the desegregation of schools. However, it did not require desegregation in other public areas across the U.S., nor did it set a time limit for schools.

Writing from a Critical Race Theory perspective, Derrick Bell (1980) argued that the Supreme Court decision was an example of interest convergence. Bell's argument was that, given that World War II had not long ended, and the Korean War (discussed in chapter 3 of this volume) had just ended, the U.S. feared mass domestic upheaval if African American service personnel, who had been prominent in both wars, faced violent racism in the U.S. In addition, this was the period of the so-called "Cold War" between the U.S. and the Soviet Union, with much of the developing world (inhabited by people of color) up for grabs. As Delgado and Stefancic (2001, p. 19) explain:

> It would ill serve the U.S. interest if the world press continued to carry stories of lynchings, racist sheriffs, or murders like that of Emmett Till [a fourteen-year-old African American boy who was shot, beaten, and had his eye gouged-out before being thrown into the river with a weight tied to his neck with barbed wire]. It was time for the United States to soften its stance toward domestic minorities. The interests of whites and blacks, for a brief moment, converged.

It should be pointed out that it was not just the world press that carried such stories. As Dudziak (1988, cited in Taylor, 2006, p. 76) explains:

> the relatively new medium of television had beamed shocking images of U.S. racial brutality around the world. The Soviet Union, China, and India regularly carried stories and pictures of the Ku Klux Klan, lynchings, and the government suppression of the civil rights movement, including police dogs tearing the flesh of young, peaceful protesters, and sparked an international sensation. Just as the United States was attempting to position itself as the leading force of anticommunism, this information threatened to undermine its position as the model of democracy.

The president of the U.S. at the time of the Brown v. Board of Education decision, Dwight D. Eisenhower, condemned it and promised that he would not enforce school desegregation (Baptiste and Sanchez, 2004). Believing that issues of civil rights should be handled by the states, and should vary from state to state, he allowed himself distance from desegregation and racism (ibid.). H. Prentice Baptiste and Rebecca Sanchez (2004) explain that Eisenhower felt himself to be a "moderate" with respect to "race." He wanted to uphold the Supreme Court, but did not want to upset his many Southern friends, so did not want to use the RSAs to enforce the law, allowing the segregationists to convince themselves that Eisenhower would never act (Ambrose, 1984, cited in Baptiste and Sanchez, 2004). While it is true that in 1957 Eisenhower sent in the army to the Little Rock school where the Arkansas National Guard was preventing the entry of nine black students and enabled successful entry of the students, Baptiste and Sanchez (2004) argue that he had no choice, since he would have been accused of defying the orders of the Supreme Court and disobeying his oath of office. They sum up Eisenhower's position on racism and civil rights as follows:

> Eisenhower has been highly criticized for his reluctance to get involved in the civil rights movement and the desegregation of schools…his personal feelings of white superiority and racism, and his need for approval from his Southern friends got in the way of the desegregation of a nation…His silence and his decisions to look the other way were no doubt his biggest failures as President of the United States. (Baptiste and Sanchez, 2004)

Thandeka K. Chapman (2006, p. 68) notes that Brown v Board of Education had the most immediate effect in southern states. Citing J. T. Patterson (2001, p. xx), Chapman (2006, p. 69) points out that Brown "took direct aim only at the South and those border regions where segregation was *de jure*—sanctioned explicitly in laws," with the *Brown v. Board of Education* decision not a challenge to the North, where de facto "racial" segregation in schooling was widespread.

Rockford, Illinois: a case study

Chapman (2006, p. 69) gives the example of Rockford, Illinois as "a microcosm that exemplifies the socio-political events that took place in many cities in the northern United States." As she explains, Rockford's history of desegregation efforts follows a pattern of economic decline in the late 1950s and parental action against school districts in the late 1960s (Chapman, 2006, p. 72). Parents of color were involved in court action there for nearly thirty years from 1968. During that period, they took their board regularly to court, attended school board meetings, boycotted meetings, held rallies, and sponsored political candidates (ibid., p. 69). The greatest obstacles they faced, like other people in similar situations in other cities, was proving that urban schools had deliberately participated in maintaining segregated schooling, and that it was not the result of other factors such as segregated housing (ibid., pp. 73–74). Eventually, in 1993, Rockford was found guilty on eleven counts of "willful discrimination" (ibid., p. 79).

However, seven years later, in a study of parents who had withdrawn their children from Rockford public schools, Taylor and Alves (2000), cited in Chapman, 2006, p. 85, found that:

> 47 percent of white parents and 64 percent of parents of color believed that the school board was undermining controlled choice in the district, and 68 percent of white parents and 67 percent of parents of color saw the district's actions as harmful to students.

As Chapman (her comments on this chapter) explains, the responses of the white parents are not necessarily a result of enlightened attitudes about social justice. Controlled choice was through strict quotas for student percentages, and parents balked at the quotas because it meant that their child might not be allowed to move from school to school. Later, when the district started unraveling the workings of the court order, their decisions concerning school choice and enrollments were clearly arbitrary and capricious. Parents were unhappy because of the effects the shifts had on their children.

As Chapman (2006, p. 86) concludes, although the populations of color in Rockford continue to grow—the 2000 census revealed that nearly 73 percent of the population were white, just over 17 percent African American [2010 Census figures for the white and African American populations are unchanged]; a little over 10 percent Latina/o; just over 2 percent Asian; less than 0.4 percent Native American; and 0.04 percent Pacific Islander—there has been little change in the white teachers and administrators of thirty years ago. Racism remains entrenched.

While meaningful school desegregation did occur the between 1964 and 1988 after the 1964 Civil Rights Act under the presidency of Lyndon Baines Johnson—rated by Baptiste et al. (2005) as number one among the ten most effective presidents in regards to social justice—this wave of progress toward school integration was short-lived due to a series of antidesegregation court rulings (McNeal, 2009, p. 566).

Resegregation

It is understandable that, in recent years, many parents, educators, policy makers, and other stakeholders have begun to question whether Brown v. Board of Education was substantive or merely symbolic (ibid., pp. 562–563). Large numbers of school systems remain under court-ordered mandates to desegregate (ibid., p. 564). According to the U.S. Department of Justice (2008, cited in ibid.), more than two hundred and fifty school districts still operate dual school systems. Segregated schools are growing, particularly in urban settings with high-poverty, high minority student populations (ibid.). Exemplifying how little things have changed in the twenty-first century, McNeal (2009, p. 564) cites a number of researchers who show how segregated minority schools continue to be characterized by "substandard academic achievement outcomes, low graduation rates, and poor teacher quality." For example, three of the largest segregated school districts—Detroit, Baltimore, and New York City—graduated fewer than 40 percent of students during the 2005–2006 academic year (Swanson, 2006, cited in McNeal, 2009, p. 564).

Moreover, McNeal (2009, p. 563) has drawn attention to the fact that schools are rapidly resegregating. She points out that four Supreme Court cases shaped and influenced this. Collectively, *Dowell* (1991), *Freeman* (1992), and *Missouri* (1995) "established that it is permissible for desegregation orders to end when a school district has demonstrated that it has complied with the court mandate, even if removing the desegregation order results in re-segregation" (McNeal, 2009, pp. 566–567). In 2007, the decision of the Supreme Court in the case of *Parents Involved in Community Schools v. Seattle School District No. 1* ruled that "school districts may not assign or deny students to schools on the basis of race, even if the intent is to achieve racial integration" (ibid., p. 570). McNeal (ibid., p. 570) concludes that this sends "a symbolic message that is likely to end affirmative action programs in public education, which is problematic because it will hinder current efforts to prevent the continued trend of separate and unequal schooling systems."

Lau v. Nichols *1970 and bilingual education*

The foundation ruling for bilingual education in the U.S. occurred in *Lau v. Nichols* in 1970 in San Francisco, where Chinese American students had been taught in English, a language they did not understand. After meetings and protests, the school district responded with an hour per day of English as a Second Language, but not for everyone (FindLaw, 2010). In May 1970, a lawsuit was filed against the president of the school board and the district, where it was argued that "[t]aking people who are the same and treating them differently is one type of discrimination but taking people who are different and treating them the same, is subtler, but, is equally discriminating," and that this violated the Civil Rights Act and the Fourteenth Amendment. This is a form of aversive racism where the children were excluded from the lessons routinely and treated less favorably in day-to-day interactions (see the discussion on the nine features of modern-day racism in the Introduction to this volume). As a result the schools signed a consent decree agreeing to provide bilingual education for Chinese, Filipina/o, and Latina/o children (FindLaw, 2010).

Underachievement and No Child Left Behind (NCLB)

One of the main legacies of over a century of de jure and de facto segregated and adversely differentiated schooling has been underachievement. As Edward Taylor (2006, p. 77) points out, the "racial disparity in school performance, known as the achievement gap, is evident in standardized test scores, grades, graduation rates, college completion and career tracking." Following Thompson and O'Quinn (2001), Taylor (2006, p. 77) notes that when children enter kindergarten, the gap is already about half its ultimate size. Moreover, despite their proven effectiveness in reducing the achievement gap, high-quality early childhood programs are rarely in place for minority children (Thompson and O'Quinn, 2001, cited in Taylor, 2006, p. 77).

In light of concerns expressed about the achievement gap between students of color and white students, in January 2002, President George W. Bush signed the No Child Left Behind Act (NCLB), designed "to improve student achievement and change American school culture" (Jones and Hancock, 2005, cited in Snipes and Waters, 2005, pp. 107–108). This act provided an increase to states of federal money to "improve low-performing schools." It required the states to implement student testing, collect and disseminate subgroup results, employ highly qualified teachers, and guarantee that all students from all socioeconomic backgrounds achieve academic proficiency by the 2014–2015 school year (National Conference of State Legislatures [NCSL, 2004, cited in Snipes and Waters, 2005, p. 108).

NCLB uses "high stakes" standardized tests, that as Au (2009a, p. 3, citing Kornhaber and Orfield, 2001) points out, have, over the last 25 years, become the central tool for public education "reform" in the U.S. Au (2009a, p. 3) poses the question as to whether such tests can reveal inequality and augment equality. Answering "no" to both questions, he (2009a, p. 4) notes the relationship between high-stakes testing and dropout rates, which have a disproportionate effect on working-class students and students of color. He cites a number of findings that show that, while all children are affected, high-stakes standardized testing "falls heaviest on the shoulders of low income students and students of color who are consistently found to be negatively and disproportionately affected" by them (Au, 2009a, p. 3).

Tracing the history of standardized tests since their inception in the late 1800s, Au (2009a, pp. 34–35) discusses their origins in the eugenics movement of the late nineteenth and early twentieth centuries that held that "intelligence" is genetic and certain "races" are biologically inferior to whites. Racial tracking and ability grouping in NCLB, as Edward Taylor (2006, p. 80) argues, has the effect of stigmatizing students of color and contributing to the achievement gap. Moreover, belonging to a group that is believed to be intellectually inferior means greater stress, anxiety, and self-consciousness, which themselves cause underachievement (Taylor, 2006, p. 80) (in chapter 6 of this volume I argue against fixed ability and for learning without limits).

Au (2009a, pp. 3–4) gives a current example of the state of Texas, which became the blueprint for NCLB, pointing out that the high-stakes testing and accountability movement witnessed dropout rates of at least 40 percent in 2001, the vast majority of which were African American and Latina/o students (Au, 2009a, p. 4).

NCLB has imposed harsh penalties against schools that do not make "adequate yearly progress" (AYP). Under NCLB, individual states are allowed to restructure schools, to change the curriculum, extend the length of the school day or year, and replace personnel responsible for the failure to make AYP (National Conferences of State Legislatures. 2004, cited in Snipes and Waters, 2005, p. 109).

Greaves et al. (2007) have assessed the economic and ideological imperatives inherent in NCLB, noting that the struggle between classes, in part played out in schooling, cannot be eradicated by state provision. For Marxists, they go on, although it can be used as a site of struggle and can make reforms, the state can never be neutral while serving a capitalist economy. As they put it:

> State involvement in education represents the attempt at regulation, harmonization, and rationalization. The standardizing and centralizing powers of the state allow for a practical and ideological correlation between national educational provision and national economic need. The state turns the interests of capital into national educational strategies. (ibid.)

The rhetoric of government policies such as that of NCLB, they argue, conceals other rationales such as political competitive vote-winning considerations. There is also the issue of maintaining and enhancing the meritocratic ideology. Where economic inequality is high and increasing, upward mobility between social classes has to be seen to be attainable—"the message is work hard and you'll be rewarded" (ibid.). In Althusserian terms, if such interpellation works for the impoverished masses, then they are more likely to tolerate the wealth of the few. However, "if these meritocratic messages of attainable riches, and advancement through a meritocratic education system are not widely accepted, then this poses legitimacy—and political survival problems—for political and economic elites" (ibid.). In Gramscian terminology, this aspect of the role of the capitalist state is a central aspect of ongoing attempts to maintain hegemonic control and to undermine counter-hegemonic struggle.

Moreover, with respect to pedagogy, the focus of NCLB testing is on mathematics and reading, which means that if it is not part of the test, it is not taught. This has led to the marginalization of social studies, thus further limiting space for counter-hegemonic pedagogy (Malott, 2006) (see chapter 6 of this volume for practical suggestions for counter-hegemonic pedagogy).

Another important aspect of NCLB, as Curry Malott (2006) argues, is its role in serving the needs of capital as part of the neoliberal business plans for the privatization of education. As Malott (2006) explains, "it is argued by its creators and proponents that NCLB is a policy to increase the academic performance of underperforming schools, which disproportionately serve working class and minority students, through an increase in high-stakes standardized tests to ensure accountability." However, these tests not only have high stakes for students who can be held back if they do not pass, they also have high stakes for schools that face privatization if pass rates are not high enough.

NCLB also endorses "choice" and "vouchers," whereby students can opt out of "failing" schools and invest their state and federal education monies in privately run charter schools, thus further "contributing to the privatization and commodification of public schools." School "choice" thus effectively transfers much-needed funds away from already under-funded schools attended by working-class students and students of color (Malott, 2006).

Using Gramscian analysis, Au (2009a, pp. 65–72) argues that hegemony operates through "common sense," by NCLB's making appeals to social equality, but actually serving the interests of the ruling class. In Althusserian terminology, the American people are interpellated to see NCLB as obviously a good thing because the government is intent on making sure no child is left behind. This serves to mask the real effects of the NCLB project.

President Obama has promised a number of changes to NCLB. Key features will be retained, including the annual requirement for reading and mathematics tests. Major changes have been summarized by Sam Dillon (2010) and include the following:

- replacing the pass-fail school grading system with one that would measure individual students' academic growth and judge schools not only on test scores but also on indicators such as student attendance, graduation rates, and learning climate;
- more vigorous interventions in failing schools;
- rewarding top performers and lessening federal interference in tens of thousands of "reasonably well-run schools"; and
- replacing the requirement that every child reach proficiency in reading and math with a new national target: that all students should graduate from high school prepared for college and a career.

The reality, according to Dana Milbank (2010), is that Obama has taken the worst aspect of Bush's No Child Left Behind, "an obsession with testing— and amplified it." As he explains, despite evidence that such practices are harmful, Obama "has expanded the importance of standardized testing to determine how much teachers will be paid, which educators will be fired and which schools will be closed." This prompted a coalition of civil rights groups, including the NAACP and the National Urban League (an organization dedicated to economic empowerment in order to elevate the standard of living in urban communities) to call in July 2010 for an end to "federally prescribed methodologies that have little or no evidentiary support" and that use minority communities as "testing grounds" (cited in Milbank, 2010). Also in July 2010, the American Federation of Teachers issued a statement to the effect that the Obama administration was encouraging "bad teacher evaluation systems," while a coalition of community organizing group (Communities for Excellent Public Schools) chided the administration for continuing "rigid, top-down solutions that are not supported by research" (ibid.). Later in July, Obama responded in a speech to the Urban

League, saying that his critics are "comfortable with the status quo" and have "a general resistance to change" (ibid.).

Milbank (2010) cites an education official in Bush's administration, Diane Ravitch, who has stated that "[t]he curriculum will be narrowed even more than under George W. Bush's No Child Left Behind," since:

> [t]here will be even less time available for the arts, science, history, civics, foreign language, even physical education. Teachers will teach to the test. There will be more cheating, more gaming the system.

The tests, Ravitch argues, are "simply not adequate" to separate good teachers and schools from bad (cited in Milbank, 2010).

Obama's ideological position on schooling, Giroux and Saltman (2008) claim, is exemplified by his choice of Arne Duncan as secretary of education. They are scathing of Duncan, arguing, in the face of considerable evidence gathered from when Duncan was chief education officer of the Chicago public schools, that he "embodies this utterly punitive, anti-intellectual, corporatized and test-driven model of schooling." They describe his views on schooling as follows:

> Duncan largely defines schools within a market-based and penal model of pedagogy...he does not have the slightest understanding of schools as something other than adjuncts of the corporation at best or the prison at worst.

As in other U.S. cities, as Brown et al. (2009) point out, Chicago has handed over public services to the market and privatized them, with public education in the forefront. Duncan, they go on, "closed schools in low-income neighborhoods of color with little community input, limiting local democratic control, undermining the teachers union, and promoting competitive merit pay for teachers."

With respect to charter schools, as Malott (2011b) explains, while NCLB provided what many have termed a "backdoor maneuver" that set schools up to fail through a system of high-stakes testing, allowing private, for-profit management companies to take over public education, Obama's "Race to the Top" policy goes a step further, threatening that any district or state that does not take steps to increase the number of charter schools could potentially lose federal funding. Districts that oppose charter schools or private interests controlling public education therefore risk swift sanctions. While charter schools are popping up everywhere, they are emerging most forcefully in those schools and districts that are performing at the lowest levels, according to standardized test scores. These schools tend to be in traditionally oppressed communities; that is, where the people are working class: predominantly, African American, Caribbean, refugee/immigrant, and/or Latina/o. Charter schools such as KIPP exist in neighborhoods such as the Bronx and Brooklyn. Principals of these schools have told Malott at their recruitment "happy hours," that as much as 40 percent of instruction is focused on "character" such as mannerisms and interaction styles, because, as he was told, "these students have many opportunities; they just don't know how to act right." Given the recent economic collapse and the subsequent increase in poverty and suffering, he concludes, it is not surprising that capitalist education, through charter schools, is intensifying this indoctrinating function. The last thing ruling class profiteers want is a worker rebellion (Malott, 2011b). Malott (2011b) compares these schools to the boarding schools for Native Americans that were designed to destroy Native American culture and create wage slaves (see chapter 3 of this volume).

Assessing Obama's impact on schooling as a whole, Au (2009b, p. 316) argues that parts of it must be hailed as progressive, such as the "economic stimulus package" that includes $115 billion for pre-K (pre-kindergarten) through college education (up from a total budget of $68 billion in 2008). Au (ibid.) also reminds us of the positive impact Obama's election has had on young people of color. It additionally needs pointing out that Obama is constrained by the forces of the capitalist system. As Malott (2011a) puts it, while Obama promised jobs and the alleviation of poverty and hardships experienced by an increasing number of Americans—whites as well as people of color—such promises cannot be delivered because there is nothing he can do to solve the failing capitalist neoliberal system:

> This is not only because the government has little disciplinary control over large, global corporations, but it is due to the fact that Obama and politicians in general are dependent on corporate sponsorship to win elections. It is therefore not surprising that when it came to education, Obama's administration enacted policies exactly in line with what elite, corporate interests want.

Gramscian optimism of the will is revealed in Au (2009b, p. 318)'s conclusion. Au argues, following Anyon, 2005, that ultimately it is the people who need to forge anti-hegemonic practice:

> We—youth, youth organizers, parent activists, progressives within teachers unions, veterans of the civil rights movement, rank=and-file social justice-minded teachers, and progressive academics—just need to build a national movement for educational justice ourselves.

"Hopefully," he concludes, "that movement is what the Obama election might really mean for public education."

Multicultural Education and Education Against Racism in the U.S.

Multicultural Education

Peter McLaren (1995, p. 119) identified three forms of multicultural education in the U.S.: conservative (or corporate) multiculturalism; liberal multiculturalism; and left-liberal multiculturalism.[15] Given that in the U.S. there are a large number of varieties of multicultural education, McLaren's typology, useful in conceptual analysis, should be seen as "ideal-typical[16] labels meant to serve only as a 'heuristic' device" (ibid.). As such they are useful in conceptual analysis.

Conservative (or corporate) multiculturalism is about disavowing racism while upholding corporate power (Ladson-Billings, 2005, p. 53). As Ladson-Billings puts it, "[c]orporate or conservative multiculturalism has a veneer of diversity without any commitment to social justice or structural change" (ibid.). She gives the example of Sears, the major U.S. retail outlet, which has targeted black and Latina/o consumers (ibid., p. 50). With respect to schooling, she argues that even though there may be representations of minority groups in texts and school curriculum, they may well be marginalized (ibid., p. 53). Ladson-Billings (ibid.) cites a typical textbook strategy of placing information about subordinated groups in a "special features" section while the main text, carrying the dominant discourse, remains "uninterrupted and undisturbed by 'multicultural information.'"

Liberal multiculturalism, on the other hand, in McLaren's (1995, p. 124) words, is based on the premise of "intellectual 'sameness'" among the races...that permits them to compete equally in a capitalist society." In other words, it is predicated on meritocracy and equal opportunities within capitalism (Ladson-Billings, 2005, p. 53). As Ladson-Billings explains, most campuses offer programs for all groups, but in isolation, and white middle class norms prevail (ibid.). Moreover, as she concludes, "[b]y acknowledging the existence of various groups while simultaneously ignoring the issues of power and structural inequity, liberal multiculturalism functions as a form of appeasement" (ibid.).

McLaren's (1995, pp. 124–125) third form of multiculturalism, the "left-liberal" variety, in Ladson-Billings' (2005, p. 54) words, exoticizes cultural differences. In an earlier paper with William Tate (Ladson-Billings and Tate, 1995, p. 61), this form of multicultural education is described as trivia: "artefacts of cultures such as eating ethnic or cultural foods, singing songs or dancing, reading folktales" (as we saw earlier in this chapter, the dominant form of multicultural education in the U.K. is very similar to this approach).

None of these forms of multicultural education in the U.S. (as in the U.K.) poses any real challenge to institutional racism. Indeed, in refusing to name racism and racialization, they have the effect, if not the intention, of perpetuating and exacerbating racism and racialization. Not one of the three, of course, is counter-hegemonic to capitalism and imperialism, past or present. Indeed, with respect to the deployment of terminology in this volume, they would, as noted above in the case of the U.K., be more aptly described as multicultural *schooling*. By using people of color for profit or as marginal, as in the case of conservative multiculturalism; or promoting the ideologies of meritocracy and equal opportunities, as in the case of liberal multiculturalism; or cultural trivia, as with left-liberal multiculturalism, these varieties of multicultural education are conducive to the maintenance and furtherance of the racialized capitalist state.[17]

Revolutionary Multiculturalism

Perhaps the closest to U.K. Marxist-based antiracist education is revolutionary multiculturalism as currently advocated by McLaren and his co-authors. Thus McLaren and Ramin Farahmandpur (2005, p. 147) champion revolutionary multiculturalism as a framework "for developing a pedagogical praxis...[which] opens up social and political spaces for the oppressed to challenge on their own terms and in their own ways the various forms of class, race, and gender oppression that are reproduced by dominant social relations." Echoing the position taken in this volume, McLaren and Scatamburlo-D'Annibale (2010) argue that, while racism often does take on a life of its own, its material basis can be traced to the means and relations of production within capitalist society—to the social division of labor that occurs when workers sell their labor-power for a wage to the capitalist (i.e., to the ownership of the means of production). To ignore class exploitation when you are talking about racism is a serious mistake.

The educational implications are that it is important to bring education into conversation with movements that speak to the larger totality of capitalist social relations and that challenge capital's social universe. The strategic focus for Marxist educators, if we are to have effective antiracist, anti-sexist, anti-homophobic struggles [I would add anti-disablism struggles], should be, they argue, on capitalist exploitation (ibid.). Nonrevolutionary multiculturalism, they continue, fails to foreground the fundamental importance of the social division of labor in the capitalist production process as a key factor in understanding racism. "The reason we need to focus on a critique of political economy in our anti-racist efforts," they argue, "is that racism in capitalist society results from the racialization of the social relations of capitalist exploitation" (ibid.).

McLaren is unequivocal in his commitment to a class analysis, and to the struggle for socialism. As Suoranta, McLaren, and Jaramillo (2000) put it:

> Our own attempts to develop a radical humanistic socialism—in part by dewriting socialism as a thing of the past—assumes the position that socialism and pedagogical socialist principles are not dead letters, but open pages in the book of social and economic justice yet to be written or rewritten by people struggling to build a truly egalitarian social order.

For revolutionary educators the pedagogical is the political, and creating pedagogical spaces for self- and social transformation are co-constitutive of building socialism for the twenty-first century (McLaren, 2008, p. 480).

Although it is central to Left radical versions of multicultural education, antiracist education as a descriptive term is not one that has been widely used in the U.S., particularly without the hyphen as it is commonly used in the U.K. This is emphatically not to deny the significant minority antiracist activity practiced daily in U.S. schools (see, for example, Au, (ed.) 2009;

see also the radical left journal, *Rethinking Schools,* available at http://www. rethinkingschools.org/index.shtml).

Conclusion

In this chapter I began by making a distinction between schooling and education. I went on to look at racism as it relates to schooling in the U.K., from the imperial curriculum of the (early) twentieth century, through the coming home to roost of the British Empire in the post-World War II period. I then addressed antiracist education, and ongoing threats to it historically and up to the present ConDem government.

I then turned my attention to racism and schooling in the U.S., examining developments from Plessy v. Ferguson (1896) up to the present, my particular focus being on segregation and underachievement. I concluded the chapter with a consideration of multicultural and antiracist initiatives in the U.S. Although multicultural education was proclaimed to reach all children, and to undermine inequalities in both U.K. and U.S. schools, because it was divorced from sociopolitical concerns, it lost much of its meaning; and initiatives centralizing antiracism (whether that is the describing term or not), informed by Marxism, I believe, are more conducive to progressive change. However, given advances in technology, most significantly the World Wide Web to enable authentic voices to be heard, counter-hegemonic *multicultural antiracist education* as part of a curriculum that also includes the case for socialism, is now, I suggest, a viable proposition (this is developed in chapter 6 of this volume). Before turning to a consideration of such practice, I look in chapter 5 to Venezuela to determine what can be learned from experiences there.

Chapter 5

Twenty-First-Century Socialism and Education in the Bolivarian Republic of Venezuela

In chapter 4, I made a distinction between schooling, on the one hand, and education on the other, with the former referring to the processes by which young people are attuned to the requirements of capitalism both in the form and the content of schooling, and the latter, "a more liberatory process from birth to death, a process of human emancipation and socialism." In many ways, the whole Bolivarian project of twenty-first-century socialism is *in its very essence* education in that sense of the word. As we shall see, the revolutionary president of Venezuela has described the country as "a giant school." In order to understand how this extraordinary project came about, it is necessary to look briefly at some economic and political historical antecedents before addressing the advent of the government of Hugo Chávez, the ensuing ascendancy of social democracy, and the move toward socialism. After that I address some of the forces opposing the Bolivarian Revolution. I then assess Chávez's call for a Fifth International, in light of previous Socialist Internationals, discussed in chapter 1 of this volume. Given the unique scenario of Chávez's call for the abolition of the state that he represents, I return to a consideration of the (neo-)Marxist theory of the capitalist state, and suggest a possible amendment of the theory. I then address racism and anti-racism in Venezuelan society in general, before concluding with a consideration of the effects of the overall Bolivarian educational processes at the level of individual educational institutions. As a case study, I outline the work of revolutionary socialist educators in an alternative school started by residents and activists in Barrio Pueblo Nuevo in Mérida, Western Venezuela.

The Bolivarian Revolution

Education, as what I have called "a liberatory process from birth to death, a process of human emancipation and socialism," is articulated by Hugo Rafael Chávez Frías, president of the Bolivarian Republic of Venezuela. In

2010, Chávez described knowledge and education as the first of three forms of power in the revolutionary process, the others being political power and economic power:

> When we talk about power, what are we talking about…The first power that we all have is knowledge. So we've made efforts first in education, against illiteracy, for the development of thinking, studying, analysis. In a way, that has never happened before. Today, Venezuela is a giant school, it's all a school. From children of one year old until old age, all of us are studying and learning. And then political power, the capacity to make decisions, the community councils, communes, the people's power, the popular assemblies. And then there is the economic power. Transferring economic power to the people, the wealth of the people distributed throughout the nation. I believe that is the principal force that precisely guarantees that the Bolivarian revolution continues to be peaceful.[1] (cited in Sheehan, 2010)

In Gramscian terms, what Chávez is describing is the fostering of the development of organic intellectuals of the working class.

Earlier in 2010, Chávez asserted that, as well as a Christian, he was also a Marxist (Chávez, 2010a), describing Marxism as "the most advanced proposal toward the world that Christ came to announce more than 2,000 years ago" (Suggett, 2010).

Some historical antecedents

In order to make sense of the Bolivarian revolution and its educational process both at the level of the society as a whole, and at the level of the individual educational institution, it is necessary to dwell briefly on some economic and political antecedents. Diana Raby (2006, pp. 140–141) documents events in Venezuela in the wake of the collapse of the international price of oil in 1982. She notes that spending on social programs and a state-sponsored industrialization plan by the previous president, Carlos Andrés Pérez (1974–1979), had been financed by massive oil revenue (part of which had also been squandered on consumption and corruption) but also by international credit. In 1983, under the presidency of Luis Herrera Campins, Venezuela's credit ran out, and after 1983, investment collapsed, inflation rose, and the Venezuelan rich transferred their money to the U.S. The currency was devalued, and the government was soon forced to accept IMF deflationary packages and austerity measures. This marked the end of the boom of the 1970s, and the economic and social situation deteriorated steadily, with devaluation producing a vicious circle in which production fell and inflation and unemployment rose. As a result, poverty increased among the poor in the barrios, and the middle classes felt their comfortable lifestyles threatened (Raby, 2006, pp. 140–141).[2]

In this critical scenario, Pérez returned to the scene, and in the course of the 1988 election, promised reforms to protect living standards. His attempts to evoke memories of the boom years of his presidency in the 1970s worked and he once again became president (ibid., p. 141).

Early in 1989, Pérez reneged on his promises and initiated a number of policies formulated in the U.S., which became known as the "Washington Consensus." These were based squarely on neo-liberal capitalist principles (see chapter 1, Note 1 of this volume), and were foisted on Latin American and Caribbean governments as a condition for their obtaining international loans; and also by threats (Victor, 2009).[3] The country worst effected, Victor (2009) goes on, was the country that most thoroughly applied them— Venezuela. The first popular uprising against the measures took place all over that country in February 1989, and about three thousand people were killed by armed troops (ibid.). The Caracazo, as it became known, seemed to intuit that in reaction to the adjustment measures imposed by the Pérez government, a new future was possible. This was a key moment in the events leading up to the election of Chávez as president of Venezuela in 1998. The overall counter-hegemonic responses of the people in 1980s and 1990s in Latin America, however, as William Robinson (2006) argues, represented not uprisings, but in Gramscian terms a "war of position" in civil society (involving a long cultural and ideological struggle—a battle of ideas— whereby socialists attempt to expose the real nature of the system and put forward their alternative). At the same time, the new transnationally oriented elites successfully engaged in cemented hegemony over political society.

But by the late 1990s, however, Robinson goes on, the neo-liberal states of Latin America were coming under assault from the popular classes, who themselves had been transformed and reorganized by new forms of globalization (Robinson, 2006). Throughout the region mass social movements and new leftist groups challenged the state in what appears to be a renovated Gramscian "war of maneuver" (a frontal attack aimed at winning quickly) under novel circumstances of the global economy and society (ibid). Robinson cites the mass struggles of indigenous people in Bolivia, the rise of Lula in Brazil, the Broad Front in Uruguay, the resurgence of the Party of the Democratic Revolution in Mexico, and the Bolivarian revolution in Venezuela.

These counter-hegemonic responses, Robinson (2006) concludes, point to the inability of the neo-liberal states to put in place a viable model of capital accumulation or to achieve legitimacy and stability, in short, to their impending breakdown.

Hugo Chávez, Social Democracy, and Twenty-First-Century Socialism

By 1998, as a result of the aforementioned neo-liberal policies, Victor (2009) describes Venezuela thusly: "this oil-rich country's economy was in ruins, schools and hospitals were almost derelict, and almost 80 percent of the population was impoverished." In that year, Hugo Chávez won the presidential elections in Venezuela by a landslide, and inaugurated a participatory democracy.

In representative democracies such as the U.K. and the U.S., political participation is by and large limited to parliamentary politics—which represent the
imperatives of capitalism, rather than the real needs and interests of the people.
Participatory democracy, on the other hand, involves direct decision-making
by the people. Victor (2009) concisely summarizes Chávez's impact:

> Immediately the elites and middle classes opposed him as an upstart, an
> Indian who does not know his place, a Black who is a disgrace to the position.[4]
> Hugo Chávez established a new Constitution that re-set the rules of a govern-
> ment that had been putty in the hands of the elites. Ratified in overwhelming
> numbers, the Constitution gave indigenous peoples, for the first time, the
> constitutional right to their language, religion, culture and lands. It estab-
> lished Human Rights, civil and social, like the right to food, a clean environ-
> ment, education, jobs, and health care, binding the government to provide
> them. It declared the country a participatory democracy with direct input of
> people into political decision making through their communal councils and it
> asserted government control of oil revenues: Oil belongs to the people.

Vast oil revenues and reserves, Victor (2009) goes on, have been used to
meet the real needs of the Venezuelan people. Little over ten years have seen
the virtual eradication of illiteracy, a dramatic lowering of infant mortality,
the lowest rate of malnutrition in South America, and the lowest unemployment in decades. At the same time, "the great majority of the people have
direct access to free health care, free schools, a network of daycare, a subsidized food distribution network, and subsidized medicines" (Victor, 2009;
see also Willgress, 2010, pp. 4–5 for the statistics). The "missions," a series
of social justice, social welfare, anti-poverty, and educational programs, have
massively reduced poverty and greatly increased educational opportunities,
all essential in the creation of organic intellectuals of the working class (for a
discussion of the missions, see, for example, Cole, 2009a, pp. 125–127).

As Victor (2009) points out, the revolutionary government of the
Bolivarian Republic of Venezuela has also brokered the beginning of solid,
true integration of the Latin American continent and the Caribbean in the
creation of the following:

- TeleSUR, a TV channel fed by the state TV stations of the continent, so
  that people learn from one another and enjoy Latin American news, art,
  and music, directly, and not through the mediation of CNN;
- ALBA (Alianza Bolivariana para los Pueblos de Nuestra América), an association of solidarity where economic projects are geared toward social justice and human development.
- PETEROSUR, a consortium of the state oil companies of Latin America
  to make sure that the oil and gas is used not just to fuel the growth of
  richer nations, but to help the infrastructure needed at home.
- Petrocaribe, an initiative to provide much-needed fuel to the smaller
  Caribbean nations with preferential financial arrangements and a fund for
  joint projects.

- The Banco del Sur, representing the liberation of Latin America from the usury and hegemony of the IMF, World Bank, and other international banks and organizations, the loans of which have imposed neo-liberal capitalist policies on governments.
- UNASUR (Unión de Naciones Suramericanas), a defense organization of Latin America, that asserts that it alone assumes the defense of the region. UNASUR has an energy council to put in place safeguards for the supply of energy for the region to protect the natural environment. UNASUR rejects the Monroe Doctrine of 1823, which effectively asserted the U.S.'s sole right to defend the region.

All of these measures, of course, entail a massive educational project *for* the Venezuelan people, and other peoples in the region, and indeed the world. They represent a major challenge to U.S. imperial hegemony, and its attendant ideological and repressive apparatuses.

While the innovations allow the export of socialist ideas and ideals, they are, of course, in themselves classic social democracy (see Note 12 of chapter 1 of this volume) rather than socialism, somewhat akin to the policies and practice of the postwar Labour governments in the U.K. What makes Venezuela unique, however, is that whereas these British Labour governments were posing social democracy as an *alternative* to socialism, and, indeed, attempting to fight off attempts by revolutionary workers to move toward socialism, Chávez is presenting reforms as a *prelude* to socialism. These reforms are seen both by sections of the Chávez government and by large sections of the Venezuelan working class[5] as a step on the road to true socialist revolution. At the same time, Chávez is promoting genuine participatory democracy that is laying the foundations for the socialist project. Thus for Chávez, "[t]he hurricane of revolution has begun, and it will never again be calmed" (cited in Contreras Baspineiro, 2003). Elsewhere, Chávez asserted: "I am convinced, and I think that this conviction will be for the rest of my life, that the path to a new, better and possible world, is not capitalism, the path is socialism, that is the path: socialism, socialism" (Lee, 2005).

As Victor (2009) argues, one of the biggest achievements of the Bolivarian Revolution is existential: "a new sense of identity, a new sense of belonging...The great majority of Venezuelans feel they are now in control of their own government and destiny—despite the continuous attacks from the oligarchy and its satellites. Now the Chávistas frame all the political discourse and its name is Socialism of the 21st Century." Socialism cannot be decreed from above (see the comment on this by Gerardo in the case study toward the end of this chapter). The people discuss Chávez and they support him, but they are aware that they are the motor of the revolution. It is worth quoting Victor (2009) at length:

> For the first time since the fall of the Berlin Wall, a country in the world repudiates the barbaric version of capitalism that has prevailed since Ronald Reagan and Margaret Thatcher, and embraces a new socialism, one that has its

roots in the indigenous people's socialism, in Liberation Theology[6] which was born in Latin America, in Humanism, in the inspiration of Cuba, as well as the works of Marx, but not exclusively in European socialism. It is not Stalinism, it is not a copy of what has passed for socialism to date, but Venezuela's own brand infused with the idea that the people are the protagonists of democracy, that the economy should serve people, not the other way around, and that only their active and direct participation in political decision making will free the country from corruption and inequality.

Writing toward the end of 2009, Luke Stobart (2009) argues that there were positive developments in that year when organized workers at the biggest factories in the country won several major battles for nationalization, including partial or total workers' control. Chávez supported the struggles, arguing that nationalized "state capitalist" firms need workers' democracy to become "socialist."

More recently (October 2010), Chávez announced the nationalization of the Spanish agro company, Agroisleña, which will be renamed Agropatria; the privately owned oil and derivatives company, Venoco; and the agro industrial company Fertinitro. In addition, complete control will be taken of hundreds of thousands of hectares of land, including some 130,000 head of cattle, owned by La Compañía Inglesa (The English Company), which is controlled by the Vestey Group (Rosales, 2010) . Chávez also announced a new housing program, and repeated calls to "banish bureaucracy and inefficiency" in the state apparatus. Finally, new "revolutionary laws" are promised to be imminent (ibid.).

Forces Opposing the Bolivarian Revolution

The Bolivarian Revolution faces three major opponents. First, international capitalism, particularly the U.S. Empire; second, the organized political opposition in Venezuela representing Venezuelan capital, and itself aligned to U.S. imperialism and capitalism; third, self-aggrandizement, corruption, and racism (for "racism," see later in this chapter) within the Venezuelan governmental and political state apparatuses.

International capitalism

With respect to this first oppositional force, the ideological apparatuses of the U.S., the U.K., and other states are engaged in a major propaganda campaign against Chávez. Capitalists and their political supporters are intent on spreading disinformation about him. In particular, there are numerous attempts to label Chávez nondemocratic or "dictatorial." As Pablo Navarrete (2010) has pointed out, both the right wing and more liberal communications ISAs give Chávez negative coverage. Thus Rupert Murdoch's right wing Fox News channel in the U.S. regularly refers to Chávez as a dictator, despite the fact that there have been twelve national elections during his time as president, "most of which received unprecedented levels of scrutiny by international observers and were systematically deemed as free and fair." At the same time, the supposedly more neutral U.K.-based BBC News online has been researched by Lee Salter (2009). As Navarrete (2010) notes of Salter's work, of 304 BBC reports on Venezuela between 1998 and 2008, "only three mentioned any of the Chavez government's positive reforms—such as poverty reduction programmes that have more than halved the poverty rate from 46.5% in 1998 to 23% in 2009." Instead the BBC has tended to insinuate that Chávez lacks electoral support, and in one instance compared him to Hitler. Chávez (2010b) has responded personally to accusations of dictatorship:

> I am against dictatorships...I've been elected one, two, three, four times, by popular vote. In Venezuela, we have elections all the time. Every year, we have elections in Venezuela. One time, Lula, the president of Brazil...when he was in Europe, someone asked him "Why are you friends with that dictator Chavez?" And Lula said a big truth: "In Venezuela, there is an excess of democracy. Every year there are elections. And if there aren't any, Chavez invents them." Referendums, popular consultations, elections for governors, mayors. Right now, soon we are starting national assembly elections, this year. In 2012 there is going to be a presidential election again. What dictator is elected so many times? What dictator convenes referendums? I'm an anti-dictator. I am a revolutionary. A democratic revolutionary. (cited in Cindy Sheehan, 2010)

On February 15, 2009, more than eleven million Venezuelans, out of almost seventeen million who were eligible, voted by a clear majority to end presidential term limits—the number of terms a person may serve in a particular elected office, allowing Chávez to be elected or *not elected* without limit. Ideological state apparatuses throughout the world, as well as opposition groups within Venezuela, maliciously portrayed this as Chávez wanting to stay in power forever, as his attempt at virtual unending dictatorship. Luis Perdomo, founding member of the Network of Afro-Venezuelan Organizations (see later in this chapter) has reflected on this referendum. As he puts it, "[t]his was not about the reelection of Chávez, this was about the reelection of the political process, because as Chávez himself stated: he is only a piece of the revolution. It's not that Chávez is going to reelect himself. No, it's the people that are going to reelect him" (cited in Martinez et al., 2010, p. 226).

With respect to the repressive apparatus of the state, the U.S. has positioned thirteen military bases around Venezuela (Ramonet, 2010). In addition, refusing to disclose the recipients, the U.S. government poured millions of dollars into Venezuela, via USAID, as the noncovert part of their funding for the opposition in the 2010 election to the National Assembly (Weisbrot, 2010).

Venezuelan Political Opposition

The result of this election was an increase in the number of seats for the anti-Chávez Coalition. Given that the last legislative elections, in 2005, were boycotted by this opposition in an attempt to delegitimize the government, their participation in 2010 was bound to result in an increase in their presence in the government. It was the recognition that the opposition would make attempts to block progressive legislation in the new parliament in January 2011 that provided the impetus for the aforementioned announcements in October 2010 of major nationalizations.

As far as the complexion of this organized internal political opposition is concerned, Raby (2006, p. 167) points out that it "finally tore off 'ts' democratic mask" in the military coup of 2002, after which the head of Fedecámaras (the Federation of Chambers of Commerce) Pedro Carmona Estanga swore himself in as "provisional president" and renamed the country "the Republic of Venezuela" (no longer the "Bolivarian Republic"). Carmona's junta immediately dissolved the Congress, dismissed all elected officials, got rid of the Supreme Court, the National Election Tribunal, and the office of the Ombudsman. Civil liberties were suspended and a witch hunt undertaken against Chávistas. However, the coup was defeated within forty hours by a mass popular uprising supported by progressive people in the military. It involved Chávez's supporters descending from the barrios surrounding Caracas on April 13, 2002 to defend their president (Martinez et al., 2010, p. 24) and successfully demanding his release from prison and return to office.

As far as the *supporters* of the antisocialist parties are concerned, Edward Ellis (his comments on this chapter) has referred to the ideological barriers blocking the revolutionary process. He argues that the upper and middle classes (in the sociological sense of the term), their perceptions shaped by U.S. and European capitalism, view their own excessive "consumerism and material gain" almost as "a birthright" owing to the country's oil wealth. "The opposition," Ellis goes on, "is a cultural manifestation of exactly what Chávez wants to get rid of" but finds difficult due to the pervasiveness of the capitalist ideology in the country. Such an ideology, Ellis suggests, also pervades the mentality of some Chávez supporters.

Chávez is accused of trying to exert hegemonic control of the communications ISA, specifically by repressing the media, even though most of it is in the hands of the opposition. As Mark Weisbrot (2010) points out, the media is far more in opposition to the Bolivarian government than that in the U.S., and in most of the world. Referring to Chávez's shutting down of illegal radio stations, Weisbrot notes, "[i]n Washington D.C., if I try to broadcast on an FM radio frequency without a legal broadcast license, I will be shut down. When this happens in Venezuela, it is reported as censorship."

Corruption and self-aggrandizement within the Bolivarian Revolution

As far as the third form of opposition to the Bolivarian Revolution is concerned, while there are genuine revolutionaries with a socialist vision within the pro-Chávez political and governmental state apparatuses, there is also corruption and self-aggrandizement within these apparatuses. Grassroots organizers have described this as a "bureaucracy," "the endogenous right," "the Fourth Republic within *Chavismo*," "the Boli-bourgeoisie" (Martinez et al., 2010, p. 23). As Luis Perdomo has argued, many government officials, on becoming ministers or heads of a department in an institution, act as if they own that institution. As he puts it, "[b]eing a revolutionary is modelled by the attention given to the people...We don't want to be a deck of cards shuffled by someone else...we want to shuffle the deck. We want to construct along with the president and the assembly representatives, and the ministers as well" (cited in ibid., pp. 230–231).

Greg Wilpert (2007, 2010, p. viii) has also described the practices of "clientelism-patronage" and "personalism," the former referring to politicians' use of government resources such as jobs or material benefits to favor their own supporters against political opponents; the latter to the tendency among both citizens and political leaders to place greater importance on loyalty to politicians than to political programs.

It should be pointed out that Chávez showed awareness that some of the delegates present at his call for a Fifth International (see immediately below in this chapter) had been elected by irregular means and that some people were only interested in getting elected to parliament or becoming mayors and governors. He described this as unacceptable (Woods, 2009).

The Call for a Fifth International

Addressing delegates at the "International Encounter of Left Parties" that took place in Caracas in November 2009, Chávez stated, "the time has come for us to convoke the Fifth International" (cited in Fuentess, 2009). Faced with the capitalist crisis and the threat of war that is putting the future of humanity at risk, Chávez went on, "the people are clamoring for" greater unity of left and revolutionary parties willing to fight for socialism (cited in ibid.).

As Fuentess, 2009 puts it, "[l]ike his call in 2005 to build '21st Century Socialism' and his call in 2006 for the creation in Venezuela of a new, mass revolutionary party—the United Socialist Party of Venezuela (PSUV)—Chavez's call to unite the left in a new International is historic." This builds on the experiences of the four previous Socialist "Internationals," the first of which, as we saw in chapter 1 of this volume, included Karl Marx, and was founded in 1864.[7]

Given the political kudos of those centrally associated with previous Socialist Internationals, and the current stature of Chávez, Fuentess (ibid.) is surely correct in claiming this intervention to be "also historic because of the political authority of Chávez himself: the leader of a revolutionary movement made up of millions struggling for a socialist society." However, it should also be stressed, as Alan Woods (2009) argues, that Chávez's intervention clearly "reflects the enormous pressure from the masses below who are getting tired of talk about socialism, while real progress towards genuine change appears to be frustratingly slow." Woods suggests that this highlights the central problem: "[a]fter 11 years there are signs that the masses are becoming impatient and frustrated with the slow pace of the revolution." "The crisis of capitalism," Woods goes on, "is having an effect, and many are disgusted with the bureaucracy and corruption they see everywhere, including [as discussed in this chapter] within the Bolivarian Movement itself."

A majority of the delegates passed the following resolution founding the Fifth Socialist International:

> as a space for socialist-oriented parties, movements and currents in which we can harmonize a common strategy for the struggle against imperialism, the overthrow of capitalism by socialism. (cited in Fuentess, 2009)

Fuentess (ibid.) points out that there were delegates from fifty-five parties from more than thirty countries, including of course the PSUV, and representatives from other Latin American countries, but also comrades from Africa and the Middle East, from Asia and Europe.

Chávez reaffirmed the call for a Fifth International in front of over 700 delegates of the PSUV at the party's first "Extraordinary Congress," also in November 2009. The majority of the delegates were workers, peasants, and students, elected by around 2.5 million grassroots voters (the total membership of the PSUV is seven million) (Woods, 2009). Chávez insisted that the debates must be democratic, and take different opinions into account. He also insisted that delegates must report back to the rank and file and then discuss with them all the different proposals and documents (Woods, 2009). Chávez also made it clear that the discussion "must go out to the people, to the social organizations and other forms of popular power in the country," and will be discussed by Left parties around the world, with a view to building a mass revolutionary party" (cited in Fuentess, 2009.).

Chávez argued at the "International Encounter of Left Parties" that the conditions to build socialism are ripe: "[t]hat is why I ask...that you allow me continue to go forward, together with those who want to accompany me, in the creation of the Fifth Socialist International"—a new international without manuals and impositions, explained Chávez, where differences are welcomed (ibid.). Chávez sharply criticized the example of the Communist Party of the Soviet Union, a party that imposed its dogmas such as "socialism in one country" (ibid.). In rejecting the failed projects of "real socialism" and social democracy, Chávez argued that a new International should embody the spirit and the accumulated heritage left to humanity by the founders of the first Four Internationals as well as Latin American radicals such as Simon Bolivar, Francisco Morazán, Maurice Bishop, and Augusto Sandino[8] (ibid.).

Fuentess concludes that, while various parties expressed their reservations, the response in favor of the proposal was very strong. A special resolution to create a "working group comprised of those socialist parties, currents, and social movements who endorse the initiative, to prepare an agenda which defines the objectives, contents, and mechanisms of this global revolutionary body" was approved, as was a document entitled the "Caracas Commitment" (ibid.). This document stated that in the face of a "structural crisis of capital, which combines the economic crisis, with an ecological crisis, a food crisis, and an energy crisis, and which together represents a mortal threat to humanity and the mother earth," the only alternative possible is "Socialism of the 21st Century" (ibid).

Stressing the lessons to be learned from the first Four Internationals at the PSUV Congress, Chávez pointed out that all of them had been convened in Europe, "where the thesis of scientific socialism emerged with force in the heat of the great popular workers' struggles, and the domination of the bourgeoisie." Today, however, he pointed out:

> the epicenter of revolutionary struggle is in our America. And Venezuela is the epicenter of this battle. It is up to us to assume the role of the vanguard and we have to assume it, so that we realize and become aware of the huge responsibility we have on our shoulders. (cited in Fuentess)[9]

Making further reference to the current world capitalist crisis, Chávez condemned Western governments' attempts to save capitalism, adding that task should be to destroy it (Woods, 2009). Acknowledging that in Venezuela, capitalism had not been destroyed, and that the Venezuelan state remained a capitalist state, he argued that things were moving in that direction of socialism, and announced the state takeover of seven banks (ibid.). As Alan Woods (2009) explains, "[w]aving a copy of Lenin's *State and Revolution* (which he recommended all the delegates to read), he said that he accepted Lenin's view that it was necessary to destroy the bourgeois state and replace it with a revolutionary state, and this task remained to be carried out."

Chávez also talked of revolutionary trade unionism, and the need for the working class to play a leading role in the revolution. As he put it, "[t]he consciousness of the working class is key to the building of socialism." He added that there must be a close alliance between the party and the workers (Woods, 2009).

Woods (2009) concludes:

> It is clear that Chavez is attempting to use the congress to breathe new life into the revolution. Let us hope that this will be the starting point for a new advance of the Bolivarian Revolution, which can only succeed by going onto the offensive, breaking radically with capitalism, striking blows against the reactionary oligarchy and establishing a genuine workers' state as the necessary condition for advancing to socialism and launching a revolutionary wave throughout the Americas and on a world scale.

(Neo-)Marxist Theory, the Venezuelan State, and the Communal Councils

"The revolution within the revolution" is commonly used to describe the role of grassroots activists in pressuring government officials and institutions to remain committed to participatory and revolutionary democracy—central to the Bolivarian Revolution as defined by Chávez, as opposed to representative democracy, common to capitalist parliamentary democracy.[10] While representative democracy entails the retention of the capitalist state, whether it be in its social democratic or neo-liberal mode, participatory and revolutionary democracy, on the Bolivarian model, means overthrowing the capitalist state, a project to which, as we have seen earlier in this chapter, Chávez is committed (see also, for example, references to Chávez's speeches in Cole, 2009a, pp. 127–130). This is in line with (neo-)Marxist theory—the capitalist state must be overthrown rather than reformed.[11] As Althusser (1971, p. 141) puts it:

> the proletariat must seize State power in order to destroy the existing bourgeois State apparatus and, in a first phase, replace it with a quite different proletarian, State apparatus, then in later phases set in motion... the end of State power, the end of every State apparatus.

In January 2007, Chávez created "communal councils," and referred to "the revolutionary explosion of communal power" (Socialist Outlook Editorial, 2007). This is a project for rebuilding or replacing the bourgeois administrative machinery of local and state governments with a network of communal councils, where the local populations meet to decide on local priorities and how to realize them (ibid.). "With the communal councils," Chávez said, in perhaps his most clearly articulated intention to destroy the existing state:

> we have to go beyond the local. We have to begin creating...a kind of confederation, local, regional and national, of communal councils. We have to head towards the creation of a communal state. And the old bourgeois state, which is still alive and kicking—this we have to progressively dismantle, at the same time as we build up the communal state, the socialist state, the Bolivarian state, a state that is capable of carrying through a revolution. (cited in ibid)

"Almost all states," Chávez continued, "have been born to prevent revolutions. So we have quite a task: to convert a counter-revolutionary state into a revolutionary state" (cited in Piper, 2007, p. 8).

The communal councils represent the bringing together of two hundred to four hundred families to discuss and decide on local spending and development plans. Thirty thousand communal councils are intended, and provide, in the words of Roland Dennis, an historic opportunity to do away with the capitalist state (ibid.). While the communal councils provide the *legal* mechanism to organize locally, the construction of popular power has also taken the form of the creation of cooperatives, the taking over of factories, the occupation of urban and rural lands, the launching of communal TV and radio stations, the building of centers for popular education and culture, and many other initiatives (Martinez et al., 2010, p. 3). As Carlos Martinez et al. (2010, pp. 3–4) point out, many of these acts have been motivated by the words of Chávez, or have been facilitated by the Chávez government, while, at the same time, those behind such actions need to continue to pressure the government for support to succeed or survive. The crucial fact is that the Chávez government, in forging ahead with the creation of organic intellectuals of the working class, is supporting revolution from below.

Althusser's analysis did not extend to the possible existence of heads of states who advocate their own state's destruction. Chávez's advocacy of the destruction of the bourgeois state that he heads may require a rethinking of (neo-)Marxist theory.

Venezuela and Racism

The colonial legacy

As Victor (2009) points out, institutional racism from the late sixteenth to the mid-nineteenth centuries entailed Spanish colonizers methodically attempting to substitute Latin American cultures for a European one. "The colonial elites" that emerged, she argues, took their cue from the Spanish aristocracy. In other words, "[t]hey had little interest in developing agriculture or industry except in as much as it allowed them to live in opulence."

Colonial society was based on a rigid legalized system of dominative institutionalized racialization, with ruling class whites the dominating elite possessing documents "to prove the 'purity' of their Spanish blood if they wanted to attain certain positions of power or join the professions" (Victor, 2009). Whites of lower socioeconomic class were limited to "lesser occupations and positions," while the rest were considered "mixed" and "inferior peoples," or "pardos," legally classified by this "racial mix" in the following way:

> [M]ulattos were white and black, Tercerones were mulatto and white; Cuarterones were Terceron and white; Quinteron were white and Cuarteron; and Zambo were Indian with mulato or black. (ibid.)

Covert dominative institutional racism was such that "colonial rules micro-managed all social life and any education or cultural expression were those approved by the elites," all of which was in turn subject to Spanish censorship, "ubiquitous in literature, history and the arts" (ibid.).

Throughout the colonial era, indigenous and black people were considered lazy, unreliable, and wicked, with Spain justifying their subjugation to "itself and the world, as part of the evangelization of otherwise savage peoples" (ibid.). As Victor (2009) concludes, two objectives were foremost: the destruction of any traditional religion that was not their version of Christianity, and the eradication of indigenous languages, more than one thousand of which disappeared in five hundred years; in other words, two per year (Baez, 2008, p. 103, cited in Victor, 2009).

Like the rest of Latin America, Venezuela's history is scarred by colonialism's and imperialism's racist legacies.

Racism, antiracism, and twenty-first-century socialism

With the gains being made by the Chávez government and the growing mass revolutionary movement, Venezuela is now in a position to seriously and effectively confront this racist legacy. However, combating racism is no easy task for at least three reasons.

First and foremost, institutionalized racism remains in Venezuelan society. As founding member of the Network of Afro-Venezuelan Organizations Luis Perdomo has put it, there is "institutional racism in the midst of the revolutionary process" (cited in Martinez et al., 2010, pp. 229–230). Perdomo is, in part, referring to racism in "whole institutions," such as schools that are still not teaching children "their history and culture as afro-descendants" (cited in ibid., p. 229). Representative of the Afro-Venezuelan Youth Network, Freddy Blanco (cited in ibid.), has also highlighted the institutional racism of the prison system, when he notes that the vast majority of the Venezuelan prison population (as in the U.K. and the U.S.) is made up of Afro-descendants.

Perdomo's reference to "institutional racism in the midst of the revolutionary process" also indicts the National Assembly. He points out that the two times he went to speak with representatives in the assembly, he was met first in the front entrance of the building, and second, at the back entrance, whereas others, including members of the opposition, have been received in the National Assembly Hall. Blanco also makes the point that people working in all of the government ministry offices mostly have phenotypically European features, and many of them treat Afro-Venezuelans as "inferior" (cited in ibid., p. 230). For these reasons, the network is proposing a national law against racism and discrimination (cited in ibid., pp. 229–230) (see chapter 4 of this volume for a discussion of the excellent, though threatened, U.K. Race Relations [Amendment] Act, 2000).

Blame for such institutional racism needs hopefully to be leveled solely at rump elements within the Chávez government. It certainly cannot be directed at Chávez himself. Indeed, Chávez was the first Venezuelan president ever to claim and honor his African and indigenous ancestry, something he declares ceaselessly. Chávez is also committed to antiracism and multiculturalism. He articulated this when he stated:

> We've raised the flag of socialism, the flag of anti-imperialism, the flag of the black, the white and the Indian...I love Africa. I've said to the Venezuelans that until we recognise ourselves in Africa, we will not find our way...We have started a hard battle to bring equality to the African descendents, the whites and the indigenous people. In our constitution it shows that we're a multicultural, multiracial nation. (Chávez, 2008, cited in Campbell, 2008, p. 58)

The second obstacle to challenging racism is the myth of "racial harmony," which is embedded in Venezuelan culture. This belief holds that through history, Europeans, Africans, and indigenous peoples of the colonial era blended or coexisted and created a new nation where all lived together equally (Lasso, 2007, pp. 9–15, cited in Martinez et al., 2010, p. 220). This belief is reinforced by claims that various "ethnic features" can be found in many Venezuelan families (ibid.).

The third obstacle relates to Venezuelan elites today, who as Victor (2009) points out, are profoundly racist. Some of their "intellectuals" refer to colonization as positive ("the golden legend"). "Encomiendas," the "enslavement of Indigenous peoples to work for particular landowners" is viewed merely "as a way of taking care of them." Many such accounts have also glossed over the role of enslaved Africans in Latin American economies and culture (Victor, 2009). The racism is such that current attempts to recognize and challenge racism are seen by some as *racist*! In other words, some of the elite have denounced Chávez, claiming that, by bringing the issues of racism out into the open, he has created racism, where none existed before (ibid).

Despite these major obstacles, there are grounds for optimism. The Bolivarian Constitution of 1999, which unequivocally stated the need for a truly participatory and multicultural republic, along with Chávez's constant declaration of his Afro-Venezuelan and indigenous roots, has provided Afro-Venezuelan and indigenous peoples with unprecedented political space. As Lauren Carroll Harris (2007) puts it:

> in Venezuela the space for frank discussion about how to move forward in the context of a mass movement has been opened up by the ongoing revolutionary process, and genuine gains have been made by indigenous and Afro-Venezuelan movements to eliminate the systemic nature of racism from Venezuelan life.

As an example Harris (2007) explains that the ambitious land and agrarian reforms embedded in the 1999 constitution have been especially beneficial to Afro-Venezuelan and indigenous communities. The constitution declares that idle, uncultivated private land over a certain size can be transformed into productive units of land for common social benefit. "By prioritizing socially productive land use over monopolistic private land ownership and redistributing idle land to the landless, Chávez has promoted independence, food sovereignty and local agricultural development" (Harris, 2007).

The struggle against racism and for socialism is, of course, a common struggle, but it is also specific. Luis Perdomo puts this well:

> [T]his is all our struggle...but [we also take] into consideration the contribution of our indigenous brothers and sisters, who were always present...Chávez has called up everyone, as is stated in the new constitution, to construct the revolution...the indigenous, the Spanish, the African, and all those more recently arrived ethnicities (cited in Martinez et al., 2010, pp. 222, 224–225).

Racism and antiracism today: Afro-Venezuelans

One organization at the forefront of the antiracist movement is the Network of Afro-Venezuelan Organizations, which emerged in response to the

1999 constitution. This lobby represents thirty to forty organizations of Afro-descendents. Working in their various communities and via the government, Afro-Venezuelans have initiated a number of projects and proposals. Both Luis Perdomo and Freddy Blanco are based in the San José de Barlovento Cumbe.[12] Barlovento covers six municipalities along the coast of Venezuela, east of Caracas. Once dominated by a wealthy landowning elite who worked thousands of enslaved Africans, Barlovento was largely ignored by previous governments (ibid., p. 220). Martinez et al. (2010, p. 220) inform us that "this exclusion is still present in physical form, embodied in the poor infrastructure of many of [Venezuela's] cities." However, the region today is "alive with Afro-Venezuelan culture," with the Network of Afro-Venezuelan Organizations "demanding inclusion in the politics of the central government and seeking to transform the cultural landscape of the entire country" (ibid.).

The network also successfully campaigned for the creation of a presidential commission against racism in 2005, the establishment of a number of cocoa-processing plants and farming cooperatives run by black Venezuelans, and for Afro-Venezuelan Day on May 10 of each year (Harris, 2007).

Afro TV is a socialist television station on *Facebook* that celebrates Afro-Venezuelan customs and cultures, and seeks to strengthen connections with the African diaspora. As Luis Perdomo explains (cited in Martinez et al., 2010, p. 229), "[t]raditionally we have only been cast as servants and criminals," whereas now, as part of the Bolivarian Revolution, Afro-Venezuelans can:

> tell our own stories, present the way we conceive the world and the way we organize ourselves, and give the people in our communities the space to provide their opinions on the Bolivarian Process—all from their perspectives as afro-descendants.

It should be stressed, however, that the network has yet to achieve either the inclusion of Afro-Venezuelan history in the school curriculum, which was proposed by Chávez in 2008 but was not approved following protests from the opposition (Blanco, 2010, cited in ibid., pp. 227–228), or their primary demand, which is to be included in the Venezuelan constitution as a distinct "ethnic group," similar to indigenous peoples (Martinez et al., 2010, pp. 220–221). This latter proposal was put forward when the new constitution was being formulated between 1998 and 1999, by the Union of Black Women, led by Nirva Camacho and Reina Arratia; and the Fundación Afroamerica, led by Jesús "Chucho" García, both organizations later to become part of the network. It was actually pushed forward by Chávez himself and supported by indigenous peoples, but ultimately rejected by the constituent assembly because many felt "it was not necessary to include afro-descendents in the constitution in the way that indigenous people were." Perdomo believes that this was to do with a lack of understanding of the proposal, but also that there was an element of racism in assembly's decision

(Luis Perdomo, cited in ibid., pp. 225–226). While it has made a number of gains under the Chávez government, the network maintains that "a genuinely revolutionary process is impossible if the historical realities of racial exploitation are not confronted" (Martinez et al., 2010, p. 221).

Racism and antiracism today: indigenous peoples

As the Embassy of the Bolivarian Republic of Venezuela to the U.K. and Ireland (undated) points out, over five hundred thousand indigenous people inhabit Venezuela (2.2 percent of the national population), representing more than thirty different ethnic groups. While nearly 90 percent of the population of Venezuela lives in the northwestern half of the country, indigenous peoples make up almost 50 percent of the huge southeastern state, Amazonas (Lee Van Cott, 2005, p. 183, cited in ibid., p. 194).

As noted above, the rights of Venezuela's indigenous people were first entrenched in the 1999 Bolivarian constitution. For the first time, indigenous land rights were identified as being collective, inalienable, and non-transferable, recognizing the rights of the indigenous peoples over the land they traditionally and ancestrally occupied (cited in Harris, 2007). Historically marginal in the national politics of Venezuela (Minority Rights Group International, 2007), indigenous people, also for the first time, had a whole chapter of the Constitution devoted to their rights (Embassy of the Bolivarian Republic of Venezuela to the U.K. and Ireland [undated]). In addition, as Harris (2007) points out:

> Article 9 stipulates that while Spanish is Venezuela's primary language, "indigenous languages are also for official use for indigenous peoples and must be respected throughout the Republic's territory for being part of the nation's and humanity's patrimonial culture." The 1999 constitution also affirms that "exploitation by the state of natural resources will be subject to prior consultation with the native communities," that "indigenous peoples have the right to an education system of an intercultural and bilingual nature," that indigenous people have the right to control ancestral knowledge over "native genetic resources" and biodiversity, and that three indigenous representatives are ensured seats in the country's National Assembly (these were elected by delegates of the National Council of Venezuelan Indians in July 1999).

A People's Ministry for Indigenous Peoples was launched in 2007, headed by a Ye'kuana indigenous woman from the Amazon and eight indigenous deputy-ministers. Thirty-nine indigenous languages share with Spanish the status of official languages in Venezuela.

While indigenous peoples recognize the unprecedented opportunities provided by these measures, there remain a number of obstacles preventing the fulfillment of these new rights (Martinez, 2010 et al., p. 196). For example, as Mecheduniya, who is Ye'kuana and from the Alto Ventuari sector of Amazonas, explains, many ministers, some of whom are indigenous, "are not responding to the needs of the people" (cited in ibid., p. 202). Mecheduniya complains of "excessive bureaucracy" and the refusal of the minister to listen or support the community (cited in ibid., p. 203), while Jorge Montiel, a member of the Wayúu community, explains that when indigenous people begin to go through the process of self-demarcation (a right under the Constitution), sometimes they are "asked to sign a [false] demarcation agreement…that [does] not include the territory that [is] rightfully theirs." He also claims that The Mining Law supersedes other laws and "allows miners to enter sacred sites and ancient cemeteries of indigenous peoples" (cited in ibid., p. 213). While Montiel is wary of factors within the Bolivarian government that are counterrevolutionary, and while he recognizes the money that can potentially be made of mining, he notes that Chávez has "on many occasions as a result of the pressure that we have placed on him" "said no to coal" (cited in ibid., p. 215).

There is, as Martinez et al. (2010, p. 196) put it, a "fragile and complicated relationship between Venezuelan social movements and the state," albeit one of general overall support for the considerable spaces the Bolivarian Revolution is providing for socialist advancement. This is best summarized by Martinez et al. (ibid., p. 8): "[t]hey recognize that a significant political space has been opened, and they are asking themselves how to achieve the change that they believe is necessary to build the society of which they dream."

It should be pointed out that the above antiracist developments in the Bolivarian Republic of Venezuela are not confined to the country itself. Chávez has also been building alliances with other marginalized communities in the Americas, including providing food, water, and medical care to 45,000 Hurricane Katrina victims in areas surrounding New Orleans, and supplying discounted heating and diesel oil to schools, nursing homes, and hospitals in poor communities in the U.S. (Harris, 2007).

Education in Venezuela

As we saw in chapter 1, according to Althusser (1971, pp. 152–153), the dominant ideological state apparatus (ISA) in mature capitalist social formations is the educational ISA. As we have also seen, Chávez, in 2010, designated knowledge and education as the first form of power in the revolutionary process, and described Venezuela as "a giant school" (cited in Sheehan, 2010). That the educational ISA is being used in the Bolivarian Republic of Venezuela to promote socialism rather than capitalism may need a further modification of the neo-Marxist theory of the state, as formulated by Althusser. Certainly, the concept of "a giant school" accords with Gramsci's revolutionary strategy of "education for socialism" as formulated by Allman (1988, p. 99) and referred to in the previous chapter of this volume.

Venezuela as "a giant school" and "education for socialism" is exemplified by the Revolutionary Reading Plan launched by Chávez in 2009 (Pearson, 2009). "A change in spirit hasn't been achieved yet," Chávez suggested, and argued that the plan will be the "base for the injection of consciousness through reading, with which our revolution will be strengthened even more" (cited in ibid.).

The plan involves the distribution by the government of 2.5 million books to develop the communal libraries. Chávez said that part of the plan was a "rescuing of our true history for our youth," explaining that many standard textbooks do not acknowledge the European imperialist genocide of the indigenous peoples and their resistance (Pearson, 2009). Chávez went on to recommend that people do collective reading and exchange knowledge, mainly through the communal councils and the popular libraries. He called on communal councils as well as "factory workers, farmers, and neighbors, to form revolutionary reading squadrons," one of whose tasks is to have discussions in order to "unmask the psychological war...of the oligarchy" (cited in ibid.).

"Read, read and read, that is the task of every day. Reading to form conscious and minds," Chávez noted, "[e]veryday we must inject the counter revolution a dose of liberation through reading" (cited in MercoPress, 2009). Moreover, the revolutionary reading plan is intended to reaffirm values leading to "the consolidation of the new man and the new woman, as the foundations for the construction of a Socialist motherland, unravelling the capitalist imaginary" (ibid.).

As far as more "formal" education is concerned, the Venezuelan Ministry of Culture stated on its website that the plan will help schoolchildren get rid of "capitalist thinking" and better understand the ideals and values "necessary to build a Socialist country and society" (ibid.). Education is increasingly put forward by the state as a social good, and a central factor in shaping the system of production (Griffiths and Williams, 2009, p. 37). In line with the Bolivarian Constitution, in addition to the urban and rural poor, access has been extended to traditionally disadvantaged or excluded groups, such as those of African descent and indigenous communities, though, as we have seen in this chapter, there is still much to do.

Tom Griffiths and Jo Williams (2009) outline the essential factors in the Bolivarian Revolution's approach to education that make it truly counter-hegemonic. The Venezuelan approach, they argue, draws on concepts of critical and popular education within the framework of a participatory model of endogenous socialist development (Griffiths and Williams, 2009, p. 41.). At the forefront, they note, is "the struggle to translate policy into practice in ways that are authentically democratic, that promote critical reflection and participation over formalistic and uncritical learning" (ibid.).

As in the U.K. and the U.S., formal school education in Venezuela is based on an explicit, politicized conception of education and its role in society (ibid., pp. 41–42). However, whereas in the U.K. (e.g., Beckman et al., 2009) and the U.S. (e.g., Au, 2009a), the capitalist state increasingly uses formal education merely as a vehicle to promote capitalism, in the Bolivarian Republic of Venezuela, "the political" in education is articulated *against* capitalism and imperialism and *for* socialism. In 2008, a draft national curriculum framework for the Bolivarian was released. It stated that the system is "oriented toward the consolidation of a humanistic, democratic, protago-nistic, participatory, multi-ethnic, pluri-cultural, pluri-lingual and intercul-tural society" (Ministerio del Poder Popular Para la Educación, 2007, p. 11, cited in Griffiths and Williams, 2009, p. 42). It went on to critique the for-mer system for reinforcing "the fundamental values of the capitalist system: individualism, egotism, intolerance, consumerism and ferocious competi-tion...[which also] promoted the privatisation of education" (Ministerio del Poder Popular Para la Educación, 2007, p. 12, cited in ibid., p. 42).

One central message of the Bolivarian Revolution tells us is that a fundamental counter-hegemonic shift in the political economy towards socialism, including *universal* free access to education, with a high degree of equity in terms of opportunity and outcomes, can be achieved quite quickly (Griffiths and Williams, 2009, p. 34). As Griffiths and Williams conclude, the Bolivarian system consistently refers these back to the underlying project to promote the formation of new republicans, with cre-ative and transformational autonomy, and with revolutionary ideas; and with a positive attitude toward learning in order to put into practice new and original solutions for the endogenous transformation of the country (Ministerio del Poder Popular Para la Educación 2007, p. 16, cited in ibid., 2009, pp. 42–43).

The Theoretical Underpinnings of Bolivarian Education

Venezuelan academic and political activist Luis Bigott (2009) argues that Bolivarian education in Venezuela is based on the twentieth-century Latin American critical/liberatory work of Orlando Fals Borda and Paolo Freire, both of whose work focused on the extension of education for the transfor-mation of society (ibid., p. 43). I will deal with each in turn.

Fals Borda

It is not surprising that Fals Borda, a Latin American socialist, born in Colombia, and an advocate of liberation theology, should figure promi-nently in Bolivarian education. Fals Borda was of the founders of par-ticipatory action research (PAR). PAR combines research and theory with political participation. Fals Borda's focus was the subordinated conditions of the Latin American societies. A sociologist, he outlined four guidelines for researchers:

- Do not monopolize your knowledge nor impose arrogantly your tech-niques, but respect and combine your skills with the knowledge of the researched or grassroots communities, taking them as full partners and co-researchers;
- Do not trust elitist versions of history and science which respond to domi-nant interests, but be receptive to counter-narratives and try to recapture them;

- Do not depend solely on your culture to interpret facts, but recover local values, traits, beliefs, and arts for action by and with the research organizations; and

- Do not impose your own ponderous scientific style for communicating results, but diffuse and share what you have learned together with the people, in a manner that is wholly understandable and even literary and pleasant, for science should not be necessarily a mystery nor a monopoly of experts and intellectuals (cited in Gott, 2008).

As Griffiths and Williams (2009, p. 43) explain, a decidedly Venezuelan version of PAR is currently being put into practice by academics and teachers. They give the example of the Bolivarian University (UBV). Founded in 2003 as part of a major attempt to extend access to higher education, UBV is free to all students and "seeks to fundamentally challenge the elitism of many of the traditional universities." Social justice and equality are "at the core of all educational content and delivery," and all courses taken there use PAR methodology, "described as a multidisciplinary approach linking practice and theory." PAR methodology bases UBV students in their local communities, working alongside a mentor on a community project, which is a core part of their formal studies (ibid.). Griffiths and Williams (2009, p. 43) give the examples of "Community Health students working with doctors within the *Barrio Adentro* health mission" (see later in this chapter); "Legal studies students establishing a community legal centre to advise and support families with civil law issues,"; and education students working with a teacher/mentor in schools in their local community.

Classes are undertaken in the evenings, where all UBV students relate theory to their experiences in the project. As Griffiths and Williams (ibid., pp. 43–44) explain:

> The approach is designed to place day-to-day decision-making and problem solving in the hands of local communities, as part of the broader societal reconstruction underway, with all participants gaining skills through the process. The intent is that the PAR methodology places researchers in positions of political leadership, but with the projects being democratically controlled and driven by the communities themselves and their own leaders, and aimed at realising the objectives of the community based organisations.

Griffiths and Williams (ibid., p. 44) conclude that while the evening discussions are interesting, what is most important is *who* is taking part in them. This is not only "social and economic inclusion" but *political* inclusion, with educational decision-making in the hands of staff, students, parents/carers, *and the community at large.*

I had the privilege to teach a course at UBV for a week in 2006. The course I wrote and taught was titled *Introduction To World Systems: Global Imperial Capitalism or International Socialist Equality: Issues, and Implications for Education.* Standards at UBV I found are very high—with seminar discussions and debate comparing more than favorably with universities in which I have taught in the U.K. and around the world. However, at UBV, as we have seen, advanced theory is very much linked to practice; that is, to improving the lives of people in the communities from where the students come. Students are almost 100 percent working class at UBV. While teaching there, I met a police officer who was studying for his master's degree. He told me how the Chávez government was humanizing the police force. He estimated that Chávez has the support of about 75 percent of the Caracas police.

One thing that symbolizes the Bolivarian Revolution for me was the way in which, at the start of my last seminar at UBV, one of the caretakers arrived to unlock the seminar room, and then sat down, listened to, and actively contributed to the seminar. His question was what percentage of the British working class did I think were revolutionary socialists. When I told him that the percentage was very, very small indeed, he seemed somewhat bemused.

A focus on "community" is also apparent at the Indigenous University of Venezuela. Mecheduniya, who is Ye'kuana and writing an undergraduate thesis there on the cosmovision—traditional worldview—of his people, explains how students "analyze the situation in each of our communities and how we should be contributing to them as the Indigenous University because we are all part of our communities" (cited in Martinez et al., 2010, p. 200). Everyone at the university learns "how to be responsible, disciplined, and to live in solidarity with one another." He also points out how students learn how to use modern technology, as well as traditional culture such as indigenous history, law, ethnology, ethnobotany, and agroecology. After finishing at the university, Mecheduniya will return to his community "because that is the responsibility we have" (cited in ibid.).

Arguing in a similar vein, but about his work as a teacher and organizer for the community, rather than as a university student, and thus exemplifying Chávez's concept of Venezuela as "a giant school," Montiel, a member of the Wayúu community, stresses that everything he learns, he takes back into his community:

> It is the role of all of us to help with everything that is necessary for our community. Rather than talk about "I," we talk about "us." However, this is difficult because the habits of today have made us all more individualistic. So we are always learning how to share, how to be collective, and how to organize ourselves. (cited in Martinez et al., 2010, pp. 208–209)

PAR principles of making "community" central to education are applicable to the whole of the education system. As we shall see shortly, it is pivotal in the work of the revolutionary teachers at the alternative school in Barrio Pueblo Nuevo.

Paulo Freire

Like Fals Borda, Paulo Freire is a Latin American socialist born in Brazil, and a liberation theologian. Exemplifying this, in an online video (Freire,

2007; Freire actually died in 1997), he makes reference to his belief in Marx with respect to the world and Christ as far as the "transcendental" is concerned. Freire is generally recognized as the founder of "critical pedagogy." As Peter McLaren (2000, p. 141) explains, Freire was able to link globally education and "a radical politics of historical struggle." He was able to provide the illiterate with "both a language of critique and a language of hope" (ibid., p. 155). For Freire, literacy was both a critique of capitalism, and an introduction to a better way of life, a life of caring for others (ibid.). Literacy programs for disempowered peasants devised by Freire and his colleagues are now used all over the world.

Freire was a keen advocate of "dialogic education," which entails a democratic learning environment and the *absence* of authoritarianism (p. 102, cited in Freire and Shor, 1987).

His work is axiomatic to *democratic* socialism, and like Chávez, Freire denied that Stalinist authoritarianism was intrinsic in socialism. As he once put it:

> I refuse to accept that the presence of authoritarianism within socialism is due to some ontological incompatibility between human beings and the essence of socialism. That would be the same as saying: "So averse is human nature to the fundamental virtues of socialism that only under coercion would it be possible to make it work." That which human ontology rejects, on the contrary, is authoritarianism, regardless of what attributes it may receive. (Freire, 1998a, p. 49)

As McLaren (2000, p. 141) has argued, Freire "was one of the first internationally recognized educational thinkers who fully appreciated the relationship among education, politics, imperialism, and liberation," arguing that they "abut to one another as well as flash off each other."

Freire (1972) also formulated the concept of "banking education," where the teacher deposits information into an "empty account," and students are required to memorize the content and reproduce it. In this system the student who reproduces the information most accurately gets the highest grade. Freire urged teachers to detach themselves from capitalism where banking education is the norm, and to reinvent schools as democratic public spheres where meaningful *dialogue* can take place.

Another of Freire's (1970, 1972) concepts is that of conscientization, a developing consciousness by which, as knowing subjects, people achieve a deepening awareness of the sociocultural reality that shapes their lives. This also entails the consciousness that they have the capacity and the power to transform that reality. The relevance of this concept to the Bolivarian Revolution should, by now, be self-evident.

It should be stressed at this stage that, in terms of actual practice in the schools and universities, education based on the above revolutionary principles is by no means universal. Indeed, as Griffiths and Williams (2009, p. 44) point out, discussions with education academics and activists during fieldwork in Caracas in 2007, 2008, and 2009, repeatedly raised the challenge of the political and pedagogical conservatism of existing teachers, often in opposition to the government's Bolivarian socialist project (e.g., Griffiths, 2008).

Revolutionary Education in an Alternative School in Barrio Pueblo Nuevo, Mérida

Creating Space[13]

The school is a small project, started by committed socialist revolutionary residents and activists of Barrio Pueblo Nuevo, perhaps the poorest community in the city of Mérida in western Venezuela. It caters to students aged between eight and fifteen, and since it has been operating for only six months, it is very much in its initiatory phase. The teachers want to create an alternative for young people who have been left behind in the public school system and reengage them in participatory pedagogy consistent with socialist and democratic values. The school is currently linked to the Ministry of Education under the title of "alternative school" and receives some state funding.

Reflecting on the overall context of his fieldwork at the school, Edward Ellis (2010) points out that the fact that the school is the exception rather than the rule as far as education in the country as a whole is concerned "need not be understood as distressing. It can be seen...as a great opportunity to empower and encourage new forms of change." He underlines one of the central themes of this chapter; namely, the spaces that the Chávez government has opened up–in this case for "independent and autonomous...new projects to grow and develop." As Gerardo, a part-time collaborator at the school, a longtime community activist from the barrio, and an organic intellectual of the working class par excellence states: "ten years ago this wouldn't have been possible. This would have been called 'terrorist' and would have to be underground." As he puts it, revolutionary teachers, unlike before, can advance faster, no longer having "to worry about being hunted down."

Gerardo points out that the school has opened many doors for people and that there are "a lot of expectations" from the Ministry of Education, which is hoping that the school might work as "a model for other schools."

Twenty-first-century socialist praxis

Gerardo is committed to socialist praxis, noting that "socialism is done, not decreed." Given that the words "revolution" and "socialism" are omnipresent in Venezuelan society, and can be used "without much thought," Gerardo is working on the *construction* of socialism in the school, being "a bit more responsible in this sense." As he explains, "here we practice socialism with concrete elements from everyday life...sharing, working in a collective way, friendship, getting along, the fundamental bases of socialism with praxis." Having seen societies torn apart in a capitalist system based on consumption, and underlining Chávez's stress on participatory democracy, Gerardo notes that the teachers are trying to teach the children to be "critical and proactive"—"not just criticism but how things can be changed," "we are trying to show that the children have a participatory role in society, and that this role can be transformative." Communication tools are crucial in this process—"the radio, the television, the written word...these things can lead to the transformation of society."

Lisbeida, a university student studying criminology, and a dance instructor, working at the school and in the community as a volunteer, says of twenty-first-century socialism, it "is being redefined, something that is flexible. I believe there are new understandings of what socialism is and how it can be implemented":

> But basically, the core concepts are the same: equality, social justice, elimination of class differences, more horizontal processes, all of this inside our school is an intrinsic part of what we are doing. It's our base...So we are trying to transmit these values of equality, solidarity, cooperation, collective work.

James Suggett, a writer for venezuelanalysis.com,[14] who is also a community activist and a volunteer at the school, reflects Freireian analysis when he says he is critical of those teachers who view socialism as being authoritarian, those who believe they should be getting students into line. For Suggett, "socialism means creating a democratic space in the classroom," encouraging people "to recognize oppression and overcome it."

Communal, cooperative, and democratic living and learning

At the Alternative School in Barrio Pueblo Nuevo, each day starts with a communal breakfast, after which students are brought together to discuss what will take place that day. Sometimes communal cleaning of the community center where the classes are held ensues; sometimes the day starts with group activities, focused on reading, writing, or mathematics, depending on what students wish to work on, or need to improve.

Addressing the socialist roots of Venezuela's indigenous communities, Gerardo illustrates Freire's process of conscientization as he points out that indigenous peoples have a tradition of companionship, solidarity, respect, and sharing, and that private property did not exist, and how the teachers are trying to break the paradigms of Western society that value "capital more than people," and that prioritize individualism and competition. The school aims to provide the children with a point of departure so that they can all advance together toward socialism. Gerardo points to the use of a pedagogy that "involves the children in collective work and thinking" and includes cooperative games. When the teachers meet with the children, as Jeaneth (the main teacher of the school, a member of the community whose children are studying at the school) explains, the teachers try to emphasize "that we are a collective and if something happens to the group it affects us all."

UNIVERSITY OF WINCHESTER
LIBRARY

Learning at the school is in line with Freire's advocacy of "dialogic educa-tion," which, as we have seen, entails a democratic learning environment and the *absence* of authoritarianism, "banking education" and grades. As Jeaneth puts it:

> we plan activities and then ask the children which they would like to work on. They choose the area. We have some basic parameters that they need to work in but they choose. Also, when we leave the school for a trip, we propose the idea to them and they take part in the discussion about how to plan the trip.

Tamara Pearson, like Suggett, a writer for venezuelanalysis.com, and also a volunteer teacher of reading at the school, points out that:

> no one is forced to do anything and there are no punishments. If they don't want to participate in an activity, they can simply go somewhere else, or sit and watch. Hence, the weight is on the teacher to properly motivate the students and draw them in through the activity rather than discipline and threats of lower grades or whatever.

"There is no grading or competition," Pearson explains, "there's simply no sense of them competing with others." "The idea of the school," she believes, "is to teach using more creative and dynamic methods, without the usual competition and grades and failure and passing and who is first etc, with teachers who are very supportive and friendly, while also involving the community in school life, and vice versa."

Socialism and the community

As Edward Ellis states, "there is a real emphasis on trying to increase stu-dents' participation in all activities." He gives the example of how "the stu-dents watched a movie and then discussed how to organize a screening of that same film in their community. A group conversation was held to iden-tify what the steps necessary would be to put on this screening." As Ellis explains, "there is a lot of collaboration on the part of the community and different activities are led by different folks ... It is quite common for the students to leave the classroom to attend an event in the community." In addition, as Lisbeida points out, the school's "activities [are] open to the entire community so that the community is a protagonist in what happens in the school. In that way, the dance group which is part of the school is also part of the community." Emphasizing how PAR works in the community and school, Lisbeida explains:

> the idea is that the children have an impact in their community, carrying with them this experience to their homes and to their families so that their families also become integrated in the educational process that the school is trying to carry out. So there's a kind of feedback that we are trying to accom-plish between the community and the school. And school-community means

family, workers, etc. There is an important interaction which is very relevant to the educational process in the school.

This is not to glamorize the students' community. As Gerardo explains, some of the students come from homes where there are problems of violence, alcohol, or drugs, or unemployment and its attendant problems. However, as Lisbeida believes, this can also be a source of strength for the students:

> As these students come from backgrounds that are very difficult, I think that this gives them the ability to see certain social realities with more clarity: justice, the marked differences between violence and love. I see this as a potential to create criticisms and questions with more meaning. Because they have experienced very difficult things, they are not going to be afraid and they are going to have a very strong base to be critical of things.

Gerardo points out that there is help from some government missions, such as Mission Barrio Adentro (literally "mission inside the barrio"), which provides comprehensive publicly funded health care, and sports training to poor and marginalized communities. Barrio Adentro delivers de facto universal health care from cradle to grave.

In addition, the teachers are trying to improve human relations, not only with cooperative games, from which the teachers are also learning, but there are physical spaces "with a community vision," such as a community library and a community radio station. As Lisbeida puts it:

> we've noticed that the children are arriving at their house with new attitudes, and although we don't have a way to scientifically measure it, we can feel a difference in the attitude of the parents as well...how they treat their children. Something very interesting is happening. Things are changing...[the children] learn things based on what they already know and live. In this way, they can also learn that they have the potential to change the reality that surrounds them.

The students at the alternative school in Barrio Pueblo Nuevo are clearly being empowered, and already there are signs of progress. As Lisbeida enthuses, "one of the things that we have seen with this process in the school is that the ones who were thought to be completely without potential or capacity to learn are making people turn their heads. They are doing some incredible things." As Gerardo concludes:

> we've only had a short time operating but I have noticed a change in the way the children see things. Before, their world was just the barrio, but now they are looking a little bit beyond this. And I have seen that the children are speaking now, they are conversing...Before everything was resolved through violence. Now there is more talking. There are still some very sharp words, but we are working on it. This has opened many doors for people. There are a lot of expectations...And there are many things that we have learned about ourselves due to the students.

Thus, in launching the school and in teaching there, the teachers are learning too. Suggett concludes that this empowerment arises from the challenge of teaching the students in the school every day. As he puts it, "the revolution is there in what they're doing and in their transformation process."

Racism

The comments on racism made by the teachers at the alternative school in Barrio Pueblo Nuevo underline observations made earlier in this chapter. A few examples will suffice. Lisbeida talks of institutional racism in Venezuelan society, and relates it to social class:

> We can see very contradictory things. It seems that the problem has more to do with class. We see that the people from the barrios, the people in the countryside and in the coastal areas are more indigenous and black. Since colonization, the upper class has been composed of lighter-skinned people. So when there are families from the upper and middle classes that have mestizo roots, there is a rejection of the people from the barrios and the lower classes and this has to do with their appearance, with indigenous or African traits.

Lisbeida believes that "within the poorer social groups, there is not much discrimination."

Gerardo explains how the school is attempting to challenge this institutional racism, which the students see in society in general, and in the movies:

> there are some problems with racism, especially in the Andean region. When the people see an afro-venezolano or an indigenous person, they think that they are inferior, whereas someone blonde is seen as positive. These are concepts that have been handed down by the family and there is definitely racism present. But these ideas can't be erased in one day, and we've tried to have the children recognize this and have them interpret these things. And little by little we have been dealing with this theme. The first thing to do is for us to recognize ourselves. We have a mixed group of children. Some are light skinned and others dark, and we recognize that we are all equal, that we think the same, that we are the same.

Edward Ellis gives one example of the school's antiracist initiatives. In March 2010, the students attended a photo exhibit in a gallery in the city of Mérida. Here they were hosted by a professor of photography of the University of the Andes. The exhibit was called "Ancestral Wisdom" and touched upon the themes of local knowledge and native experiences, with photographs of elder community members who maintain local customs and traditions. During the visit, the professor of photography gave a short talk to the students emphasizing the need to recognize as Venezuelans the beauty within themselves—dark-skinned and native. He pointed out that Venezuelan people should not be looking to ideals of blond-haired, light-skinned Europeans as models for growth and development, but rather being proud as Latina/os and Venezuelans of different colors and backgrounds.

Finally, Lisbeida explains, the values the school is trying to promote have to do with respect, solidarity, cooperation, integration, and understanding of differences. For her, antiracism is about respecting others. In Venezuela, she believes, the theme of racism is different from the global North:

> Here when there exists a rejection of someone for their indigenous features, what is happening in reality is that we are rejecting ourselves. Because our way of being and our culture has these roots. So when this happens, the impact is different. It's like beating ourselves up. And this is the case even more in a community like the school where so many are dark skinned and look a lot alike.

Conclusion

The government of the Bolivarian Republic of Venezuela, led by Hugo Chávez, represents, I believe, the best currently existing model in the world for a future socialist society. However, as stressed by Gerardo, the part-time collaborator in the alternative school in Barrio Pueblo Nuevo, and by Chávez himself, the revolution will not be decreed from above. From a (neo-)Marxist perspective, it is important to stress the Chávez government's dialectic and symbiotic relationship with the Venezuelan working class. However, as Martinez et al. (2010, p. 2) argue, President Chávez continues to be "the defining political factor" as revealed "by the typical political labels that...divide many Venezuelans between *Chavistas* and *anti-Chavistas*." It is "precisely in the relationship and tension between the Venezuelan government and the social movements that the process of building a participatory democracy comes alive most vividly." Greg Wilpert (2010, pp. viii-ix) underlines this fact:

> To learn about...the movements that stand behind the Chávez phenomenon is...as important as learning about the Chávez government itself. One cannot truly make sense of one without the other. And making sense of and defending what is happening in Venezuela is perhaps one of the most important tasks for progressives around the world today, since Venezuela is at the forefront in the effort to find a real progressive alternative to capitalism, to representative democracy, and to U.S. imperialism.

Central to the Bolivarian Revolution, as we have seen, is the idea of participatory democracy, as opposed to representative democracy, which has been a pillar of Chávez's philosophy since his first election victory in 1998.

While much remains to be done, particularly with respect to the full implementation of indigenous and Afro-Venezuelan rights (consistently acknowledged by Chávez, though not the whole of the Chávez government), there seems to be an abundance of hope for the future at the local and societal levels *despite* the forces opposing the revolution outlined earlier in this chapter.

With respect to education, we have witnessed that, viewed as a life-long liberatory process, education is a key pillar of the revolution. I have noted how this is manifested in Chávez's concept of Venezuela as "a giant school." At the "formal" institutional level of education, the principles of the revolution have not been fully put into practice. Moreover, given the aforementioned conservatism of many teachers discovered by Griffiths and Williams, the challenge for Venezuelan revolutionary teachers to continue their counter-hegemonic struggle against capitalism, racism, and imperialism remains paramount.

As noted earlier in this chapter, the overall societal reforms with respect to the "missions" and the other ameliorative measures are precisely that—*reforms*. However, just as these societal reforms need to be seen in the context of the country having a revolutionary socialist president and millions of pro-Chávez workers, who are *or have the potential to become* revolutionary socialists, so do the reforms at the level of education in general, and at the level of the alternative school in Barrio Pueblo Nuevo. In the same way that the societal reforms are reminiscent of those of the post-World War II Labour governments in the U.K., the educational reforms being carried out in Barrio Pueblo Nuevo recall those that took place, for example, in the Inner London Education Authority (ILEA) and other progressive authorities, referred to in chapter 4 of this volume. Indeed, in some ways these U.K.-based educational reforms were more progressive, particularly with respect to antiracist policies, as are antiracist policies embedded in U.K. equalities legislation today (see chapter 4 of this volume for a discussion).

In Mérida, there are, however, revolutionary teachers fostering, in Freire's terms, a deepening awareness of the sociocultural reality that shapes their students' lives, including the racism still institutionalized in Venezuelan society. To reiterate, unlike the U.K. and the U.S., either historically or contemporaneously, the promotion in future workers of the consciousness that they have the capacity and the power to transform that reality is supported in Venezuela by a revolutionary movement and a revolutionary president.

Good socialist education in the U.K. tends to get undermined or banned, as was ILEA, against the wishes of the parents/carers, by the undemocratic government of Margaret Thatcher. In the Bolivarian Republic of Venezuela, socialist education is promoted by and is pivotal to the revolutionary process. Whereas the liberation of the working class in the U.K. and the U.S. is, for the foreseeable future, forestalled, in Venezuela, for Chávez, the epicenter of the revolution, socialism is unstoppable. Whatever the final outcome of twenty-first-century socialism, in Venezuela's "giant school," conscientization is providing the working class, current and future, with the certainty that a different world is possible.

The practical implications of how U.K. and U.S. revolutionary teachers might move forward in promoting socialism of the twenty-first century, a socialism in which racism and *all* other equalities are consistently confronted challenged and overcome, is addressed in the next chapter.

In various ways, we all have much to learn from each other. The revolutionary teachers in the school in Mérida have expressed a desire for open collaboration with revolutionary pedagogical scholars and theorists outside of Venezuela (personal correspondence). The U.K. has a history of working-class militancy, currently hindered by the ideological and repressive apparatuses of the British state, particularly since the advent of the Thatcher government, and accelerated under Tony Blair, and under the ConDem government. Blair's mantra, "education, education, education," in essence creating a flexible workforce for capitalism, represents the antithesis of the forms of popular education advocated by Chávez. The U.K. also has an ongoing tradition of antiracist education, a form of education under threat by dominant interpretations of "community cohesion," from which we can all learn (see chapter 4 of this volume).

With respect to the U.S., San Juan Jr. (2010, p. xiv) has suggested that among other factors, the lack of a viable labor-union tradition has distorted historical materialist principles there. Hence, among many leftist academics, "there is no mention of the working class as a significant force for overthrowing capitalism, much less initiating a socialist revolution" (San Juan Jr., 2010, p. xiv). It is, in part, for this reason that a non-Marxist interpretation of Critical Race Theory (CRT) is so preeminent among U.S. antiracist academics (for a Marxist critique of CRT, and a discussion of some of its strengths, see Cole, 2009a). Nevertheless, despite all this, as we have seen in chapter 4 of this volume, revolutionary thought continues to exist among some key educationists in the U.S.

San Juan Jr. (2010, p. xiv) shows awareness of how events in Venezuela may serve as a positive example to people in the U.S., when he suggests that it is instructive to contrast the trend among those leftists in the U.S. who have abandoned the socialist cause with the revolutionary promotion of popular literacy in Venezuela, "a pedagogical experiment of historic significance for all anti-capitalist militants" (San Juan Jr., 2010, p. xiv).

As part of the more general process of conscientization for all workers, intercontinental collaboration between revolutionary teachers and revolutionary academics surely captures a key element in the spirit of the Fifth International as proposed by Chávez. Some suggestions as to how this might translate into practice in educational institutions are addressed in the final chapter of this volume.

Chapter 6

Implications for Multicultural Antiracist Socialist Practice in Educational Institutions

In this final chapter, I make some suggestions for practice in educational institutions to promote education *against* racism; and political education that includes arguments *for* socialism. I begin by establishing some fundamental underlying principles that I believe Marxist and other Left radicals should adopt. These include efforts to promote the process of conscientization; a radical conception of pedagogy that centralizes dialogical education; participatory action research; the replacement of the fixed-ability paradigm with a commitment to learning without limits; and a structurally located sense of student empowerment. I go on to make suggestions for content, focusing on media education in order to resist processes of interpellation, and to be able to recognize and challenge hegemonic discourse; on multicultural antiracist education; and on political education.

Underlying Principles

Conscientization

In the course of my discussion about twenty-first-century socialism in the Bolivarian Republic of Venezuela in chapter 5 of this volume, I introduced Paolo Freire's concept of conscientization (*conscientização*, in his native Portuguese), or critical consciousness—a developing consciousness by which people gain a deepening awareness of the sociocultural reality that shapes their lives. Crucially conscientization also entails people's awareness that they have the capacity and the power to transform that reality (Freire, 1970, 1972). In chapter 5, I also demonstrated the processes of conscientization and counter-hegemonic education taking place at various levels in Venezuela, from that of the society as a whole (Chávez's description of the country as "a giant school") to the work being carried out in the alternative school in Barrio Pueblo Nuevo in Mérida.

Conscientization can enable an awareness that people do not possess defined "racial" characteristics; and that racialization is *constructed* in ways that are related to economic and political processes, processes in turn related to capitalism and imperialism.

Conscientization should be central to good practice in educational institutions for Marxists and other Left radical teachers everywhere.[1] Despite the very successful interpellation processes in the U.K. and the U.S. described throughout this book, and notwithstanding the overall dominance, albeit fragile, of neoliberal capitalism and imperialism in most of the world, there remains as always, Gramscian "optimism of the will" in the face of "pessimism of the intellect." Indeed events in Venezuela since the election of President Hugo Chávez in 1998 demonstrate that conscientization is a living twenty-first-century reality, and that another world is possible.

Conscientization may be thought of as the pedagogical process by which counter-hegemonic awareness is achieved, and by which students in the U.K. and the U.S. can come to realize that capitalism is but one stage in the development of human society; that there is no reason why it should be permanent; that there is a viable alternative model—a model based on need rather than profit.[2]

Radical Pedagogy

In chapter 4, following Wrigley and Hick (2009, p. 36), I advocated a model of pedagogy that includes more than just teaching methods, and requires attention to social, ethical, and affective as well as cognitive domains, and involves reflection about the changing nature of society. Such a definition fits well with Freire's concept of conscientization.

Freire favored dialogical education, which as noted in chapter 5 of this volume, entails a democratic learning environment (Freire, 1987, p. 102, cited in Freire and Shor, 1987). James Beane and Michael Apple (1999, p. 8) are surely correct in claiming that many people believe that democracy refers only to a form of government, and that it does not apply to schools or to young people. To their assertion, I would add: the overwhelming majority of people think in terms only of pro-capitalist representative democracy rather than participatory democracy (for an explanation of the distinction between the two forms of democracy, and for some examples of participatory democracy in action, see chapter 5 of this volume).

For Freire, learning environments, as democratic spaces, entail an absence of authoritarianism (Freire, 1987, p. 102, cited in Freire and Shor, 1987). Such an absence is not to be confused with a lack of authoritativeness. As Peter Ninnes (1998) points out, Freire (1998b) explains the importance of teachers being authoritative, rather than being weak and insecure or being authoritarian. In addition to democracy, dialogic education centralizes the need to develop an open dialogue with students, and requires a balance between "talking to learners and talking with them" (Freire, 1998b, p. 63, cited in Ninnes, 1998). Freire maintains that only through talking with and to learners can teachers contribute to the "[development of] responsible and critical citizens" (ibid., p. 65, cited in Ninnes, 1998). Freire makes a distinction between the progressive and democratic teacher, on the one hand, which he favors, and the permissive or authoritarian teacher, on the other, which he rejects.

In chapter 5, I also outlined participatory action research (PAR) as developed by Fals Borda, and I demonstrated how this was in use in the alternative school in Mérida, Venezuela. As noted, PAR involves respecting and combining one's skills with the knowledge of the researched or grassroots communities; taking them as full partners and coresearchers; not trusting elitist versions of history and science that respond to dominant interests; being receptive to counter-narratives and trying to recapture them; not depending solely on one's own culture to interpret facts; and sharing what one has learned together with the people, in a manner that is wholly understandable (Gott, 2008). PAR should guide Marxist and other Left radical teachers in all their pedagogical activities. Thus the communities where the students live should be fully involved in the educative process, should fully contribute to them, and should fully benefit from them. Here the role of the teacher as authoritative is crucial if confronted with reactionary (anti-social progress) politics emanating from certain groups of people in certain communities.

Empowerment

In chapter 5 of this volume, I pointed out that Paulo Freire (1972) urged teachers to detach themselves and their pupils from the idea that they are agents of capital, where *banking education* is the norm, and to reinvent schools as democratic public spheres where meaningful *dialogue* can take place.

If, as educators, we wish to empower the working class beyond the very necessary refusal to accept limits to learning (see the next section of this chapter), we need to be precise about what empowerment entails. "Empowerment" can mean all things to all people. For Hart et al. (2004, e.g., pp. 180, 186, 222–223) empowerment seems to be restricted to learning. What I have in mind is something on the lines of Colin Lankshear's (1995) adaptation of Feinberg's notion of "elliptical" statements. Empowerment, for me, represents far more than psychologistic notions of "sensing that one has more power." Empowerment needs to be situated structurally. The empowered person needs to know who she or he is; where she or he is coming from; what she or he is up against; how she or he can move forward; and what the end result of empowerment might look like. As Lankshear puts it:

> the full version of elliptical statements about empowerment will require attention to at least four variables. Adequate accounts will be required of (1) the SUBJECT of empowerment; (2) the power STRUCTURES in relation to which, or in opposition to which, a person or group is becoming empowered; (3) the PROCESSES or "achievement" by which empowerment arguably

occurs; and (4) the ENDS or OUTCOMES of becoming thus empowered. (Lankshear, 1995, p. 303)

From a Marxist perspective, in the educational context the student and her or his community are the subjects of empowerment; the power structures are the exploitative and oppressive racialized (and gendered and disablist) capitalist state; the processes are conscientization and counter-hegemonic awareness; and the ends are counter-hegemonic practices.

Learning without limits[3]

Well into the twenty-first century, a belief in notions of fixed ability remains fully enshrined in both the U.K. and the U.S. schooling systems. This is reinforced by a narrow focus on "standards" rather than achievement in its wider sense (Hart et al., 2004, p. 226). In this ability-focused paradigm, *differentiation* becomes essential to "effective pedagogy," and is sanctioned by the educational ideological state apparatuses in order that people are schooled according to the changing requirements of the capitalist economy. It is working-class young people, including those who are racialized, who are most adversely affected by the fixed-ability paradigm. We have seen throughout this volume how racialized groups are considered de facto lacking in "ability." Having made the assumption that children differ in ability, teachers teach them up to their perceived maximum ability at best, prior to their being ejected "into production" (Althusser, 1971, p. 155) or into unemployment.

The Learning Without Limits (LWL) project, which was set up at the University of Cambridge School of Education in 1999, aims to challenge notions of fixed ability, and "to build a new agenda for school improvement around the development of effective pedagogies that are free from ability labelling" (Hart et al., 2004, p. 21).

Promoting the LWL paradigm is particularly apposite in education against racism to counter the racist assumptions made about racialized groups having predetermined levels of ability.

More generally, the rejection of fixed ability is integral to the Marxist view of humankind. Indeed, Marxism is predicated on a belief in the unlimited potential of the working class. From a Marxist perspective, it is the working class that is at the forefront of the struggle for a qualitatively better world. The transition for the working class to a *class for itself* (acknowledging its exploitation and willing to challenge the capitalist system), in addition to being a *class in itself* (an *objective* fact because of workers' shared exploitation—see Appendix 1 to chapter 1 of this volume for a discussion of the labor theory of value) means that only the working class are in a position to create a classless society. In liberating themselves, workers are able to liberate humanity.

It is essential, therefore, to contest the fixed-ability paradigm. As Gramsci (1978, p. 9) famously remarked, in sexist language characteristic of his time, "[a]ll men are intellectuals but not all men have in society the function of intellectuals." The Learning Without Limits paradigm is a most useful development, and its rejection of "fixed ability" is a rallying cry for all teachers who share this progressive view of children and young people.[4]

Content

Media Education

I will now make the case that content is a crucial terrain for counter-hegemonic practice in schools. Throughout this volume, I have argued that the communications ISA, and in particular the media, plays a major role in interpellation and in forging hegemony. Radical Left media education is essential to help young people deconstruct and decode the dominant discourse inherent in the interpellation process. For example, students could be given copies of coverage of the same issue in right-wing tabloids and socialist newspapers respectively, and discussion could focus on what is being said and why. One example for the U.K. is coverage of Gypsy Roma and Traveller communities; one for the U.S. is segregation issues; one for both is immigration and border controls. Thus when Rupert Murdoch's right-wing *Sun* newspaper, describing Gypsies in the U.K., reports that "crafty gypsies" in caravans "swarmed" on to a field in a "Gypsy Nightmare" (as related in chapter 2 of this volume); or Murdoch's Fox News channel in the U.S. refers to Chávez as a dictator, despite evidence to the contrary (as discussed in chapter 5 of this volume), students can be enabled to respond in Althusserian terms as "bad subjects" and declare: "that's most dubious! That's wrong! That's a lie."

Students in the U.K. might be encouraged to compare the reporting of political news, about immigration, for example, in, say, *The Sun* or *The Daily Mail* (a newspaper with similar politics to *The Sun* but aimed more at the middle classes—here used in a sociological sense) with *Socialist Worker*, the weekly newspaper of the Socialist Workers Party (SWP), in order to contrast the voices of hegemony with those of counter-hegemony. A similar exercise could be carried out in the U.S. by looking at differing perspectives on the same topic from Fox and the biweekly *Socialist Worker*, published by the International Socialist Organization (the U.S.-based sister organization of the U.K.-based SWP).

Multicultural antiracist education

For a number of years I argued against multicultural education, because of its aforementioned stress on relatively superficial elements of culture (see chapter 4 of this volume), and because it tended to be taught by people outside of the culture they were teaching. In chapter 4, I argued that given advances in technology—most significantly the World Wide Web that enables authentic voices to be heard—counter-hegemonic *multicultural antiracist education* is now a viable proposition. Given the multiple, though country-specific, forms that racism takes in the U.K. and the U.S. (as analyzed in chapters 2 and 3 respectively), there is much work to do here.

As far as the antiracist component of multicultural antiracist education is concerned, we should be equipping students with the knowledge and where-withal to understand and to resist interpellation, to have the capacity and the confidence to engage in counter-hegemonic struggle against racism.

With respect to content, I would suggest that a basic education against racism should include awareness of the following key concepts: racism, racial-ization, and institutional racism. These are all discussed in the Introduction to this volume.

Education against racism should also encompass the history of racism in the U.K., as outlined in chapter 2 of this volume; and in the U.S., as outlined in chapter 3. Without such knowledge it is impossible to understand contem-porary racism. The plethora of different forms of contemporary racism in the U.K. and the U.S., respectively, are also discussed in chapters 2 and 3. While in no sense underestimating color-coded racism in the U.K., it should be stressed that there is also noncolor-coded racism. With respect to the U.S., while anti-black racism is a key feature, it should be pointed out that racism exists far beyond the black-white binary.

Education against racism should also include a critical analysis of impe-rialism, both historic and contemporary. Students will need to be aware of the realities of imperialism in the past and the impact of these realities on racism today. Students will also need skills to evaluate the new imperialism and "the permanent war" being waged by the U.S. with the acquiescence of Britain.

According to neo-Conservative Niall Ferguson (2003):

> Empire is as "cutting edge" as you could wish…[It] has got everything: eco-nomic history, social history, cultural history, political history, military history and international history—not to mention contemporary politics (just turn on the latest news from Kabul). Yet it knits all these things together with…a "metanarrative."

For Marxists, an understanding of the metanarrative of imperialism, past and present, does much more than this. It takes us to the crux of the trajec-tory of capitalism from its inception right up to the twenty-first century; and this is why Marxists should endorse the teaching of imperialism old and new. Of course, young people are interpellated by the media to have a positive view, at least of new imperialism, although it is not labeled as such (Ferguson and a few other pro-imperialists excepted), thus underlying the need for Left radical media education.

In chapters 2 and 3 of this volume, I discussed Islamophobia, noting that it is closely related to both old U.K. and new U.S. imperialisms. Only Marxism adequately explains the connections, and why Islamophobia, the "war on terror" and other forms of racism are necessary to keep the popu-lace on task for "permanent war" and the accumulation of global profits.

Elsewhere (e.g., Cole, 2004c) I have dealt at length, from a Marxist perspective, with the teaching of imperialism in schools.

It is also important to stress historical interconnections between the treatment of racialized minorities. In chapter 2 of this volume I showed how, related to varying requirements of capitalism and accompanying migration patterns, different minority groups became and have become racialized at different periods in history. In chapter 3, I cited Edward Taylor, who described the U.S. history of racism as entailing white people having unalienable rights to property and capital, and black people, Native Americans, and other people of color providing these rights—in the form of land (Native Americans) and labor (enslaved/oppressed people), the justification being based on a broad consensus that Europeans were innately superior.

To exemplify the multicultural element of multicultural antiracist education, it may be useful to refer back to my discussion in chapter 4 of this volume. Here I suggested the way in which an antiracist version of the Australian bi-centennial of 1988 might have been taught in primary (elementary) schools. To show what I mean by *multicultural* antiracist education, I have added in italics how multiculturalism could be woven into the description given in that chapter.

Multicultural antiracist education would focus on the fact that the indigenous peoples of Australia and their supporters view what happened two centuries ago as an imperialist colonial invasion. *The children would discover that, at the time of the invasion, there were up to four hundred indigenous nations and over two hundred languages, clearly indicating a plethora of cultural formations.* Given access to a comprehensive range of resources pertaining to life in Australia, children would discover that in reality, multicultural Australia is a racialized capitalist society stratified on lines of ethnicity, class, and gender, with Australian-born and English-speaking white male immigrants at the top of the hierarchy and Aboriginal women at the bottom. *They would find out that the dominant culture is the culture of Anglo-Australians, and that Aboriginal art, for example, is used as a selling point for tourism, while indigenous communities continue to live in the most appalling conditions.* Children would learn about "land rights" and other counter-hegemonic struggles, and the economic and ecological arguments pertaining to these rights. *They would be able to relate these arguments to traditional spiritual beliefs that have links with socialism and Marxism: the land belongs to the people and the people belong to the land.* They would discover that Aboriginal communities have faced ongoing exploitation and oppression since the invasion, and how this has intensified in recent years. *In 2009, an Aboriginal representative body in New South Wales complained of a failure to protect Aboriginal culture and heritage from ongoing destruction and stated that this will continue without fundamental reform.* Children would relate Australian indigenous struggles against injustice to other struggles for social justice in Australia, and to struggles worldwide. *The children would find out that struggles against imperialism worldwide have a strong cultural dimension in the sense of counter-hegemonic resistance to Americanization, that is, white corporate U.S. hegemony.* The children would be encouraged to resist racist interpellations from the ISAs that attempt to distort and mask these realities. *This would include refusing to accept ongoing attempts to denigrate specified racialized groups and their cultures.*

Political education

Neo-liberal capitalism, in being primarily about expanding opportunities for large multinational companies, has undermined the power of nation-states and exacerbated the negative effects of globalization on such services as healthcare, education, water and transport (Martinez and García, 2000). However, the current hegemonic role of business in schooling is paramount in convincing workers and future workers that socialism is off the agenda. Marxist educators and other Left radicals should expose this myth. Students have a *right* to discuss different economic and political systems such as twenty-first-century democratic socialism. This is particularly pressing given the current economic recession. It is easier in general for discussion in schools to embrace issues of gender, "race," disability, sexual orientation, and social class *when social class relates just to attainment* than to address social class in the context of overthrowing capitalism, and replacing it with world democratic socialism, where participatory democracy is central. The latter may thus be seen as *the last taboo,* and, of course, understandably so. It is time to move forward and bring such discussions into schools, colleges, and universities. Marxist and other Left educators can make the case that such considerations are a perfectly reasonable democratic demand. Global capitalism is out of control, and the very survival of our planet is dependent on dialogical education that considers the socialist alternative, an alternative distanced from the distortions of Marx by Stalinism.

No longer can socialism be divorced from environmental and ecological issues. McLaren and Houston (2005, p. 167) have argued that "escalating environmental problems at all geographical scales from local to global have become a pressing reality that critical educators can no longer afford to ignore." They go on to cite "the complicity between global profiteering, resource colonization, and the wholesale ecological devastation that has become a matter of everyday life for most species on the planet." Following Kahn (2003), they state the need for "a critical dialogue between social and eco-justice" (McLaren and Houston 2005, p. 168). They call for a dialectics of ecological and environmental justice to reveal the malign interaction between capitalism, imperialism, and ecology that has created widespread environmental degradation that has dramatically accelerated with the onset of neo-liberalism.

World capitalism's environmentally racist (Bullard et al., 2007) effects in both the "developing" and "developed" world should be discussed openly and freely in the educational institutions. As far as the "developing world" is concerned, there are, for example, such issues as the environmentally devastating method of extraction of natural resources utilized by multinational corporations in numerous "developing" countries that have devastated eco-systems and destroyed cultures and livelihoods (World Council of Churches, 1994, cited in Robinson, 2000), with toxic waste polluting groundwater, soil and the atmosphere (e.g., Robinson, 2000). In addition, there is trans-boundary dumping of hazardous waste by developed countries to develop-ing nations, usually in sub-Sahara Africa (e.g., Ibitayo et al., 2008; see also Blanco, 2010 on Latin America).

As far as the "developed" world is concerned, in the U.S., for example, people of color are concentrated around hazardous waste facilities–more than half of the nine million people living within two miles of such facilities are minorities (Bullard et al., 2007).

Finally, there is the ubiquitous issue of climate change, itself linked to the totally destructive impact of capitalism. Joel Kovel (2010) has described cli-mate change as "a menace without parallel in the whole history of humanity." However, on a positive note, he argues that "[it]s spectacular and dramatic character can generate narratives capable of arousing general concern and thus provide a stimulus to build movements of resistance." Climate change is linked to loss to the planet of living things—also a rallying point for young people. For Marxist educators, this provides a good inroad for linking envi-ronment, global capitalism, and arguments for the socialist alternative. As Kovel (2010) puts it, "[o]nly within the framework of a revolutionary ecoso-cialist society can we deal with the twinned crises of climate change and spe-cies loss—and others as well—within a coherent program centered around the flourishing of life."

Capitalism and the destruction of the environment are inextricably linked, to the extent that it is becoming increasingly apparent that saving the environment is dependent on the destruction of capitalism. Debate should therefore include a consideration of the connections between global capital-ism and environmental destruction, as well as a discussion of the socialist alternative.

The need for environmental issues to be allied to socialism is paramount. As Nick Beams (2009) notes, all the "green" opponents of Marxism view "the overthrow of the capitalist system by means of the socialist revolution as the key to resolving the problems of global warming" as either "unrealis-tic," "not immediate enough," or believe that socialism is hostile to nature. Beams (ibid.) argues that, in reality, "the system of market relations is based on the separation of the producers from the means of production, and it is this separation—the metabolic rift between [human beings] and nature—that is the source of the crisis." In other words, instead of the real producers of wealth (the working class) having control over what they produce and rationally assigning this to human need, goods are irrationally produced for profit. Beams (ibid.) quotes Marx (1894 [1966] p. 959) as follows:

> Freedom...can consist only in this, that socialised man, the associated pro-ducers, govern the human metabolism with nature in a rational way, bringing it under their collective control instead of being dominated by it as a blind

power; accomplishing it with the least expenditure of energy and in conditions most worthy and appropriate for their human nature.

As Beams (2009) concludes, "[f]ar from Marx being outdated, the world has, so to speak, caught up with Marx."

As far as linking students up with actually existing socialist practice, the Internet, of course, provides possibilities for doing this. For example, students in the U.K. and the U.S. can communicate with students and socialist teachers in Venezuela and elsewhere, where the role of indigenous peoples (whose lives, like Native Americans, are intimately connected to the environment) is crucial in the creation of twenty-first-century socialism, and in which ecosocialism is central. Announcing the formation of the United Socialist Party of Venezuela (PSUV) in 2007, Hugo Chávez recounted how the pioneer Peruvian socialist José Carlos Mariátegui had pointed to the socialist project's roots in the indigenous societies of America. The indigenous peoples, Chávez recalled, "lived in socialism for centuries." He referred to indigenous Venezuelans as "the bearers of the socialist seed in our land, our nation, our America" (cited in Riddell, 2007).

In this volume, I have examined racism as it relates to schooling in the U.K. and the U.S., and differentiated this from education against racism and for socialism, using the model of democratic socialism in the Bolivarian Republic of Venezuela as an example. In this final chapter, I have provided some suggestions as to what might guide practice in educational institutions, based on the arguments presented throughout this volume. What Marxist and other radical Left educators are able to do will, of course, depend on various institutional constraints. However, whatever the nature of such constraints, the struggle against racism and for socialism will continue unabated.

Referring to the U.S. (but equally applicable to the U.K. and other countries implicated in U.S. aggression), Eric Mann (2002) has succinctly identified the central role that education against racism and imperialism plays in the struggle against capitalism:

> Right now the U.S. is financing its war against the world by super-exploiting the entire world, subjecting more than three billion people to abject poverty. In that racism and imperialism are at the heart of the U.S. ideological framework, antiracism and anti-imperialism are the central ideological concepts of contestation, the essence of counterhegemonic political education work. (cited in San Juan Jr., 2003)

Conclusion

In this volume I have made use of (neo-)Marxist analysis to try to understand racism as it relates to schooling in the U.K. and the U.S., and have used its insights to make suggestions for educating against racism, imperialism, and capitalism and for socialism. Capitalism, as a failed social system, is there for all to see especially in its current crisis. That capitalism is inherently destabilizing was recognized by Marx and Engels a century and a half ago:

> The bourgeoisie cannot exist without constantly revolutionising the instruments of production, and thereby the relations of production, and with them the whole relations of society. Conservation of the old modes of production in unaltered form, was, on the contrary, the first condition of existence for all earlier industrial classes. Constant revolutionising of production, uninterrupted disturbance of all social conditions, everlasting uncertainty and agitation distinguish the bourgeois epoch from all earlier ones. All fixed, fast-frozen relations, with their train of ancient and venerable prejudices and opinions, are swept away, all new-formed ones become antiquated before they can ossify. All that is solid melts into air, all that is holy is profaned. (Marx and Engels, (1847) [1977]

Global capitalism, exacerbated by the new imperialism, creates unprecedented inequalities. As Bill Van Auken (2010b) puts it:

> [t]he "poverty summit" that concluded at the United Nations [in September, 2010] served to expose capitalism's responsibility for the poverty and hunger confronting billions of people across the planet. Despite vows by the UN and the major powers over the past decade to ameliorate these conditions, the desperation and misery of the world's most oppressed layers have only deepened as a result of imperialist predations and the shocks arising from the global financial crisis.

Global economic integration, he goes on, while enabling an immense growth in technology, production, and communications, "has been totally subordinated to the profits of the banks and corporations and the accumulation of obscene amounts of wealth by a tiny financial aristocracy" (Van Auken, 2010b). To put this in perspective, it is informative to point out that the three richest people in the world have more money than the gross domestic product (GDP) of forty-eight of the world's poorest nations, and over two thousand of the richest people earn more than the total income of nearly 50 percent of the total world population (Smith, 2009). The masses of the world's poor have suffered a series of catastrophes as social inequality has grown (Van Auken, 2010b). Over the last ten years the number of people living on the brink of starvation has increased from 830 million to 915 million, with 980 million people living on less than a dollar a day. At the same time, over nine million children still do not live past their fifth birthday, mainly because of malnutrition and preventable disease, and half a million women die each year from complications in pregnancy and childbirth (Van Auken, 2010b).

As an alternative to these crimes against humanity, I have advocated twenty-first-century socialism, and have commended events in the Bolivarian Republic of Venezuela as a viable way forward for the planet. In making the case for *democratic* socialism based on participatory democracy, in the pages of this volume I have distanced myself from the distortions of Stalinism.

Jean-Paul Sartre (1960) described Marxism as a "living philosophy" continually being adapted and adapting itself "by means of thousands of new efforts." To Sartre's observation, Crystal Bartolovich (2002, p. 20) added, Marxism is not "simply a discourse nor a body of (academic) knowledge" but a living project. In the barrios of Caracas and elsewhere in Venezuela, "the people have awoken" (Martinez et al., 2010, p. 24), and everywhere else where the poor live and the spark of socialism has been lit, people are engaging with the possibility of a *practical* democratic socialism.

Women of color are prominent leaders of the Bolivarian revolution. Let me leave the last word to one resident in the Caracas barrio of Baruta, who joined the hundreds of thousands of people, maybe a million, descending from the barrios around Caracas, successfully demanding the reinstatement of Chávez after the military coup in 2002 (Blough, 2010):

> We love our president, but this is not his revolution. This is our revolution and it will always be the revolution of the people. If President Chávez goes, we will miss him dearly but we will still be here. We are revolutionaries and we will always be here. We will never go back! (cited in Blough, 2010)

Notes

Introduction

1. Venezuela was re-designated "The Bolivarian Republic of Venezuela" in the new constitution enacted after the election of socialist president Hugo Chávez Frías in 1999. The new constitution, written with the direct participation of the Venezuelan people, was approved in a popular referendum by 70 percent of the vote. The country was named after the Venezuelan Simon Bolivar, who helped liberate Venezuela from the Spanish in the nineteenth century.

2. The original main title of this book was *Racism, Schooling, and Education in the U.K. and the U.S.* However, it was felt that the inclusion of the word "Schooling" would make the title clumsy and ambiguous. While the focus of the book is the years of compulsory attendance at schools rather than further or higher education, education has the potential to be a liberatory process, society-wide rather than just in educational *institutions* in the conventional sense of the term. This societal process of liberation is occurring currently in Venezuela (see chapter 5 of this volume).

3. It is not my intent here to provide overviews of the work of Gramsci and Althusser. For analyses of Gramsci, see, for example, Giuseppe, F. (1970); Boggs (1976); Buci-Glucksmann (1980). For Althusser, see, for example, Callinicos (1976); Kaplan and Sprinkler (eds.) 1993; Elliott (2006).

4. Stalinism refers to political systems that have the characteristics of the Soviet Union from 1928 when Joseph Stalin became leader (his leadership lasted until 1953). The term refers to a repressive and oppressive from of government by dictatorship, which includes the purging by exile or death of opponents, mass use of propaganda, and the creation of a personality cult around the leader.

5. My views on the concept of "ethnicity" are dealt with at length in Cole (2003).

6. The following analysis of racism draws on and develops Cole, 2009a, pp. 38–41.

7. "Ideological" when used by Marxists means ideas that act in the interests of the capitalist class.

8. The thrust of Herrnstein and Murray's (1994) arguments in *The Bell Curve* is an unabashed defense of social inequality, attributing wealth and poverty to superior versus inferior genetically determined intellectual abilities. The political conclusion of *The Bell Curve* is a rejection of all policies aimed at ameliorating social injustice. Attempts to reduce inequality do not work, they conclude, because of inequality of endowments. It is thus "time for America once

again," they argue, "to try living with inequality" (Herrnstein and Murray, ibid., p. 551).

9. Ellis, erstwhile lecturer in Russian and Slavonic Studies at Leeds University, told the student newspaper that he supported the theory developed by Herrnstein and Murray that white people are more intelligent than black people. (He also said that women did not have the same intellectual capacity as men [Taylor, M., 2006.] According to Matthew Taylor, Ellis first came to prominence in 2000 "when he traveled to the U.S. to speak at the American Renaissance conference, an event described by anti-fascist campaigners as a three-day rally bringing together the scientific racism movement." Apparently the event attracts organizations such as the Ku Klux Klan. In one of his books, Ellis states that the fascist British National Party (BNP) "is the only party in Britain that has consistently attacked the scandalously high levels of legal and illegal immigration" (ibid.).

10. Miles's discussions of racism, as an exemplar of neo-Marxist analysis, are probably the most widely cited in the U.K. I should point out that my definition of racism is different from that favored by Miles and his associates who are totally against inflating the concept of racism (see the Appendix to this Introduction for a discussion).

11. Steve Fenton (2003, p. 164) has used the term "ethnic majoritarian thinking" to describe the process of making a distinction between the (ethnic) majority, an almost unspoken "us," and members of minority ethnic communities. This way of thinking is perhaps epitomized in the use of "our" in the title of the (1981) U.K. Rampton Report, *West Indian Children in Our Schools* (see chapter 4, pp. 118–119 of this volume). This distinction is underlined more recently by the fact that in Britain, for example, British Muslims have to substantiate their allegiance to Britain. After the Forest Gate terror raid (where the police raided the home of two innocent Muslim brothers, one of whom was shot, though not fatally; see Cole and Maisuria, 2010), the media highlighted the fact that the brothers stated they were "born and bred" East Londoners and they "loved Britain" (Getty, 2006, p. 5) (for a discussion of "Britishness," see chapter 4 of this volume).

12. The "Tea Party" movement is named after the 1773 rebellion in Boston, Massachusetts, which preceded the American Revolution (see chapter 3 of this volume) and signaled the end of British colonial rule. As Gary Younge (2010) argues, what unites the "Tea Party" is not an agenda, but anger. As he explains, many "are regular anti-tax, small-government social conservatives," but some, who tend to be the loudest, "believe Obama is a Muslim communist who was not born in the US." The Southern Poverty Law Center, the most prominent civil rights group focused on hate organizations, noted that a recent poll found that the Tea Party movement is viewed in more positive terms than either the Democratic or Republican parties (SPLC, 2010a). The movement is heavily funded by Republican oil billionaires, the Koch brothers (Goldenberg, 2010).

13. Fascism is a political philosophy based on racism and a strong patriotic belief in the nation. Once in power fascists centralise authority under a dictatorship, and promote belligerent nationalism. Workers and their organizations are smashed, as is any form of opposition through terror and censorship. Fascism tends to arise when capitalist democracy becomes unable to sustain capitalism. As Leon Trotsky put it, "[t]he historic function of fascism is to

smash the working class, destroy its organizations, and stifle political liberties when the capitalists find themselves unable to govern and dominate with
the help of democratic machinery" (Trotsky, 1944).

14. Maria Papapolydorou (2010) has pointed out that for Miles (1989) racism is
    associated with modes of production but not limited to *capitalist* modes of
    production, and that, according to Miles, racialization and racism predate
    capitalist societies. As Miles, 1989, p. 99, puts it, neither are "exclusive 'prod-
    ucts' of capitalism but have origins in European societies prior to the devel-
    opment of the capitalist mode of production." While I acknowledge this, my
    focus in this volume is specifically on the way in which racialization connects
    to capitalist modes of production (and to patterns of migration). This is not
    to say, of course, that all instances of racism are directly or even indirectly
    linked to capitalism, economics and politics. In racialized societies, racism is
    experienced with massive and constant frequency in countless situations. The
    point I am making is that without the neo-Marxist concept of racialization, it
    is impossible to have a full understanding of racism historically and contem-
    poraneously. For a discussion of different uses of the concept of racialization,
    both (neo-) Marxist and non-Marxist, see Murji and Solomos (eds.) 2005.

15. Sexist language was the norm before the advent of the twentieth-century
    feminist movement. I will thus resist the temptation to comment each time
    it occurs in citations in this volume. Today sexist language tends to be absent
    from the printed word. When it occurs, one must presume it is there out of
    ignorance, or because the writer is deliberately being sexist.

16. The Stephen Lawrence Inquiry Report (Macpherson, 1999) followed a
    lengthy public campaign initiated by the parents of black teenager Stephen
    Lawrence, murdered by racist thugs in 1993. A bungled police investigation
    means that there have been no convictions. The report looked at racism in
    the Metropolitan Police and other British institutions, and acknowledged
    the existence of institutional racism in the police, the education system, and
    other institutions in the society. In subsequent years, the concept of insti-
    tutional racism has been under sustained political attack in the U.K. (see
    chapter 4 of this volume for a discussion).

17. I have included continent-wide and global institutions in my definition. The
    former, for example, would incorporate xeno-racism and xeno-racialization
    in the case of Europe, in light of the enlargement of the European Union
    (see chapter 2 of this volume for a discussion). With respect to the global
    dimension, modes of production throughout the world have become globally
    racialized in new ways and have created new institutionally racist structures.
    In an analysis, which is essentially postmodern but informed by Marxism,
    Bhattacharyya et al. (2002) have provided a number of insights that can aid
    in the development of our understanding of a Marxist concept of racializa-
    tion. Their argument is that, in the global economy, racialization has taken
    on new forms; for example, the way in which the World Trade Organization
    has supported multinationals against developing world farmers (ibid., p. 30);
    how "downsizing" has spawned a revival of old-fashioned sites and forms of
    production like "sweatshops" and homeworking (p. 31); and the general way
    in which high street goods on sale in the West are produced by excessively
    exploited labor in developing countries (pp. 32–33). Bhattacharyya et al.
    make interesting observations on new forms of institutional racism, such as
    the "prison-industrial complex," which "performs the oldest management

tricks in the book—undercuts wages, exploits the most constrained work-force imaginable and, through this, disrupts the organization of workers on the outside" (ibid., p. 43), and on the role of the WTO and the IMF in the debt crisis (pp. 111–136). The spatial proximity of the racialized poor and the rich, they point out, is needed "because insurance companies, law firms, banks, etc., need cleaners, porters and gardeners: they also need entertainment both for their own workforce and for their international clients" (p. 131). In addition, they attempt to extend Marxist analysis by noting the way in which biotechnology and genetic modification extends the idea of ownership to the organic world (pp. 116–121).

18. I use "Latina/o" in order to be inclusive of both women and men. Where "Latino" appears on its own in this volume, I am citing someone who, for whatever reason, has not used the inclusive term.

19. Since my primary purpose is to examine the contribution of Gramsci and Althusser to theorizing racism, schooling, and education, I do not deal in this volume with theoretical developments that have taken place in (neo-) Marxist educational theory since the interventions of Gramsci and Althusser. I have, however, addressed some of this work in Cole (ed.) (1988) and Cole, 2008a, chapter 3. For a more comprehensive analysis of theoretical developments that have taken place in (neo-)Marxist educational theory since Althusser and Gramsci, see Allman (2007, pp. 51–68), Rikowski (2002, pp. 18–20; and 2007) and Small (2005, pp.169–187).

20. While CRT has its strengths, it also has a number of weaknesses. For example, some Critical Race Theorists (e.g., Gillborn, 2009; Mills, 2009) caricature Marxism as being largely insensitive to racism. For a response to and a rebuttal of this view, see, for example, Cole, 2009a, b, c, d. For a comprehensive Marxist response to CRT, see Cole, 2009a.

21. "Barrio" is a Spanish word meaning district or neighborhood. In the Venezuelan context, the term commonly refers to the outer rims of big cities inhabited by poor working class communities.

22. I put "imperialisms" in the plural in order to make a distinction, for example, between old U.K., Spanish, and U.S. imperialism (discussed in chapters 2 and 3 of this volume) and current "new imperialism," in which the U.S. is hegemonic.

23. In the context of increasing political and academic awareness of human rights in general, Marxists should not allow workers' rights to be excluded from the equation. Workers' rights are human rights that we have because we are human (Gross, 2006).

24. In Marxist terminology, the dialectic refers to contradictions between opposing forces and their solutions (the dialectic is referred to and developed throughout this volume).

25. One contributor suggested that we should use "Englishness" rather than "racism." His argument was that "Englishness" helps to explain the contemporaneous incorporation of previously racialized groups. My response would be that the connection between "racism" and "nationalism" implicit in "Englishness" might be particularly close in the English context, as noted by Miles (see p. 55 of this volume). Thus while the concept of "Englishness" may explain a form of *racism* (excluding others not considered to be "English") at a specific juncture, for example, what *may have been* occurring, in certain contexts, in England in 2006, "racism" is a more useful *general* term to

describe discourse, actions, processes, and practices, both historically and contemporaneously.

26. The concept of xeno-racialization is discussed in chapter 2 of this volume. Essentially, in *my* usage of the term, it refers to that form of racialization currently meted out to Eastern European workers in the U.K.

27. It should already be clear that (neo-)Marxism is a "broad church" encompassing varying interpretations of Marxist theory.

1 Socialism, Marxism and Neo-Marxism

1. For a fuller discussion of utopian socialism, see Cole, 2008a, pp. 13–21, on which this section of the chapter is based. My focus is on Europe because the utopian socialists, which Marx and Engels critiqued in their development of scientific socialism (see below), were Europeans. This is not to imply that socialist thought was not occurring elsewhere in the world—to take just one example, see Tecumseh's (1810) thoughts cited on p. 68 of this volume. Marxism has been accused of Eurocentrism. However, I would argue that one of the major strengths of Marxism is that it is non-Eurocentric. As I have argued elsewhere (Cole, 2008a, p. 76), while Eurocentricity may be true of modernism in general, Marxism is not Eurocentric. That this is the case is attested to by the "fact that many of the most brilliant, prominent, and effective anticolonial activists have insistently pronounced themselves Marxists" (Bartolovich, 2002, p. 15). While accusations of lack of awareness in the North's complicity in the underdevelopment of the South, of Euro-American genocide, and the lack of dialogue between the North and the South are valid when directed at many "modernists," they also do not apply to Marxism, particularly *current* Marxist analyses, which do engage with such issues. Top priorities for modern-day Marxists include the way in which the economic situation in the South is a direct result of decisions made in the North, particularly with respect to impoverishment as a result of debt burdens; and the violence practiced as a result of the economic and political trajectory of neo-liberal capitalism. This is the form of capitalism where the market rules; public expenditure is cut; governments reduce regulation of everything that could diminish profits; state-owned enterprises, goods and services are sold to private investors; and the concept of "the public good" or "community" is eliminated (Martinez and García [2000]). Neo-liberal capitalism is accompanied by (U.S.) imperialism. Connections need to be made and lessons learned with respect to resistance to U.S. imperialism and Left political and economic developments in countries such as Cuba, and in Latin America (Cole, 2008a, p. 76; see chapter 5 of this volume for a discussion of twenty-first-century socialism in the Bolivarian Republic of Venezuela).

2. A dialectical conception of history sees societies moving forward through stages of struggle. Thus out of opposing forces (thesis and antithesis), a new form of society arises (synthesis). This in turn generates a new thesis and antithesis, and ultimately a new synthesis and so on and so on (this is discussed further, later in this chapter).

3. The word "communism" is a greatly misunderstood one. It was used by Marx to refer to the stage after socialism when the state would have withered away and when we would live communally. In the period after the Russian Revolution up to the demise of the Soviet Union, the Soviet Union and other

Eastern European countries were routinely referred to as "communist" in the West. The Soviet Union, founded in 1922, actually referred to itself, following Marx, as "socialist." Some Marxists (e.g., Cliff, 1974) have described what became of the Soviet Union and other Eastern European countries as "state capitalist." It is ironic that the West falsely designated these states "communist." In reality (despite the fact that many had a number of positive features—full employment, housing for all, free public and social services, safety for women to walk the streets at night, and so on), they were undemocratic dictatorships with special privileges for an elite and drudgery for the many. These Eastern European societies were not real socialist states, and were also far removed from Marx's vision of communism. Marx and Engels also made reference to early pre-capitalist social formations—stages of communal living—for example, "the ancient communal and State ownership which proceeds especially from the union of several tribes into a city by agreement or by conquest, and which is still accompanied by slavery" (Marx and Engels, 1845–46).

4. Terry Eagleton (2002, p. 3) makes a distinction between the term *proletariat* (originally those who served the state by producing children) and the term *working class*. While the former refers primarily to any kind of subservient labor, the latter denoted a position within the social relations of production. However, in current usage, the two terms have become synonymous.

5. "Forcible" does not necessarily imply or involve excessive violence (a charge often leveled at Marxists). Engels, for example, stated: "if the social revolution and practical communism are the necessary result of our existing conditions—then we will have to concern ourselves above all with the measures by which we can avoid a violent and bloody overthrow of the social conditions" (Engels, 1845 [1975], p. 243). Engels believed that education could play a role in a peaceful transformation of society: "the calm and composure necessary for the peaceful transformation of society can...be expected only from an *educated* working class" (ibid.). While Marxists recognize that violence has been perpetrated on a grand scale *in the name of Marxism*, it is, in fact, neo-liberal capitalism that is currently unleashing unabashedly an orgy of violence, hitherto unprecedented, causing masses of avoidable deaths from world poverty and imperialist conquest (for a discussion of Marxism, social revolution, and violence, see chapter 10 of Cole, 2008a).

6. Lenin is more circumspect about the transition from socialism to communism, or from the "first phase of communism" where "every worker...receives from society as much as he has given to it" (1918 [2002], pp. 98–99) to the higher phase where the rule will be "[f]rom each according to his ability to each according to his needs" (ibid., p. 103). As he puts it, "it has never entered the head of any socialist to 'promise' that the higher phase of the development of communism will arrive'" (ibid.) (for a discussion, see Lenin, 1918 [2002], pp. 91–109). Elsewhere, however, he appears to possibly contradict himself. Thus in 1920 [2002], p. 192, he writes, "Marx studied the laws of development of human society and realised the inevitability of the development of capitalism towards communism."

7. History has confirmed that while "stages" hold true as a *general* description of history, different stages can exist in a given country at the same time (Marx, Engels and Lenin were acutely aware of this), and that it is possible to go backward or forward, for example, from socialism to capitalism, or from capitalism to feudalism, or indeed from capitalism to fascism and vice versa.

8. For Lenin, as indeed for Marx, a period of the "dictatorship of the proletariat" was necessary in the transition from capitalism to socialism. As Lenin argues, unlike bourgeois democracy which, as we saw in the Introduction to this volume, Lenin defined as the oppressed being allowed to decide every few years who will repress them in parliament (Lenin, 1917 [2002], p. 95), under the dictatorship of the proletariat, "democracy...passes into an entirely new phase...and the class struggle rises to a higher level, dominating each and every form" (Lenin, 1919 [2002], p. 176). For Lenin, as for Marx, the dictatorship of the proletariat is a *temporary* phase necessary to consolidate and defend the revolution from inevitable challenges from capitalists, both nationally and overseas. The ultimate aim is the abolition of social class per se. As Lenin (1919, [2002] p. 172) puts it, "[s]ocialism means the abolition of classes" (for a discussion, see Lenin, 1919 [2002], pp. 153–154). Despite Lenin's heartfelt hopes that the dictatorship was temporary, it actually intensified and continued in various forms until the demise of the Soviet Union in 1991.

9. From the stance taken in this book where education is viewed as "liberating" and schooling as "conforming" young people to the requirements of capitalism (see chapter 4), it make more sense to think of the "educational ISA" as "the schooling ISA." It is clear from a reading of Althusser, 1971 that it is the schools that Althusser has in mind. However, given that "educational ISA" is the term that he used, I will retain it.

10. Althusser's use of a capital "S" here represents a religious analogy, as in the Subject (capital "S," the Father). People "must be obedient to God, to their conscience, to the priest, to de Gaulle [the French president at the time he was writing this passage], to the boss" (Althusser, 1971, p. 181).

11. For Althusser (1971, p. 182), it is this very phrase, "*So be it!*" that "registers the effect to be obtained" and "proves that it *has* to be so."

12. Rather than having the aim of overthrowing capitalism with a socialist revolution, social democratic policies entail the attempt to *reform* capitalism through parliamentary and democratic processes; to regulate the market; and to implement state-sponsored programs to ameliorate and remove the inequalities and injustices caused by capitalism.

13. Clause IV stated that the aim of the Labour Party was:
    To secure for the workers by hand or by brain the full fruits of their industry and the most equitable distribution thereof that may be possible upon the basis of the common ownership of the means of production, distribution and exchange, and the best obtainable system of popular administration and control of each industry or service.

14. What Blair meant was that in his use of terminology, the grand ideology of socialism is over, but not the grand ideology of capitalism. He repeated this belief in his aforementioned speech to the (British) Labour Party Conference, on October 2, 2001, when, in reaffirming his belief in meritocracy, he declared that "ideology...in the sense of rigid forms of economic and social theory...is dead." (*Guardian*, October 3, 2001, p. 5). From a Marxist perspective, where, as we have seen, ideology represents ideas and beliefs that uphold and maintain capitalist hegemony, it is in fact the idea of *meritocracy*—that people advance on merit—within capitalism that is ideological. In their classic treatment of the relationship between schooling and capitalist America, Samuel Bowles and Herbert Gintis (1976, p. 103)

demonstrate how schooling legitimates economic inequality by providing an *ostensibly* meritocratic mechanism for assigning individuals to unequal economic positions. For Bowles and Gintis, both meritocracy and equal opportunities within capitalism are ideological. In reality schooling mirrors the inherently unequal structure of the capitalist economy.

15. The cuts, which are, in reality, not even necessary (e.g., Basketter, 2010; Hari, 2009) have been described by Steve Bundred, chief executive of the Audit Commission and the U.K.'s "chief accountant," as unavoidable. As he put it in classic interpellative style, "[d]on't believe the shroud-wavers who tell you grannies will die and children starve if spending is cut. They won't. Cuts are inevitable and perfectly manageable." Bundred earned nearly £250,000 in 2008 (*Socialist Worker,* July 11, 2009, pp. 1 and 2).

16. Conventionally, from a (neo-)Marxist perspective, the capitalist state needs to be overthrown, and replaced by socialism, rather than socialism being established through parliamentary change (but see chapter 5 of this volume for the interesting case of Venezuela, where Hugo Chávez is advocating the overthrow of the state of which he is president). For this reason, Marxists would normally vote for socialist parties in order to spread socialist ideas rather than in the hope that such parties can enact socialism through parliament.

17. VAT (value added tax) is like a sales tax, based on the estimated market value added to a product during each stage of its manufacture.

18. In October 2009, BNP leader Griffin appeared on the BBC current affairs "Question Time," a program in which a panel with a "cross section" of views answers questions from the audience. Griffin stated that Islam was incompatible with life in Britain; admitted sharing a platform with the Ku Klux Klan (see chapter 3 of this volume); and described gay men kissing in public as "really creepy." He said that "legal reasons" prevented him from explaining why he had previously sought to play down the Holocaust and that he had now changed his mind. He was challenged by Jack Straw, the then Justice Secretary and a fellow panelist, who said there was no law preventing him for giving an explanation.

19. Derrick Bell's (1980) concept of "interest convergence" has been defined by Critical Race Theorists Richard Delgado and Jean Stefancic (2000, p. xvii, cited in Gillborn, 2008, p. 32) as the tolerance of or encouragement for "racial advances" for black people "only when such advances also promote white self-interest." It is a key concept in the lexicon of Critical Race Theory. For a key example, Brown v. Board of Education in 1954, see chapter 4 of this volume.

20. This is another of Derrick Bell's concepts, and refers to "those situations where an inequity becomes so visible and/or so large that the present situation threatens to become insurmountable" (Gillborn, 2008, p. 32). In Bell's 1985, p. 32 words, such cases "serve as a shield against excesses in the exercise of white power, yet they bring no real change in the status of blacks" (cited in Gillborn, 2008, p. 32).

21. Traditional intellectuals regard themselves as an autonomous and independent group, and are seen as such by the public, whereas in fact they tend to be conservative and allied and supportive of the ruling group. Organic intellectuals, on the other hand, grow organically with both dominant and subordinate groups classes in society, and are their thinking and organizing

elements. For Gramsci, organic intellectuals are produced by the educational system to perform a function for the dominant social group in society. It is through organic intellectuals that the ruling class maintains its hegemony over the rest of society. Gramsci argued that it was important for the working class to produce its own organic intellectuals, and also that a significant number of "traditional intellectuals" come over to the revolutionary cause (see Burke, 2005, for an analysis).

22. Marx argues that the origins of the capital held by capitalists lie in the forcible seizure of feudal and clan property, the theft of common lands and state lands, and the forced acquisition of church property at nominal price. In other words, capitalism has its origins in theft and continues on the same basis (see Marx, 1887 [1965], pp. 717–733).

23. This Appendix is adapted from Cole, 2009a, pp. 115–116.

24. Marx's views on religion are well known. As he famously put it: "Religion is the sigh of the oppressed creature, the heart of a heartless world, and the soul of soulless conditions. It is the opium of the people" (Marx, 1843–1844). The editors of the Marx Internet Archive (MIA) (cited with this extract from Marx) explain that in the nineteenth century, opium was widely used for medical purposes as a painkiller, and thus Marx's dictum did not connote a delusionary state of consciousness, but rather a way of easing the pain of capitalism. Although Marx and Marxism have traditionally been associated with atheism, my own view is that this needs amending. While religion, as opposed to theism (belief in a God or Gods that intervene in the world) or deism (belief in a God who does not intervene in the world) has often been and continues to be form of oppression and conservatism, there have been and are large numbers of people who identify with a religious or spiritual belief who also identify with Marxism or socialism (millions of Roman Catholics in Venezuela; for example, see chapter 5 of this volume). There are also, of course, many Marxists who are atheists or agnostics. Whatever our beliefs or lack of beliefs, it is my view that our energies should be devoted primarily to the creation of equality and happiness on earth. This becomes increasingly imperative as capitalism and imperialism intensify their ravages.

2   Racism in the U.K.

1. An earlier, shorter, and less theorized version of this chapter was published as Cole (2009e).

2. In June 2009, a conference titled, "Critical Race Theory in the U.K. What is to be learnt? What is to be done?" was held at the Institute of Education, University of London. Over thirty papers were presented, and the conference included contributions from leading U.K. Critical Race Theorists David Gillborn, Namita Chakrabarty, and John Preston. There was a significant undercurrent of "black exceptionalism" (see the beginning of chapter 3 of this volume). One of the main conference organizers, Kevin Hylton, heralded the birth of "BritCrit."

3. For a critique of the concept of "white supremacy" as deployed by Critical Race Theorists, see Cole, 2009a, pp. 23–33; see also Cole, 2009b, pp. 247–255. For a CRT response, see Mills, 2009. The importance of differentiating the traditional use of the term "white supremacy" to describe the ideology of fascists and other far right racists from "everyday racism" was underlined for

me in the 2009 elections to the European Parliament (discussed in chapter 1 of this volume).

4. The concept of "the colonial schema" is Etienne Balibar's (see Balibar, 1991, p. 12).

5. I recall seeing ads in shop windows for accommodation in Hammersmith, West London in the 1960s that (before it was made illegal) ended with "No coloureds. No Irish." Such racialization was typical and rampant at that time.

6. At the time of writing (spring 2010), a report by The Equality and Human Rights Commission found black people were at least six times more likely and Asian people about twice as likely to be stopped and searched than white people. The commission said it could not rule out legal action against some forces (BBC News, 2010). The evidence suggested that racial stereotyping and discrimination were significant factors behind these higher rates of stops and searches (ibid.). Black and ethnic minority youths were also overrepresented in the criminal justice system (ibid.). Additionally police were more likely to give white young people more lenient reprimands or fines, while black young people were more likely to be charged. Along with the continued racialization of black and Asian constituencies, the racialization of the Irish also continues (see Delaney, 2007; Mac An Ghaill, 2000; see also the discussion in this chapter of anti-Gypsy and Roma Traveller racism).

7. Not all forms of racism discussed in this paper under the heading of "non-color-coded racism" are necessarily definitively non-color-coded. There are, for example, dark-skinned Jewish people who may experience color-coded racism rather than or alongside antisemitism. The point is that the forms or racism discussed under this heading are not *necessarily* color-coded.

8. This concept is also Etienne Balibar's (see Balibar, 1991, p. 12). However, whereas Balibar puts a hyphen between "anti" and "semitism," I have omitted it, on the grounds that Jewish communal organizations in the U.K.—such as the Community Security Trust—use the unhyphenated "antisemitism." This more closely reflects Wilhelm Marr's use of the word that he and others advocate to describe a policy toward Jews based on "racism" (Langmuir, 1990, p. 311, cited in Iganski and Kosmin, 2003, pp. 6–7). Not using a hyphen or a capital "S" denotes that antisemitism is a form of racism directed at Jewish people per se, and not at those who speak a Semitic language per se. Semitic languages are spoken by nearly five hundred million people across large parts of the Middle East, North Africa, and Northeast Africa. The most widely spoken Semitic language is Arabic.

9. I use the term "mainly" because there were settlements of colonial citizens in various parts of the U.K. during the colonial era (Fryer, 1984).

10. The rest of Kern's (2009) article takes an anti-Left, pro-Israel stance.

11. While the reference to "jihad" *could* imply the involvement of antisemitic radical Islamists, there is no evidence that contemporary antisemitic attacks are predominantly the work of "extremist groups." Indeed such attacks, including the daubing of swastikas on synagogues and graves, are prompted not "by a particular ideological conviction or volition but instead unthinkingly manifest a commonsense antisemitism" (Iganski, 2009, p. 138).

12. The mode of production in Nazi Germany involved the state exercising ultimate control of the economy, with the seizure of the property of Jewish people. Selected corporations, which supported the state in its program, operated

with monopoly power. This mode of production also involved the slave labor of Jewish people and others deemed by the fascist state to be subhuman.

13. David Latchman (2010, cited in Reisz, 2010) has expressed concerns about antisemitism among some parts of the Muslim population in the U.K., and what he describes as "far Left" "antisemitism." It is my view that those who claim to be anti-imperialist and anti-Zionist and on the Left, but also express antisemitism in any form, are not truly on the Left and certainly not modern-day Marxists.

14. I deal with anti-Gypsy Roma and Traveller racism under the main heading of "Non-color-coded racism" because my focus is the U.K. I am aware, of course, that many European Roma people have darker skins, and that this will be a component in the racism directed at them. An example of anti-Roma racism occurred in Belfast in June 2009, when there were violent attacks on a Roma community from Romania (Shilton, 2009). One of those affected stated, "[t]hey made signs like they wanted to cut my brother's baby's throat. They said they wanted to kill us." Reports claimed that there was graffiti in the area containing the slogans of the neo-Nazi Combat 18 group. It was also reported that extracts from Hitler's *Mein Kampf* had been put through letterboxes (ibid.). Attacks were also directed against those seeking to help the Roma people (ibid.). The fascists also wrote texts connecting racism against the Roma with xeno-racism, thanking "all true loyalists for forcing Romanian Muslims out of Belfast and also Polish in mid Ulster out of their homes! These foreign nationals are a threat to Britain's Britishness" (see later in this chapter for a discussion of xeno-racism).

15. "Pikey" is a racist term of abuse directed at the Gypsy Roma and Traveller communities in the U.K. The U.S. terms "white trash" and "trailer trash" are used in a similar perjorative way, though the stereotypes differ. The U.S. terms are used to describe people perceived to be of lower socioeconomic class, relating to the belief that people of lower socioeconomic class tend to live in trailers or mobile homes.

16. As Thomas Acton has pointed out, "if official statistics about 'Gypsies'" health relate only to poor caravan-dwelling people who have come to the notice of the authorities, they omit those Romani people who are living in houses or who use private caravan sites (his comments on this chapter).

17. Fekete's centralizing of "the economic" accords with the neo-Marxist formulation of racialization (see the Introduction to this volume).

18. Of course, there may be overlap between xeno-racism, anti-asylum-seeker racism, and Islamophobia. For example, some Eastern European workers are Muslim, as are many asylum seekers (see the next section of this chapter).

19. My focus here on *current* anti-asylum-seeker racism, under the heading "Newer Hybridist Racism" is not of course to underestimate the fact that this form of racism has a long history in the U.K. and elsewhere (for an analysis, see, for example, Schuster, 2002).

20. I recognize the problematic nature of the term "asylum-seeker." It forms part of a "discourse of derision" (Ball, 1990, p. 18) in the communications ISA, and in the political ISA in the pronouncements of certain politicians. "Forced migrants" (Rutter, 2006) might be a more appropriate term.

21. Islamophobia as a concept is not without its problems, with some commentators making the case for different terms. For example, the Commission on the Future of Multi-ethnic Britain (2000) and Arun Kundnani (2007) prefer

"anti-Muslim racism," while others (e.g., Etienne Balibar, cited in Modood, 2005) favor Muslimophobia. However, as Robin Richardson (2009, p. 11) points out, Islamophobia is widely used in the U.K. and in the deliberations and publications of international organizations, and "[d]espite its disadvantages, the term Islamophobia looks as if it is here to stay" (for a thorough analysis of Islamophobia and related concepts and terms, see Richardson, 2009).

3   Racism in the U.S.

1. Althusser's analysis of RSAs and ISAs pertains to the unified (French) capitalist state in the sixth decade of the twentieth century operating on home soil. The five hundred years of institutional racism described in this chapter, however, occurred in a variety of "state formations" beginning with a colonial administration, as part of the British Empire, based in London. After U.S. independence in 1776, when the central state became unified (if not united), institutional racism was in large part administered by individual local states of the United States. Institutional racism continues in the United States, with the RSAs and ISAs operating from individual states as well as the central U.S. state apparatus.

2. Wayne Au has pointed out that it may be more appropriate to use the term, "enslaved Africans," both for historical accuracy, and as a reminder that being enslaved was not Africans' normal state of being (his comments on this chapter). I agree with this point, and will use it where appropriate.

3. This occurred forty-two years before the English colony at Jamestown, Virginia, and fifty-five years before the landing of the Pilgrims on Plymouth Rock in Massachusetts, making it the oldest permanent European settlement on the North American continent (Oldcity.com, 2009).

4. The town of Wounded Knee, site of probably the most famous Sioux massacre, in 1890, was seized by the American Indian Movement (AIM), a Native American activist organization in 1973.

5. The different identity-specific forms of CRT are useful in this chapter to focus on the concerns of specific racialized groups. However, CRT is not without its problems. I have already noted that a central tenet of Critical Race Theory is the use of the term "white supremacy" to describe everyday racism in certain societies, rather than the conventional restriction of the term to describe the views of extremist groups, and have made reference to my critiques of the concept. Another central tenet of CRT is the primacy of "race" over social class. I have also extensively critiqued this tenet elsewhere (see Cole, 2009a, b, c, d). Further weaknesses are CRT's continuing attempts to caricature Marxism as being insensitive to racism, and CRT's inability (beyond vague references to "human liberation," "the struggle," "a vision of hope for the future," "social transformation") to envisage a future world (see Cole, 2009a, pp. 149–150 for a discussion).

6. Old films about "cowboys and Indians," and indeed "Texans and Mexicans" replayed endlessly on television on both sides of the Atlantic serve to reinforce imperialism and colonialization, as do "cowboy outfits" and "Indian outfits" readily available for sale in retail stores and on the Internet.

7. The origin of the term "Jim Crow" is often attributed to "Jump Jim Crow," a "song-and-dance" caricature of African Americans first performed by a white actor in 1832. "Jim Crow" subsequently became a derogatory expression for

black Americans. Hence the racial segregation laws became known as "Jim Crow laws" (Woodward et al., 2001, p. 7).

8. "White supremacy" is used here in its traditional, and in my view correct sense, as opposed to the CRT usage that uses the term to describe, in certain contexts, everyday racism experienced by people of color (see Gillborn, 2008 for a defense of CRT usage of the term; for a critique of CRT usage, see, for example, Cole 2009d).

9. The National Association for the Advancement of Colored People held its 101st National Convention in March 2010. While it combats all forms of racism, it is oriented toward the defense and advancement of black Americans (NAACP, 2010).

10. As this book goes to press, the 2010 U.S. Census figures (available from the U.S. Census Bureau: http://www.census.gov/) are gradually becoming available. I have inserted the 2010 figures throughout this chapter where they are available.

11. Mulatta/o is a Spanish colonial term referring to a person with one black and one European parent, Mestiza/o to someone of mixed European and Indian origin.

12. I differentiate schooling (the work of the educational ISA) from education (a potentially expansionary liberating process) (see chapter 4 of this volume).

13. It is important not to forget that indigenous peoples from Mexico and other parts of Central America tend to be wrongly subsumed under the label "latina/o." As Olin Tezcatlipoca (2008) points out Nican Tlaca (indigenous) people are 180 million strong, of which 32 million reside in the United States. Nican Tlaca people are projected to be over 50 percent of the U.S. population in the next one hundred years.

14. Space constraints prevent my providing more than a brief consideration of the large number of constituencies of Asian Americans, which I will discuss in alphabetical order. For more comprehensive analyses, see, for example, Takaki, 1989; Zia, 2000; Wu, 2002; Perea et al. 2007; Asian-Nation, 2010.

15. Asian-Nation (2010) also includes "Native Hawaiians and Pacific Islander Americans" (NHPIs) as being constituencies of "Asian Americans." However, as we shall see, in response to representations from Native Hawaiian and Pacific Islander activists, since 2000, NHPIs are now a sixth "racial category." For this reason I consider this group separately from "Asian Americans."

16. From 1913 to 1948, thirty out of the then 48 states of the United States prohibited "interracial couples." This included whites and blacks, and in many states, also relationships and the intermarriage of whites with Native Americans or Asians (Loving Day, 2009). Antimiscegenation legislation continued in some states until the outlawing of "interracial" relationships and marriage was made illegal in 1967.

17. The "model minority" myth is discussed under the heading "Asian Americans Today" later in this chapter. Perea (1995, cited in Perea et al. 2007, p. 1102) goes on to identify a fourth media image: groups of Latina/o people rushing from stores clutching stolen goods. Perea (1995, cited in Perea et al., 2007, p. 1102) points out how this image works to mask the fact that Latina/o people were also part of the riots. He points out that this is hardly surprising since half the population of South Central Los Angeles was Latina/o and faced similar life conditions to African Americans. The needs of Latina/o

communities there, however, were not part of the picture (Perea, 1995, cited in Perea et al., 2007, p. 1102).

18. This last group includes the Hmong who, given that they comprise a separate entry in the U.S. census, are discussed separately in this chapter.

19. The forthcoming 2010 census makes it clear that "race" is not considered in a biological way. As the "United States 2010 Census Constituent FAQs" spell out: "The racial categories included in the census form generally reflect a social definition of race recognized in this country, and are not an attempt to define race biologically, anthropologically or genetically. In addition, it is recognized that the categories of the race item include racial and national origin or socio-cultural groups."

20. I should point out for the benefit of U.K. readers that, in this volume, I use "public school" in the literal sense of the term to differentiate that system from private education. It is a (historical) peculiarity of educational usage in the U.K. that "public school" implies an elite private school such as Eton or Harrow.

4   Racism, Schooling, and Education Against Racism in the U.K. and the U.S.

1. Since "the compulsory years" are my major focus. I tend, in this volume, to use *schooling* in the restricted U.K. sense of the compulsory years of attendance at *schools* rather than the wider North American usage of "school" that can include colleges and universities. However, quite clearly, colleges and universities in both the U.K. and the U.S. increasingly and overtly attempt to prepare students for capitalist conformity and jobs, consistent with the changing demands of the capitalist economy.

2. Barry Burke (2005) points out that Gramsci's writings on schooling are not always easy to understand, are confusing, and are open to misinterpretation. In a well-known study, Harold Entwistle (1979) argues that Gramsci paradoxically promotes conservative schooling for a radical politics. This has drawn considerable adverse criticism (e.g., Apple, 1980; Giroux, 1980; Borg and Mayo, 2006). The editors of the *Prison Notebooks*, Quintin Hoare and Geoffrey Nowell Smith, make the point that Gramsci's apparent " 'conservative' eulogy of the old curriculum [in Italy] in fact often represents a device which allowed Gramsci to circumvent the prison censor" (Gramsci, 1971 p. 24). However, as Burke (2005) argues, "this device has had the effect of perplexing more than his captors."

3. Terry Wrigley and Peter Hick (2009, p. 36) have argued that the word *pedagogy* is relatively new in English-speaking countries, and that it is often used with limited understanding. In most European languages and education systems, they argue the concept means more than just teaching methods. It requires "an articulation of educational aims and processes in social, ethical and affective as well as cognitive terms, and involves reflection about the changing nature of society or the value of human existence." It is in this sense that I am using it here.

4. Given current U.S. and U.K. imperialism's obsessive designs on Afghanistan, this historical reference is telling, to say the least.

5. Maud Blair worked as an advisor for multicultural education, and as late as 1989 was helping schools identify books with outdated colonial theories and racist views and images. Not only were there history and geography books,

but story books and well-intentioned books by non-governmental organizations (NGOs) such as Oxfam. Some published as late as the 1970s still presented images that were demeaning to Asian and black peoples (Cole and Blair, 2006, p. 85).

6. The rest of this section of the chapter draws heavily on Cole, 2009a, pp. 72–75.

7. I have deliberately chosen this traditional nomenclature, given that I am describing the monocultural approach.

8. Antiracist education in the U.K. has shown awareness of equality issues other than "race" for over twenty years (e.g., Cole, 1986a, b; Troyna, 1987).

9. It should be recorded that there were local government exceptions. For example, the left-wing Inner London Education Authority (ILEA), eventually abolished by Thatcher in 1988, published a number of equality documents in the 1980s, including *Race, Sex and Class: 4. Anti-Racist Statement and Guidelines* (ILEA, 1983), and distributed the pamphlets to all of its schools. (For an analysis of the political climate in the years of the radical Right, see, for example, Hill, 1989, 1997; see also Jones, 2003; Tomlinson, 2005).

10. This was all part of a concerted radical Right attack on teacher education that was assumed to be a hotbed of Marxism (see Hill, 1989, 1994, 2001, 2007a; see also Cole, 2004d, pp. 150–163). This legacy continues to this day. For example, the term "trainee" rather than "student teacher" relates to the radical Right notion that teacher *training* is not a theoretical enterprise, but a combination of love of subject and practical skills. For similar reasons it is the *Training and Development Agency* that oversees teacher education. However, progressive equalities legislation (see Equality and Human Rights Commission Website, 2010) has required departments of education in universities, university colleges, and colleges to verse their student teachers in equality issues (for suggestions on promoting equality in the primary/elementary school, see Hill and Helavaara Robertson (2009), and for ideas for the secondary/high school, see Cole (ed.) (2009).

11. Gillborn (2008, p. 133) is careful to stress his awareness that his analysis could be seen as disrespectful to the Lawrence family's ongoing battle for justice, and of victories won along the way. He underlines that this is neither his intent, nor, he hopes the outcome of his analysis, and lists a number of such victories (ibid., pp. 133–134). "The Lawrence Inquiry," he notes, "has delivered considerable advances and holds out the possibility of further progress, but it is a start not an end" (ibid., p. 135).

12. "PC" or "Political correctness" is a pernicious concept invented by the radical Right, which, to my dismay, has become common currency in the U.K. and the U.S. The term was coined to imply that there exist (Left) political demagogues who seek to impose their views on equality issues' in particular, appropriate terminology, on the majority. In reality, nomenclature changes over time. Thus, in the twenty-first century, terms such as "negress" or "negro" or "colored," nomenclatures that at one time were considered quite acceptable, are now *generally* considered offensive. There are some exceptions. According to the U.S. Bureau of the Census, some people still use the nomenclature "negro." In addition, as pointed out in the Introduction to this volume, the NAACP retains "colored" in the title of its organization. Egalitarians are concerned with *respect* for others and, therefore, are careful to acknowledge changes in nomenclature, changes

that are decided by oppressed groups themselves, bearing in mind that there can be differences among such oppressed groups. Thus, for example, it has become common practice to use "working class" rather than "lower class"; "lesbian, gay, bisexual, and transgender" rather than "sexually deviant"; "disability" rather than "handicap," "gender equality" rather than "a woman's place." Using current and acceptable nomenclature is about the fostering of a caring and inclusive society, not about "political correctness" (Cole, 2008a, p. 142–143).

13. There will also be increased privatization, and, as with all other public services, there will be cuts. As far as privatization is concerned, all English primary and secondary schools will be encouraged to become academies; that is, state-maintained but free of local authority control and independently run and open to control by private companies. In addition, there will be "free schools," "all-ability, state-funded schools, set up in response to parental demand." These schools will also be academies, and are modeled on U.S. "charter schools" (see later in this chapter). Although the government has talked about protecting schools, in reality the cuts will have a devastating effect on schools. Attacks are already being made on additional funding outside the core schools budget, and there will be a total real reduction in the Education Department's spending of 3 percent by 2014 to 2015. Teachers are facing a pay freeze and cuts to pensions (Darke, 2010). Clearly all this will have a major financial and demoralizing impact on both students and teachers. Gove has commented about the closure of playgrounds: "[p]lay has to make its contribution to tackling the deficit" (cited in Orr, 2010, p. 10). As suggested in chapter 1 of this volume, we are witnessing a qualitative shift in the sense of a generalized offensive against the working class with economic restructuring going further than even Thatcher dared (Orr, 2010, p. 12).

14. Gloria Ladson-Billings (2006, p. viii) describes CRT "chronicles" as constructed narratives in which evidence and other forms of data are embedded. For a critical appraisal of the CRT concept of "chronicle" written from a Marxist perspective, see Cole, 2009a, pp. 50–51.

15. In his 1995 writing, in opposition to these three forms of multiculturalism, McLaren (pp. 126–144) outlined the central features of what he called "critical and resistant multiculturalism." He described this as "a resistance post-structuralist approach to meaning…located within the larger context of postmodern theory (ibid., p. 126). According to McLaren, critical and resistance multiculturalism "stresses the central task of transforming the social, cultural, and institutional relations in which meanings are generated" (ibid.). Resistance multiculturalism "doesn't see diversity itself as a goal but rather argues that diversity must be affirmed within a politics of cultural criticism and a commitment to social justice" (ibid.). Like post-structural and postmodern analyses in educational theory in general, there is much talk of social change and social justice in McLaren's mid-1990s analysis, but no concrete suggestions for societal change. Elsewhere (Cole, 2008a, chapter 5) I have examined the work of some leading poststructuralists/postmodernists. I argue that, while many questions are asked, and there are many claims for moving toward social change and social justice, no specific indications are given except at the local level. One of the great strengths of Marxism is that it allows us to move beyond appearances and to look beneath the surface *and* to move forward collectively: local, nationally, and internationally.

16. The term "ideal type" is associated with the work of the sociologist Max Weber. It is an analytical construct that allows us to see similarities in different approaches to a given topic.

17. The above analysis by McLaren and his co-writers, summarized here, is considered in more detail in Cole, 2009a, pp. 65–71.

5   Twenty-First-Century Socialism and Education in the Bolivarian Republic of Venezuela

1. A common criticism leveled at Marxism, as we saw in Note 5 of chapter 1 of this volume, is that it is inherently "violent." As we also saw in Note 5, Engels, like Chávez, believed that that education could play a role in a peaceful transformation of society.

2. "Middle class" is used here in the sociological sense of relatively rich people in relatively high-status jobs. A distinction needs to be made between sociological and Marxist usages of "social class." Sociologists such as Max Weber use the term to describe people according to status, occupation, and earnings. For Marxists, the working class consists of *all* those who need to sell their labor power to survive rather than living off the labor power of others (see Appendix 1 to chapter 1 of this volume). Both Weberian and Marxist definitions have their advantages. For example, the Weberian definition allows us to differentiate between the working conditions, including income, of those working in a given society at a given time, or over time. The Marxist definition reminds us that those who sell their labor power are all workers, even though within a given society and from one capitalist society to another, some are more privileged than others.

3. The "consensus" entailed a package of policies aimed at extending markets further into areas previously run by governments, its rhetoric being that multinational private enterprises were better at protecting the public interest than "the inept governments" of Latin America and the Caribbean (Victor, 2009). The "Washington Consensus" "prescribed privatization of public services, widespread deregulation, lifting of tariffs, unrestricted investment flows, and free access of large corporations to public contracts and domestic markets" (ibid.). Maria Paez Victor (2006) has noted how the "Consensus" spectacularly failed the people by stunting the growth of income per person in the region (it fell from 82 percent to 9 percent to 1 percent and increasing the number of poor by 14 million, while at the same time bringing corresponding spectacular success for capitalism in the form of $1 trillion in profits from Latin America for U.S. banks and corporations. As Victor (2009) argues, the U.S. historically has played, and continues to play, a major role in political and economic events in Latin America. However, as she puts it, "US hegemony was not easy and did not come without a price for Latin America." Since the end of the nineteenth century, she points out, the U.S. has "invaded, overthrown, and destablized [*sic*] governments in the region about 90 times." Indeed, every one of the twentieth-century dictatorial governments in Latin America (and the Caribbean) has been backed by the U.S. (Victor, 2009).

4. As we shall see later in this chapter, Chávez has consistently expressed pride in his indigenous and African roots.

5. The Venezuelan working class should not be viewed as constituting a traditional industrial proletariat, as detailed, for example, in the discussion of

Lenin in chapter 1 of this volume. Some 60 percent of Venezuelan workers are involved in the informal economy (street vendors and so on), primarily in the barrios from where Chávez draws his support (Dominguez, 2010).

6. Liberation theology began as a movement within the Catholic Church in Latin America in the 1950s, achieving prominence in the 1970s and 1980s. It emphasizes the role of Christians is aligning themselves with the poor and being involved in the struggle against economic, political, and social inequalities. In Chávez's view, "[t]he people are the voice of God" (cited in Sheehan, 2010). Chávez is referring to the Venezuelan revolutionary masses. Two advocates of liberation theology, Fals Borda and Paulo Freire, as guiding educational theorists and practitioners, are discussed later in this chapter. See Note 2 of Appendix 2 to chapter 1 of this volume for some comments on Marx's views on religion.

7. For a discussion of the First, Second, Third, and Fourth Socialist Internationals, see chapter 1, pp. 20–32 of this volume.

8. That Bolivar helped liberate Venezuela from the Spanish in the nineteenth century has already been noted. Morazán attempted to transform Central America into one large and progressive nation, also in the nineteenth century. Maurice Bishop was a Marxist revolutionary and prime minister of the People's Revolutionary Government of Grenada from 1979 to 1983. Augusto Sandino was a Nicaraguan revolutionary and leader of a rebellion against U.S. military presence in Nicaragua between 1927 and 1933.

9. Chávez's reference to this "huge responsibility" is reminiscent of Engels' reference to "the momentous act" that the working class is "called upon to accomplish," but without the same implication of inevitability (see chapter 1, pp. 23–24 of this volume), and *with* the foresight of mistakes made by others in the past. It is true that scientific socialism was originally led by white European men (see chapter 1 of this volume for a discussion), and as such has been described as Eurocentric (see Note 1 of chapter 1 of this volume for a refutation). There then followed, however, anticolonial developments in Asia and Africa and elsewhere that were by definition not Eurocentric. Chávez is correct to assert that the current epicenter of socialist struggle is in Latin America, and in particular, Venezuela, where as noted later in this chapter, people of color, of which Chávez is a prominent example, are central, if contested, players.

10. As noted in the Introduction to this volume, Lenin characterized capitalist democracy as the process by which oppressed workers are allowed once every few years to decide which particular representatives of the oppressing class will represent them and repress them in parliament. In an interview in which she explains the centrality of the communes—created not by the government but "by the people for the people," the aim being to build socialism on a permanent basis —o the success of the revolution, Antenea Jimenez (2010) argues that "the advance of participatory democracy is irreversible," and that there is no going back to "representative democracy."

11. It should be reiterated here, however, that, for (neo-)Marxists, the state represents more than "the government," and includes the various apparatuses of the state, repressive and ideological as outlined by Althusser. These various apparatus will have to be won over to, in order to "convert a counter-revolutionary state into a revolutionary state." It should also be pointed out that there is no single (neo)-*Marxist theory of the state*. Notwithstanding some

communist parties historically (e.g., those associated with Euro-communism when the Stalinist regimes still existed in Europe) that advocated the parliamentary road to socialism, the general Marxist and neo-Marxist position is that the capitalist state has to be overthrown in order to move toward socialism. With respect to capitalist states in general in the twenty-first century, this becomes even more apparent as, in the current crisis in capitalism, these states bail out the international banks at the expense of the working classes of the world, and play more and more the role of an executive committee for managing the common affairs of the whole bourgeoisie (Marx and Engels (1847) [1977], p. 37; Beams, 2010). Some earlier neo-Marxist theories of the state in capitalist society where the state is seen as "relatively autonomous" from the economic base (e.g., Poulantzas, 1972) do not hold water in the current climate.

12. "Cumbe" is the name given to liberated spaces created by liberated slaves (cited in Martinez et al., 2010, p. 221).

13. The fieldwork at this school was carried out on my behalf by Edward Ellis. I am most grateful to him for this. The subheadings in this section of the chapter reflect the main issues and concerns that arose in Ellis's interviews.

14. Venezuelanalysis.com, in its own words:

> is an independent website produced by individuals who are dedicated to disseminating news and analysis about the current political situation in Venezuela. The site's aim is to provide on-going news about developments in Venezuela, as well as to contextualize this news with in-depth analysis and background information. The site is targeted towards academics, journalists, intellectuals, policy makers from different countries, and the general public.

6 Implications for Multicultural Antiracist Socialist Practice in Educational Institutions

1. I use the term "other Left radical" to describe those teachers who are against the values of capitalism and wish to use their role as teachers to promote a more equal world, but do not identify themselves as Marxists. This could be, for example, because of a lack of awareness of what being a Marxist entails; it could be because they have internalized a distorted view of Marxism; or because they embrace a different Left thought system such as anarchism (for a discussion of the principle tenets of anarchism, see, for example, Ward, 2004; Marshall, 2010).

2. A common response from students and others is likely to be a rejection of Marxism. See Cole, 2009a, pp. 115–132, where I raise some common objections to Marxism, and attempt to respond to them from a Marxist perspective.

3. The following discussion of Learning Without Limits (LWL) draws on Cole, 2008b, pp. 453–463; for a response from one of the LWL team members, and a reply from myself, see Yarker, 2008, pp. 464–469.

4. It should be pointed out, however, that the LWL paradigm, as formulated by Hart et al. 2004, is lacking, in my view, in two major interrelated respects. First, implicit in the paradigm seems to be an accommodation with social democratic politics, and a reluctance to make connections with capitalism—local, national, or international. This means that while LWL promotes the

achievement of the working class, a noble aim in itself, this promotion is (by default) within the confines of a global system—capitalism. Second, the notion of empowerment in LWL is confined to pedagogy to enhance individual and collective (academic) achievement and excludes a consideration of emancipatory *content* that can increase the class consciousness of the working class. This critique of Learning Without Limits is developed in Cole, 2008b. I would like to reiterate that my critical appraisal of Hart et al. (2004) as a whole should be viewed very much as a development of, rather than a rejection of, their work.

References

African American English (2010) "History Matters: Arizona and English-Only." *Word*, May 28. http://africanamericanenglish.com/2010/05/28/history-matters-arizona-and-english-only/ (accessed October 30, 2010).

Allman, P. (1988) "Gramsci, Freire and Illich: Their Contributions to Education for Socialism," in T. Lovett (ed.), *Radical Approaches to Adult Education: A Reader*, London: Routledge.

—— (2007) *On Marx: An Introduction to the Revolutionary Intellect of Karl Marx*, Rotterdam/Taipei: Sense.

Althusser, L. (1969) *For Marx,* translated by Ben Brewster, London: Allen Lane. http://www.marxists.org/reference/archive/althusser/1965/introduction.htm (accessed July 27, 2009).

——(1971) "Ideology and Ideological State Apparatuses," in *Lenin and Philosophy and Other Essays,* London: New Left Books. http://www.marx2mao.com/Other/LPOE70NB.html (accessed December 19, 2009).

Ambrose, S. (1984) *Eisenhower the President*, New York: Simon & Schuster.

American Civil Liberties Union (2008) "School to Prison Pipeline: Talking Points," June 6. http://www.aclu.org/racial-justice/school-prison-pipeline-talking-points (accessed September 28, 2010).

American Federation of State, County and Municipal Employees (AFSCME) (2008) "Dr. Martin Luther King, Jr. on Labor," A FSCME. http:// www.afscme.org/about/1550.cfm (accessed February 4, 2011).

Anderson, B. (1983) *Imagined Communities: Reflections on the Origin and Spread of Nationalism,* London: Verso.

Anderson, B., M. Ruhs, B. Rogaly, and S. Spencer (2006) *Fair Enough? Central and East European Migrants in Low-Wage Employment in the UK,* York: Joseph Rowntree Foundation.

Anderson, B., N. Clark, and V. Parutis (2007) "New EU Members? Migrant Workers' Challenges and Opportunities to UK Trade Unions: A Polish and Lithuanian Case Study," London: TUC. http://www.tuc.org.uk/extras/migrantchallenges.pdf (accessed June 6, 2009).

Anyon, J. (2005). *Radical Possibilities: Public Policy, Urban Education, and a New Social Movement,* New York: Routledge.

Asian-Nation (2008) "Taiwanese Americans" http://www.asian-nation.org/taiwanese.shtml (accessed April 7, 2011).

—— (2010) Asian Nation: Asian American History, Demographics, and Issues. http://www.asian-nation.org/index.shtml (accessed August 1, 2010).

Au, W. (2009a) "Obama, Where Art Thou? Hoping for Change in U.S. Education Policy," *Harvard Educational Review,* 79 (2), Summer, pp. 309–320.

Au, W (ed.) (2009b) *Rethinking Multicultural Education: Teaching for Racial and Cultural Justice,* Milwaukee, Wisconsin: Rethinking Schools.

—— (2009c) *Unequal by Design: High-Stakes Testing and the Standardization of Inequality,* New York: Routledge.

Baez, F. (2008) El saqueo cultural de América Latina: Random House.

Balibar, E. (1991) "Racism and Politics in Europe Today," *New Left Review,* 186, pp. 5–19.

Ball, S. (1990) *Politics and Policymaking in Education,* London: Routledge.

BAMN (Coalition to Defend Affirmative Action, Integration, and Immigrant Rights And Fight for Equality by Any Means Necessary) (2001) "Asian Pacific Americans and Affirmative Action: From the Trial Transcript of Professor Frank Wu." http://www.bamn.com/doc/2001/010212-apas-and-aa-wu-excerpts.pdf (accessed August 15, 2010).

Bankston, C. L. III (2010) "Cambodian Americans." http://www.everyculture.com/multi/Bu-Dr/Cambodian-Americans.html (accessed August 3, 2010).

Baptiste, H. P., H. Orvosh-Kamenski, and C. J. Kamenski (2005) "American Presidents and Their Attitudes, Beliefs, and Actions Surrounding Education and Multiculturalism," *Notes and Abstracts in American and International Education,* September 22. http://www.thefreelibrary.com/American+presidents+and+their+attitudes%2c+beliefs%2c+and+actions...-a0154459382 (accessed August 29, 2010).

Baptiste, H. P. and R. Sanchez (2004) "American Presidents and Their Attitudes, Beliefs, and Actions Surrounding Education and Multiculturalism," *Multicultural Education,* Spring.

Bartolovich, C. (2002) "Introduction," in C. Bartolovich and N. Lazarus (eds.), *Marxism, Modernity and Postcolonial Studies,* Cambridge: Cambridge University Press.

Basketter, S. (2010) "They're Out to Tear Down the Welfare State," Socialist Worker online, October 26. http://www.socialistworker.co.uk/art.php?id=22851 (accessed March 20, 2011)

BBC News (2005) "US Immigrants Stage Boycott Day," May 2. http://news.bbc.co.uk/1/hi/world/americas/4961734.stm (accessed October 17, 2010).

—— (2007) "Quick Guide: The Slave Trade: Who Were the Slaves?" http://news.bbc.co.uk/1/hi/world/africa/6445941.stm (accessed May 3, 2010).

—— (2008a) "Attack on House Treated as Racist." http://news.bbc.co.uk/1/hi/northern_ireland/foyle_and_west/7452233.stm (accessed July 27, 2008).

—— (2008b) "Cash Raised after Racist Attack." http://news.bbc.co.uk/1/hi/england/shropshire/7304198.stm (accessed July 27, 2008).

—— (2008c) "Gang Attack Polish Man with Knife." http://news.bbc.co.uk/1/hi/england/lincolnshire/7299238.stm (accessed December 18, 2008).

—— (2008d) "Man in Unprovoked Racist Assault." http://news.bbc.co.uk/1/hi/scotland/edinburgh_and_east/7350036.stm (accessed July 27, 2008).

—— (2008e) "Pole Subjected to 'Racist Attack.'" http://news.bbc.co.uk/1/hi/scotland/north_east/7358197.stm (accessed July 27, 2008).

—— (2008f) "Prison for Racist Polish Attack." http://news.bbc.co.uk/1/hi/scotland/edinburgh_and_east/7433720.stm (accessed July 27, 2008).

—— (2008g) "Rise in Racist Attacks Reported." http://news.bbc.co.uk/1/hi/northern_ireland/7266249.stm (accessed July 27, 2008).

—— (2009a) "'More Needed' to Tackle NI Racism." http://news.bbc.co.uk/1/hi/northern_ireland/8129460.stm (accessed March 23, 2010).

—— (2009b) "Plea after 'Brutal' Racist Attack." http://news.bbc.co.uk/1/hi/scotland/north_east/8147157.stm (accessed December 4, 2009).

—— (2009c) "Polish Man Attack 'Was a One Off.'" http://news.bbc.co.uk/1/hi/scotland/north_east/8152527.stm (accessed March 23, 2010).

—— (2009d) "Prison for Racist Polish Attack." http://news.bbc.co.uk/1/hi/scotland/edinburgh_and_east/7433720.stm (accessed March 23, 2010).

—— (2009e) "Racist Link to Town Gang Attack." http://news.bbc.co.uk/1/hi/northern_ireland/7838319.stm (accessed March 23, 2010).

—— (2010) "Police Stop and Search 'Target Minorities.'" http://news.bbc.co.uk/1/hi/uk/8567528.stm (accessed April 17, 2010).

Beams, N. (2009) "Marxism, Socialism and Climate Change," *World Socialist Web Site (WSWS)*, December 22. http://www.wsws.org/articles/2009/dec2009/etnb-d22.shtml (accessed September 21, 2010).

—— (2010) "The Second Stage of the Global Capitalist Crisis," *World Socialist Web Site (WSWS)*, April 12. http://www.wsws.org/articles/2010/apr2010/bnrt-a12.shtml (accessed April 13, 2010).

Beane, J. A. and M. W. Apple (1999) "The Case for Democratic Schools," in M. W. Apple and J. A. Beane (eds.), *Democratic Schools: Lessons from the Chalk Face*, Buckingham: Open University Press.

Beckman, A., C. Cooper, and D. Hill (2009) "Neoliberalization and Managerialization of 'Education' in England and Wales—A Case for Reconstructing Education," *Journal for Critical Education Policy Studies*, 7 (2), November. http://www.jceps.com/PDFs/07-2-12.pdf (accessed April 16, 2010).

Behrendt, S. (1999). "Transatlantic Slave Trade," *Africana: The Encyclopedia of the African and African American Experience*, New York: Basic Civitas Books.

Bell, D. (1976) [2000] "Serving Two Masters: Integration Ideals and Client Interests in School Desegregation Litigation," in Delgado, R. and J. Stefancic (eds.), *Critical Race Theory: The Cutting Edge*, Philadelphia: Temple University Press.

—— (1980) "Brown v. Board of Education and the Interest Convergence Dilemma," *Harvard Law Review*, 93, pp. 518–533.

—— (1985) "Foreword: The Civil Rights Chronicles (the Supreme Court, 1884 Term)," *Harvard Law Review*, 99, pp. 4–83.

Berki, R. N. (1975) *Socialism*, Letchworth: Aldine Press.

Berlin, I. (2003) *Generations of Captivity: A History of African-American Slaves*, Cambridge, MA: Belknap Press of Harvard University Press.

Berryhill and Sturgeon Ltd. (undated) "1912 Canada Prime Minister Robert Borden Signed Letter." http://berryhillsturgeon.com/Archives/Canada/Borden/Borden1912.html.

Bhattacharyya, A. (2008) "The Movement behind Obama," *Socialist Worker*, November 15. http://www.socialistworker.co.uk/art.php?id=16399 (accessed October 28, 2010).

—— (2009) The Daily Mail vs. the Nazis? *Socialist Worker*. http://www.socialist-worker.co.uk/art.php?id=19454 (accessed October 28, 2010).

Bhattacharyya, G., J. Gabriel and S. Small. (2002) "Race and Power: Global Racism in the Twenty-First Century," London: Routledge.

Bigott, L. (2009) "Popular Education in Venezuela and Latin America," Presentation to a delegation of visiting education academics to Venezuela, coordinated by Tom Griffiths and Jo Williams, in January 2009. Caracas: National Assembly Building.

Black American History, a History of Black People in the United States: Montgomery Bus Boycott (undated) http://www.africanaonline.com/montgomery.htm (accessed May 20, 2010).

Blair, T. (1995) "Speech at NewsCorp Leadership Conference," Hayman Island, Australia, July 7.

Blanco, H. (2010) "Online Video: Hugo Blanco Urges Greens: End Capitalism before It Ends Us." http://links.org.au/taxonomy/term/441 (accessed September 20, 2010).

Blassingame, J. W. (ed.) (1977) *Slave Testimony: Two Centuries of Letters, Speeches, Interviews and Autobiographies*, Baton Rouge: Louisiana State University Press.

Blough, L. (2010) "Bolivarian Republic of Venezuela: It Is Not Chavez. It Is the People. Axis of Logic," April 14. http://axisoflogic.com/artman/publish/Article_59344.shtml (accessed April 24, 2010).

Boggs, C. (1976) *Gramsci's Marxism*, London: Pluto Press.

Booth, R. (2010) "Rise in Hate Crime Follows BNP Council Election Victories," *The Guardian*, January 15. http://www.guardian.co.uk/politics/2010/jan/15/hate-crime-bnp-local-council-elections (accessed January 30, 2010).

Borg, C. and P. Mayo (2006) *Learning and Social Difference. Challenges for Public Education and Critical Pedagogy*, Boulder: Paradigm.

Bowles, S. and H. Gintis (1976) *Schooling in Capitalist America*, London: Routledge and Kegan Paul.

Brayboy, B. (2005) "Toward a Tribal Critical Race Theory in Education." *The Urban Review*, 37 (5) December, pp. 425–446.

Bron Davis, D. (2006) *Inhuman Bondage: The Rise and Fall of Slavery in the New World*, Oxford: Oxford University Press.

Brown, J., E. Gutstein, and P. Lipman (2009) "Arne Duncan and the Chicago Success Story: Myth or Reality?" *Rethinking Schools*, http://www.rethinkingschools.org/restrict.asp?path=archive/23_03/arne233.shtml (accessed September 11, 2010).

Bruce, I. (2008) *The Real Venezuela: Making Socialism in the 21st Century*, London: Pluto Press.

Bucholtz, M. (2004) "Styles and Stereotypes: The Linguistic Negotiation of Identity among Laotian American Youth," *Pragmatics*, 14 (2/3), pp. 127–147. http://elanguage.net/journals/index.php/pragmatics/article/viewFile/430/362 (accessed August 12, 2010).

Buci-Glucksmann, C. (1980) *Gramsci and the State*, translated by David Fernbach, London: Lawrence and Wishart.

Bullard, R. D., P. Mohai, R. Saha, and B. Wright (2007) *Toxic Wastes and Race at Twenty: 1987–2007: Grassroots Struggles to Dismantle Environmental Racism in the United States*, Cleveland, OH: Justice and Witness Ministries, United Church of Christ. http://www.ejnet.org/ej/twart.pdf (accessed September 17, 2010).

Buras, K. L. (2008) *Rightist Multiculturalism*, New York: Routledge.

Burke, B. (2005) "Antonio Gramsci, Schooling and Education." http://www.infed.org/thinkers/et-gram.htm (accessed August 19, 2010).

Callinicos, A. (1976) *Althusser's Marxism*, London: Pluto Press.

—— (2009) "Labour's Policies Boost the Racists," *Socialist Worker*, November 21, p. 4.

Camara, B. (2002) "Ideologies of Race and Racism," in P. Zarembka (ed.), *Confronting 9–11, Ideologies of Race, and Eminent Economists*, Oxford: Elsevier Science.

Campbell, N. (2008) "When the Supermodel Met the Potentate," *GQ Magazine*, February, pp. 56–61.

Cankú Lúta (2009) "Help Stop the Exploitation of Indian Ceremonies and Culture." http://www.canku-luta.org/oldnews/exploitation.html (accessed May 3, 2010).

Carrasco, G. P. (1997) "Latinos in the United States: Invitation and Exile," in J. F. Perea (ed.), *Immigrants Out! The New Nativism and the Anti-Immigrant Impulse in the United States*, New York and London: New York University Press.

Castagno, A. and S. Lee (2007) "Native Mascots, Ethnic Fraud, and Interest Convergence: A Critical Race Theory Perspective on Higher Education," *Equity and Excellence in Education*, 40 (1), pp. 3–13.

Chan, S. (1991) *Asian Americans: An Interpretive History*, Boston: Twayne.

Chancellor, V. (1970) *History for Their Masters*, Bath: Adams and Dart.

Chang, E. T. (2003) "Korean Americans." *Asian-Nation: The Landscape of Asian America*. http://www.asian-nation.org/korean.shtml (accessed August 7, 2010).

Chang, R. S. (2000) "Toward an Asian American Legal Scholarship: Critical Race Theory, Post-structuralism, and Narrative Space," in R. Delgado and J. Stefancic (eds.), *Critical Race Theory: The Cutting Edge* (2nd Edition), Philadelphia, PA: Temple University Press.

Chang, B. and W. Au (2007–2008) "Unmasking the Myth of the Model Minority," *Rethinking Schools*, 22 (2), pp. 15–19.

Chang, R. S. and N. Gotanda (2007) "Afterword: The Race Question in LatCrit Theory and Asian American Jurisprudence," *Nevada Law Journal*, 7, November 16, pp. 1012–1029.

Chapman, F. (2010) "Some Sobering Notes on African American Equality," politicalaffairs.net: Marxist Thought Online. http://politicalaffairs.net/article/articleview/9338/ (accessed July 2, 2010).

Chapman, T. K. (2006) "Pedaling Backward: Reflections of *Plessy* and *Brown* in Rockford Public Schools' De Jure Desegregation Efforts," in A. D. Dixson and C. K. Rousseau (eds.), *Critical Race Theory in Education: All God's Children Got a Song*, New York and London: Routledge.

Chávez, H. (2010a) "Coup and Countercoup: Revolution!" http://venezuela-us.org/2010/04/11/coup-and-countercoup-revolution/ April 11 (accessed April 14, 2010).

——— (2010b) Online Video. http://www.caracaschronicles.com/node/2281.

Choonara, E. (2009) "BNP Gains Led to This Racist Attack," *Socialist Worker*, July 4.

Chuong, C. H. and H. T. Minh (2003) "Vietnamese Americans," *Asian-Nation: The Landscape of Asian America*. http://www.asian-nation.org/vietnamese.shtml (accessed August 9, 2010).

Churchill, W. (2004) *Kill the Indian, Save the Man: The Genocidal Impact of American Indian Residential Schools*. San Francisco, CA: City Lights.

Clark, C. (2006a) "Conclusion," in C. Clark and M. Greenfields, *Here to Stay: The Gypsies and Travellers of Britain*, Hatfield: University of Hertfordshire Press.

——— (2006b) "Introduction," in C. Clark and M. Greenfields. *Here to Stay: The Gypsies and Travellers of Britain*, Hatfield: University of Hertfordshire Press.

——— (2006c) "Who Are the Gypsies and Travellers of Britain?" in C. Clark and M. Greenfields, *Here to Stay: The Gypsies and Travellers of Britain*, Hatfield: University of Hertfordshire Press.

Cliff, T. (1974) *State Capitalism in Russia*. http://www.marxists.org/archive/cliff/works/1955/statecap/index.htm (accessed November 28, 2009).

Clink, C. F. (ed.) (1961) *Tecumseh: Fact and Fiction in Early Records*, New Jersey: Englewood Cliffs.

CNN.com/US (2009) "Hispanic Population Boom Fuels Rising U.S. Diversity."
    http://edition.cnn.com/2009/US/05/14/money.census.diversity/ (accessed
    June 2, 2010).
Cobb, C. D. and G. V. Glass (2009) "School Choice in a Post-Desegregation World,"
    Peabody Journal of Education, 84 (2), April, pp. 262–278.
Coben, D. (1999) "Common Sense or Good Sense: Ethnomathematics and the
    Prospects for a Gramscian Politics of Adults' Mathematics Education," in M. van
    Groenestijn & D. Coben (eds.), *Mathematics as Part of Lifelong Learning. The
    Fifth International Conference of Adults Learning Maths—A Research Forum,
    ALM-5* (pp. 204–209). London: Goldsmiths College, University of London, in
    Association with ALM. http://www.alm-online.net/images/ALM/conferences/
    ALM05/proceedings/ALM05-proceedings-p204-209.pdf?7c979684e0c0237f9
    1974aa8acb4dc29=36f0is6pst9523pt8acs48p337 (accessed June 7, 2010).
——— (2002) "Metaphors for an Educative Politics: 'Common Sense,' 'Good Sense'
    and Educating Adults," in C. Borg, J. Buttigieg, and P. Mayo (eds.), *Gramsci and
    Education*, Lanham, MD: Rowman and Littlefield.
Cochran, S. (2010) "Civil Rights Hero—Cesar Chavez" Bella Online: The Voice
    of Women, http://www.bellaonline.org/articles/art32934.asp (accessed June 5,
    2010).
Coffer, W. E. (a.k.a. Koi Hosh) (1979) *Phoenix: The Decline and Rebirth of the Indian
    People*, New York and London: Van Nostrand Reinhold.
Cohen, J. (2010) "The Naming of America: Fragments We've Shored against
    Ourselves," July 12. http://www.umc.sunysb.edu/surgery/america.html
    (accessed July 13, 2010).
Cohen, S. (1985) "Anti-Semitism, Immigration Controls and the Welfare State,"
    Critical Social Policy, 13, Summer.
Cole, G. D. H. (1971) *A History of Socialist Thought, Volume 1: The Forerunners,
    1789–1850*, London and Basingstoke: Macmillan Press.
Cole, M. (1986a) "Multicultural Education and the Politics of Racism in Britain,"
    Multicultural Teaching, Autumn.
——— (1986b) "Teaching and Learning about Racism: A Critique of Multicultural
    Education in Britain," in S. Modgil, G. K. Verma, K. Mallick, and C. Modgil
    (eds.), *Multicultural Education: The Interminable Debate*, Barcombe, UK: Falmer
    Press.
——— (1992) *Racism, History and Educational Policy: From the Origins of the
    Welfare State to the Rise of the Radical Right*. Unpublished PhD thesis, University
    of Essex.
——— (1998) "Racism, Reconstructed Multiculturalism and Antiracist Education,"
    Cambridge Journal of Education, 28 (1), Spring, pp. 37–48.
——— (2003) "Ethnicity, 'Status Groups' and Racialization: A Contribution to
    a Debate on National Identity in Britain," *Ethnic and Racial Studies*, 26 (5),
    September, pp. 962–969.
——— (2004a) "F*** You—Human Sewage: Contemporary Global Capitalism
    and the Xeno-racialization of Asylum Seekers," *Contemporary Politics*, 10 (2),
    pp. 159–165.
——— (2004b) "'Brutal and Stinking' and 'Difficult to Handle': The Historical
    and Contemporary Manifestations of Racialisation, Institutional Racism, and
    Schooling in Britain," *Race Ethnicity and Education*, 7, 1, March, pp. 35–56.
——— (2004c) "'Rule Britannia' and the New American Empire: A Marxist
    Analysis of the Teaching of Imperialism, Actual and Potential, in the British

School Curriculum," *Policy Futures in Education,* 2 (3 and 4), pp. 523–538. http://www.wwwords.co.uk/pfie/content/pdfs/2/issue2_3.asp#7 (accessed September 17, 2010).

————(2004d) "Rethinking the Future: The Commodification of Knowledge and the Grammar of Resistance," in M. Benn and C. Chitty (eds.), *For Caroline Benn: Essays in Education and Democracy,* London: Continuum.

————(2005) "New Labour, Globalization, and Social Justice: The Role of Education," in G. E. Fischman, P. McLaren, H. Sünker, and C. Lankshear (eds.), *Critical Theories, Radical Pedagogies, and Global Conflicts,* Lanham, MD: Rowman and Littlefield.

———— (2008a) *Marxism and Educational Theory: Origins and Issues,* London: Routledge.

————(2008b) "Learning without Limits: A Marxist Assessment," *Policy Futures in Education,* 6 (4), pp. 453–463. http://www.wwwords.co.uk/pdf/validate.asp? j=pfie&vol=6&issue=4&year=2008&article=7_Cole_PFIE_6_4_web (accessed February 9, 2011).

————(2009a) *Critical Race Theory and Education: A Marxist response,* New York: Palgrave Macmillan.

————(2009b) "Critical Race Theory Comes to the UK: A Marxist Response," *Ethnicities,* 9 (2), pp. 246–269.

———— (2009c) "The Color-Line and the Class Struggle: A Marxist Response to Critical Race Theory in Education as It Arrives in the United Kingdom," *Power and Education,* 1 (1), pp. 113–124.

———— (2009d) "On 'White Supremacy' and Caricaturing, Misrepresenting and Dismissing Marx and Marxism: A Response to David Gillborn's 'Who's Afraid of Critical Race Theory in Education,'" *Journal for Critical Education Policy Studies,* 7 (1), pp. 29–49 (accessed August 27, 2009).

———— (2009e) "A Plethora of 'Suitable Enemies': British Racism at the Dawn of the Twenty-First Century," *Ethnic and Racial Studies,* 32 (9), pp. 1671–1685.

———— (forthcoming, 2011) "Racism and Education: from Empire to ConDem" in M. Cole (ed.) *Education, Equality and Human Rights: Issues of Gender, "Race," Sexuality, Disability and Social Class* (3rd Edition), London and New York: Routledge.

———— (ed.) (1988) *Bowles and Gintis Revisited: Correspondence and Contradiction in Educational Theory,* Lewes: Falmer Press.

———— (ed.) (2009) *Equality in the Secondary School: Promoting Good Practice across the Curriculum,* London: Continuum.

———— (ed.) (forthcoming, 2011) *Education, Equality and Human Rights: Issues of Gender, "Race," Sexuality, Disability and Social Class* (3rd Edition), London and New York: Routledge.

Cole, M. and M. Blair (2006) "Racism and Education: From Empire to New Labour," in M. Cole (ed.), *Education, Equality and Human Rights,* London: Routledge.

Cole, M. and A. Maisuria (2010) "Racism and Islamophobia in Post-7/7 Britain Critical Race Theory, (Xeno-) racialization, Empire and Education: A Marxist Analysis," in D. Kelsh, D. Hill, and S. Macrine (eds.), *Class in Education: Knowledge, Pedagogy, Subjectivity,* New York: Routledge.

Cole, M. and S. Virdee (forthcoming, 2011) "Racism and Resistance: From Empire to ConDem," in M. Cole (ed.), *Education, Equality and Human Rights: Issues of Gender, "Race," Sexuality, Disability and Social Class* (3rd Edition), London: Routledge.

Commission for Racial Equality (CRE) (2007) "Gypsies and Travellers: A Strategy for the CRE, 2004–2007," London: Commission for Racial Equality.

Community Security Trust (CST) (2010) "Antisemitic Incidents Report 2009." http://www.thecst.org.uk/docs/CST-incidents-report-09-for-web.pdf (accessed March 21, 2010).

Congressional Information Service (2000) Wartime Relocation of Civilians http://bss.sfsu.edu/internment/congressional%20records/19880415.html (accessed October 19, 2010).

Contreras Baspineiro, A. (2003) "Globalizing the Bolivarian Revolution Hugo Chávez's Proposal for Our América." http://www.narconews.com/Issue29/article746.html (accessed April 7, 2010).

Cookson, M. (2009) "The Peasants' Revolt Shook England's Rulers," *Socialist Worker*, September 5.

Cozzens, L. (1995) "Plessy v. Ferguson." http://www.watson.org/~lisa/blackhistory/post-civilwar/plessy.html.

——— (1998) "Brown v. Board of Education," *African American, History*, May 25. http://fledge.watson.org/~lisa/blackhistory/early-civilrights/brown.html (accessed August 24, 2010).

Crick, B. (1987) *Socialism*, Milton Keynes: Open University Press.

Cultural Survival: Australia (2009) http://www.culturalsurvival.org/australia?gclid=CL2iiOSD6aMCFVMB4wodjk6Z2A.

Dale, G. (1999) "Capitalism and Migrant Labour," in G. Dale and M. Cole (eds.), *The European Union and Migrant Labour*, Oxford: Berg.

Daniel, W. W. (1968) *Racial Discrimination in England*, Harmondsworth: Penguin.

Darder, A. and R. D. Torres (2004) *After Race: Racism after Multiculturalism*, New York and London: New York University Press.

Darke, M. (2010) "Education," *The Argus*, October 22.

Dela Cruz, M. and P. Agbayani-Siewart (2003) "Filipino Americans," *Asian-Nation: The Landscape of Asian America*. http://www.asian-nation.org/filipino.shtml (accessed August 5, 2010).

Delaney, E. (2007) *The Irish in Post-War Britain*, Oxford: Oxford University Press.

Delgado, R. and J. Stefancic (2000) "Introduction," in Delgado, R. and J. Stefancic (eds.), *Critical Race Theory: The Cutting Edge* (2nd Edition), Philadelphia, PA: Temple University Press.

Delgado, R. and J. Stefancic (2001) *Critical Race Theory: An Introduction*, New York: New York University Press.

Delgado, R., J. F. Perea, and J. Stefancic (2008) *Latinos and the Law: Cases and Materials*, St. Paul, MN: West.

Democracy Now (2005) "Chicano Leader Rodolfo 'Corky' Gonzales 1929–2005: 'He Was the Fist. He Stood for Defiance, Resistance,'" April 15. http://www.democracynow.org/2005/4/15/chicano_leader_rodolfo_corky_gonzales_1929 (accessed October 17, 2010).

Democratic Socialists of Central Ohio (2011) http://dsco1.tripod.com/ (accessed June 7, 2010).

Denevan, W. M. (1992) "Native American Populations in 1492: Recent Research and a Revised Hemispheric Estimate," in W. M. Denevan (ed.), *The Native Population of the Americas in 1492* (2nd Edition), Madison: University of Wisconsin Press.

——— (2010) Personal e-mail correspondence, June 2010.

Department for Children, Schools and Families (DCSF) "Statistical First Release" (2009) http://www.dcsf.gov.uk/rsgateway/DB/SFR/s000889/ SFR312009KS2AttainmentbyPupilCharacteristics.pdf (accessed December 19, 2009).

Department for Education, "Statistical First Release" (2010) "GCSE and Equivalent Attainment by Pupil Characteristics in England, 2009/10" http://www. education.gov.uk/rsgateway/DB/SFR/s000977/SFR37_2010.pdf (accessed April 6, 2011).

Dillon, S. (2010) "Obama Calls for Major Change in Education Law," *The New York Times*, March 13. http://www.nytimes.com/2010/03/14/education/14child. html (accessed September 1, 2010).

Diverse Herts (2009) "Travellers Community History." http://www.diverseherts. org.uk/community.php?CID=80&Title=Travellers (accessed July 24, 2009).

Dixson, A. D. (2006) "The Fire This Time: Jazz Research and Critical Race Theory," in A. D. Dixson and C. K. Rousseau (eds.), *Critical Race Theory in Education: All God's Children Got a Song*, New York and London: Routledge.

Dominguez, F. (2010) "Education for the Creation of a New Venezuela," Paper delivered at *Latin America and Education*, Marxism and Education: Renewing Dialogues XIII, Institute of Education, University of London, July 24.

Douglass, F. (1845) *Narrative of the Life of Frederick Douglass*. http://etext.lib.virginia.edu/toc/modeng/public/DouNarr.html (accessed May 6, 2010).

Du Bois, W. E. B. (1935) "The General Strike," *Black Reconstruction in America*. https://facultystaff.richmond.edu/~aholton/121readings_html/generalstrike. htm (accessed May 12, 2010).

Duffy, R. and A. Tomlinson (2009) "Education on the Hoof," Paper presented to the first Centre for Education for Social Justice Seminar at Bishop Grosseteste University College Lincoln, January 19. http://www.bishopg.ac.uk/docs/ C4E4SJ/Education%20on%20the%20Hoof.pdf (accessed February 10, 2011).

Eagleton, T. (2002) "A Shelter in the Tempest of History," *Red Pepper*, February. www.redpepper.org.uk/arts/x-feb02-eagleton.htm (accessed July 23, 2009).

East Asian Times (2010) "Vietnamese Fishermen Fear Rougher Waters Ahead after Spill," http://www.eastasiantimes.com/vietnamese-fishermen-fear-rougher-waters-ahead-after-spill.htm (accessed August 14, 2010).

Eichhoff, W. (1869) "The International Workingmen's Association. Its Establishment, Organisation, Political and Social Activity, and Growth." http://www.marx. org/archive/marx/iwma/archive/eichhoff/iwma-history/index.htm (accessed December 3, 2009).

Eley, T. (2010a) "In Cleveland Speech Obama Unveils Pro-business 'Jobs' Plan," *World Socialist Web Site (WSWS)*, September 9, 2010. http://www.wsws.org/ articles/2010/sep2010/obam-s09.shtml (accessed September 26, 2010).

—— (2010b) "Obama Seizes on Arizona Law to Push Repressive Immigration Overhaul," *World Socialist Web Site (WSWS)*, April 28. http://www.wsws.org/ articles/2010/apr2010/immi-a28.shtml (accessed July 15, 2010).

Elliott, G. (2006) *Althusser: The Detour of Theory*, Leiden: Brill.

Elliott, L. (2008) "Saving Fannie and Freddie Was Nationalisation Pure and Simple: It's the Free-Marketeers Who Are to Blame but, by Not Seizing the Moment, It's the Left that Could Well End Up Carrying the Can," *The Guardian*, September 9. http://www.guardian.co.uk/commentisfree/2008/sep/09/ freddiemacandfanniemae.subprimecrisis (accessed September 12, 2008).

UNIVERSITY OF WINCHESTER LIBRARY

Elliott, L. and T. Clark (2010) "Public Backs Coalition on Economy—Poll," *The Guardian,* August 18, pp. 1–2.

Ellis, E. (2010) *Field Study Report: Alternative School, Barrio Pueblo Nuevo, Mérida, Venezuela,* unpublished field work undertaken especially for this book.

Eltis, D. (2007) "A Brief Overview of the Trans-Atlantic Slave." http://www.slavevoyages.org/tast/assessment/essays-intro-08.faces (accessed February 4, 2011).

——— (2008) "The U.S. Transatlantic Slave Trade, 1644–1867: An Assessment," *Civil War History,* 54 (4), December, pp. 347–378.

Embassy of the Bolivarian Republic of Venezuela to the UK and Ireland (undated) *Indigenous Peoples as Revolutionary Protagonists.* http://www.venezlon.co.uk/pdf/fc_indigenous.pdf (accessed April 11, 2010).

Encyclopaedia Britannica (2010) "Hispanic Heritage in the Americas." http://www.britannica.com/hispanic_heritage/article-9052384 (accessed June 6, 2010).

Engels, F. (1845) [1975] "Speeches in Elberfeld," *Marx and Engels, Collected Works, Volume 4.* www.marxists.org/archive/marx/works/1845/02/15.htm (accessed November 28, 2009).

——— (1877) [1962] *Anti-Dühring: Herr Eugen Dühring's Revolution in Science,* Moscow: Foreign Language Press.

——— (1886) [1965] "Preface to the English Edition," *Capital, Volume 1,* Moscow: Progress.

——— (1892) [1977] "Socialism: Utopian and Scientific," in *Karl Marx & Frederick Engels: Selected Works in One Volume,* London: Lawrence and Wishart.

Equality and Human Rights Commission Website (2010) http://www.equalityhumanrights.com/ (accessed August 24, 2010).

Espinoza, L. and A. P. Harris (2000) "Embracing the Tar-Baby: LatCrit Theory and the Sticky Mess of Race," in R. Delgado and J. Stefancic (eds.), *Critical Race Theory: The Cutting Edge,* Philadelphia, PA: Temple University Press.

Fekete, L. (2009) *A Suitable Enemy: Racism, Migration and Islamophobia in Europe,* London: Pluto.

Feldman, P. and C. Lotz (2004) *A World to Win: A Rough Guide to a Future without Global Capitalism,* London: Lupus Books.

Fenton, S. (2003) *Ethnicity,* Cambridge: Polity Press.

Ferguson, N. (2004) "American Empire—Who Benefits?" *Empire and the Dilemmas of Liberal Imperialism,* CD accompanying *Prospect,* March 2004.

——— (2005) "Admit It, George Dubya's Medicine Is Not all Bad," *Times Higher Education Supplement,* March 18, 2005. http://www.timeshighereducation.co.uk/story.asp?storyCode=194801&sectioncode=26 (accessed August 22, 2010).

FindLaw (2010) "Lau vs. Nichols." http://www.stanford.edu/~kenro/LAU/IAPolicy/IA1aLauvNichols.htm (accessed September 9, 2010).

Fine, M. (2006) "The Morning After, and the Morning After That," in Teachers College Press and M. Grolnick (eds.), *Forever After: New York City Teachers on 9/11,* New York: Teachers College Press.

Fitzgerald, I. (2007) "Working in the UK: Polish Migrant Worker Routes into Employment in the North East and North West Construction and Food Processing Sectors," London: TUC.

Fourier, C. (1820) *Theory of Social Organization,* www.fordham.edu/halsall/mod/1820fourier.html (accessed September 2, 2009).

Freire, P. (1970) *Cultural Action for Freedom,* Harmondsworth: Penguin.

——— (1972) *Pedagogy of the Oppressed,* Harmondsworth: Penguin.

——— (1998a) *Pedagogy of the Heart,* New York: Continuum.

——— (1998b). *Teachers as Cultural Workers: Letters to Those Who Dare Teach*, translated by D. Macedo, D. Koike, and A. Oliveira, Boulder: Westview Press.

——— (2007) Paulo Freire—Karl Marx (subtitled), Video, June 5. http://www.youtube.com/watch?v=pSyaZAWIr1I&feature=related (accessed November 8, 2011).

Freire, P. and I. Shor (1987) *A Pedagogy for Liberation: Dialogues on Transforming Education*, London: Macmillan Education.

Fryer, P. (1984) *Staying Power: The History of Black People in Britain*, London: Pluto Press.

Fuentess, F. (2009) "Chavez's Historic Call for a Fifth Socialist International," *Monthly Review*, November 28. http://mrzine.monthlyreview.org/fuentes281109.html (accessed December 1, 2009).

Gair, R. (2006) "Ellis Faces Disciplinary Charges." http://campus.leeds.ac.uk/newsincludes/newsitem3675.htm (accessed September 2, 2009).

Gandin, L. A. and M. W. Apple (2002) "Challenging Neo-liberalism, Building Democracy: Creating the Citizen School in Porto Alegre, Brazil," *Journal of Education Policy*, 17, (2), April, pp. 259–279.

Getches, D., C. F. Wilkinson, and R. A. Williams, Jr. (2005) *Cases and Materials on Federal Indian Law* (5th Edition), Eagan, MN: West.

Getty, S. (2006) "East Enders Say They Love London," *The Metro*.

Gibson, R. and G. Rikowski (2004) *Socialism and Education: An E-Dialogue*, conducted between July 19 and August 8, at Rich Gibson's *Education Page for a Democratic Society*, http://www.pipeline.com/~rougeforum/RikowskiGibsonDialogueFinal.htm (accessed December 5, 2009).

Gillborn, D. (2008) *Racism and Education: Coincidence or Conspiracy?* London: Routledge.

——— (2009) "Who's Afraid of Critical Race Theory in Education? A Reply to Mike Cole's 'The Color-Line and the Class Struggle,'" *Power and Education*, 1, 1, pp. 125–131.

——— (2010) "The White Working Class, Racism and Respectability: Victims, Degenerates and Interest-Convergence," *British Journal of Educational Studies*, 58 (1), pp. 3–25.

Gilroy, P. (1987) *There Ain't No Black in the Union Jack*, London: Hutchinson.

Giroux, H. A. and K. Saltman (2008) "Obama's Betrayal of Public Education? Arne Duncan and the Corporate Model of Schooling," *truthout*. http://www.truthout.org/121708R (accessed September 10, 2010).

Giuseppe, F. (1970) *Gramsci, Life of a Revolutionary*, London: New Left Books.

Glover, J. (2009) "Voters Want Tory Spending Axe to Fall, Poll Shows," *The Guardian*, July 13. http://www.guardian.co.uk/politics/2009/jul/13/public-spending-poll-cuts (accessed January 31, 2011).

Goldenberg, S. (2010) "Tea Party Movement: Billionaire Koch Brothers Who Helped It Grow," *The Guardian*. http://www.guardian.co.uk/world/2010/oct/13/tea-party-billionaire-koch-brothers (accessed October 14, 2010).

Gott, R. (2008) "Orlando Fals Borda: Sociologist and Activist Who Defined Peasant Politics in Colombia," *The Guardian*, August 26. http://www.guardian.co.uk/world/2008/aug/26/colombia.sociology (accessed April 16, 2010).

Gramsci, A. (1921) "Unsigned, L'Ordine Nuovo," March 4, 1921, in *Antonio Gramsci, "Selections from Political Writings (1921–1926),"* translated and edited by Quintin Hoare (Lawrence and Wishart: London 1978), transcribed to the World Wide Web with the kind permission of Quintin Hoare. http://www.marxists.org/archive/gramsci/1921/03/officialdom.htm (accessed September 12, 2010).

——— (1978) *Selections from Prison Notebooks*, London: Lawrence and Wishart.

Grande, S. (2009) "Red Pedagogy: Indigenous Theories of Redistribution (a.k.a. Sovereignty)," in M. W. Apple, W. Au, & L. A. Gandin (eds.), *The Routledge International Handbook of Critical Education*, London: Routledge.

Grant, W. (2009) "Venezuela's Revolutionary Reading," BBC News, August 2. http://news.bbc.co.uk/1/hi/8113388.stm (accessed April 7, 2010).

Greaves, N. M., D. Hill, and A. Maisuria (2007) "Embourgeoisment, Immiseration, Commodification—Marxism Revisited: A Critique of Education in Capitalist Systems," *Journal for Critical Education Policy Studies* 5 (1), May. http://www.jceps.com/print.php?articleID=83 (accessed September 1, 2010),

Greenfields, M. (2006) "Stopping Places," in C. Clark and M. Greenfields, *Here to Stay: The Gypsies and Travellers of Britain,* Hatfield: University of Hertfordshire Press.

Griffiths, T. G. (2008) "Preparing Citizens for a 21st Century Socialism: Venezuela's Bolivarian Educational Reforms," Paper presented at the Social Educators Association of Australia National Biennial Conference, Newcastle, Australia.

Griffiths, T. G. and J. Williams (2009) "Mass Schooling for Socialist Transformation in Cuba and Venezuela," *Journal for Critical Education Policy Studies,* 7 (2), pp. 30–50. http://www.jceps.com/index.php?pageID=article&articleID=160 (accessed April 12, 2010).

Griswold del Castillo, R., I. Ortiz, and R. Gonzalez (2000) "What Was the Lemon Grove School Desegregation Case All About?" http://aztlan.sdsu.edu/chicano-history/chapter07/c07s02.html (accessed September 9, 2010).

Gross, J. A. (2006) "A Logical Extreme: Proposing Human Rights as the Foundation for Workers' Rights in the United States," in R. N. Block, S. Friedman, M. Kaminski, and A. Levin (eds.), *Justice on the Job: Perspectives on the Erosion of Collective Bargaining in the United States,* Kalamazoo, MI: Upjohn Institute Press.

——— (ed.) (2006). *Workers' Rights as Human Rights.* Albany, NY: ILR Press.

Gu, C-J (2003) "Unbearable Racial Othering: Taiwanese Americans' Working Experiences, Relations, and Mental Health," Paper presented at the annual meeting of the American Sociological Association, Atlanta Hilton Hotel, Atlanta, Georgia, August 16.

Gypsy Roma Traveller Leeds (2007) "Strategy on Gypsies and Travellers." http://www.grtleeds.co.uk/information/CRE.html (accessed March 22, 2010).

Hall, S. (1978) "Racism and Reaction," in BBC/CRE, *Five Views of Multi-Racial Britain,* London: BBC/CRE.

——— (2010) "Interpreting the Crisis: Doreen Massey and Stuart Hall Discuss Ways of Understanding the Current Crisis," in R. S. Grayson and J. Rutherford (eds.), *After the Crash—Re-inventing the Left in Britain,* London: Lawrence and Wishart (a Soundings ebook).

Harding, N. (1977) *Lenin's Political Thought,* London: Macmillan.

Hardy, J. (2009) "Migration, Migrant Workers and Capitalism," *International Socialism,* 122, pp. 133–153.

Hardy, J. and N. Clark (2007) "EU Enlargement, Workers and Migration: Implications for Trade Unions in the UK," Geneva: International Labour Organisation.

Hari, J. (2009) "Britain's Not Bust. So Don't Use It as an Excuse to Impose Cuts," *The Independent,* October 8. http://www.independent.co.uk/opinion/commentators/johann-hari/johann-hari-britains-not-bust-so-dont-use-it-as-an-excuse-to-impose-cuts-1799217.html (accessed October 13, 2009).

Harris, L. C. (2007) "Real Rights and Recognition Replace Racism in Venezuela," July 13. http://www.venezuelasolidarity.org/?q=node/182 (accessed April 10, 2010).

Harris, P. (2008) "Forty Years after the Shot Rang Out, Race Fears Still Haunt the US." http://www.guardian.co.uk/world/2008/mar/30/race.uselections2008 (accessed February 4, 2011).

Harrity, J. (2004) "Dr. King Dedicated His Life to the Causes of Working People," *International Association of Machinists and Aerospace Workers,* January 16.

Hart, S., A. Dixon, M. J. Drummond, and D. McIntyre (2004) *Learning without Limits.* Maidenhead: Open University Press.

Hasan, M. (2010) "Thatcherism Gilded with Piety," *New Statesman,* August 18. http://www.newstatesman.com/blogs/mehdi-hasan/2010/08/david-hare-cameronism-crisis (accessed August 20, 2010).

Hayward, S. (2010) "6 Bankers Share £23M," *Sunday Mirror,* September 26.

Hearne, R. (2005) "World Social Forum 2005—The Movements Fight On." http://www.swp.ie/socialistworker/2005/sw236/socialistworker-236-3.htm.

Heath, A. and J. Ridge (1983) "Social Mobility of Ethnic Minorities," *Journal of Biosocial Science,* Supplement, 8, pp. 169–184.

Herrnstein, R. J. and C. Murray (1994) *The Bell Curve,* New York: Free Press.

Hickey, T. (2002) "Class and Class Analysis for the Twenty-first Century," in M. Cole (ed.), *Education, Equality and Human Rights,* London: Routledge/Falmer.

——— (2006) "'Multitude' or 'Class': Constituencies of Resistance, Sources of Hope," in M. Cole (ed.), *Education, Equality and Human Rights* (2nd Edition), London: Routledge.

Higgins, C. (2010) "Rightwing Historian Niall Ferguson Given School Curriculum Role," *The Guardian,* May 30. http://www.guardian.co.uk/politics/2010/may/30/niall-ferguson-school-curriculum-role (accessed August 22, 2010).

Hill, D. (1989) *Charge of the Right Brigade: The Radical Right's Attack on Teacher Education,* Brighton: Institute for Education Policy Studies. http://www.ieps.org.uk.cwc.net/hill1989.pdf (accessed July 5, 2008).

——— (1994) "Initial Teacher Education and Ethnic Diversity," in G. Verma and P. Pumfrey (eds.), *Cultural Diversity and the Curriculum, Vol 4: Cross-Curricular Contexts, Themes and Dimensions in Primary Schools,* London: Falmer Press.

——— (1997) "Equality in Primary Schooling: The Policy Context, Intentions and Effects, of the Conservative 'Reforms'", in M. Cole, D. Hill and S. Shan (eds.), *Promoting Equality in Primary Schools,* London: Cassell.

——— (2001) "Equality, Ideology and Educational Policy," in D. Hill and M. Cole (eds.), *Schooling and Equality: Fact, Concept and Policy,* London: Kogan Page.

——— (2005) "State Theory and the Neoliberal Reconstruction of Schooling and Teacher Education," in G. Fischman, P. McLaren, H. Sünker, and C. Lankshear (eds.), *Critical Theories, Radical Pedagogies and Global Conflicts.* Boulder, CO: Rowman and Littlefield.

Hill, D. and L. H. Robertson (eds.) (2009) *Equality in the Primary School: Promoting Good Practice Across the Curriculum,* London and New York: Routledge.

History Place, the (1999) "Genocide in the 20th Century: Pol Pot in Cambodia 1975–1979 2,000,000 Deaths." http://www.historyplace.com/worldhistory/genocide/polpot.htm (accessed August 3, 2010).

HM Chief Inspector of Prisons (2009) Report on an unannounced short follow-up inspection of Tinsley House Immigration Removal Centre. July 13–15, London: Her Majesty's Inspectorate of Prisons.

Ho, C. (2003) "The Model Minority Awakened: The Murder of Vincent Chin—Part 1," USAsians.net. http://us_asians.tripod.com/articles-vincentchin.html (accessed October 31, 2010).

Hobsbawm, E. J. (1977) "Gramsci and Political Theory," *Marxism Today*, http://www.amielandmelburn.org.uk/collections/mt/index_frame.htm (accessed September 2, 2009).

Holmes, C. (1979) *Anti-Semitism in British Society 1876–1939*, London: Edward Arnold.

Horseman, R. (1981) *Race and Manifest Destiny*, Cambridge, MA: Harvard University Press.

Ibitayo, O. (2008) "Transboundary Dumping of Hazardous Waste," *The Encyclopedia of Earth*, August 26. http://www.eoearth.org/article/Transboundary_dumping_of_hazardous_waste (accessed September 17, 2010).

Iganski, P. (2009) "The Banality of Anti-Jewish 'Hate Crime," in R. Blazak (ed.), *Hate Crime Offenders*, Westport, CT: Praeger.

Iganski, P. and B. Kosmin (2003) "The New Antisemitism Debate: Background and Context," in P. Iganski and B. Kosmin (eds.), *A New Antisemitism? Debating Judeophobia in 21st Century Britain*, London: Profile Books.

In Defence of Marxism (2007) "Imperialism—From Marxism and the USA," March 16. http://www.marxist.com/imperialism-marxism-usa.htm (accessed June 6, 2010).

Institute of Race Relations (IRR) (2010) *Driven to Desperate Measures*, London: IRR.

Irvin, G. (2008) *Super Rich: The Rise of Inequality in Britain and the United States*, Cambridge: Polity Press.

Islamophobia Watch (2010) http://www.islamophobia-watch.com/ (accessed July 3, 2010).

Jackson, J. (2010) "The Dream Is Still Alive and Kicking," *The Sunday Times Magazine*, October 3.

JCOR (Jewish Council for Racial Equality (2010) http://www.jcore.org.uk/about.php?src=ab&mid=1 (accessed May 3, 2010).

Jessop, B. (2002) *The Future of the Capitalist State*, Cambridge: Polity Press.

———— (2008) *State Power*, Cambridge: Polity Press.

Jimenez, A. (2010) "Building Socialism from Below: The Role of the Communes in Venezuela." Atenea Jimenez Interviewed by Susan Spronk and Jeffrey R. Webber, http://links.org.au/node/1745 (accessed August 6, 2010).

Jones, K. (2003) *Education in Britain: 1944 to the Present*. Cambridge: Polity Press.

Jones, J. and C. Hancock (2005) "Brown v Board of Education at 50: Where Are We Now?" *The Negro Educational Review*, 56 (1), pp. 91–98.

Jordan, B. and F. Düvell (2002) *Irregular Migration, the Dilemmas of Transnational Mobility*, Cheltenham: Edward Elgar.

Kahn, R. (2003) "Paulo Freire and Eco-Justice: Updating *Pedagogy of the Oppressed* for the Age of Ecological Calamity." http://getvegan.com/ecofreire.htm (accessed February 9, 2011).

Kaplan, E. A. and M. Sprinkler (eds.) (1993) *The Althusserian Legacy*, London: Verso.

Kern, S. (2009) "Anti-Semitism Sweeps Europe in Wake of Gaza Operation," *The Brussels Journal* http://www.brusselsjournal.com/node/3745# (accessed May 4, 2009).

Kershen, A. (ed.) (2000) *Language, Labour and Migration*, Aldershot: Ashgate.

Kincaid, S. (2009) "Fighting the Nazis in the Workplaces," *Socialist Worker*, September 26.

Kirk, N. (1985) *The Growth of Working Class Reformism in Mid-Victorian England*, London: Croom Helm.

Kishore, J. (2010) "Afghanistan: Obama's Escalation Begins," *World Socialist Web Site (WSWS)*, February 17. http://www.wsws.org/articles/2010/feb2010/pers-f17.shtml.

Kolakowski, L. (1978) *Main Currents of Marxism*, Trans, P. S. Falla, 3 Vols., Oxford: Oxford University Press.

Kolchin, P. (1995) *American Slavery 1619–1877*, London: Penguin Books.

Kornhaber, M. L. and G. Orfield (2001) "High-Stakes Testing Policies: Examining Their Assumptions and Consequences," in G. Orfield and M. L. Kornhaber (eds.), *Raising Standards or Raising Barriers?: Inequality and High-Stakes Testing in Public Education*, New York: Century Foundation Press.

Kovel, J. (1988) *White Racism: A Psychohistory*, London: Free Association Books.

—— (2010) "Ecosocialism as Holistic Earth Care: Redefining Our Role as Environmental Agents—An Interview with Joel Kovel," *Canadian Dimension*, August 16. http://canadiandimension.com/articles/3265 (accessed September 17, 2010).

Kraus, G. (1969) "Chinese Laborers and the Construction of the Central Pacific," *Utah Historical Quarterly*, 37 (1), Winter, pp. 41–57. http://cprr.org/Museum/Chinese_Laborers.html (accessed October 18, 2010).

Kreis, S. (2006) "The Utopian Socialists: Charles Fourier (1)." www.historyguide.org/intellect/lecture21a.html (accessed September 2, 2009).

Kundnani, A. (2007) *The End of Tolerance: Racism in 21st Century Britain*, London: Pluto Press.

Lacan, J. (1949) [1977] *The Mirror Stage as Formative of the Function of the I as Revealed in Psychoanalytic Theory* London: Tavistock.

Laclau, E. (1977) *Politics and Ideology in Marxist Theory*, London: New Left Books.

Ladson-Billings, G. (2005) "New Directions in Multicultural Education: Complexities, Boundaries, and Critical Race Theory," in J. A. Banks and C. A. M. Banks (eds.), *Handbook of Research on Multicultural Education*, San Francisco: Jossey Bass.

Ladson-Billings, G. (2006) "Foreword: They're Trying to Wash Us Away: The Adolescence of Critical Race Theory in Education," in Dixson A. D. and C. K. Rousseau (eds.), *Critical Race Theory in Education: All God's Children Got a Song*, New York: Routledge.

Ladson-Billings, G. and W. F. Tate (1995) "Toward a Critical Race Theory of Education," *Teachers College Record*, 97 (1), pp. 47–68.

Lai, E. (2003) "Taiwanese Americans," *Asian-Nation: The Landscape of Asian America*. http://www.asian-nation.org/taiwanese.shtml (accessed August 9, 2010).

Lamb, C. (2010) " 'Crazy Carl' and His Mad Dog Lure Voters," *The Sunday Times*, October 3.

Langston, D. H. (2006) http://www.indybay.org/newsitems/2006/03/21/18095451.php.

Lasso, M. (2007) *Myths of Harmony: Race and Republicanism During the Age of Revolution, Colombia 1795–1831*, Pittsburgh: University of Pittsburgh Press.

Lavalette, M., G. Mooney, E. Mynott, K. Evans, and B. Richardson (2001) "The Woeful Record of the House of Blair," *International Socialism*, 90. http://pubs.socialistreviewindex.org.uk/isj90/lavalette.htm (accessed August 25, 2010).

Lawrence, E. (1982) "Just Plain Common Sense: The 'Roots' of Racism," in Centre for Contemporary Cultural Studies (ed.), *The Empire Strikes Back: Race and Racism in 70s Britain*, London: Hutchinson.

Leano, R. (2010) "Sandiwa National Alliance of Filipina/o American Youth Marches in Solidarity with Youth & Students in the U.S. Rallying against Massive Budget Cuts in Education." http://sandiwa.wordpress.com/2010/03/05/sandiwa-national-alliance-of-filipinao-american-youth-marches-in-solidarity-with-youth-students-in-the-u-s-rallying-against-massive-budget-cuts-in-education/ (accessed August 5, 2010).

Lee, F. J. T. (2005) "Venezuela's President Hugo Chavez Frias: 'The Path is Socialism.'" http://www.handsoffvenezuela.org/chavez_path_socialism_4.htm (accessed May 4, 2007).

Lee Van Cott, D. (2005) *From Movements to Parties in Latin America: The Evolution of Ethnic Politics,* Cambridge: Cambridge University Press.

Lemberg, I. (2010) "Anti-Semitic Incidents Rise Sharply in 2009, Study Says," CNN. http://edition.cnn.com/2010/WORLD/meast/04/12/anti.semitic.study/index.html (accessed April 26, 2010).

Lenin, V. I. (1917 [1997]) *Imperialism: The Highest Stage of Capitalism,* New York: International Publishers.

——— (1925) "Lecture on the 1905 Revolution." http://www.marxists.org/archive/lenin/works/1917/jan/09.htm (accessed August 25, 2010).

———(2002) *On Utopian and Scientific Socialism,* Amsterdam: Fredonia Books.

Lesage, J., A. L. Ferber, D. Storrs, and D. Wong (2002) *Making a Difference: Students of Color Speak Out,* Oxford: Rowman and Littlefield.

Levy, C. (2009) "Antonio Gramsci, Anarchism, Syndicalism and *Sovversivismo,*" *Challenges for Democracy in a Global Era,* 59th Political Studies Association Political Studies Association Annual Conference, April 7–9, http://www.psa.ac.uk/2009/pps/Levy.pdf (accessed September 2, 2009).

Ling-chi Wang, L. (2010) "Chinese Americans." http://www.everyculture.com/multi/Bu-Dr/Chinese-Americans.html (accessed August 4, 2010).

Litwack, L. F. (1961) *North of Slavery: The Negro in the Free States,* Chicago: University of Chicago Press.

Loewen, J. W. (1996) *Lies My Teacher Told Me: Everything Your American History Textbook Got Wrong,* New York: Touchstone.

Love, B. J. (2004) "Brown Plus 50 Counter-Storytelling: A Critical Race Theory Analysis of the 'Majoritarian Achievement Gap' Story," *Equity & Excellence in Education,* 37, pp. 227–246.

Love Music Hate Racism (2009) http://www.lovemusichateracism.com/ (accessed October 15, 2009).

Loving Day (2009) "Legal Map." http://lovingday.org/legal-map (accessed August 5, 2010).

Lowles, N. (2009) "The Way Forward," *Searchlight,* July. http://www.searchlightmagazine.com/index.php?link=template&story=284 (accessed September 2, 2009).

Mac An Ghaill, M. (2000) "The Irish in Britain: The Invisibility of Ethnicity and Anti-Irish Racism," *Journal of Ethnic and Migration Studies,* 26 (1), pp. 137–147.

MacFarquhar, N. (2006) "Pakistanis Find U.S. an Easier Fit Than Britain," *The New York Times,* August 21. http://www.nytimes.com/2006/08/21/us/21devon.html?pagewanted=1&_r=1 (accessed August 1, 2010).

Mackenzie, J. M. (1984) *Propaganda and Empire: The Manipulation of British Public Opinion 1880–1960,* Manchester: Manchester University Press.

MacKenzie, N. (1967) *Socialism,* London: Hutchinson.

Macpherson, W. (1999) *The Stephen Lawrence Enquiry, Report of an Enquiry by Sir William Macpherson*, London: HMSO. http://www.archive.official-documents. co.uk/document/cm42/4262/4262.htm (accessed January 30, 2011).

Malott, C. (2006) "Schooling in an Era of Corporate Dominance: Marxism against Burning Tires," *Journal for Critical Education Policy Studies*, 4 (1), March. http://www.jceps.com/index.php?pageID=article&articleID=58.

—— (2011a) *Critical Pedagogy and Cognition: An Introduction to a Postformal Educational Psychology*. New York: Springer.

—— (2011b). "Part II: Introduction," in R. Brock, C. Malott, and L. Villaverde (eds.), *Teaching Joe Kincheloe*, New York: Peter Lang.

Mann, E. 2002. *Dispatches from Durban*, Los Angeles, CA: Frontlines Press.

Mannix, D. P. with M. Cowley (1962) *Black Cargoes: A History of the Atlantic Slave Trade, 1518–1865*, New York: Viking Press.

Marshall, P. (2010) *Demanding the Impossible: A History of Anarchism*, Oakland, CA: PM Press.

Martin, P. (2008) "Forty Years On, Some Lessons from the Life—and Death—of Dr. Martin Luther King Jr." *World Socialist Web Site (WSWS)* April 7. http://www.wsws.org:80/articles/2008/apr2008/king-a07.shtml (accessed October 16, 2010).

—— (2010) "Arizona Immigration Bill: A Frontal Assault on Democratic Rights," *World Socialist Web Site (WSWS)*, April 26. http://www.wsws.org/articles/2010/apr2010/pers-a26.shtml (accessed July 15, 2010).

Martinez, C., M. Fox, and J. Farrell (2010) *Venezuela Speaks: Voices from the Grassroots*, Oakland, CA: PM Press.

Martinez, E. and A. García (2000) "What Is 'Neo-Liberalism': A Brief Definition," *Economy 101*. www.globalexchange.org/campaigns/econ101/neoliberalDefined. html (accessed April 4, 2010).

Marx, K. (1843–1844) "A Contribution to the Critique of Hegel's Philosophy of Right Introduction." http://www.marxists.org/archive/marx/works/1843/critique-hpr/intro.htm (accessed December 5, 2009).

—— (1852) *The Eighteenth Brumaire of Louis Bonaparte*. http://www.marxists.org/archive/marx/works/1852/18th-brumaire/ (accessed July 3, 2009).

—— (1859) "Preface to *A Contribution to the Critique of Political Economy*." http://www.marxists.org/archive/marx/works/1859/critique-pol-economy/preface.htm.

—— (1862) "A London Workers' Meeting," *Marx and Engels Collected Works, Volume 19*. http://www.marxists.org/archive/marx/works/1862/02/02.htm (accessed August 25, 2010).

—— (1870) [1978] *Ireland and the Irish Question*, Moscow: Progress.

—— (1885) [1976] "The Eighteenth Brumaire of Louis Bonaparte," in K. Marx and F. Engels, *Selected Works in One Volume*, London: Lawrence and Wishart.

—— (1887) [1965] *Capital, Volume 1*, Moscow: Progress.

—— (1894) [1966] *Capital, Volume 3*, Moscow: Progress.

Marx, K. and F. Engels (1845–46) *The German Ideology*, http://artsci.wustl.edu/~anthro/courses/361/GermanIdeology.html (accessed September 7, 2009).

—— (1846 [1977]). "Letters: Marx to P. V. Annenkov in Paris," in K. Marx and F. Engels, *Selected Works in One Volume*, London: Lawrence and Wishart.

—— (1847) [1977] "The Communist Manifesto," in Marx K. and F. Engels, *Selected Works in One Volume*, London: Lawrence and Wishart.

—— (1965) *Selected Correspondence*, Moscow: Progress.

McClain, C. J. (1994) *In Search of Equality: The Chinese Struggle against Discrimination in Nineteenth-Century America*, Berkeley, CA: University of University of California Press.

McGreal, C. (2010) "US Facing Surge in Rightwing Extremists and Militias," *The Guardian*, March 4. http://www.guardian.co.uk/world/2010/mar/04/us-surge-rightwing-extremist-groups (accessed March 20, 2010).

McGregor, D. and E. Moy 2003. "Native Hawaiians and Pacific Islander Americans," *Asian-Nation: The Landscape of Asian America*. http://www.asian-nation.org/hawaiian-pacific.shtml (accessed August 9, 2010).

McLaren, P. (1995) *Critical Pedagogy and Predatory Culture: Oppositional Politics in a Postmodern Era*, London and New York: Routldege.

—— (2000) *Che Guevara, Paulo Freire, and the Pedagogy of Revolution*, Lanham, MD: Rowman and Littlefield.

—— (2005) *Capitalists and Conquerors: A Critical Pedagogy against Empire*, Lanham, MD: Rowman and Littlefield.

—— (2008). "*This Fist Called My Heart*," Antipode, 40 (3), pp. 472–481.

McLaren, P. and D. Houston (2005) "Revolutionary Ecologies: Ecosocialism and Critical Pedagogy," in P. McLaren, *Capitalists and Conquerors: A Critical Pedagogy against Empire*, Lanham MD: Rowman and Littlefield.

McLaren, P. and R. Farahmandpur (2005) *Teaching against Global Capitalism and the New Imperialism: A Critical Pedagogy*, Oxford: Rowman and Littlefield.

McLaren, P. and V. Scatamburlo-D'Annibale (2010). "Class-ifying Race: The 'Compassionate' Racism of the Right and Why Class Still Matters," in Z. Leonardo (ed.), *Handbook of Cultural Politics and Education*. Boston: Sense.

McNeal, L. R. (2009) "The Re-Segregation of Public Education Now and After the End of Brown v. Board of Education," *Education and Urban Society*, 41 (5), July, pp. 562–574. http://www.electricprint.com/edu4/classes/readings/294readings/resegregation.pdf (accessed August 28, 2010).

McVeigh, T. (2009) "Detention of Children at Immigration 'Prisons' Attacked by MPs," *The Observer*, November 10. http://www.guardian.co.uk/uk/2009/nov/29/child-immigrant-detention-select-committee (accessed July 3, 2010).

Memarian, O. (2009) "Islamophobia Alive and Well in the U.S.," *IPS News*. http://ipsnews.net/news.asp?idnews=46620 (accessed July 3, 2010).

Menchaca, M. (1997) "Early Racist Discourses: The Roots of Deficit Thinking," in R. Valencia (ed.), *The Evolution of Deficit Thinking: Educational Thought and Practice*, New York: Routledge.

MercoPress (2009) "To School for Reading Classes with Karl Marx and Che Guevara," MercoPress, May 17. http://en.mercopress.com/2009/05/17/to-school-for-reading-classes-with-karl-marx-and-che-guevara. (accessed February 10, 2011).

Messina, A. (1989) *Race and Party Competition in Britain*, Oxford: Clarendon Press.

MIA: Encyclopedia of Marxism (undated a) "Congresses of the Communist International." http://www.marxists.org/glossary/events/c/comintern.htm#first-congress.

—— (undated b) "Glossary of Organisations." http://www.marxists.org/glossary/orgs/f/i.htm (accessed December 2, 2009).

Milbank, D. (2010) "On Education Policy, Obama Is Like Bush," *The Washington Post*, August 15, 2010. http://www.washingtonpost.com/wp-dyn/content/article/2010/08/13/AR2010081303197.html (accessed September 9, 2010).

Miles, R. (1982) *Racism and Migrant Labour*, London: Routledge and Kegan Paul.

———(1989) *Racism*, London: Routledge.

———(1993) *Racism after "Race Relations,"* London: Routledge.

Mills, C. W. (2009) "Critical Race Theory: A reply to Mike Cole," *Ethnicities*, 9 (2), pp. 270–281.

Ministerio del Poder Popular Para la Educación (2007). "Currículo Nacional Bolivariano: Diseño Curricular del Sistema Educativa Bolivariano." http://www.me.gov.ve/media.eventos/2007/dl_908_69.pdf.

Ministry of Justice (2009) *Statistics on Race and the Criminal Justice System 2007/8: A Ministry of Justice publication under Section 95 of the Criminal Justice Act 1991*, April. http://www.justice.gov.uk/publications/docs/stats-race-criminal-justice-system-07-08-revised.pdf (accessed August 27, 2009).

Minority Rights Group International (2007) *World Directory of Minorities and Indigenous Peoples—Venezuela: Overview. http://www.unhcr.org/refworld/docid/4954ce6821.html* (accessed April 11, 2010).

Modood, T. (2005) *Multicultural Politics: Racism, Ethnicity and Muslims in Britain*, Edinburgh: Edinburgh University Press.

Morris, R. (2006) "Nomads and Newspapers," in C. Clark and M. Greenfields, *Here to Stay: The Gypsies and Travellers of Britain*, Hatfield: University of Hertfordshire Press.

Murji, K. and J. Solomos (eds.) (2005) *Racialization: Studies in Theory and Practice*, Oxford: Oxford University Press.

National Association for the Advancement of Colored People (NAACP) (2010) *101 One Nation One Dream.* http://www.naacp.org/events/convention/100th/index.htm (accessed May 30, 2010).

National Conferences of State Legislatures (NCSL) (2004) *No Child Left Behind: History.*

Native American Heritage Programs (2010) http://www.lenapeprograms.info/Articles/brief_bkg.htm (accessed June 7, 2010).

Navarrete, P. (2010) "Venezuela Deserves a Fair Hearing," *The Guardian*. http://www.guardian.co.uk/commentisfree/cifamerica/2010/apr/09/venezuela-hugo-chavez (accessed June 2, 2010).

Nederveen Pieterse, J. (1986) "Amerindian Resistance: The Gathering of the Fires," *Race and Class*, 27, Spring, pp. 35–51.

Ninnes, P. (1998) "Freire, Paulo," *Teachers as Cultural Workers: Letters to Those Who Dare Teach*, translated by D. Macedo, D. Koike, and A. Oliveira, Boulder: Westview Press, *Education Review*, August 4. http://www.edrev.info/reviews/rev28.htm (accessed September 12, 2010).

Observer, The (2010) "New Wave of Evictions Threatens Gypsies," August 1, http://www.guardian.co.uk/society/2010/aug/01/gypsies-evictions-planning.

Okihiro, G. Y. (1994) *Margins and Mainstreams: Asians in American History and Culture*, Washington: University of Washington Press.

Oldcity.com (2009) "St Augustine History: The City that Was Never Conquered." http://www.oldcity.com/history-information.cfm (accessed November 12, 2009).

Olmos, J. (2009) "In Defiance of US Federal Order: Arizona Sheriff Carries Out Immigrant Raid," *World Socialist Web Site (WSWS)*, October 27. http://www.wsws.org/articles/2009/oct2009/ariz-o27.shtml (accessed July 15, 2010).

——— (2010) "Obama Administration Boasts of Increased Repression of I Immigrants," *World Socialist Web Site (WSWS)*, October 12. http://www.wsws.org/articles/2010/oct2010/depo-o12.shtml.

Olmstead, F. L. (1861) *The Cotton Kingdom: A Traveller's Observations on Cotton and Slavery in the American Slave States,* New York: Mason Brothers.

Online Etymology Dictionary (2001) http://www.etymonline.com/index.php? (accessed June 6, 2009).

Orr, J. (2010) "Tories Declare War," *Socialist Review,* September, pp. 10–14. http://www.socialistreview.org.uk/article.php?articlenumber=11369 (accessed September 5, 2010).

Ovenden, K. (2005) "Malcolm X: 'Show Me a Capitalist and I'll Show You a Bloodsucker,'" *Socialist Worker,* February 25. http://www.socialistworker. co.uk/art.php?id=5915

Owen, R. (1820) *Report to the County of Lanark,* web.jjay.cuny.edu/jobrien/reference/ob50.html (accessed September 2, 2009).

Papapolydorou, M. (2010) Review of "*Critical Race Theory and Education: A Marxist Response* by Mike Cole," *Race and Class,* 51(4), pp. 109–111.

Patterson, J. T. (2001) *Brown v. Board of Education: A Civil Rights Milestone and Its Troubled Legacy,* New York: Oxford University Press.

PBS (Public Broadcasting Service) (undated) "The African Slave Trade and the Middle Passage." http://www.pbs.org/wgbh/aia/part1/1narr4.html (accessed June 13, 2010).

Pearson, T. (2009) "Venezuela Opens National Art Gallery and Launches National Reading Plan," Venezuelanalysis.com http://venezuelanalysis.com/news/4402 (accessed April 7, 2010).

Pelaez, V. (2008) "The Prison Industry in the United States: Big Business or a New Form of Slavery?" http://www.globalresearch.ca/index.php?context=va&aid=8289 (accessed July 3, 2010).

Perea, J. (1997) "Panel: Latina/o Identity and Pan-Ethnicity: Toward Lat Crit Subjectivities: Five Axioms in Search of Equality," *Harvard Latino Law Review,* 231, Fall, pp. 231–237.

Perea, J. F. (1995) "Los Olvidados: On the Making of Invisible People," *New York University Law Review,* 70, 4, pp. 965–991.

Perea, J. F., R. Delgado, A. P. Harris, J. Stefancic, and S. M. Wildman (2007) *Race and Races: Cases and Resources for a Diverse America,* St. Paul, MN: Thomson/West.

Perlo, A. (2010) "African Americans and the Jobs Crisis," *politicalaffairs.net: Marxist Thought Online,* February. http://www.politicalaffairs.net/article/view/9272/1/385/ (accessed June 17, 2010).

Permanent Revolution (2008) "Columbus and the Discovery of Latin America," August 23. http://www.permanentrevolution.net/entry/2267 (accessed October 3, 2009).

Pfeifer, M. E. (2003) "Hmong Americans," *Asian-Nation: The Landscape of Asian America.* http://www.asian-nation.org/hmong.shtml (accessed August 6, 2010).

Phapphayboun, T. (2003). "Laotian Americans," *Asian-Nation: The Landscape of Asian America.* http://www.asian-nation.org/laotian.shtml (accessed August 8, 2010).

The Philippine History Site (undated) http://opmanong.ssc.hawaii.edu/filipino/riots.html. (accessed 10 February).

Pilger, J. (2010) "The Kidnapping of Haiti," *New Statesman,* January 28. http://www.newstatesman.com/international-politics/2010/02/haiti-pilger-obama-venezuela (accessed April 9, 2010).

Pilkington, A. (2008) "From Institutional Racism to Community Cohesion: The Changing Nature of Racial Discourse in Britain," *Sociological Research Online,* 13 (3), p. 6 http://www.socresonline.org.uk/13/3/6.html.

Piper, S. (2007) "After the Elections: A New Party for the Venezuelan Revolution," *International Viewpoint*, January.

Platt, L. (2007) "Poverty and Ethnicity in the UK." http://www.jrf.org.uk/publications/poverty-and-ethnicity-uk (accessed May 16, 2009).

——— (2009) *Ethnicity and Child Poverty: Department for Work and Pensions Research Report No 576*, London: Department of Work and Pensions.

Poulantzas, N. (1972) "Problems of the Capitalist State," in Blackburn R. (ed.), *Ideology and Social Science*, London: Fontana.

——— (1978) *State, Power, Socialism*, London: Verso.

Poynting, S. and V. Mason (2001) "The Resistible Rise of Islamophobia: Anti-Muslim Racism in the UK and Australia before 11 September 2001," *Journal of Sociology*, 43 (1), pp. 61–86.

Preston, J. (2007) *Whiteness and Class in Education*, Dordrecht: Springer.

Proyect, L. (2009) "G. A. Cohen (1941–2009)," Louis Proyect: The Unrepentant Marxist August 7. http://louisproyect.wordpress.com (accessed August 13, 2009).

Raby, D. L. (2006) *Democracy and Revolution: Latin America and Socialism Today*, London: Pluto Press.

Radhikaranjan (2009) "Bangladesh, Post-independence," *MARXIST: An Encyclopedia of Countries from Poorest*, September 29. http://radhikaranjan-marxist.blogspot.com/2009/09/bangladesh-post-independence.html (accessed August 2, 2010).

Ramdin, R. (1987) *The Making of the Black Working Class in Britain*, London: Gower.

Ramonet, I. (2010) "Venezuela Surrounded," *Venezuela Solidarity Campaign*, Spring.

Rampton Report (1981) *West Indian Children in Our Schools*, Cmnd 8723, London: HMSO.

Rao, K. V. (2003) "Indian Americans," *Asian-Nation: The Landscape of Asian America*. http://www.asian-nation.org/indian.shtml (accessed August 6, 2010).

Reeves, T. J. and C. E. Bennett (2004) *We the People: Asians in the United States: Census 2000 Special Reports*. http://www.census.gov/prod/2004pubs/censr-17.pdf (accessed August 5, 2010).

Refugee Action (2009) "The Global Perspective." http://www.refugee-action.org.uk/information/challengingthemyths1.aspx (accessed May 23, 2009).

Refugee and Migrant Justice (2010) *Safe at Last? Children on the Front Line of UK Border Control*, London: Refugee and Migrant Justice. http://refugee-migrantjustice.org.uk/downloads/RMJ%20Safe%20at%20Last%20WEB.pdf (accessed March 23, 2010).

Reisz, M. (2010) "Library that Helped Bring Nazis to Justice to Relocate," *Times Higher Education*, January 14. http://www.timeshighereducation.co.uk/story.asp?storyCode=409956&sectioncode=26 (accessed February 4, 2011).

Rhodes, M. (2009) "The Forsyth Saga," *Holyrood Magazine*, September. http://www.holyrood.com/index.php?option=com_holyrood&func=article&artid=2872&edition=219&brick=3.

Richardson, R. (2009) "Islamophobia and Anti-Muslim Racism—Concepts and Terms, and Implications for Education," *Race Equality Teaching*, 27 (1), pp. 11–16.

Riddell, J. (2007) "Chávez Calls for United Socialist Party of Venezuela: Rank-and-File Committees to Be Building Blocks for New Organization," January 11. http://www.socialistvoice.ca/?p=149 (accessed September 18, 2010).

Rikowski, G. (2001) "The Importance of Being a Radical Educator in Capitalism Today," Guest Lecture in Sociology of Education, The Gillian Rose Room, Department of Sociology, University of Warwick, Coventry, May 24. Institute for Education Policy Studies, http://www.ieps.org.uk/PDFs/rikowski2005a.pdf (accessed December 5, 2009).

——— (2002) "Prelude: Marxist Educational Theory after Postmodernism," in D. Hill, P. McLaren, M. Cole, and G. Rikowski (eds.), *Marxism against Postmodernism in Educational Theory*, Lanham, MD: Lexington Books.

———(2004) "Marx and the Education of the Future," *Policy Futures in Education*, 2 (3 and 4), pp. 559–571. http://www.wwwords.co.uk/pdf/validate.asp?j=pfie& vol=2&issue=3&year=2004&article=10_Rikowski_PFEO_2_3-4_web (accessed December 5, 2009).

——— (2007) "Marxist Educational Theory Unplugged," Paper prepared for the Fourth Historical Materialism Annual Conference, November 9–11, School of Oriental & African Studies, University of London. http://www.flowideas. co.uk/?page=articles&sub=Marxist%20Educational%20Theory%20Unplugged (accessed August 20, 2009).

Rismukhamedov, I. (2009) "Inventory // The Political Theory of Antonio Gramsci." http://www.chtodelat.org/index.php?option=com_content&task=view&id=279 &Itemid=125 (accessed August 20, 2009).

Robinson, D. M. (2000) "Environmental Racism: Old Wine in a New Bottle," *Echoes* 17. http://www.wcc-coe.org/wcc/what/jpc/echoes/echoes-17-02.html (accessed September 17, 2010).

Robinson, S. (2010) "Travellers Resist Tory Assault on Their Rights," *Socialist Worker*, September 11.

Robinson, W. (2006) "From War of Position to War of Manoeuvre: The Popular Assault on the Neo-Liberal State in Latin America," Paper presented at the annual meeting of the International Studies Association, Town & Country Resort and Convention Center, San Diego, California, March 22. http://www.allacademic. com/meta/p_mla_apa_research_citation/1/0/0/2/2/p100220_index.html (accessed July 26, 2009).

Roman, E. (1997) "Empire Forgotten: The United States' Colonization of Puerto Rico," *Villanova Law Review* 1119, pp. 1151–1156.

Rosales, A. (2010) "Chávez Revving Up Revolution with Land Takeovers," Venezuelanalysis.com. http://venezuelanalysis.com/analysis/5716 (accessed October 24, 2010).

Rose, S. and H. Rose (2005) "Why We Should Give Up on Race: As Geneticists and Biologists Know, the Term No Longer Has Meaning," *The Guardian*, April 9. http://www.guardian.co.uk/comment/story/0,,1455685,00.Html (accessed November 2, 2009).

Rosen, M. (2009) "Why Nick Griffin Shouldn't Be on Question Time: No Platform for Nazis," *Socialist Worker*, September 22. http://www.socialistworker.co.uk/ art.php?id=19072 (accessed January 31, 2011).

Rosengarten, F. (2011) "An Introduction to Gramsci's Life and Thought." http:// www.internationalgramscisociety.org/about_gramsci/biograpy.html (accessed January 31, 2011).

Ruddick, S. (2009) "Myths and Migrants," *Socialist Worker*, August 8, p. 8.

Rutter, J. (2006) *Refugee Children in the UK*, Buckingham, UK: Open University Press.

Ryder, M. (2009) "The Police Need to Stop and Think about Stop and Search," *The Observer*, May 3. http://www.guardian.co.uk/commentisfree/2009/may/03/matthew-ryder-police-stop-and-search (accessed May 10, 2009).

Saint-Simon, H. (1817) [1975] "Declaration of *Principles*' (*L'Industry, Volume 2*). www.eco.utexas.edu/~hmcleave/368simonprinciples.html (accessed September 2, 2009).

Salter, L. (2009) "A Decade of Propaganda? The BBC's Reporting of Venezuela." http://venezuelanalysis.com/analysis/5003 (accessed June 2, 2010).

San Juan Jr., E. (2003) "Marxism and the Race/Class Problematic: A Re-Articulation," *Cultural Logic*, 6. http://clogic.eserver.org/2003/sanjuan.html (accessed November 30, 2009).

—— (2009) "Re-visiting Race and Class in 'The Age of Obama,'" remarks delivered at the Thames Foley Institute, Washington State University, Pullman, Washington, April 18.

—— (2010) "Foreword" to D. Kelsh, D. Hill, and S. Macrine (eds.), *Class in Education: Knowledge, Pedagogy, Subjectivity*, London and New York: Routledge.

Sandmeyer, E. C. (1991) *The Anti-Chinese Movement in California*, Urbana, IL: University of Illinois Press.

Sartre, J. P. (1960) *The Search for Method (1st Part). Introduction to Critique of Dialectical Reason.* http://www.marxists.org/reference/archive/sartre/works/critic/sartre1.htm (accessed July 2, 2009).

Sarup, M. (1986) *The Politics of Multicultural Education*, London: Routledge and Kegan Paul.

Schmitt, D. A. (ed.) (2009) *Contemporary Literary Criticism, Volume 106.* http://www.enotes.com/contemporary-literary-criticism/althusser-louis (accessed September 7, 2009).

Schuster, L. (2002) "Asylum and the Lessons of History," *Race and Class*, 44 (2), pp. 40–56.

Sheehan, C. (2010) "Transcript of Cindy Sheehan's Interview with Hugo Chavez," March 30. http://venezuelanalysis.com/analysis/5233 (accessed August 1, 2010).

Sheppard, R. (2006) "The Assassinations of Malcom X and Martin Luther King, Jr.," *Fightback: The Marxist Voice of Labour and Youth*, June 14. http://www.marxist.ca/content/view/161/50/ (accessed February 4, 2011).

Shilton, J. (2009) "Northern Ireland: Racist Attacks Force 100 Roma Out of Belfast," *World Socialist Web Site (WSWS)*, July 4. http://www.wsws.org/articles/2009/jul2009/roma-j04.shtml (accessed August 1, 2010).

Shinn Sunoo, S. (2002) *Korean Picture Brides: 1903–1920: A Collection of Oral Histories*, Bloomington, IN: Xlibris Corp.

Short, G. and B. Carrington. (1996) "Anti-Racist Education, Multiculturalism and the New Racism," *Educational Review*, 48 (1), pp. 65–77.

Shufelt S. (1850) [2003] "The California Gold Rush, 1849," *EyeWitness to History*. http://www.eyewitnesstohistory.com/californiagoldrush.htm (accessed August 3, 2010).

Singh, J. 2003. "Bangladeshi & Pakistani Americans," *Asian-Nation: The Landscape of Asian America.* http://www.asian-nation.org/bangladeshi-pakistani.shtml (accessed August 1, 2010).

Sivanandan, A. (1982) *A Different Hunger: Writings on Black Resistance*, London: Pluto Press.

Sivanandan, A. (1990) *Communities of Resistance: Writings on Black Struggles for Socialism,* London: Verso.

———(2000) "UK: Reclaiming the Struggle," *Race and Class,* 42 (2), pp. 67–73.

———(2001) "Poverty Is the New Black," *Race and Class,* 43 (2), pp. 1–5.

———(2009) "Foreword" to Fekete, L. (2009) *A Suitable Enemy: Racism, Migration and Islamophobia in Europe,* London: Pluto.

Slave Voyages. http://slavevoyages.org/tast/assessment/estimates. faces?yearFrom=1501&yearTo=1866

Small, R. (2005) *Marx and Education,* Aldershot: Ashgate.

Smith, D. G. (2009) "Critical Notice: Engaging Peter McLaren and the New Marxism in Education," *Interchange,* 40 (1), pp. 93–117.

Smith, D. J. (1977) *Racial Disadvantage in Britain,* Harmondsworth: Penguin.

Smith, M. (2010) "Nazis in the Election, Racists on the Streets...the BNP and EDL," *Socialist Review,* March.

Snipes, V. T. and R. D. Waters (2005) "The Mathematics Education of African Americans in North Carolina: From the Brown Decision to No Child Left Behind," *The Negro Educational Review,* 56 (2–3), July, pp. 107–126.

The Socialist Equality Party (2010) "After the General Election: Where Is Britain Going?" *World Socialist Web Site (WSWS),* May 6. http://www.wsws.org/articles/2010/may2010/pers-m06.shtml (accessed January 31, 2011).

Socialist Outlook Editorial (2007) "Chavez: I Am Also a Trotskyist," *Socialist Outlook Editorial,* Spring. http://www.isg-fi.org.uk:80/spip.php?article430 (accessed June 20, 2009).

Southern Poverty Law Center (2009) *Under Siege: Life for Low-Income Latinos in the South.* http://www.splcenter.org/get-informed/publications/under-siege-life-for-low-income-latinos-in-the-south (accessed July 12, 2010).

Southern Poverty Law Center (2010a) "Antisemitism." http://www.splcenter.org/search/apachesolr_search/antisemitism (accessed April 27, 2010).

——— (2010b) "Hate Map." http://www.splcenter.org/get-informed/hate-map (accessed April 27, 2010).

——— (2010c) "Intelligence Report," Spring, 137, "Rage on the Right: The Year in Hate and Extremism" by Mark Potok. http://www.splcenter.org/get-informed/intelligence-report/browse-all-issues/2010/spring/rage-on-the-right (accessed March 20, 2010a).

Spartacus Educational (undated) "Black Panthers." http://www.spartacus.school-net.co.uk/USApantherB.htm (accessed February 9, 2011).

Stobart, L. (2009) "Letter from Venezuela," *Socialist Review,* October. http://www.socialistreview.org.uk/article.php?articlenumber=11001.

StoptheWarCoalition(2009)http://stopwar.org.uk/content/blogcategory/24/41/ (accessed October 25, 2009).

Suggett, J. (2010) "Chávez's Annual Address Includes Minimum Wage Hike, Maintenance of Social Spending in Venezuela." http://venezuelanalysis.com/news/5077 (accessed August 5, 2010).

Suoranta, J., P. McLaren, and N. Jaramillo (2000) "Not Neo-Marxist, Not Post-Marxist, Not Marxian: In Defence of Marxist Cultural Critique in the Process of Becoming a Critical Citizen," in H. Alexander, H. Pinson, and Y. Yonah (eds.), *Citizenship, Education and Social Conflict,* New York and London: Routledge.

Swain, D. (2010) "From Class War to Imperialist Slaughter," *Socialist Worker,* February 13, p. 6.

Swann Report (1985) *Education for All: Report of the Committee of Inquiry into the Education of Children from Minority Ethnic Groups*, London: HMSO.

Takaki, R. (1989) *Strangers from a Different Shore: A History of Asian Americans*, Boston: Little, Brown.

Taylor, E. (2006) "A Critical Race Analysis of the Achievement Gap in the United States: Politics, Reality, and Hope," *Leadership and Policy in Schools*, 5, pp. 71–87.

——— (2009) "The Foundations of Critical Race Theory in Education: An Introduction," in E. Taylor, D. Gillborn, and G. Ladson-Billings (eds.), *Foundations of Critical Race Theory in Education*, New York and London: Routledge.

Taylor, M. (2006) "University Suspends Lecturer in Racism Row Who Praised BNP," *The Guardian*, March 24, http://www.guardian.co.uk/uk/2006/mar/24/raceineducation.highereducation (accessed September 2, 2009).

Taylor, D. G. and Alves, M. J. (2000) "Implementing Controlled Choice and the Search for Educational Equity in the Rockford, Illinois Public Schools: A Survey of Parents Who Withdrew from the Rockford Public Schools after the 1998–99 School Year," *Equity and Excellence in Education*, 33 (2), pp. 81–94.

Tezcatlipoca, Olin (2008) *The Crimes of Hispanic And Latino Racist Labels*. http://www.mexica-movement.org/timexihcah/thecrime.htm (accessed March 24, 2010).

Thane, P. (1982) *Foundations of the Welfare State*, London: Longman.

Thatcher, M. (1982) "Speech to Conservative Rally at Cheltenham," The Thatcher Foundation. http://www.margaretthatcher.org/document/104989 (accessed August 25, 2010).

——— (1993) *The Downing Street Years*, London: HarperCollins.

Thayer-Bacon, B. (2008) *Beyond Liberal Democracy in Schools: The Power of Pluralism*, New York: Teachers College Press.

Thompson, C. L. and O'Quinn, S. D. (2001) *First in America special report: Eliminating the Black-White ahievement gap*. Chapel Hill: North Carolina Education Research Council.

Time magazine (1969) "The Little Strike that Grew to La Causa," July 4. http://www.sriettc.org/tah/Year_3_Documents/Primary%20Documents_2010/The%20Little%20Strike%20that%20Grew%20to%20La%20Causa,%20Time%20Magazine,%20July.pdf (accessed June 5, 2010).

Toji, D. S. (2003) "Japanese Americans," *Asian-Nation: The Landscape of Asian America*. http://www.asian-nation.org/japanese.shtml (accessed August 7, 2010).

Tomlinson, S. (2005) *Education in a Post-welfare Society* (2nd Edition), Buckingham, UK: Open University Press.

Townsend, M. (2009) "Rise in Antisemitic Attacks 'the Worst Recorded in Britain in Decades,'" *The Guardian*. http://www.guardian.co.uk/world/2009/feb/08/police-patrols-antisemitism-jewish-community (accessed August 27, 2009).

——— (2010) "English Defence League Forges Links with America's Tea Party," *The Observer*, October 10. http://www.guardian.co.uk/uk/2010/oct/10/english-defence-league-tea-party (accessed October 10, 2010).

The Trans-Atlantic Slave Trade Database—Voyages (2009): "Assessing the Slave Trade." http://slavevoyages.org/tast/assessment/estimates.faces? yearFrom=1501&yearTo=1866 (accessed May 8, 2010).

Travis, A. (2003) "Blunkett: Racism Tag Is Aiding Racists." *The Guardian*, January 16.

Trilling, D. (2010a) "BNP Suffers a Crushing Defeat at the Ballot Box," *New Statesman*, May 7. http://www.newstatesman.com/blogs/the-staggers/2010/05/bnp-party-councillors-losses (accessed May 8, 2010).

Trilling, D. (2010b) "Gone to the Dogs," *New Statesman,* April 16. http://www.newstatesman.com/uk-politics/2010/04/bnp-party-barking-hodge (accessed May 8, 2010).

Trotsky, L. (1944) *Fascism: What It Is and How to Fight It.* http://www.marxists.org/archive/trotsky/works/1944/1944-fas.htm (accessed February 21, 2011).

Troyna, B. (1987) "Antisexist/Antiracist Education—A False Dilemma: A Reply to Walkling and Brannigan." *Journal of Moral Education,* 16 (1), January, pp. 60–65.

——— (1993) *Racism and Education,* Buckingham: Open University Press.

Troyna, B. and B. Carrington (1990) *Education, Racism and Reform,* London: Routledge.

Tsosie, R. (2005–2006) "Engaging the Spirit of Racial Healing within Critical Race Theory: An Exercise in Transformative Thought," *Michigan Journal of Race and Law,* 11 (21), pp. 21–49.

Tuan, M. (1999) *Forever Foreigners or Honorary Whites?: The Asian Ethnic Experience Today.* New Brunswick, NJ: Rutgers University Press.

Unite Against Fascism (UAF) (2010) http://uaf.org.uk/about/ (accessed February 4, 2011).

United States 2010 Census Constituent FAQs (2010). http://2010.census.gov/partners/pdf/SandL_ConstituentFAQ.pdf (accessed August 10, 2010).

United States Census 2010 "Official Form" (2010) http://2010.census.gov/partners/pdf/langfiles/2010_Questionnaire_Info_Copy.pdf (accessed August 10, 2010).

United States History (undated) "Immigration Act of 1924." http://www.u-s-history.com/pages/h1398.html (accessed August 10, 2010).

United States Immigration Legislation Online (2007) http://library.uwb.edu/guides/USimmigration/1965_immigration_and_nationality_act.html (accessed August 4, 2010).

Van Auken, B. (2010a) "Obama Signs Law to Militarize US-Mexico Border," *World Socialist Web Site (WSWS),* August 14. http://www.wsws.org/articles/2010/aug2010/immi-a14.shtml (accessed October 30, 2010).

——— (2010b) "UN 'Poverty Summit' Exposes Failure of World Capitalism," *World Socialist Web Site (WSWS),* 23 September. http://www.wsws.org/articles/2010/sep2010/pers-s23.shtml (accessed September 23, 2010).

Vann Woodward, C. (1966) "Seeds of Failure in Radical Race Policy," *Proceedings of the American Philosophical Society,* 110 (1), February 18, pp. 1–9.

Vasagar, J. (2010) "Historian Schama to Bring Story of UK Back to Classroom," *The Guardian,* October 6.

Verma, R. (2008). *Backlash: South Asian Immigrant Voices on the Margins.* Rotterdam: Sense Publishers.

Victor, M. P. (2006) "Mr. Danger and Socialism for the New Milennium," *Z Net: The Spirit of Resistance of Resistance Lives.* http://www.zcommunications.org/mr-danger-and-socialism-for-the-new-milennium-by-maria-paez-victor.

——— (2009) "From Conquistadores, Dictators and Multinationals to the Bolivarian Revolution," Keynote speech at the Conference on Land and Freedom, of The Caribbean Studies Program, University of Toronto, October 31, *Venezuelanalyis,* December 4, 2009, http://www.venezuelanalysis.com/analysis/4979 (accessed April 9, 2010).

Virdee, S. (1999a) "England: Racism, Anti-racism and the Changing Position of Racialised Groups in Economic Relations," in G. Dale. and M. Cole (eds.), *The European Union and Migrant Labour,* Oxford: Berg.

——— (1999b) "Racism and Resistance in British Trade Unions: 1948–79," in P. Alexander and R. Halpern (eds.), *Labour and Difference in the USA, Africa and Britain*, London: Macmillan.

Virdee, S. and K. Grint (1994) "Black Self-organisation in Trade Unions," *Sociological Review*, 42 (2), pp. 202–26.

Walters, D. (2001) "Socialist International." http://www.marxists.org/glossary/orgs/s/o.htm (accessed December 2, 2009).

Ward, C. (2004) *Anarchism: A Very Short Introduction*, New York: Oxford University Press.

Waters, S. (2002) "The Future Lasts a Long Time," *New Statesman*, June 17. http://www.newstatesman.com/200206170034 (accessed August 24, 2009).

Watkins, W. H. (2001). *The White Architects of Black Education: Ideology and Power in America, 1865–1954*, New York: Teachers College.

Weaver, M. (2008) "Live Blog: Barack Obama's Victory Sinks In." http://www.guardian.co.uk/world/deadlineusa/2008/nov/05/barackobama (accessed July 3, 2009).

Webber, F. (1991) "From Ethnocentrism to Euro-racism," *Race and Class*, 32 (3), pp. 11–17.

Weisbrot, M. (2010) "The Anti-Venezuela Election Campaign," *The Guardian*, March 18. http://www.guardian.co.uk/commentisfree/cifamerica/2010/mar/18/venezuela-election (accessed April 15, 2010).

Weston, R. F. (1972) *Racism in US Imperialism*, Columbia, SC: University of South Carolina Press.

Wetherell, M., M. Lafleche, and R. Berkeley (eds.) (2007) *Identity, Ethnic Diversity and Community Cohesion*, London: Sage.

Wikipedia (2009) "Fourth International." November 24.http://en.wikipedia.org/wiki/Fourth_International (accessed December 3, 2009).

——— (2010) "Lemon Grove Incident." http://en.wikipedia.org/wiki/Lemon_Grove_Incident (accessed September 9, 2010).

Willgress, M. (2010) "Venezuela under Threat from US Intervention," *Latin America Forward! Adelante!*

Williams, P. (2010) "Tea Party Rhetoric Twists the Language of Emancipation," *The Observer*, September 19. http://www.guardian.co.uk/world/2010/sep/19/tea-party-language-civil-rights (accessed September 27, 2010).

Williams, R. (2009) "Muslim Men Cleared of 7/7 Plot but Jailed for Attending Terror Camps." *The Guardian*. http://www.guardian.co.uk/uk/2009/apr/30/july-7-london-bombings-trial (accessed May 4, 2009).

Wilpert, G. (2007) "Chavez Swears-In New Cabinet for 'Venezuelan Path to Socialism.'" http://www.venezuelasolidarity.org/?q=node/46(accessed March 24, 2011).

——— (2010) "Prologue," in C. Martinez, M. Fox, and J. Farrell, *Venezuela Speaks: Voices from the Grassroots*, Oakland, CA: PM Press.

Winfrey, R. H. (1986) "Civil Rights and the American Indian: Through the 1960s," PhD dissertation, Department of History, University of Oklahoma.

Woods, A. (2009) "First Extraordinary Congress of the PSUV—Chavez Calls for the Fifth International," in *Defence of Marxism*, November 23. http://www.marxist.com/first-extraordinary-congress-psuv.htm (accessed December 3, 2009).

Woodward, C. and W. McFeely (2001) *The Strange Career of Jim Crow*, Oxford: Oxford University Press.

Woolley, R. (2010) *Tackling Controversial Issues: Facing Life's Challenges with Your Learners*, London: Routledge.

World Council of Churches (1994) *Ecumenical Study Process on Racism*, Geneva: World Council of Churches.

Wrigley, T. and P. Hick (2009) "Promoting Equality: Pedagogy and Policy," in M. Cole (ed.), *Equality in the Secondary School: Promoting Good Practice across the Curriculum*, London: Continuum.

Wu, F. H. (2002) *Yellow: Race in America Beyond Black and White*, New York: Basic Books.

Yarker, P. (2008) "Learning Without Limits—A Marxist Assessment: A Response to Mike Cole, with a Reply from Mike Cole," *Policy Futures in Education*, 6 (4), pp. 464–469.

Younge, G. (2008) "Obama's Army of Supporters Must Maintain Their Level of Activism." *The Guardian*, November 10. http://www.guardian.co.uk/commentisfree/2008/nov/10/barack-obama-supporters-campaign (accessed July 3, 2009).

Younge, G. (2010) "The Tea Party Is a Dynamic Force, but It Is still Unruly and Incoherent," *The Guardian*, February 28. http://www.guardian.co.uk/commentisfree/cifamerica/2010/feb/28/obama-tea-party-republicans-opposition (accessed March 20, 2010).

Zhou, M. (2003) "Chinese Americans," *Asian-Nation: The Landscape of Asian America*. http://www.asian-nation.org/chinese.shtml (accessed August 5, 2010).

Zia, H. (2000) *Asian American Dreams*, New York: Farrar, Straus and Giroux.

Index

working class—*Continued*
    199n12, 200n13, 201n2,5,
    202n9,11, 203n4
  assault on, 32–3
  class consciousness of, 28
  as class in itself, 43–4, 176
  intellectuals of, 41, 117, 142, 144–5, 153, 164, 192n21
  as international, 21–3, 85
  and "middle class," 201n2
  and NCLB, 132–5
  and Owen, 18
  and racism, 53, 57
  and Venezuela, 142, 144–5, 151, 153, 162, 164, 169–71
  versus proletariat, 190n4
The World and its Peoples (Nelson), 117
World War I, 21, 56

World War II, 49, 52, 89, 92, 98–9, 102, 128, 139, 170
Wrigley, Terry, 174, 198n3
Wu, Frank, 5, 104, 109–10, 197n14

xeno-racialization, 7, 10, 13, 42, 47, 56–7, 62–3, 187n17, 189n26
xeno-racism, 10, 47, 54, 56, 60, 187n17, 195n14,17

YouGov, 34

Zandi, Mark, 40
Zhou, Min, 97–8
Zia, Helen, 91, 96, 100–1, 104, 107–9
Zimbabwe, 57–8
Zinn, Howard, 75–7
Zong slave ship, 74